Keys to Success

BUILDING SUCCESSFUL INTELLIGENCE

for College, Career, and Life

FIFTH EDITION

Carol Carter

Joyce Bishop

Sarah Lyman Kravits

PEARSON
Prentice
Hall

Upper Saddle River, New Jersey
Columbus, Ohio

Library of Congress Cataloging-in-Publication Data
Carter, Carol.
  Keys to success : building successful intelligence for college,
  career, and life / Carol Carter, Joyce Bishop, Sarah Lyman Kravits.
    p. cm.
  Rev. ed. of: Keys to success in college, career, and life. 4th ed. ©2003.
  Includes bibliographical references and index.
  ISBN 0-13-147421-9
  1. College student orientation—United States—Handbooks, manuals,
  etc. 2. Study skills—Handbooks, manuals, etc. 3. College students—
  United States—Life skills guides. 4. Career development—United
  States—Handbooks, manuals, etc. I. Bishop, Joyce
  (Joyce L.). II. Kravits, Sarah Lyman. III. Carter, Carol. Keys to
  success in college, career, and life. IV. Title.
  LB2343.32.C37 2006
  378.1'98—dc22   2004028280

Vice President and Publisher: Jeffery W. Johnston
Senior Acquisitions Editor: Sande Johnson
Assistant Editor: Susan Kauffman
Development Editors: Jennifer Gessner, Charlotte Morrissey
Production Editor: Holcomb Hathaway
Design Coordinator: Diane C. Lorenzo
Cover Designer: Jeff Vanik
Cover Photos: SuperStock, PhotoDisk
Interior Design: Aerocraft Charter Art Service
Production Manager: Pamela D. Bennett
Director of Marketing: Ann Castel Davis
Marketing Manager: Amy Judd

Credits and acknowledgments appear on page xviii,
which constitutes an extension of the copyright page.

This book was set in Sabon by Carlisle Communications, Ltd. It was printed by Courier Kendallville, Inc.
The cover was printed by Phoenix Color Corp.

Pearson Education Ltd.
Pearson Education Australia Pty. Limited
Pearson Education Singapore Pte. Ltd.
Pearson Education North Asia Ltd.

Pearson Education Canada, Ltd.
Pearson Educación de Mexico, S. A. de C.V.
Pearson Education–Japan
Pearson Education Malaysia Pte. Ltd.

10 9 8 7 6 5 4 3 2
0-13-147421-9

Our Mission Statement

*O*ur mission is to help students know and believe in themselves, successfully retain and use what they learn, and take advantage of resources and opportunities. With these abilities, we are confident that all students can achieve their goals, become lifelong learners, build fruitful and satisfying relationships with others, and experience the challenges and rewards that make life meaningful.

Foreword

Everyone's experience in college is different. My experience was not that of a traditional student because I volunteered for four years of military service prior to going to college full-time. The Marine Corps gave me discipline and instilled in me the motivation I needed to continue my education. By the time I had finished my enlistment, I had also finished my freshman year at the University of South Carolina.

The time I took to serve our country also gave me the opportunity to decide what type of college atmosphere best suited my needs. In the end, I chose to attend a small university with close ties to the businesses in Denver. The information in *Keys to Success* was important to my college education. While acting as student editor on this book, I learned how to be a better student, employee, and person. I graduated feeling ready for the rest of my life.

I took advantage of the worksheets and personal stories by applying them to my everyday life. After working with this book, I was more inclined to take active steps toward improving my education and my ability to learn. The most important thing I learned in college is, in fact, how to learn. I have a goal to learn throughout my lifetime. I want my life to be a series of new lessons about my profession and myself.

Someone once told me that a college education can be valued by the amount of effort the student puts into it. Anyone can go to class, take notes, and pass the tests. In my experience, the students who succeed in the long term make every assignment a learning challenge. I encourage you to take advantage of every opportunity to learn. Your efforts and dedication to learning are in direct relation to your degree of happiness and success in college, career, and life.

Best Wishes,

Dylan Lewis

UNIVERSITY OF COLORADO, DENVER

Brief Contents

Contents

Chapter 3

Chapter 4

Chapter 8

RESEARCHING AND WRITING   224
Gathering and Communicating Ideas

Chapter 9

RELATING TO OTHERS   260
Communicating in a Diverse World

NOTE: *Every effort has been made to provide accurate and current Internet information in this book. However, the Internet and information posted on it are constantly changing, so it is inevitable that some of the Internet addresses listed in this textbook will change.*

Preface

Since the last edition of *Keys to Success*, we have focused our energies and research on the following question: How can students get the most out of college and use what they learn to achieve their goals in an ever-changing world? We found an important answer in the concept of successful intelligence, developed by psychologist Robert Sternberg.[1]

This book builds successful intelligence

Successful people, says Sternberg, are more than their IQ score. Focus on the two most important parts of Sternberg's message and you can change your approach to education in a way that will maximize your learning and *life success*.

One: *Successful intelligence gives you tools to achieve important goals.* Successful intelligence goes beyond doing well on tests (analytical thinking). Only by combining that analytical skill with the ability to come up with innovative ideas (creative thinking) and the ability to put ideas and plans to work (practical thinking) will you get where you want to go.

Two: *Intelligence can grow.* The intelligence you have when you are born does not stay the same for the rest of your life. You can build and develop your intelligence in the same way that you can build and develop physical strength or flexibility.

Every chapter of *Keys to Success* helps you to build successful intelligence. How?

- *Chapter coverage:* The theme is introduced in Chapter 1 and covered in more detail in the thinking chapter (Chapter 4). Successful intelligence concepts are referenced throughout all chapters of the text.
- *In-text exercises:* Three exercises within the chapter text—"Get Analytical!," "Get Creative!," and "Get Practical!"—develop each skill in the context of the chapter material and your personal needs.
- *Synthesis exercise:* At the end of each chapter, the "Putting It All Together" exercise

gives you an opportunity to combine all three skills and apply them toward a meaningful task.

This book connects you with the ideas and experiences of others

To help you excel in a world that is increasingly diverse, this edition of *Keys to Success* introduces the concept of *cultural competence*, using the following features:

- *Chapter-opening Q & A* highlights questions posed by actual students as they begin college. Each question is answered by another person who offers ideas and advice.
- *Descriptions of real students' experiences*, often accompanied by quotes from the students, have been woven into the text in areas where they enhance the topic being discussed.
- *A focus on cultural competence*, in Chapter 9, shows the value of going beyond tolerance to actively adapt to and learn from people different from you. References to cultural competence and diversity are also woven throughout every chapter, showing how diversity is part of many aspects of school, the workplace, and personal life.
- *Personal Triumph* stories, real-life accounts of how people have overcome difficult circumstances in the pursuit of education and fulfillment, appear near the end of every third chapter. These inspiring stories motivate you to step up your personal efforts to succeed.
- *Chapter summaries* introduce a word or phrase from a language other than English

and suggest how you might apply the concept to your own life.

- *A continuing focus on multiple intelligences* highlights individual diversity and confirms that each individual has a unique way of learning, with no one way being better than another. Chapter 3 introduces and explains this concept, and subsequent chapters include grids with strategies for applying various learning styles to the chapter content.

This book provides strategies and resources that help you do your work

With successful intelligence as the foundation of this edition and cultural competence as an underlying theme, *Keys to Success* presents these learning tools and materials that will help you succeed in college and beyond:

A college primer. Because there's so much to know right off the bat, the section "Quick Start to College" appears at the beginning of this text. Quick Start helps you get a feel for the structure of your college, the people who can help you with academic and life issues, the resources available to you, and expectations from instructors, administrators, and fellow students.

Skills that prepare you for college, career, and life. The ideas and strategies that help you succeed in college also take you where you want to go in your career and personal life. The three parts of this text help you develop a firm foundation for lifelong learning.

- *Defining yourself and your goals:* Chapter 1 provides an overview of today's college experience and an opportunity to evaluate your personal starting point. Chapter 2 gets you on track with ways to manage yourself effectively, focusing on values, goal-setting strategies, time-management skills, and handling stress. Chapter 3 helps you identify complementary aspects of your learning style (your Multiple Intelligences and your Personality Spectrum), choose strategies that make them work for you, and begin to think about your major.
- *Developing your learning skills:* Chapter 4 puts your learning into action by exploring the concept of successful intelligence in

depth, helping you to build analytical, creative, and practical thinking skills and to put them together in order to solve problems, make decisions, and achieve goals. The next few chapters build crucial skills for the classroom and beyond—Reading and Studying (Chapter 5), Listening, Note Taking, and Memory (Chapter 6), Test Taking (Chapter 7), and Researching and Writing (Chapter 8).

- *Creating success:* Recognizing that success includes more than academic achievement, Chapter 9 focuses on developing the interpersonal and communication skills you need in a diverse society. Chapter 10 helps you to manage the stress and wellness issues that so many college students face, and Chapter 11 covers the money-management and career-planning skills you need in college and beyond. Finally, Chapter 12 helps you think expansively: What path have you traveled during the semester? What plans do you have for your future?

Skill-building exercises. Today's graduates need to be effective thinkers, team players, writers, and strategic planners. The set of exercises at the end of each chapter—"Building Skills for College, Career, and Life Success"—encourages you to develop these valuable skills and to apply thinking processes to any topic or situation:

- *Developing Successful Intelligence: Putting It All Together.* These exercises encourage you to combine your successful intelligence thinking skills and apply them to chapter material.
- *Team Building: Collaborative Solutions.* This exercise gives you a chance to interact, problem solve, and learn in a group setting, building your teamwork and leadership skills in the process.
- *Writing: Discovery Through Journaling.* This journal exercise provides an opportunity to express your thoughts and develop your writing skills.
- *Career Portfolio: Plan for Success.* This exercise helps you gather evidence of your talents, skills, interests, qualifications, and experience. The Career Portfolio exercises build on one another to form, at the end of

the semester, a portfolio of information and insights that will help you in your quest for the right career and job.

Particular help with test taking. At three places in the text, a segment called "Study Break" appears. Each segment features a test-taking topic and helps you to develop your test-taking skills throughout the semester in addition to your work on the test-taking chapter.

This book changes with your needs

As we revise, we are in constant touch with students and instructors who tell us how we can improve. From our work with students, student editors, instructors, and experts all over the country, we have made important changes to better focus this new edition on what you need to succeed now. Here's what's new:

- The text-wide theme of successful intelligence—the way to achieve goals and success through analytical, creative, and practical thinking
- A new focus in Chapter 1 on how to use and benefit from the text and its theme
- Three in-chapter exercises in each chapter— one building analytical thinking skill, one building creative thinking skill, and one building practical thinking skill
- A new first exercise at the end of each chapter— "Developing Successful Intelligence: Putting It All Together"—to encourage the synthesis of successful intelligence thinking skills
- Earlier placement (in Chapter 2) of values, goal setting, time management, and basic stress-management strategies
- Revision of learning styles material in Chapter 3 to more clearly delineate the two learning styles assessments and enhance their usefulness
- Extensive revision of Chapter 4—the thinking chapter—to focus on successful intelligence and how it makes problem solving and decision making happen
- Earlier placement of test-taking material (in Chapter 7) as well as in the "Study Break" segments

- Revision of Chapter 9—the diversity chapter—to focus on cultural competence, along with added cultural references throughout the text
- New student stories included within the text to heighten relevance of the material and the reader's ability to connect to it
- Newly revised end-of-chapter exercises to increase relevance and usefulness and to help students build on what they learn throughout the semester

This book is just a start—only you can create the life of your dreams

As you work through this course and move forward toward your goals, keep this in mind: Studies have shown that when students feel that they have a fixed level of intelligence, they improve less, put less effort into their work, and have a harder time in the face of academic challenges. However, students who feel that they can become more intelligent over time are more likely to improve, tend to work harder, and handle academic challenges with more success.[2] *Believe that your intelligence can grow*—and use this book to develop it this semester, throughout your college experience, and afterward as you build the future of your dreams.

Students and instructors: Many of our best suggestions have come from you. Send your questions, comments, and ideas about *Keys to Success* to Carol Carter at caroljcarter@lifebound.com or call our toll-free number at 1-877-737-8510. We look forward to hearing from you, and we are grateful for the opportunity to work with you.

Notes

1. Successful intelligence concepts from Robert Sternberg, *Successful Intelligence*. New York: Plume, 1997.
2. David Glenn, "Students' Performance on Tests Is Tied to Their Views of Their Innate Intelligence, Researchers Say," *The Chronicle of Higher Education*, June 1, 2004 [on-line]. Available: http://chronicle.com/daily/ 2004/06/ 2004060103n.htm (June 2004).

Credits and Acknowledgments

Photo Credits

Acknowledgments

This significant revision has been produced through the efforts of an extraordinary team. Many thanks to:

- Robert J. Sternberg, IBM Professor of Psychology and Education at Yale University, for his ground-breaking work on successful intelligence and for his gracious permission to use and adapt that work as a theme for this new edition.

- Our reviewers, whose input is invaluable.

Fifth edition reviewers: Peg Adams, Northern Kentucky University; Veronica Allen, Texas Southern University; Angela A. Anderson, Texas Southern University; Robert Anderson, The College of New Jersey; Joyce Annette Deaton, Jackson State Community College; Ray Emett, Salt Lake Community College; Jacqueline Fleming, Texas Southern University; Ralph Gallo, Texas Southern University; Jennifer Guyer-Wood, Minnesota State University; Laura Kauffmann, Indian River Community College; Quentin Kidd, Christopher Newport University; Patsy Krech, University of Memphis; Curtis Peters, Indiana University Southeast; Margaret Quinn, University of Memphis; Corliss A. Rabb, Texas Southern University; Rebecca Samberg, Housatonic Community College; Karyn L. Schulz, Community College of Baltimore County–Dundalk; Jill R. Strand, University of Minnesota–Duluth; Toni M. Stroud, Texas Southern University; Cheri Tillman, Valdosta State University

Reviewers from previous editions: Fred Amador, Phoenix College; Manual Aroz, Arizona State University; Glenda Belote, Florida International University; Todd Benatovich, University of Texas at Arlington; John Bennett, Jr., University of Connecticut; Ann Bingham-Newman, California State University–LA; Mary Bixby, University of Missouri–Columbia; Barbara Blandford, Education Enhancement Center at Lawrenceville, NJ; Jerry Bouchie, St. Cloud State University; Mona Casady, SW Missouri State University; Kara Craig, University of Southern Mississippi; Leslie Chilton, Arizona State University; Jim Coleman, Baltimore City Community College; Sara Connolly, Florida State University; Janet Cutshall, Sussex County Community College; Valerie DeAngelis, Miami-Dade Community College; Rita Delude, NH Community Technical College; Marianne Edwards, Georgia College and State University; Judy Elsley, Weber State University in Utah; Skye Gentile, California State University, Hayward; Bob Gibson, University of Nebraska–Omaha; Sue Halter, Delgado Community College; Suzy Hampton, University of Montana; Karen Hardin, Mesa Community College; Patricia Hart, California State University, Fresno; Maureen Hurley, University of Missouri–Kansas City; Karen Iversen, Heald Colleges; Laura Kauffman, Indian River Community College; Kathryn K. Kelly, St. Cloud State University; Nancy Kosmicke, Mesa State College; Frank T. Lyman, Jr., University of Maryland; Marvin Marshak, University of Minnesota; Kathy Masters, Arkansas State University; Barnette Miller Moore, Indian River Community College; Rebecca Munro, Gonzaga University; Sue Palmer, Brevard Community College; Bobbie Parker, Alabama State University; Virginia Phares, DeVry of Atlanta; Brenda Prinzavalli, Beloit College; Jacqueline Simon, Education Enhancement Center at Lawrenceville, NJ; Carolyn Smith, University of Southern Indiana; Joan Stottlemyer, Carroll College; Thomas Tyson, SUNY Stony Brook; Eve Walden, Valencia Community College; Marsha Walden, Valdosta State University; Rose Wassman, DeAnza College; Angela Williams, The Citadel; Don Williams, Grand Valley State University; William Wilson, St. Cloud State University; Michelle G. Wolf, Florida Southern College

- Our student editor, Dylan Lewis, for his wisdom, guidance, and hard work.

- The PRE 100 instructors at Baltimore City Community College, Liberty Campus, for their ideas and support, especially college President Dr. Jim Tschechtelin, and coordinator Stan D. Brown.

- Those who generously contributed personal stories, exhibiting courage in being open and honest about their life experiences:

Beverly Andre, Triton College; Stephen Beck, Learn-to-Learn Company; Joyce Bishop, Golden West College; Carol Carter, LifeBound Inc.; Peter Changsak, Sheldon-Jackson College; Rosalia Chavez, University of Arizona; Carol Comlish, University of Alabama; Darrin Estepp, Ohio State University; Rachel Faison, Bard College; Jacqueline Fleming, Texas Southern University; Ramona Z. Locke, Vice President Senior Financial Consultant, Merrill Lynch Private Client Group; Parisa Malekzadeh, University of Arizona; Joe A. Martin, Jr., University of West Florida; Gustavo Minaya, Community College of Baltimore County, Essex Campus; Raymond Montolvo, Jr., University of Southern California; Afsaneh Nahavandi, Arizona State University West; Nisar Nikzad, Community College of Denver; Julia Nolan, University of California, Davis; Michael Nolan, Oregon State University; Morgan Paar, Academy of Art College; Morgan Packard, Tulane University; Shyama Parikh, DePaul University; Joe Pullen, University of Detroit; Lisa Rabinowitz, Bloomfield College; Randy Ust, University of Mary; Tracy Ust, St. Cloud University; Dr. Benjamin Victorica, University of Florida; Tonjua Williams, St. Petersburg College

- Jessica Ovitz, Cynthia Nordberg, Dr. Frank T. Lyman, and Dan Laukitis for their invaluable advice and assistance.

- Michael Jackson for his writing samples and advice.

- Our terrific editor Sande Johnson, who through her leadership was able to put together a team of people whose combined efforts took this edition to a new level. Special thanks to developmental editors Jennifer Gessner and Charlotte Morrissey for their comprehensive vision, hard work, and insightful ideas, and to editorial assistant Erin Anderson for all her efforts and attention to detail.

- The education professionals who contributed to the development and enhancement of the supplementary materials for this book, including Karyn Schultz and Charlotte Morrissey (Instructor's Manual) and Susan Bierman (Companion Website).

- Alison Pendergast of Pearson Education and Phyllis Colazzo and Peter Simmons of *The New York Times* for their roles in making stellar *New York Times* photographs available for our photo program.

- The following reviewers of and contributors to the instructor's manual, for their insight:

Todd Benatovich, University of Texas at Arlington; Amy Bierman, student, Old Dominion University; Jennifer Cohen; Jodi Levine, Temple University; Geri MacKenzie, Southern Methodist University; Gene Mueller, Henderson State University; Tina Pitt, Heald College; Dan Rice, Iowa State University; Michael and Frances Trevisan, Washington State University; Karen Valencia, South Texas Community College; Eve Walden, Valencia Community College; Don Williams, Grand Valley State University; William Wilson, St. Cloud State University; Nona Wood, North Dakota State University

- Our production team for their patience, flexibility, and attention to detail, especially Gay Pauley, John Wincek, Tammy Levins, JoEllen Gohr, and Pam Bennett.

- Our marketing gurus, especially Amy Judd, our Marketing Manager; Ann Davis, Director of Marketing; and our student success sales directors Joe Hale, Deb Gravely, Brian McGarry, and Connie James.

- Publisher Jeff Johnston, President of Education, Career, and Technology Robin Baliszewski, and Prentice Hall President Tim Bozik, for their leadership and their interest in and commitment to the Student Success list.

- The Prentice Hall representatives and management team, who help us to bring our mission to instructors all over the country.

- Our families and friends, who have encouraged us and put up with our commitments.

- We extend a very special thanks to Judy Block, whose research, writing, and editing work was essential and invaluable.

Finally, for their ideas, opinions, and stories, we would like to thank all of the students and professors with whom we work. Joyce in particular would like to thank the thousands of students who have allowed her, as their professor, the privilege of sharing part of their journey through college. We appreciate that, through reading this book, you give us the opportunity to learn and discover with you—in your classroom, in your home, on the bus, and wherever else learning takes place.

Best-Selling Titles in the KEYS TO SUCCESS Series

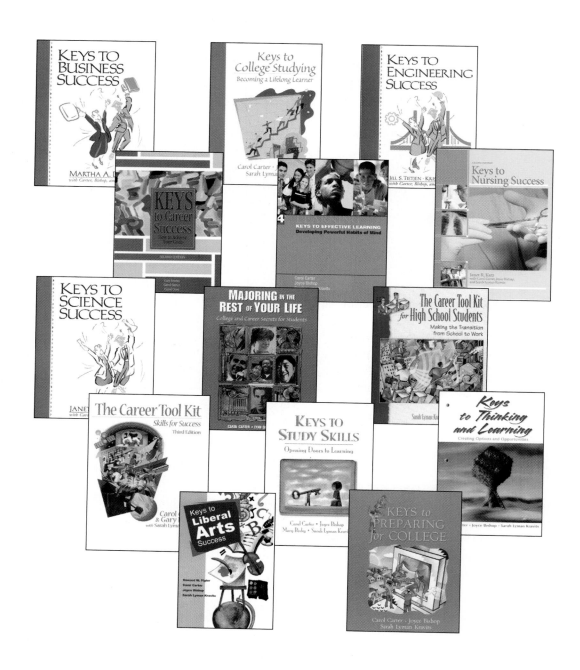

About the Authors

Carol Carter is founder of LifeBound, a career coaching company that offers individual coaching sessions and seminars for high school students, college students, and career seekers. She has written *Majoring in the Rest of Your Life: Career Secrets for College Students* and *Majoring in High School*. She has also co-authored *Keys to Preparing for College, Keys to College Studying, The Career Tool Kit, Keys to Career Success, Keys to Study Skills, Keys to Thinking and Learning*, and *Keys to Success*. She has taught welfare-to-work classes, team taught in the La Familia Scholars Program at the Community College of Denver, and conducted numerous workshops for students and faculty around the country. Carol is a national college and career expert and is interviewed regularly in print, on the radio, and for television news programs. In addition to working with students of all ages, Carol thrives on foreign travel and culture; she is fortunate enough to have been a guest in more than 40 foreign countries. Please visit her Web site and write her at www.lifebound.com.

Joyce Bishop holds a Ph.D. in psychology and has taught for more than 20 years, receiving a number of honors, including Teacher of the Year for 1995 and 2000. For five years she has been voted "favorite teacher" by the student body and Honor Society at Golden West College, Huntington Beach, California, where she has taught since 1987 and is a tenured professor. She worked with a federal grant to establish Learning Communities and Workplace Learning in her district, and she has developed workshops and trained faculty in cooperative learning, active learning, multiple intelligences, workplace relevancy, learning styles, authentic assessment, team building, and the development of learning communities. Joyce is currently teaching on-line and multimedia classes, and she trains other faculty to teach on-line in her district and region of 21 colleges. She co-authored *Keys to College Studying, Keys to Success, Keys to Thinking and Learning*, and *Keys to Study Skills*. Joyce is the lead academic of the Keys to Lifelong Learning Telecourse, distributed by Dallas Telelearning.

Sarah Lyman Kravits comes from a family of educators and has long cultivated an interest in educational development. She co-authored *Keys to College Studying, The Career Tool Kit, Keys to Success, Keys to Thinking and Learning*, and *Keys to Study Skills* and has served as Program Director for LifeSkills, Inc., a nonprofit organization that aims to further the career and personal development of high school students. In that capacity she helped to formulate both curricular and organizational elements of the program, working closely with instructors as well as members of the business community. She has also given faculty workshops in critical thinking. Sarah holds a B.A. in English and drama from the University of Virginia, where she was a Jefferson Scholar, and an M.F.A. from Catholic University.

Quick Start to College

A Guide to Knowing What to Do, How to Do It, and Where to Get Help

Welcome to college! Ahead of you are opportunities to learn more than you can imagine. Over the next years, you will explore the world of ideas, acquire information, and develop skills that will last a lifetime.

With these wonderful opportunities comes the challenge of adjusting to the realities of college. It may help you to know that nearly every college student—no matter what age or level of experience—feels overwhelmed as college begins.

Quick Start to College is designed to help you feel in control as you start the most important educational journey of your life. As you read, consult your college handbook and/or Web site to learn about the specific resources, policies, and practices of your college. The exercises interspersed throughout Quick Start will also help you focus on your school.

Remember that you, along with instructors, advisors, administrators, support personnel, and fellow students, are a full participant in the educational process. Take the first steps toward a future filled with opportunity by

- taking an active role in your courses from the first day of class.
- being in charge of your learning, which involves setting goals, managing your time, completing assignments on schedule, and seeking help, if necessary.
- striving to do your best and making a commitment to quality.
- being an advocate for yourself as you relate to others.
- taking care of your mind, body, and relationships.
- getting involved in activities that interest you and that help develop your talents.
- deciding what you want to study—what you are passionate about.
- pursuing meaningful academic goals (honors or awards, involvement in academic organizations, internships or other work experiences that support your academic path).

One of the first steps in creating your own success is learning what your college expects of you—and what you have a right to expect in return as a consumer of higher education.

What your college *expects of you*

If you get clear before classes start on what it means to be a college student, you will minimize surprises that may be obstacles later on. What is expected of you may be different from anything you encountered in high school or in other educational settings.

Specific expectations involve understanding curriculum and graduation requirements, registering for classes, pursuing academic excellence, following school procedures, getting involved in extracurricular activities, and mastering the college's computer system. Do your best to understand all these areas and, if you need it, ask for help—from instructors, administrators, advisors, mentors, experienced classmates, and family members.

Understand curriculum and graduation requirements

Every college has degree requirements stated in the catalog and Web site. Among the requirements you may encounter are:

- Number of credits needed to graduate, including credits in major and minor fields
- Curriculum requirements, including specific course requirements
- Departmental major requirements, including the cumulative average needed for acceptance as a major in the department

Among the degrees granted by two-year and four-year colleges are Bachelor of Arts, Bachelor of Science, Associate of Arts, Associate of Science, and Associate of Applied Science.

Choose and register for classes

Your course selections define what you will learn and who will teach you. Course registration can be both exciting and challenging, especially the first time. Scan the college catalog and Web site and consider these factors as you make your selections:

- core/general requirements for graduation
- your major or minor or courses in departments you are considering
- electives that sound interesting, even if they are out of your field

In most schools, you can choose to attend a class without earning academic credit by *auditing* the class. The main reason students choose to audit is to explore different areas without worrying about a grade, although tuition charges are generally the same.

Once you decide on courses, but before you register, create a schedule that shows daily class times. If the first class meets at 8:00 A.M., ask yourself if you will be at your best at that early hour. Create one or more backup schedules in case courses or sections you want fill up before you register. Show your ideas to your advisor for comments and approval.

Actual course registration varies from school to school. Registration may take place through your school's computer network, via an auto-

EXPLORING YOUR CURRICULUM AND GRADUATION REQUIREMENTS

Use your college catalog and Web site to explore your course requirements, and then complete the following:

- What are your course requirements for graduation?

  _____

  _____

  _____

- What are the requirements to major in a department that interests you? List, on a separate page if necessary, the courses in the order they must be taken.

  _____

  _____

  _____

- What grade point average must you maintain in order to remain in good standing at your college and to major in your area of interest? Identify two study-related activities you will start in the next month to help ensure that you will achieve that GPA.

  GPA: _____

  1. _____

  2. _____

mated phone system, or in the school gym or student union. When you register, you may be asked to pay tuition and other fees. If you receive financial aid, make sure that checks from all aid sources have arrived at the college before registration.

Pursue academic excellence

Pursuing academic excellence means doing your very best in every course. You can accomplish this through a series of small but important steps that lead you to success:

- Read all assigned text material ahead of time.
- Attend every class with a positive attitude.
- Arrive on time.
- Complete assignments on schedule.
- Listen attentively, take notes, and participate in discussions.
- Study for exams.
- Seek help if you need it.

When you receive grades, remember that they reflect your work, not your self-worth. A D or an F does not diminish you as a person, but rather tells you that your efforts or products are below what the instructor expects.

Letter Grade	A	A−	B+	B	B−	C+	C	C−	D+	D	F
Numerical Grade	4.0	3.7	3.3	3.0	2.7	2.3	2.0	1.7	1.3	1.0	0.0

Similarly, an A does not inflate your value as a person, but recognizes the high quality of your academic performance.

Most schools use grading systems with numerical grades or equivalent letter grades (see Key QS.1). Generally, the highest course grade is an A, or 4.0, and the lowest is an F, or 0.0. In every course, you earn a certain number of college credits, called semester hours. For example, Accounting 101 may be worth three hours, and Physical Education may be worth one hour. These numbers generally refer to the number of hours the course meets per week. When you multiply each numerical course grade by the number of hours the course is worth, take the average of all these numbers, and divide by the total number of semester hours you are taking, you obtain your grade point average, or GPA.

Learn the minimum GPA needed to remain in good standing and to be accepted and continue in your major. At some schools, for example, courses with grades below 2.0 may not be counted toward your major requirement. Key QS.2 shows you how to calculate your GPA.

Inherent in the pursuit of academic excellence is honest, ethical behavior. Your school's academic integrity policy defines the behavioral standards that are expected of you in your studies and in your relationships with faculty, administrators, and fellow students. The values that are the foundation of academic integrity are examined in Chapter 2, and Chapter 8 discusses the serious offense of plagiarism.

Follow school procedures

Your college has rules and regulations, found in the college handbook and on the Web site, for all students to follow. Among the most common procedures are:

Adding or dropping a class. This should be done within the first few days of the semester if you find that a course is not right for you or that there are better choices. Late-semester unexcused withdrawals (almost any withdrawal after a predetermined date) receive a failing grade. However, course withdrawals that are approved for medical problems, a death in the family, or other special circumstances have no impact on your GPA.

Taking an incomplete. If you can't finish your work due to circumstances beyond your control—an illness or injury, for example—many colleges allow you to take a grade of Incomplete. The school will require approval from your instructor and your commitment to make up the work later.

Transferring schools or moving from a two-year to a four-year college. If you want a change, check out the degree requirements of the new college and

How to calculate your GPA.

COURSE	SEMESTER HOURS	GRADE	GRADE POINTS
Chemistry 1	4	C	4 credits × 2 points = 8
Freshman Writing	3	B+	3 credits × 3.3 points = 9.9
Spanish I	3	B−	3 credits × 2.7 points = 8.1
Introduction to Statistics	3	C+	3 credits × 2.3 points = 6.9
Social Justice	2	A−	2 credits × 3.7 points = 7.4

Total semester hours: 15
Total grade points for semester: 40.3

GPA for semester (total grade points divided by semester hours): 40.3 divided by 15 = 2.68
Letter equivalent grade: C+/B−

complete an application. If you are a student at a community college and intend to transfer to a four-year school, be sure to take the courses required for admission to that school. In addition, be sure all your courses are transferable, which means they will be counted toward your degree at the four-year school. At most community colleges, advisors are available to help students through this process.

Taking a leave of absence. There are many reasons students take a leave of absence for a semester or a year and then return. You may want time away from academics to think through your long-term goals, or you may be needed for a family emergency. If you are in good standing at your college, leave is generally granted. However, students with academic or disciplinary problems who take a leave may have to reapply for admission afterward.

Get involved

Extracurricular activities give you a chance to meet people who share your interests and to develop teamwork and leadership skills. These activities also give you the chance to develop skills that may be important in your career. In addition, being connected to friends and a supportive network of people is one of the main reasons people stay in school.

Some freshmen take on so many activities that they become overwhelmed. Pace yourself the first year. You can always add more activities later. As you seek the right balance, consider this: Studies have shown that students who join organizations tend to persist in their educational goals more than those who don't branch out.[1]

Master your college's computer system

A large part of the communication and work that you do in college involves the computer. Here are just some examples:

- registering for classes
- accessing a course syllabus and required-readings list
- e-mailing instructors for assignment clarification; receiving e-mail responses
- tapping into library databases and the Internet for research
- completing assignments and writing papers
- submitting papers via e-mail to instructors
- creating spreadsheets for math and science
- e-mailing classmates to schedule group/team meetings
- receiving schoolwide announcements via the college computer network
- taking interactive quizzes

In most colleges, it is no longer possible to manage without a computer—your own, one borrowed from school, or one available in computer labs. Most dorm rooms are now wired for computers, which gives students access to the campus network. Here are some suggestions for using your computer effectively:

- **Get trained.** Start by getting help to connect to your college network. Then, take training classes to master word processing, data and spreadsheets, and the Internet. If you encounter technical problems, talk to technicians in the computer lab.
- **Use computers to find information.** If you have specific questions about your school, check the college Web site. You may find the information or the e-mail address of a contact person.
- **Be a safe and cautious user since computers sometimes fail.** To safeguard your work, create regular backups by saving your work periodically onto the hard drive or a diskette, CD, or flash drive. In addition, use an antivirus program.
- **Use computers for appropriate tasks.** During study time, try to stay away from Internet surfing and computer games. Set time limits at other times to keep your academic focus.
  - **Protect yourself from trouble.** Avoid revealing personal information, including financial data, to strangers you meet on the Internet.

A word about e-mail

You may be required to communicate with your instructor, submit assignments, and even take exams via e-mail. Following are suggestions for improving your communication:

- **Use your college's e-mail system.** Register for an e-mail account at your school as soon as possible. You'll need this connection to receive schoolwide e-mails and possibly to access the college library.
- **Use effective writing techniques.** To make the best impression—especially when writing to an instructor—take the time to find the right words. Organize your thoughts and use correct spelling, punctuation, and grammar. To make your e-mails easy to read, get to the point in the first paragraph, use short paragraphs, use headings to divide long e-mails into digestible sections, and use lists. Always proofread before hitting "send."

- **Be careful of miscommunication.** Try to be diplomatic and pleasant, and think before you respond to upsetting messages. If you write back too quickly, you may be sorry later.
- **Rein in social e-mailing.** Prioritize your e-mailing. Respond to the most important and time-sensitive messages first. Save personal e-mail for when you have down time.

No matter what school or extracurricular activity you are involved in, you will find people who are eager to help you succeed.

Connecting with people and support services

Instructors, administrators, advisors, and a range of support staff are available to help you. This overview will help you identify and connect to the people and services around you. As you read, keep in mind that the names of offices and personnel titles may vary, and remember that some colleges do not offer every resource.

Teaching and learning take center stage

The primary mission of most colleges and universities is teaching—communicating to students the knowledge and thinking skills they need to succeed in school and beyond. Responding as an active, engaged learner is your role and responsibility as a student.

In every course, you'll meet one—or sometimes several—instructors. Although the term "instructor" is used in this text, teachers have official titles that show their rank within your college. Instructors with the highest status are full professors. Moving down from there are associate professors, assistant professors, lecturers, instructors, and assistant instructors, more commonly known as teaching assistants or TAs. Adjuncts may teach several courses, but are not official staff members.

Administrators provide support

The administrative staff enables your college—and the student body—to function. Large universities may be divided into schools with separate administrative structures and staffs—for example, a School of Business or a School of Social Work. Each school normally has its own dean, and each department within the school has a chairperson—an instructor who heads the department.

One of the most important administrative offices for students is the Office of the Dean of Student Affairs, which, in many colleges, is the center for student services. Staff members there can answer your questions or direct you to others who can help.

Administrative offices dealing with tuition issues and registration

Among the first administrative offices you will encounter are those involved with tuition payments, financial aid, and registration.

- The *bursar's office* (also called the office of finance, the accounting office, and cashiering services) issues bills for tuition and room and board and collects payments from students and financial aid sources.
- The *financial aid office* helps students apply for financial aid and understand the eligibility requirements of different federal, state, and private programs.
- The *registrar's office* handles course registration, sends grades at the end of the semester, and compiles your official transcript, which is a comprehensive record of your courses and grades. Graduate schools require a copy of your offical transcript before considering you for admission, as do many employers before considering you for a job.

Student-centered services

A host of services helps students succeed in college and deal with problems that arise. Here are some you may find.

Academic enhancement centers, including reading, writing, math, and study-skills centers. These centers offer consultations and tutoring to help students improve skills at all levels.

Academic computer center. Most schools have computer facilities that are open every day, usually staffed by technicians who can assist with computer-related problems. Many facilities also offer training workshops.

Student housing or commuter affairs office. Residential colleges provide on-campus housing for undergraduate students, with many schools requiring lower classmen to live on campus. The housing office handles room and roommate placement, establishes behavioral standards, and deals with special needs (for example, an allergic student's need for a room air conditioner) and problems. Schools with commuting students may have transportation and parking programs.

Health services. Health services generally include sick care, prescriptions for common medicines, routine diagnostic tests, vaccinations, and first aid. All clinics are affiliated with nearby hospitals for emergency care. In addition, psychological counseling is sometimes offered through health services, or you may find it at a separate facility or via the college Web site. Although services are available, you have to seek them out. Many colleges require proof of health insurance at the time of registration.

Career services. This office helps students find part-time and full-time jobs, as well as summer jobs and internships. Career offices have reference files on careers and employers. They also help students learn to write résumés and cover letters and search job sites on the Internet. Career offices often invite employers to interview students on campus and hold career fairs to introduce companies and organizations. Summer internships and jobs are snapped up quickly, so check the office early and often to improve your chances.

Services for students with disabilities. Colleges must provide students with disabilities full access to facilities and programs. For students with documented disabilities, federal law requires that assistance be provided in the form of appropriate accommodations and aids. These range from interpreters for the hearing impaired to ramps for students in wheelchairs. If you have a disability, visit this office to learn what is offered. Remember, also, that this office is your advocate if you encounter problems. For specifics on learning disabilities, see Chapter 3.

Veterans' affairs. The Office of Veterans' Affairs provides veterans with various services, including academic and personal counseling and current benefit status, which may affect tuition waivers.

While affording college isn't easy, certain financial-aid resources can help ease the burden. Every school has a system in place to help you understand and apply for financial-aid opportunities. The following overview will help you explore them.

Understanding and applying for *financial aid*

Financing your education—alone or with the help of your family—involves gathering financial knowledge and making financial decisions. Visit your school's financial aid office in person or on the Internet, research the available options and decide what works best, and then apply early. The types of aid available are student loans, grants, and scholarships.

Student loans. As the recipient of a student loan, you are responsible for paying back the amount you borrow, plus interest, according to a predetermined payment schedule. The amount you borrow is known as the *loan principal,* and *interest* is the fee that you pay for the privilege of using money that belongs to someone else. Loan payments usually begin after graduation, after a grace period of between six months and a year, and generally last no more than 10 years.

The federal government administers or oversees most student loans. To receive aid from any federal program, you must be a citizen or eligible noncitizen and be enrolled in a program that meets government requirements. Individual states may differ in their aid programs, so check with the financial aid office for details. Key QS.3 describes the main student loan programs to which you can apply.

Grants and scholarships. Unlike student loans, neither grants nor scholarships require repayment. Grants, funded by federal, state, or local governments as well as private organizations, are awarded to students who show financial need. Key QS.4 describes federal grant programs. In contrast, scholarships are given for various abilities and talents. They may reward academic achievement, exceptional abilities in sports or the arts, citizenship, or leadership. Scholarships are sponsored by federal agencies and private organizations.

Researching financial aid. Start digging at your financial aid office and visit your library, bookstore, and the Internet. Guides to funding sources catalog thousands of opportunities.

Get the details on federal student loan programs.

QS.3

LOAN	DESCRIPTION
Perkins	Low, fixed rate of interest. Available to those with exceptional financial need (determined by a government formula). Issued by schools from their allotment of federal funds. Grace period of up to nine months after graduation before repayment, in monthly installments, must begin.
Stafford	Available to students enrolled at least half-time. Exceptional need not required, although students who prove need can qualify for a subsidized Stafford loan (the government pays interest until repayment begins). Two types of Staffords: the direct loan comes from federal funds, and the FFEL (Federal Family Education Loan) comes from a bank or credit union. Repayment begins six months after you graduate, leave school, or drop below half-time enrollment.
PLUS	Available to students enrolled at least half-time and claimed as dependents by their parents. Parents must undergo a credit check to be eligible, or may be sponsored through a relative or friend who passes the check. Loan comes from government or a bank or credit union. Sponsor must begin repayment 60 days after receiving the last loan payment.

Additional information about federal grants and loans is available in the current version (updated yearly) of *The Student Guide to Financial Aid*. This publication can be found at your school's financial aid office, or you can request it by mail or phone (1-800-433-3243). The publication is also available on-line at www.ed.gov/prog_info/SFA/StudentGuide/.

You can find the Free Application for Federal Student Aid (FAFSA) form at your library, at the Federal Student Aid Information Center, through your college's financial aid office or Web site, or via the U.S. Department of Education's Web site at www.ed.gov/finaid.html.

If you are receiving aid from your college, follow all the rules and regulations, including meeting application deadlines and remaining in academic good standing. In most cases, you will have to reapply for aid

Get the details on federal grant programs.

QS.4

GRANT	DESCRIPTION
Pell	Need-based; the government evaluates your reported financial information and determines eligibility from that "score" (called an expected family contribution, or EFC). Available to undergraduates who have earned no other degrees. Amount varies according to education cost and EFC. Adding other aid sources is allowed.
Federal Supplemental Educational Opportunity (FSEOG)	Need-based; administered by the financial aid administrator at participating schools. Each participating school receives a limited amount of federal funds for FSEOGs and sets its own application deadlines.
Work-study	Need-based; encourages community service work or work related to your course of study. Pays by the hour, at least the federal minimum wage. Jobs may be on campus (usually for your school) or off (often with a nonprofit organization or a public agency).

every year. Even if you did not receive a grant or scholarship as a freshman, you may be eligible as a sophomore, junior, or senior. These opportunities often are based on grades and campus leadership, and they may be given by individual college departments.

You are beginning the journey of your college education and lifelong learning. The work you do in this course will help you achieve your goals in your studies and in your personal life and career. Yale University Professor Robert J. Sternberg, the originator of the concept of *successful intelligence* that is the theme of *Keys to Success*, said that those who achieve success "find their path and then pursue it, realizing that there will be obstacles along the way and that surmounting these obstacles is part of their challenge."[2]

Finally, think about what Josh Billings, a nineteenth-century American writer, said over 100 years ago: "Everyone who does the best he can do is a hero." In college and beyond, be your own personal hero.

LEARN MORE ABOUT THE FINANCIAL AID PROCESS

You'll find detailed information about the financial aid application process in your college catalog, on the college Web site, and in federal publications and Web sites mentioned in Quick Start. Use these resources to complete the following:

- List the deadlines to submit FAFSA applications during the next year:

Term/Semester	FAFSA Filing Date
Fall 200_	_____
Spring 200_	_____
Summer 200_	_____

- Endowed scholarships may be available through your college. Find out about two scholarships for which you are eligible and describe them here:

    1. _____

    _____

    2. _____

    _____

- Make a commitment to take three actions in the coming year to apply for these scholarships. Describe these actions in the space below.

    1. _____

    _____

    2. _____

    _____

    3. _____

    _____

SUGGESTED READINGS

Chany, Kalman A. *Paying for College Without Going Broke*. New York: Princeton Review, 2004.

Gottesman, Greg, Daniel Baer, et al. *College Survival: A Crash Course for Students by Students*, Fifth edition. New York: Macmillan, 1999.

Greene, Howard R. and Matthew Greene. *Ten Principles for Paying for College*. New York: St. Martin's Press, 2004.

Light, Richard J. *Making the Most of College: Students Speak Their Minds*. Cambridge, MA: Harvard University Press, 2001.

Rozakis, Laurie. *The Complete Idiot's Guide to College Survival*. New York: Alpha Books, 2001.

INTERNET RESOURCES

Prentice Hall Student Success Supersite (information about student life, student-to-student bulletin boards, personal stories, opinion polls, and more): www.prenhall.com/success

ENDNOTES

1. Alexander W. Astin, *Preventing Students from Dropping Out*. San Francisco: Jossey-Bass, 1976.

2. Robert J. Sternberg, *Successful Intelligence: How Practical and Creative Intelligence Determine Success in Life*. New York: Plume, 1997, p. 19.

Keys to Success

BUILDING SUCCESSFUL INTELLIGENCE

for College, Career, and Life

FIFTH EDITION

1

you will explore answers to the
following questions:

Welcome to College
OPENING DOORS TO SUCCESS

Welcome—or welcome back—to your education. You are embarking on a new phase of life—one that presents challenges, promises hard work, and offers extraordinary rewards. As you contemplate the course of the next two to five years, you may wonder: How am I going to get from freshman orientation to graduation? How am I going to make it?

Here's one important part of the answer to that question: *With the help of this book.* Why? Because it will make your life easier. This book, and the course for which you are reading it, have a primary goal: To help you learn successfully, graduate, and reap the personal and professional rewards of a solid education. This chapter gives you an overview of how that will happen—how being a successfully intelligent, motivated, and forward-thinking student will help you face the challenges of college and achieve more than you could have imagined.

On the following page, read about student Joe Pullen, who is wondering how much grades matter and how hard he will have to focus to earn good grades in college.

- Where are you now—and where can college take you?
- How can successful intelligence help you achieve your goals?
- How will *Keys to Success* help you build successful intelligence?
- What will motivate you to make the most of college?
- How can what you learn now help you succeed in school, work, and life?

3

How important is it to have a high GPA in your first year?

In high school I was considered a pretty smart student but I didn't try that hard. I always waited to the last minute to do things, but I got them done. My GPA was okay but I feel it could have been twice as good. I'm nervous about what will happen in my first year of college. Everyone tells me that freshman year is fun but distracting. Knowing myself, I don't think I can take too much distraction.

I am a very energetic person so I try to get involved in everything I can. In high school I was active in the basketball team, football team, school newspaper, student council, forensics, chess team, student chapel organization, and baseball. I was able to balance athletics and academics in my high school but in college it seems like it will be different. Can I get involved in as many activities as I can without hurting my grades? How important is having a high GPA going to be for me to be able to continue my education?

Joe Pullen
Freshman, University of Detroit

Grades reflect the depth and focus of your learning.

You expect college to be more challenging than high school, and you are right! College As may be harder to earn. They may also represent greater commitment to subject and depth of understanding. Although a poor grade may reflect a lack of commitment, sometimes it means that you were exploring a subject in which you were not gifted but were brave enough to try!

When I began college, I found the courses more demanding than in high school. There was harder reading and more of it, more preparation required before class, more participation in class, and the teachers had higher expectations. Attractive events and activities distracted me. I had to study much harder and there never seemed to be enough time before an exam.

To get good grades, I learned, you have to make time—to write and revise papers, work out answers to problems, or plan and then finish a challenging project. Getting good grades shows that you have eliminated distractions, made school work a priority, demonstrated some natural or hard-earned ability in the subject, and met the professor's requirements.

It's important for you, and for all freshmen, to understand how grades work at your college. How free are you to study in an area that you are weak in but that interests you? Can you take a course for pass–fail? Do you need a certain GPA to major and/or to graduate? When you are not doing well in a course, can you drop it without facing a penalty? Remember, it is always a good idea to meet with your professor about problems and to avoid dropping a course unless you have consulted with your professor and your advisor.

So, back to your question: You don't want fear of a bad grade to prevent you from exploring whatever interests you, but you need to adjust your time to put your best effort into your academics. Good grades and a high GPA show that you are meeting college standards. You are right to be concerned, not because the grade itself is everything but because making smart choices about grades reflects maturity and growth as a learner.

Lisa Rabinowitz, Ed. D., Chair, Creative Arts and Technology, Bloomfield College, Bloomfield, New Jersey

Where are you now— and *where can college take you?*

You are standing at the gateway to a new phase of life. Before you think about moving forward, though, take a look at the road that brought you here. You completed high school or its equivalent. You may have built life skills from experience as a partner or parent. You may have been employed in one or more jobs or completed a tour of duty in the armed forces. You have enrolled in college, found a way to pay for it, signed up for courses, and shown up for class. And, in deciding to pursue a college degree, you made the choice to believe in your ability to accomplish important goals. You have earned this opportunity to be a college student!

What college can do for you

Part of what will make your sacrifices worthwhile is for you to under-stand—and aim to achieve—what you want out of your experience. Students have many different reasons for starting, or returning to, college. The following are just some of many possibilities:

- *"I want to earn a better living."*
- *"I want to get a degree so that I can move ahead in a career."*
- *"I want to spend time learning new subjects."*
- *"I just lost my job, so I want to learn new skills."*
- *"I want to make my parent or spouse happy, and they want me to go to college."*
- *"I don't really know why I'm here."*

Almost all of these reasons for attending college have a specific goal lying within—a degree, earning power, new skills, learning. These goals may change as students gain knowledge and experience through the semesters. Being straight with yourself about why you are here will help you define what you want and begin thinking about how to achieve it over the course of your college years. As for those of you who don't know quite why you are here, even if you don't have a goal now, the experience of college will help you find one.

How can you define your goals so that they give purpose to your educational experience? Looking at the big picture of what college can do for you will give you somewhere to start.

How education promotes life success

If your work in college only helped you succeed in the classroom, the benefit of your learning wouldn't last beyond graduation day. However, learning is a tool for life, and a college education is designed to serve you far beyond the classroom. Here are a few important "life success goals" that college can help you achieve:

Life Success Goal: Increased employability and earning potential. Getting a degree greatly increases your chances of finding and keeping a high-level, well-paying job. College graduates earn, on average, around $20,000 more per year than those with a high school diploma (see Key 1.1). Furthermore, the unemployment rate for college graduates is less than half that of high school graduates (see Key 1.2).

Life Success Goal: Preparation for career success. Your course work will give you the knowledge and hands-on skills you need to achieve your career goals. It will also expose you to a variety of careers related to your major, many of which you may not have even heard of. Completing college will open career doors that are closed to those without a degree.

Life Success Goal: Smart personal health choices. The more educated you are, the more likely you are to take care of your physical and mental health. A college education prepares you with health-related information that you will use over your lifetime, helping you to practice wellness through positive actions and to avoid practices with the potential to harm.

Life Success Goal: Active community involvement and an appreciation of different cultures. Going to college prepares you to understand complex political, economic, and social forces that affect you and others. This understanding is the basis for good citizenship and encourages community involvement. Your education also exposes you to the ways in which people and cultures are different and how these differences affect world affairs.

Thinking about these big-picture goals should help you begin to brainstorm, in more detail, what you want out of college. What courses

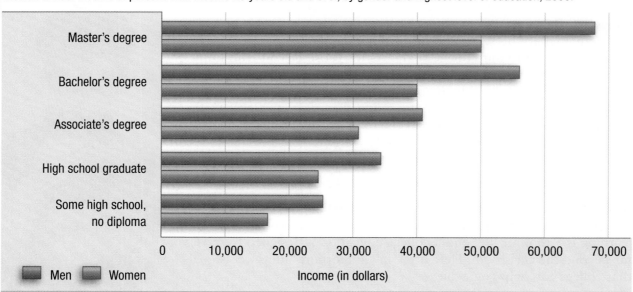

key 1.1

More education is likely to mean more income.

Median annual income of persons with income 25 years old and over, by gender and highest level of education, 2000.

Source: U.S. Department of Commerce, Bureau of the Census, *Current Population Reports*, Series P-60, "Money Income of Households, Families, and Persons in the United States," 2002.

More education is likely to mean more consistent employment.

Unemployment rates of persons 25 years old and over, by highest level of education, 2001.

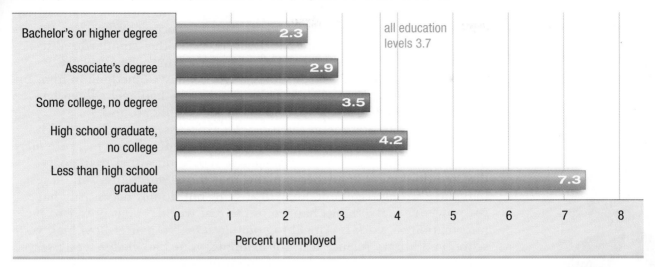

	Percent unemployed
Bachelor's or higher degree	2.3
Associate's degree	2.9
Some college, no degree	3.5
High school graduate, no college	4.2
Less than high school graduate	7.3

all education levels 3.7

Source: U.S. Department of Labor, Bureau of Labor Statistics, Office of Employment and Unemployment Statistics, unpublished tabulations of annual averages from the Current Population Survey, 2002.

do you want to take? What kind of schedule do you want? What degree or certificate are you shooting for? Think about academic excellence and whether honors and awards are important goals. If you have a particular career in mind, then consider the degrees and experience it may require. Finally, consider personal growth, and think about the importance of developing friendships with people who will motivate and inspire you.

A journey of a thousand miles begins with a single step.

LAO TZU

Now you have an idea of your starting point—where you are now—and you are beginning to develop a picture of your ending point—what you want to have gained by the end of your college experience. The biggest question remains: What gets you from here to there? Not everyone arrives successfully. However, with dedication, hard work, and the power that comes from something called *successful intelligence*, you can make it.

How can *successful intelligence* help you achieve your goals?

Think about how you would define *intelligence*. Chances are, like many people, you believe that people are born with a certain, unchangeable amount of intelligence, and that this has a significant effect on the ability to succeed. Another fairly common belief is that standardized tests, such as IQ (intelligence quotient) tests, accurately measure a person's intelligence and are predictors of success.

Psychologist and Yale professor Robert J. Sternberg views intelligence differently. His life experiences convinced him that traditional intelligence measurements lock people into poor performances and often do not accurately reflect their potential for life success. When test anxiety caused Sternberg to score poorly on IQ and other standardized tests during elementary school, he delivered exactly what was expected of him—very little. In the fourth grade, a teacher saw something in him. By letting him know that she expected more than he had ever shown he could give, she provided a spark that turned his life around.

According to Sternberg, the IQ, Scholastic Assessment Test (SAT), American College Test (ACT), and other standardized tests measure *inert intelligence*—that is, they require passive repetition rather than goal-directed thinking. He further explains that those who score well on tests may have strong recall and analytical skills but do not necessarily have the power to make things happen in the real world.[1] That power to put information to work is critical to your success. No matter how high you score on a library science test, for example, your knowledge won't serve you unless you can use it to research a topic successfully.

Defining successful intelligence

In Sternberg's view, intelligence is not a fixed quantity; people have the capacity to increase intelligence as they learn and grow. In his book *Successful Intelligence: How Practical and Creative Intelligence Determine Success in Life*, Sternberg focuses on what he calls *successful intelligence*—"the kind of intelligence used to achieve important goals."[2] Successful intelligence better predicts life success than any IQ test because it focuses on actions—what you *do* to achieve your goals—instead of just on recall and analysis.

Everyone knows people who fit the conventional definition of "smart." They score well on tests and get good grades. Teachers expect them to achieve academically, and they do. However, these students may have limited success outside the classroom if they can't translate their "smarts" into real-world actions.

In contrast, other students have a hard time making the grade but are seen as "offbeat," "creative," or "street smart." Some of these students use their practical or creative intelligence to lift themselves above the crowd. Successful people such as Bill Gates, Ellen DeGeneres, and Woody Allen, despite difficulties in school, built extraordinary success by creatively using their strengths and developing practical ways to reach their goals.

Think about people you know who consistently achieve what they're after, whether they do so in a traditional or nontraditional way. These people demonstrate successful intelligence.

Sternberg breaks successful intelligence into three parts or abilities: *Analytical* thinking, *creative* thinking, and *practical* thinking.

- *Analytical thinking*—commonly known as critical thinking—involves analyzing and evaluating information, often in order to work through a problem or decision. Analytical thinking is largely responsible for school success and is recognized and measured through traditional testing methods.

- *Creative thinking* involves generating new and different ideas and approaches to problems, and, often, viewing the world in ways that disregard convention.
- *Practical thinking* means putting what you've learned into action in order to solve a problem or make a decision. Practical thinking enables you to accomplish goals despite real-world obstacles.

These ways of thinking work together to move you toward a goal, as Sternberg describes:

> Analytical thinking is required to solve problems and to judge the quality of ideas. Creative intelligence is required to formulate good problems and ideas in the first place. Practical intelligence is needed to use the ideas and their analysis in an effective way in one's everyday life.[3]

Here are two examples that illustrate how this works.

**Successful intelligence in a study group—
reaching for the goal of helping each other learn.**

- **Analyze** the concepts you must learn, including how they relate to what you already know.
- **Create** humorous memory games to help you remember key concepts.
- **Think practically** about who in the group does what best, and assign tasks according to what you discover.

**Successful intelligence in considering an academic path—
reaching for the goal of declaring a major.**

- **Analyze** what you do well, what you like to do. Then analyze the course offerings in your college catalog until you come up with one or more that seem to match up with your strengths.
- **Create** a dream career, then work backward to come up with majors that might support it. For example, if you want to be a science writer, consider majoring in biology and minoring in journalism.
- **Think practically** about your major by talking with students and instructors in the department, looking at course requirements, and interviewing professionals in the fields that interest you.

Why successful intelligence is your key to success

When you understand how learning helps you achieve goals that are important to you, you want to learn. When you want to learn, you work hard to make it happen. When you make the effort to learn, you are most likely to succeed.

Successful intelligence powers this entire process, from understanding to success. By helping you to focus on how your learning propels you toward specific goals, it boosts your desire to learn. By giving you an action plan with which you can think through problems or pursue goals, successful intelligence inspires you to work hard and aim high. By helping you to make the most of your strengths and compensate for or correct your weaknesses, it helps you capitalize on who you are and what you can do.

More good news for all kinds of learners lies in the fact that successful intelligence has three equally important elements. Students who have had trouble with tests and other traditional analytical skills can take heart, knowing that creative and practical thinking can help them forge new paths to success. Students who test well can turn their analytical skills into real tools for success through creative thinking and practical action plans.

How will *Keys to Success* help you build *successful intelligence?*

The goal of *Keys to Success* is to help you build the analytical, creative, and practical thinking skills that will get you where you want to go in school and in life. Each element of the book contributes to this goal.

The chapter material

Through your exploration of the various topics in *Keys to Success*, you will develop all three aspects of successful intelligence. The material will often connect a topic to analytical, creative, or practical thinking. Accounts and examples from students, professors, and professionals show how people use various analytical, creative, and practical skills to accomplish personal goals. In addition, Chapter 4—the chapter on thinking—goes into detail about how you can evaluate and build analytical, creative, and practical skills.

Key 1.3 provides some examples of the practical, analytical, and creative thinking skills that lie within chapter topics.

Keys to Success *chapters develop successful intelligence.*

key 1.3

CHAPTER	ANALYTICAL SKILLS	CREATIVE SKILLS	PRACTICAL SKILLS
2	• Thinking about whether your values reflect who you are or want to be • Analyzing how successful a time manager you are	• Coming up with creative ways to manage stress • Thinking about different paths toward a goal	• Planning steps toward a goal • Keeping an effective calendar
3	• Examining how you learn • Matching your learning style to courses, skills, and environments	• When thinking about a major, considering departments or types of majors that are off the beaten path • Opening your mind to new perceptions of you as a learner	• Creating a step-by-step plan toward declaring a major • Linking your learning style to study skills that will help you most

CHAPTER	ANALYTICAL SKILLS	CREATIVE SKILLS	PRACTICAL SKILLS
4	● Distinguishing fact from opinion ● Evaluating assumptions	● Brainstorming ● Using strategies that enhance creative abilities	● Practical problem solving ● Making a well-considered decision
5	● Evaluating arguments ● Analyzing the hidden perspectives found in all media messages	● Thinking of different ways to review reading material ● Finding innovative ways to work with study group members	● Using a practical plan—SQ3R—for maximizing reading comprehension ● Expanding your vocabulary
6	● Deciding which information is important enough to record in notes ● Examining your particular listening challenges	● Coming up with interesting mnemonic devices ● Brainstorming ways to listen more effectively when you don't agree with the speaker	● Memorizing by grouping information ● Knowing when and how to use different note-taking systems
7	● Analyzing why you made a particular mistake on a test ● Selecting the most important material to study for a test	● Brainstorming a study schedule ● Coming up with a variety of review techniques	● Knowing how to handle different types of test questions ● Combating test anxiety
8	● Examining the credibility of research sources ● Evaluating how well you support your thesis statement with examples	● Thinking up essay topics ● Freewriting to generate a flow of ideas	● Going through a writing process—plan, draft, revise, edit ● Using a basic research strategy
9	● Examining how prejudice leads to discrimination ● Evaluating the accuracy of your judgments of others	● Finding ways to think expansively about diversity ● Brainstorming methods for managing anger	● Making connections with diverse people ● Adjusting to different communication styles
10	● Thinking through the consequences of drugs and alcohol ● Evaluating options for sexual decisions	● Coming up with ways you can use resources if you need help ● Thinking of activities that reduce stress for you	● Facing and conquering addiction ● Staying disease-free
11	● Analyzing how effectively you spend your money ● Linking your learning style to related career areas	● Brainstorming careers that interest you and suit your talents ● Coming up with people with whom you can network	● Keeping credit card use under control ● Juggling work and school
12	● Reevaluating and modifying goals ● Considering the effect you can have when you help others	● Engaging creative talents as a way to learn through life ● Facing change with flexibility and creative options	● Getting involved in your community and environment ● Living your personal mission

The in-chapter activities

As you work through each chapter, you will find three activities designed to help you turn ideas you read into news you can use.

- *Get Analytical* gives you an opportunity to analyze a chapter topic.
- *Get Creative* prompts you to think creatively about chapter material.
- *Get Practical* provides a chance to consider a practical application of a chapter idea.

Working through these activities gives you a double benefit. While building successful intelligence skills, you are also deepening your understanding of chapter material, making it more useful to you in pursuing your goals.

The end-of-chapter exercises

The end-of-chapter exercises give you several opportunities to combine what you have learned and apply it to important tasks.

- *Developing Successful Intelligence: Putting It All Together* unites analytical thinking ("Think it through"), creative thinking ("Think out of the box"), and practical thinking ("Make it happen"). This exercise builds your understanding of successful intelligence as an active process and strengthens your ability to direct its elements toward a goal.
- *Team Building: Collaborative Solutions* encourages you to apply various successful intelligence elements to a group setting, building both thinking skills and your ability to work successfully with others.

get creative!

SEE YOURSELF AT YOUR BEST

Use your creative powers to improve your opinion of yourself and inspire action.

You probably have some idea of where you fit into the student body—your age, stage of life, and educational background. However, your "student status" is only a small part of who you are.

Imagine that students gained entry into college by writing personal ads and posting them on the admissions Web site. Write a personal ad that you feel would give you the best possible chance to get in. In it, talk about

- what makes you unique and anything but "average."
- what is special about you that will make the college a better place.
- how your college education will bring you personal and professional success.

- *Writing: Discovery Through Journaling* provides an opportunity to put your analysis, creative thoughts, and practical ideas down in words, building writing skills as well as thinking skills.

- *Career Portfolio: Plan for Success* is a chance to see how your analytical, creative, and practical skills will help you prepare for workplace success. Through the chapters you will build a tangible and useful portfolio—analyzing workplace opportunities, coming up with creative ideas about careers, and creating practical items that you will use in your job search.

With the power of your mind and the tools waiting for you in this book, you possess the keys to success. What remains is to turn the key and get moving toward your goals—and this requires motivation. Here are some ways to find that motivation and put it to work.

MOTIVATION

A force that moves a person to action; often inspired by an idea, a fact, an event, a goal.

What will *motivate you* to make the most of college?

Success is a process, not a fixed mark—and motivation keeps the process in motion. Successfully intelligent people find ways to motivate themselves to learn, grow, and work toward what they want.

Everyone has the potential to be motivated. Your challenge as you begin college is to identify and activate your personal *motivators*—the forces that move you forward. For example, you may be motivated to learn a marketable skill so you can support yourself and your family or to study a subject that has always fascinated you. Motivators can change with time and situations. Though good grades may be all that interest you at the beginning of the semester, as time passes you may wish to learn as much as you can about a subject you have grown to love.

The following strategies will help boost your motivation now, as you begin college, and in the future.

Focus on your self-esteem

When people believe in themselves, their self-esteem fuels their motivation to succeed. Belief, though, is only half the game. The other half is the action and effort that help you feel that you have earned your self-esteem, as basketball coach Rick Pitino explains: "Self-esteem is directly linked to deserving success. If you have established a great work ethic and have begun the discipline that is inherent with that, you will automatically begin to feel better about yourself."[4]

SELF-ESTEEM

A belief in your value as a person.

POSITIVE SELF-TALK

Supportive and positive thoughts and ideas that a person communicates to himself or herself.

Think positively

Your attitudes influence what you will learn from your courses, instructors, and fellow students. A positive attitude—reinforced by positive self-talk—can open your mind to learning and inspire you to action. How can you talk positively to yourself even when times get tough?

After working hard to win the school's first women's national title, Purdue basketball players have earned their self-esteem.

- **Stop negative talk in its tracks.** If you catch yourself thinking, "I can never write a decent paper," replace this negativity with, "I can write better than that and next time I will." Then think about specific steps you can take to improve your writing.
- **Pay yourself a compliment.** Note your successes. Be specific: "I can now create an outline that helps me organize my thoughts for a paper." Keep a list of your successes in a notebook or use calendars with daily affirmations.
- **Replace words of obligation with words of personal intent.**

I should	*becomes*	I choose to
I'll try	*becomes*	I will

COMMITMENT

(1) A pledge or promise to do something, or

(2) a dedication to a long-term course of action.

Words of intent give you power and control because they imply a personal decision to act. For example, "I have to be in class by nine o'clock" implies that someone else has power over you and has handed you a required obligation. However, "I want to be in class by nine o'clock because I don't want to miss anything" says that the choice is yours.

A nursing student at Palo Alto College in San Antonio, Texas, understands the relationship between positive self-talk and success. "To stay motivated I will always remember that I am doing this to better myself and to learn what I need to in order to be the best nurse that I can be. Making a commitment and staying true to it is not easy, but I know that an uncommitted person will never finish anything."[5]

Take action

Although thinking positively sets the tone for success, taking action gets you there. Without action, positive thoughts become empty statements.

Consider, for example, a student in a freshman composition class. This student thinks positive thoughts: "I write well. I can get at least a B+ in this class." She even posts her positive thoughts where she can see them. Then, during the semester, she misses about one-third of the class meetings, turns in papers late, and completely forgets to hand in two assignments. *She did not back up her intentions with action.* At the end of the course, when she barely passes the class, she wonders how someone with such a positive attitude could have done so poorly.

Following are some ways to get moving in a positive direction:

- **Take responsibility.** See yourself as being in charge of your success. Create personal guidelines that support that success—for example, "I pay attention to deadlines."
- **Translate general statements into specific actions.** Success will come when you make your guidelines real through action. If one of your personal guidelines is "I pay attention to deadlines," one action might be turning in assignments when they are due.

Be responsible

College requires that you take personal responsibility for your academic success in ways that you never did in high school. Even if you have lived on your own and held a job, helped raise a family, or both, college adds to that responsibility. You, as your own manager, are responsible for making decisions that keep you on track toward achieving what you want.

The theme of responsibility stands out in how several New Mexico State University students describe their personal transitions:[6]

- **Angie Miller (majoring in Biology):** "The hardest part of my freshman courses was doing all my work myself with nobody telling me every day that my homework was due. Also, there was more material covered in a shorter time, so it was more study time than in high school."

- **Jason Roach (majoring in Business Computer Systems):** "Your classes don't meet as many times a week as they did in high school. As a result, you get more homework. Since you only meet for a minimum of three hours a week, you have a great deal more time to read the book and complete the homework. It is sort of like a 'learn on your own' concept."

- **Daniel Estrada (majoring in Latin American History and Spanish):** "Are the classes harder than high school? Yes and no. I find that they can be easier because they are more to my interest since I picked them. The catch is that it is not up to the instructor to keep you on task. It is left unsaid that it is our responsibility to keep up with the reading and homework and to actually show up for class."

Taking responsibility is about living up to obligations. Through action, you prove that you are responsible—"response-able"—able to respond as efficiently as possible and to the best of your ability. Responsible college students can be trusted to fulfill obligations like these:

- attending class and participating in activities and discussions
- completing reading and assignments on time
- communicating with instructors and fellow students

Why are these basic actions the building blocks of school success? First, completing everyday responsibilities promotes good habits. The more you do something, the more it becomes second nature. Second, small accomplishments make a big impression. When you show up to class, pay attention, contribute, and put in the hours necessary to master the material, you show your instructor and fellow students that you are committed to learning.

HABIT
A preference for a particular action that you do a certain way, and often on a regular basis or at certain times.

Develop positive habits

"Bad" habits stall motivation and prevent you from reaching important goals. Some bad habits, such as chronic lateness, cause obvious problems. Other habits, such as surfing the Internet, may not seem bad until you realize that you needed to spend those hours studying.

"Good" habits bring you closer to your goals. You often have to wait longer and work harder to be rewarded for good habits, which makes them harder to maintain. If you reduce your nights out to gain study time, for example, your grades won't improve in a week.

Define and evaluate your habits to see whether you need to make a change. If a habit is getting in the way of your goals, make a decision to change it. Pick a day to make the change, and then keep it up. To become accustomed to a new habit, be consistent for at least three weeks. Use positive self-talk to encourage your progress, and reward yourself for steps in the right direction.

It's never too late to make an important change in your habits. Returning student Sunny Hobbs is determined and serious, although she had neither trait 30 years ago, when she first enrolled in college and failed nearly every course. Sunny's personal problems, including her troubled marriage, were insurmountable barriers. Now divorced, she arrives early at Joliet Junior College in Joliet, Illinois. Sitting in the second row of her intermediate-algebra course, she works hard to take comprehensive notes. Her positive habits reflect a determination to earn an associate's degree from Joliet and to transfer to the University of Saint Francis where she plans to study elementary education.[7]

Try not to get discouraged if the process seems difficult. Rarely does someone make a change without setbacks. Take it one step at a time; when you lose steam, reflect on what you stand to gain. With persistence and positive thinking, you can reach your goal.

Face your fears

Everyone experiences fear. Anything unknown—new people, experiences, situations—can be frightening because it involves risk. As you begin college, for example, you may wonder if you can handle the work, if you have chosen the right school, or if your education will prepare you for a well-paying job. Ultimately giving in to fear can keep you from living the life you envision.

Nobody succeeds beyond his or her wildest expectations unless he or she begins with some wild expectations.

RALPH CHARELL

Fear often leads to actions—perfectionism, self-criticism, putting things off—that can derail you. For example, if a student is afraid that an instructor won't like his work, he might stop participating in class, put off finishing an assignment, and so on. Students in this kind of situation may not even recognize the fear—only the symptoms. "Why am I so lazy? Why do I feel so out of it in class?"

The challenges you will face in college may require that you face your fears and push your limits. The first step is to acknowledge what you fear. Look for fears that may lurk under symptoms like putting things off and not trying very hard. Then, be specific about what you're afraid of. Focusing on a fear of working in the science lab, for example, helps you to brainstorm useful ways of coping.

Once you know what you fear, evaluate what will help you overcome it. For example, if you are concerned about working in the science lab, arrange to work with another student who is comfortable there and willing to be a mentor to you.

As you work through your fears, talk about them with people you trust. Everyone has fears, and when people share strategies, everyone benefits.

FACE YOUR FEARS[8]

Use practical skills to conquer a fear of yours that stems from the experience of starting college.
First, describe your fear—and be specific.

_____

_____

Now, list three small activities that get you closer to working through that fear. If you don't
want to start a project because you fear failure, for example, you can begin by reading a book
on the subject, brainstorming what you already know about it, or making up a project schedule.

1. _____

2. _____

3. _____

Commit yourself to one step that you will take within the next two days. State it here. Include
the time and date you will begin and how much time you will spend.

_____

_____

What reward will you give yourself for taking this step?

_____

Did taking this step help ease your fear? If so, describe how.

_____

_____

Affirm that you have taken that first step and are on the way to success by signing your name
here and writing the date.

Name _____   Date _____

What do you do if you lose motivation during the semester? Refocus
your attention on the practical steps that lead you toward your goals—
attend class, complete your assignments when due, challenge yourself to
do your best. Also, remind yourself of the connection between your work
in school and your ability to achieve goals in your life beyond graduation.

How can *what you learn now* help you succeed in school, work, and life?

I n his book *Techno Trends—24 Technologies That Will Revolu-
tionize Our Lives*, futurist Daniel Burns describes a tomorrow
that is linked to continuing education: "The future belongs to
those who are capable of being retrained again and again," he says.

"Think of it as periodically upgrading your human assets throughout your career. . . . Humans are infinitely upgradeable, but it does require an investment" in lifelong learning.[9]

The vast majority of Americans see lifelong learning as important in their own lives. In a recent survey of workers, ages 18 to 24, conducted by the country's leading labor union, the American Federation of Labor and Congress of Industrial Organizations (AFL-CIO), 85 percent of respondents viewed education and training as the nation's top economic priority, and 9 of 10 believed that the key to career advancement is ongoing education and training.[10]

In other words, you will need to continue to learn and grow in order to succeed. Here are some ways in which your college experience will develop your ability to stay open to new information and experiences.

College helps you value diversity

Most students are at least 18 when they enter college, and many are older. Yet the years students spend in college are likely to change the way they view themselves and others far more than the previous 18-plus years did. Why? Because college is a time to question the "givens" of life and to open your mind and heart to people who are different from you. Learning to appreciate the similarities and differences among people and within people, and to value diversity in all its forms, is critical for life success.

Diversity means differences among people. On an interpersonal level, diversity refers to the differences between ourselves and others, between the groups we belong to and the groups we are not part of. Differences in gender, skin color, ethnicity and national origin, age, physical characteristics and abilities, and sexual orientation define this most obvious level of diversity.

Other differences—many of which define people and affect relationships in fundamental ways—lie beneath the surface. Among these are:

Students often meet and work with instructors and other students representing a variety of ethnicities, cultural backgrounds, and stages of life.

- cultural and religious backgrounds and beliefs, reflected in different values and behaviors
- differences in educational background and socioeconomic status
- differences in family background (for example, two-parent versus single-parent households)
- differences in marital and parental status

Diversity refers to the differences within people. Another layer of diversity lies within each person. Among the factors that define this layer are:

- personality traits—Are you shy or assertive, a social butterfly or a loner, thoughtful and cautious or impulsive and a risk taker?

- learning style—Are you a verbal, visual, or logical learner? Do you learn by talking with others, thinking on your own, or performing hands-on tasks?
- strengths and weaknesses in analytical, creative, and practical abilities
- natural talents and interests

As you will see in Chapter 9, accepting people for who they are means accepting all aspects of their diversity. In Chapter 3, you will gain a greater understanding of your own and others' learning styles, and in Chapter 4 you will explore differences in analytical, creative, and practical abilities. An important benefit of learning about the diversity of others is gaining a greater appreciation for the diversity that lies within you.

College prepares you to learn from failure and celebrate success

Even the most successful people make mistakes and experience failures. In fact, failure is one of the greatest teachers. Failure provides an opportunity to realize what you didn't know so that you can improve. What you learn from a failure will most likely stay with you more intensely and guide you more effectively than many other things you learn.

Learning from failure

Learning from your failures and mistakes involves successfully intelligent thinking.

Analyze what happened. For example, imagine that after a long night of studying for a chemistry test, you forgot to complete an American History paper due the next day. Your focus on the test caused you to overlook other tasks. Now you may face a lower grade on your paper if you turn it in late, plus you may be inclined to rush it and turn in a project that isn't as good as it could be.

Come up with creative ways to change. You can make a commitment to note deadlines in a bright color in your planner and to check due dates more often. You can also try arranging your study schedule so that it is more organized and less last-minute.

Put your plan into action. Do what you have decided to do—and keep an eye on how it is working. If you rearrange your study schedule, for example, look carefully at whether it is improving your ability to stay on top of your responsibilities.

Sometimes you can't get motivated to turn things around. Here are some ways to boost your outlook when failure gets you down:

- *Believe you are a capable person.* Focus your energy on your strengths and know that you can try again.
- *Share your disappointment with others.* Blow off steam and exchange creative ideas that can help you learn from what happened.

- *Look on the bright side.* At worst, you got a lower grade because your paper was late. At best, you learned lessons that will help you avoid the same mistake in the future.

Your value as a human being does not diminish when you make a mistake. People who can manage failure demonstrate to themselves and others that they have the courage to take risks and learn. Employers often value risk takers more than people who always play it safe.

In order to succeed you must fail,

so that you know what not to do the next time.

ANTHONY J. D'ANGELO

Celebrating success

Acknowledging your successes, no matter how small, is as important as learning from your mistakes. Earning a B on a paper after you had received a C on the previous one, for example, is worth celebrating. Take a moment to acknowledge what you have accomplished, whether it is a good grade, a job offer, or any other personal victory. Let your success help you to build your confidence that you can succeed again.

As you would when working to change a habit, reward yourself when you succeed. "Take it seriously and work hard, yes. But don't forget to enjoy yourself every now and then," advises a Palo Alto College freshman

get analytical!   **LEARN FROM A MISTAKE**

Analyze what happened when you made a mistake in order to avoid the same mistake next time.

Describe an academic situation—you didn't study enough for a test, you didn't complete an assignment on time, you didn't listen carefully enough to a lecture and missed important information—where you made a mistake. What happened?

What were the consequences of the mistake?

What, if anything, did you learn from your mistake that you will use in similar situations?

taking a First Year Experience class. "Take a break and see a movie. Read a book that's deliciously trashy, not scholarly. Take a bubble bath as you pat yourself on the back for a job well done. This is a special time. It's costing you time, money, sacrifices to be in college. Enjoy it and embrace it. You're making memories now, so make it count."[11]

College helps you apply successful intelligence in a changing world

As a college student, you are making sacrifices—including a significant investment of time and money as well as a dramatic lifestyle change—to achieve success throughout your life. You are building the analytic, creative, and practical intelligence you need to cope with a changing world:

- **Knowledge in nearly every field is doubling every two to three years.** That means that if you stop learning, for even a few years, your knowledge base will be inadequate to keep up with the changes in your career.

- **Technology is changing how you live and work.** The Internet and technology will shape communications and improve knowledge and productivity during the next 20 years—and will require continual learning.

- **The global economy is moving from a product and service base to a knowledge and talent base.** Jobs of the past are being replaced by knowledge-based jobs, in the United States and abroad, that ask workers to think critically to come up with solutions.

- **Workers are changing jobs and careers more frequently.** The National Research Bureau reports that currently the average employee changes jobs every three to four years, and it is estimated that a 22-year-old college graduate in the year 2000 will have an average of 8 employers in his or her first 10 years in the workplace.[12] Every time you decide to start a new career, you need new knowledge and skills.

All of these signs point to the need to become life-long learners—individuals who continue to build knowledge and intelligence as a mechanism for improving their lives and careers. Through successful intelligence, you will maintain the kind of flexibility that will enable you to adapt to the demands of the twenty-first century. If you analyze what is happening, come up with creative approaches for handling it, and make a practical plan to put your ideas into motion, you can stay on track toward your goals. Or, you may decide to shift direction toward a new goal that never occurred to you before the change.

Facing change means taking risks. When you enter college, you accept certain challenges and risks as necessary hurdles on the path toward success. As a successfully intelligent lifelong learner, you will find ways to continue to learn and strive toward what you want. Welcome to the beginning of the road to your dreams.

In Chinese writing, this character has two meanings: One is "chaos"; the other, "opportunity." The character communicates the belief that every chaotic, challenging situation in life also presents an opportunity. By responding to challenges actively, you can discover the opportunity within the chaos.

Let this concept reassure you as you begin college. You may feel that you are going through a time of change and chaos. Take heart. No matter how difficult the obstacles, you can choose to persevere. You can build the kind of successful intelligence that helps you learn, grow, and realize your dreams.

FOR COLLEGE, CAREER, AND LIFE SUCCESS

Developing Successful Intelligence

PUTTING IT ALL TOGETHER

Make your first semester count. Academics is only part of college. Campus resources, clubs, student activity groups, and other organizations can enrich your experience. Remember that students who make social connections tend to do better in college. Put a toe in the water sooner rather than later and you will begin to benefit from what your school has to offer.

Step 1. Think it through: *Analyze your college self.* On a separate piece of paper, describe who you are as a student—your identity, interests, challenges, and goals—in a short paragraph. Here are some questions to inspire thought:

- How would you describe your culture, ethnicity, gender, age, lifestyle?
- How long are you planning to be in college?
- What family and work obligations do you have?
- What is your current living situation?
- What do you feel are your biggest challenges in college?
- What do you like to study, and why does it interest you?

Step 2. Think out of the box: *Brainstorm your ideal extracurriculars.* On a second piece of paper, write ideas about how you want to spend your time outside of class. To inspire creative ideas, try using one or more of the following questions as a starting point:

- If you had no fear, what horizon-broadening experience would you sign up for?
- When you were in elementary school, what were your favorite activities? Which activities might translate into current interests and pursuits?
- What kinds of organizations, activities, groups, experiences, or people make you think, "Wow, I want to do that"?

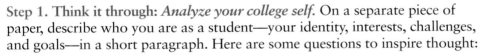

create your future

- Think about the people that you feel bring out the best in you. What do you like to do with them? What kinds of things are they involved with?
- Who are the people with whom you have little in common? How could you benefit from getting to know them?

Step 3. Make it happen: *Take practical steps toward the activities you like.* Thinking about how you have described yourself in terms of both academics and extracurricular pursuits, look in your student handbook at the resources and organizations your school offers. These may include some or all of the following:

Academic centers (reading, writing, etc.)

Academic organizations

Adult education center

Arts clubs (music, drama, dance, etc.)

Fraternities/Sororities

International student groups

Minority student groups

On-campus work opportunities

Organizations for disabled students

Religious organizations

School publications

School TV/radio stations

Sports clubs

Student associations

Student government

Volunteer groups

In the left-hand column on the grid that follows, list the five offices or organizations you most want to check out this semester. Then—through your school publications and/or a little legwork—fill in the information on the grid, answering the questions shown across the top for each item you listed. Notice that the last column requires action—fill it in when you have made initial contact with each office or organization.

Office or Organization	Location	Hours, or times of meetings	What it offers	Phone number or e-mail	Initial contact— date and what happened

Let this exercise be a jumping-off point for real involvement this semester. If after your initial contact you wish to become more involved, go for it. Remember that the activities that inspire you are often a clue to your career path—and that knowing how to work with others is one of the most important skills you will build in college.

Team Building

Motivators. Gather in a group of three to five. Together, brainstorm school motivation blockers—situations or things that most often kill your motivation to succeed in school. When you have as many problems as you have group members, each person should choose one problem and write it at the top of a blank sheet of paper.

Look at the motivation blocker on your page. Under it, write one practical idea you have about how to overcome it. When everyone is finished, pass the pages one person to the left. Then write an idea about the new blocker at the top of the page you've received. If you can't think of anything, pass the page as is. Continue this way until your page comes back to you. Then discuss the ideas as a group, analyzing which ideas might work better than others. Add other ideas to the lists if you think of them.

The last step: On your own, keeping in mind your group discussion, list three specific actions that you commit to taking in order to keep motivation high when the going gets rough.

1. _____
2. _____
3. _____

Writing

Record your thoughts on a separate piece of paper or in a journal.

Reasons for college. People attend college for technical training, the sake of learning, increased earning power, and more. Think about your own reasons. Why are you here, and what do you want out of the experience? On a scale of 1 (lowest) to 10 (highest), rank your commitment to succeeding in college. What sacrifices—in terms of time, hard work, finances—are you willing to make to get what you want and to persevere in your quest for success?

Career Portfolio

This is the first of 12 career portfolio assignments you will complete, one for each chapter. By the end of the semester, you will have compiled a portfolio of documents that will help you achieve your career goals.

Type your career portfolio work on a computer and store the documents electronically, on a disk or in a specific file on your hard drive. If you do not have access to a computer, type or write your work on sheets of paper and keep them together in one file folder. Use paper for assignments that ask you to draw or make collages.

2

Values, Goals, Time, and Stress

MANAGING YOURSELF

Achieving your most important goals depends on your ability to manage yourself. As an effective self-manager, you take charge of your life much like a CEO heads up a top-performing business. This chapter divides the indispensable skill of self-management into four parts: using values to guide your goal setting, working through a process to achieve goals, managing time in a way that propels you toward your goals, and, throughout the journey, managing the stress that will often arise.

The reality of school, workplace, and personal life will often bring problems that create obstacles and produce stress. Everyone has problems; what counts is how you handle them. Your ability to manage yourself—accompanied by a generous dose of motivation—will help you cope with what you encounter, achieve your goals, and learn lasting lessons in the process.

On the following page, read how student Rosalia Chavez is working to overcome her real-life obstacles.

- **Why is it important to know what you value?**
- **How do you set and achieve goals?**
- **How can you effectively manage your time?**
- **How do you cope with the stress of college life?**

How can I stay focused on my school goals?

I married at 18 and didn't finish high school. After our two sons were born, I decided to get my G.E.D., but my husband didn't want me to. At this point, I knew I had to start making opportunities for myself. Shortly after I had begun to further my education, my husband died. I am now taking classes full-time and I work part-time in the Chicano/Hispano Student Affairs Office. I would like to empower future generations of Hispanic women to follow their dreams by telling them my story.

I have to make daily decisions about priorities, and my life situations often get in the way of my schoolwork. Recently, I had to drop a class because my children were sick and I couldn't keep up. My son, who is 11, has ADHD (attention deficit hyperactivity disorder). I can no longer afford his medicine because I was denied state medical assistance. Can you offer suggestions about how I can manage my life and stay focused on my school goals?

Rosalia Chavez
University of Arizona,
Tucson, Arizona

The key to everything is to decide what is most important to you and let all else fall in line.

I want to applaud you for trying to do so much under difficult circumstances. First, to minimize the sense of conflict and frustration, I suggest that you sit with your children and make a *written* list of your priorities. If you have too many things on the list, eliminate some. Simplicity is an important key to life management. If your first priority is your children, then don't sweat the fact that you had to stop school when one child was sick. You can always finish school.

Second, make a *written weekly schedule* so that you can see how you spend your time. Look at the schedule as your primary problem-solving tool. Monitor it to see how well it works and what it tells you about how you are managing. If how you spend your time does not reflect your priorities, or if you do not have enough time to accomplish tasks, revise your schedule.

Third, enlist your children to help with your management activities. For instance, your 11-year-old is old enough to help with most household tasks. I know of a woman who was divorced with four children. She discovered that they could do most everything as well as she could, including cleaning and paying bills. Her children are now a rocket scientist, a doctor, and two are lawyers. She credits their having learned responsibility at an early age. See what your children can do.

Finally, your son's ADHD problem can be approached from more than one angle. Changing diet or particular exercises may be effective. You may not need the medicine eventually. In the meantime, there are companies such as Medco that provide drugs at reduced rates. You and your son should research this issue thoroughly.

Dr. Jacqueline Fleming
Director, General University Academic Center
Texas Southern University, Houston, Texas

Why is it important to know *what you value?*

You make life choices—what to do, what to believe, what to buy, how to act—based on your personal values. Your choice to pursue a degree, for example, reflects that you value the personal and professional growth that come from a college education. Being on time for your classes shows that you value punctuality. Paying bills regularly and on time shows that you value financial stability.

Values play a key role in your drive to achieve important goals, because they help you to:

- **Understand what you want out of life.** Your most meaningful goals should reflect what you value most.
- **Build "rules for life."** Your values form the foundation for your decisions. You will return repeatedly to them for guidance, especially when you find yourself in unfamiliar territory.
- **Find people who inspire you.** Spending time with people who share similar values will help you clarify how you want to live and find support as you work toward what's important to you.

Now that you have an idea of how you can use values, focus on how to identify yours.

VALUES

Principles or qualities that one considers important.

Identifying and evaluating values

Ask yourself questions: What do you focus on in a given day? What do you consider important to be, to do, or to have? What do you wish to accomplish in your life? Answers to questions like these will point you toward your values. The exercise on page 33 will help you think through values in more detail.

After you determine your values, evaluate them to see if they make sense for you. Many forces affect your values—family, friends, culture, media, school, work, neighborhood, religious beliefs, world events. No matter how powerful these external influences may be, whether a value feels right should be your primary consideration in deciding to adopt it.

Answering the following questions about a value will help you decide if it "feels right."

- Where did the value come from?
- What other different values could I consider?
- What might happen as a result of adopting this value?
- Have I made a personal commitment to this choice? Have I told others about it?
- Do my life goals and day-to-day actions reflect this value?

Even the most solid set of values needs a reevaluation from time to time. Why? Because values often change. Life experience and education give you new perspectives that may alter what you consider important. For example, a fun-loving student who is seriously injured in an auto accident may place greater value on friends and family after the accident than he did before. If you let your values shift to fit you as you grow, you will always have a base on which to build achievable goals and wise decisions.

How values affect your educational experience

Well-considered values can lead to smart choices while you are in school. Your values will help you:

- **Keep going when the going gets tough.** Translate your value of education into specific actions, as a student at Palo Alto College did. "Success takes much hard work and dedication," he says. "Since I have a hard time with writing, and I can't understand algebra, I've made a commitment to write in a journal every day and attend math tutoring at least three times a week."[1]

Great minds have purposes; others have wishes.

WASHINGTON IRVING

- **Choose your major and a career direction.** If you've always been an environmentalist, then you may choose to major in environmental science. If you feel fulfilled when you help people, then you might consider a career in social work.

- **Choose friends and activities that enrich your life.** Having friends who share your desire to succeed in school will increase your motivation and reduce your stress. Joining organizations whose activities support your values will broaden your educational experience.

- **Choose what you want out of school and how hard you want to work.** What kinds of skills and knowledge do you wish to build? Do you want to focus on coursework that will lead to career success? Do you want to learn about Egyptian archaeology simply because it interests you? Do you want to read every novel Toni Morrison ever wrote? Decide also how hard you are willing to work to achieve your goals. Going above and beyond will build your drive to succeed and hone your work habits—two items that will be useful in a competitive job market.

Finally, your values affect your success at school and beyond, because the more ethical a student you are, the more likely you are to stay in school and to build lasting knowledge and skills.

Academic integrity: How ethical values promote success at school

ACADEMIC INTEGRITY

Following a code of moral values, prizing honesty and fairness in all aspects of academic life—classes, assignments, tests, papers, projects, and relationships with students and faculty.

Having (academic integrity) promotes learning and ensures a quality education based on ethics and hard work. Read your school's code of honor, or academic integrity policy, in your student handbook. When you enrolled, you agreed to abide by it.

Defining academic integrity

The Center for Academic Integrity, part of the Kenan Institute for Ethics at Duke University, defines academic integrity as a commitment to five

get analytical!

Evaluate what you think is most important to you, and connect educational goals to your top values.

Rate each of the values in the list on a scale from 1 to 5, 1 being least important to you and 5 being most important.

___ Knowing yourself	___ Being liked by others	___ Reading
___ Self-improvement	___ Taking risks	___ Time to yourself
___ Improving physical/mental health	___ Time for fun/relaxation	___ Lifelong learning
___ Staying fit through exercise	___ Competing and winning	___ Getting a good job
___ Pursuing an education	___ Spiritual/religious life	___ Making a lot of money
___ Good relationships with family	___ Community involvement	___ Creative/artistic pursuits
___ Helping others	___ Keeping up with the news	___ Other (write below)
___ Being organized	___ Financial stability	_____

Write your top three values here:

1. _____

2. _____

3. _____

Values often affect your educational choices. Choose one top value that is a factor in an educational choice that you have made. Explain the choice and how the value is involved. Example: A student who values mental health makes a choice to pursue a degree in psychology with a future plan to work as a school counselor.

_____

_____

_____

Name an area of study that you think would help you live according to this value.

fundamental values: honesty, trust, fairness, respect, and responsibility.[2] These values are the positive actions that define academic integrity.

- **Honesty.** Honesty defines the pursuit of knowledge and implies a search for truth in your class work, papers and lab reports, and team-work with other students.

- **Trust.** Mutual trust—between instructor and student, as well as among students—makes possible the free exchange of ideas that is fundamental to learning. Trust means being true to your word.

- **Fairness.** Instructors must create a fair academic environment where students are judged against clear standards and in which procedures are well defined.

- **Respect.** In a respectful academic environment, both students and instructors accept and honor a wide range of opinions, even if the opinions are contrary to core beliefs.
- **Responsibility.** You are responsible for making choices that will provide you with the best education—choices that reflect fairness and honesty.

Unfortunately, the principles of academic integrity are frequently violated on college campuses. In a recent survey, three of four college students admitted to cheating at least once during their undergraduate careers.[3] Violations of academic integrity—turning in previously submitted work, using unauthorized devices during an exam, providing unethical aid to another student, or getting unauthorized help with a project—constitute a sacrifice of ethics that isn't worth the price.

Students who are discovered violating school policies experience a variety of consequences. In most cases, students are brought before a committee of instructors or a "jury" of students to determine whether the offense has occurred. Consequences vary from school to school and include participation in academic integrity seminars, grade reduction or course failure, suspension, or expulsion.

Why academic integrity is worth it

Choosing to act with integrity has the following positive consequences:

- **Increased self-esteem.** Self-esteem is tied to action. The more you act in respectful and honorable ways, the better you feel about yourself, and the more likely you are to succeed.
- **Acquired knowledge.** If you cheat you might pass a test—and a course—but chances are you won't retain the knowledge and skills you need for success. Honest work is more likely to result in knowledge that lasts—and that you can use to accomplish career and life goals.
- **Effective behavioral patterns.** When you condition yourself to play fair now, you set a pattern for your behavior at work and with friends and family.
- **Mutual respect.** Respecting the work of others will lead others to respect your work.

The last two bullet points reflect the positive effect that integrity has on your relationships. This is only one way in which values help you to successfully relate to, work with, and understand the people around you. Here's another way: Being open to different values, often linked with different cultures, can enhance your understanding of cultural diversity.

Values and cultural diversity

At college, you may meet people who seem different in ways that you may not expect. Many of these differences stem from attitudes and behaviors that are unfamiliar to you. These attitudes and behaviors are rooted in the values that people acquire from their culture, either from the continuing influence of family and community in the United States or from their homeland.

CULTURE

A set of values, behaviors, tastes, knowledge, attitudes, and habits shared by a group of people.

Cultural misunderstandings can interfere with the relationships and friendships you form in college, career, and life. As someone who accepts and appreciates diversity, your goal is to develop the (cultural competence) to understand and appreciate these differences so that they enhance—rather than hinder—communication.[4]

A simple model to help you avoid communication problems with people from other cultures was developed by Edward Hall, an anthropologist and an authority on cross-cultural communication. Hall linked communication styles to what he called high-context and low-context cultures:[5]

- People from *high-context* cultures rely heavily in their communication on context and situation as well as on body language and eye contact. Time (past, present, and future), fate, personal relationships and status, gender roles, trust, gestures, and sense of self and space are just some of the factors that influence communication in these cultures. High-context countries span the world and include China, Japan, Brazil, Saudi Arabia, Italy, and France.

- In contrast, people from *low-context* cultures focus on what is explicitly said or written and pay little attention to context and nonverbal cues. Countries with low-context cultures include the United States, Canada, England, Australia, Germany, and the Scandinavian countries.

As you continue to read *Keys to Success*, look for examples of how cultural diversity impacts everything from teamwork and relationships, to listening, questioning, and more. Then think of the wisdom of cultural diversity consultant Helen Turnbull on turning differences into strengths:

We must suspend our judgment. We should not judge others negatively because they are indirect, or their accents aren't clear, or their tone of voice is tentative, or they avoid eye contact. We must learn patience and suspend judgment long enough to realize these differences don't make one of us right and the other wrong. They simply mean that we approach communication from a different frame of reference and, many times, a different value system.[6]

Although clarifying your values will help you choose your educational path, goal-setting and goal-achievement skills will help you travel that path to the end. Goals turn values into tools and put them to practical use.

How do you *set and achieve* goals?

When you identify something that you want, you set a (goal.) Actually *getting* what you want—from college, career, or life—demands working to *achieve* your goals. Achieving goals, whether they are short term or long term, involves following a goal-achievement plan. Think of the plan you are about to read as a map; with it helping you to establish each segment of the trip, you will be able to define your route and follow it successfully.

CULTURAL COMPETENCE

The ability to understand and appreciate differences and to respond to people of all cultures in a way that values their worth, respects their beliefs and practices, and builds communication and relationships.

GOAL

An end toward which effort is directed; an aim or intention.

Set long-term goals

Start by establishing the goals that have the largest scope, the *long-term goals* that you aim to attain over a period of six months, a year, or more. As a student, your long-term goals include attending school and earning a degree or certificate. Getting an education is a significant goal that often takes years to reach.

Some long-term goals have an open-ended time frame. For example, if your goal is to become a better musician, you may work at it over a lifetime. These goals also invite more creative thinking; you have more time and freedom to consider all sorts of paths to your goal. Other goals, such as completing all the courses in your major, have a shorter scope, a more definite end, and often fewer options for how to get from A to Z.

The following long-term goal statement, written by Carol Carter, a *Keys to Success* author, may take years to complete:

> My goal is to build my own business in which I create opportunities for students to maximize their talents. In this business, I will reach thousands of students and teachers through books, the Internet, teacher seminars, and student-oriented programs.

Carol also has long-term goals that she hopes to accomplish in no more than a year:

> Develop and publish one book. Design three seminars for teachers with accompanying PowerPoints and other materials. Create Internet-based materials that encourage student success and use them in student seminars.

Just as Carol's goals are tailored to her personality, abilities, and interests, your goals should reflect your uniqueness. To determine your long-term goals, think about what you want to accomplish while you are in school and after you graduate. Think of ways you can link your personal values and professional aims, as in the following examples:

- Values: Health and fitness, helping others
  Goal: To become a physical therapist
- Values: Independence, financial success
  Goal: To obtain a degree in business and start a company

Basing your long-term goals on values increases your motivation. The more your goals focus on what is most important to you, the greater your drive to reach them.

Set short-term goals

Short-term goals are smaller steps that move you toward a long-term goal. Lasting as short as a few hours or as long as a few months, these goals help you manage your broader aspirations as they narrow your focus and encourage progress. If you had a long-term goal of graduating with a degree in nursing, for example, you may want to accomplish the following short-term goals in the next six months:

- I will learn the names, locations, and functions of every human bone and muscle.
- I will work with a study group to understand the muscular-skeletal system.

These same goals can be broken down into even smaller parts, such as the following one-month goals:

- I will work with on-screen tutorials of the muscular-skeletal system until I understand and memorize the material.
- I will spend three hours a week with my study partners.

In addition to monthly goals, you may have short-term goals that extend for a week, a day, or even a couple of hours in a given day. To support your monthlong goal of regularly meeting with your study partners, you may wish to set the following short-term goals:

- **By the end of today:** Call study partners to ask them about when they might be able to meet
- **One week from now:** Have scheduled each of our weekly meetings this month
- **Two weeks from now:** Have had our first meeting
- **Three weeks from now:** Type up and send around notes from the first meeting; have the second meeting

Try to pay special attention to goals that are intermediate in length—for example, one-month or one-semester goals on the way to a yearlong goal. Why? Because your motivation is at its peak when you begin to move toward a goal and when you are about to achieve that goal. If you work hard to stay motivated in the middle, you will have a more successful journey and a better result.

Reviewing animal physiology while caring for her son is just part of how this single parent and premed student juggles responsibilities on a daily basis.

As you consider your long- and short-term goals, notice how all of your goals are linked to one another. As Key 2.1 shows, your long-term goals establish a context for the short-term goals. In turn, your short-term goals make the long-term goals seem clearer and more reachable.

At any given time, you will be working toward goals of varying importance. Setting priorities helps you decide where and when to focus your energy and time.

Prioritize goals

When you (prioritize,) you evaluate everything you are working toward, decide which goals are most important, and focus your time and energy on them. What should you consider as you evaluate?

PRIORITIZE
To arrange or deal with in order of importance.

- **Your values.** Thinking about what you value will help you establish the goals that take top priority—for example, graduating in the top 25 percent of your class or developing a strong network of personal contacts.
- **Your personal situation.** Are you going to school and working part-time? Are you taking three classes or five classes? Are you a parent

Goals reinforce one another.

LONG TERM		Earn a degree	
YEAR LONG	Declare major		Pass classes
SEMESTER	Explore career areas	Work with study groups	Be in class and on time
ONE MONTH	Meet with academic advisor	Plan group meetings	Cut down on late-night socializing
THIS WEEK	Call advisor to set up appointment	Call friends from class about getting a group together	Study weeknights and go out on Friday nights

with young children who need your attention? Are you an athlete on a sports team? Every individual situation requires unique priorities and scheduling.

- **Your time commitments.** Hours of your day may already be committed to class, team practices, a part-time job, or sleep. Your challenge is to make sure these commitments reflect what you value and to establish priorities for the remaining hours.

As you will see later in the chapter, setting clear priorities will help you manage your time and accomplish more.

Goals are dreams with deadlines.

DIANA SCHARF HUNT

Work to achieve goals

When you've done all the work to think through a goal you want to achieve, these practical steps will help you achieve it. Remember, the more specific your plans, the more likely you are to fulfill them.

- **Define your goal-setting strategy:** *How do you plan to reach your goal?* Brainstorm different paths that might get you there. Choose one; then map out its steps and strategies. Focus on specific behaviors and events that are under your control and that are measurable.
- **Set a timetable:** *When do you want to accomplish your goal?* Set a realistic time line that includes specific deadlines for each step and strategy you have defined. Charting your progress will help you stay on track.

MAP OUT A PERSONAL GOAL

get creative!

Work backwards to find an interesting path toward an important goal.

Name one important personal goal you have for this year.

_____

Now imagine that you have made it to the end—you already achieved your goal—and an impressed friend asks you to describe how you did it. Write your answer here, in a paragraph, as though you were telling this person about the specific steps you took to achieve your goal.

_____

_____

_____

_____

_____

_____

_____

_____

_____

Finally, examine what you've written. You just created a potential plan! Consider putting it—or a plan similar to it—to work. As you begin, let the image of the success you created in this exercise motivate and inspire you.

- **Be accountable for your progress:** *What safeguards will keep you on track?* Define a personal reporting or buddy system that makes accountability a priority.
- **Get unstuck:** *What will you do if you hit a roadblock?* Define two ways to get help with your efforts if you run into trouble. Be ready to pursue more creative ideas if those don't work.

Through this process, you will continually be thinking about how well you are using your time. In fact, goal achievement is directly linked to effective time management.

How can you effectively *manage your time?*

Time is a universal resource; everyone has the same 24 hours in a day, every day. Depending on what's happening in your life, however, your sense of time may change. On some days you feel like you have hours to spare, while on others the clock becomes your worst enemy.

Your challenge is to turn time into a goal-achievement tool by making smart choices about how to use it. Think of each day as a jigsaw puzzle: You have all of the pieces in a pile, and your task is to form a picture of how you want your day to look. Successful time management starts with identifying your time-related needs and preferences. This self-knowledge sets the stage for building and managing your schedule, avoiding procrastination, and being flexible in the face of change.

Identify your time-related needs and preferences

Body rhythms and habits affect how each person deals with time. Some people are night owls; others are at their best in the morning. Some people are chronically late; others get everything done with time to spare. Individual tendencies become clear as people build up "records" of behavior.

A mismatch between your habits and your schedule causes stress and drains energy. For example, a person who loses steam in the mid-afternoon may struggle in classes that meet between 3:00 and 5:00 P.M. However, an awareness of your needs and preferences will help you create a schedule that maximizes your strengths and cuts down on stress. If you are a morning person, for example, look for sections of required courses that meet early in the day. If you work best at night, schedule most of your study time at a library that stays open late.

Daniel Estrada, a student at New Mexico State University, arranged his schedule to maximize his personal strengths and minimize his weaknesses. Estrada explains: "An ordinary day is getting up around 9:00 A.M. to get ready for my 10:30 A.M. class. I have two classes on Monday-Wednesday-Friday and three on Tuesday-Thursday. Knowing that the classes on Tuesdays and Thursdays are longer, I schedule my more difficult classes on those days and leave Monday-Wednesday-Friday for those that I find easier to work with."[7]

Take the following steps to identify your time-related needs and preferences:

Create a personal time "profile." Ask yourself these questions: At what time of day do I have the most energy? The least energy? Do I tend to be early, on time, or late? Do I focus well for long stretches or need regular breaks? Your answers will help you find the schedule setup that works best for you.

Evaluate the effects of your profile. Which of your time-related habits and preferences will have a positive impact on your success at school? Which are likely to cause problems?

Establish what schedule preferences suit your profile best. Make a list of these preferences—or even map out an ideal schedule as a way of illustrating them. For example, one student's preference list might read: "Classes bunched together on Mondays, Wednesdays, and Fridays. Tuesdays and Thursdays free for studying and research. Study time primarily during the day."

Next, it's time to build the schedule that takes all of this information into account, helping you maximize your strengths and compensate for your weaker time-management areas.

Build a schedule

You've set up your "goal map," with all of the steps that you need to accomplish to reach your destination. With a schedule you place each step in time and, by doing so, commit to making it happen. Schedules help you gain control of your life in two ways: They provide segments of time for tasks related to the fulfillment of your goals, and they remind you of tasks, events, due dates, responsibilities, and deadlines.

Use a planner

A planner is the ideal practical tool for managing your time. With it, you can keep track of events and commitments, schedule goal-related tasks, and rank tasks according to priority. Time-management expert Paul Timm says that "rule number one in a thoughtful planning process is: Use some form of a planner where you can write things down."[8]

There are two major types of planners. One is a book or notebook in which to note commitments. If you write detailed daily plans, look for the kind that devotes a page to each day. If you prefer to see more days at a glance, try the kind that shows a week's schedule on a two-page spread. Some planners contain sections for monthly and yearly goals.

The other option is an electronic planner or personal digital assistant (PDA). Basic PDA functions allow you to schedule days and weeks, note due dates, make to-do lists, perform mathematical calculations, and create and store an address book. You can enter information with an on-screen or attachable keyboard or handwrite with a stylus. You can also transfer information to and from a computer.

Though electronic planners are handy and have a large data capacity, they cost more than the paper versions, and their small size means they can be easy to lose. Analyze your preferences and options, and decide which tool you are most likely to use every day. A dime-store notebook will work as well as a top-of-the-line PDA as long as you use it conscientiously.

Keep track of events and commitments

Your planner is designed to help you schedule and remember events and commitments. A quick look at your notations will remind you when items are approaching.

Putting your schedule in writing will help you anticipate and prepare for crunch times. For example, if you see that you have three tests and a presentation coming up all in one week, you may have to rearrange your schedule during the preceding week to create extra study time.

Among the events and commitments worth noting in your planner are:

- test and quiz dates; due dates for papers, projects, and presentations.
- details of your academic schedule, including semester and holiday breaks.
- club and organizational meetings.
- personal items—medical appointments, due dates for bills, birthdays, social events.
- milestones toward a goal, such as due dates for sections of a project.

Although many students don't think to do so, it's important to include class prep time—reading and studying, writing and working on assignments and projects—in the planner. According to one reasonable formula, you should schedule at least two hours of preparation for every hour of class—that is, if you take 15 credits, you should study about 30 hours a week, making your total classroom and preparation time 45 hours. Surveys have shown, however, that most students study 15 or fewer hours per week, and some study even less—often not enough to master the material.

William Imbriale was such a student. As a freshman at Boston College, he had priorities other than studying and writing papers. "I got a D on my first philosophy paper," said William. "That woke me up, big time." With the aid of a professor who helped him plan his time more effectively, William found ways to increase his study time and received an A− on the final paper. He says "I felt like I earned that. The professor gave me a sense of achievement," but William was the one who did the work and put in the time.[9]

Students who hold jobs have to fit study time in where they can. Lisa Marie Webb, a University of Utah student, prepares for class while commuting from her job as a clerk at ShopKo to school and to home. Athletes, too, have to work hard to fit everything in. "I get up at 6:30, go to study hall from 7:30 to 9, have class from 9:30 to 1:15, then have practice at 2," says Ohio State defensive back A. J. Hawk. "Then we lift after practice every day through Thursday."[10] These kinds of situations demand creative time management and close attention to following your schedule.

Schedule tasks and activities that support your goals

Linking the events in your planner to your goals will give meaning to your efforts and bring order to your schedule. Planning study time for an economics test, for example, will mean more to you if you link the hours you spend to your goal of being accepted into business school. The simple act of relating what you do day to day to what you want in your future has enormous power to move you forward.

Here is how a student might translate his goal of entering business school into action steps over a year's time:

This year: Complete enough courses to meet curriculum requirements for business school and maintain class standing

This semester: Complete my economics class with a B average or higher

This month: Set up economics study group schedule to coincide with quizzes and tests

This week: Meet with study group; go over material for Friday's test

Today: Go over Chapter 3 in econ text

The student can then arrange his time to move him in the direction of his goal. He schedules activities that support his short-term goal of doing well on the test and writes them in his planner as shown in the example

Monday	Tuesday	Wednesday	Thursday	Friday	Saturday	Sunday
9 AM: Economics class Talk with study group members to schedule meeting.	3–5 PM: Study econ chapter 3.	9 AM: Economics class Drop by instructor's office hours to ask question about test	6 PM: Go over chapter 3 7–9 PM: Study group meeting.	9 AM: Economics class—Test 3:30 PM: Meet w/advisor to discuss GMAT and other business school requirements	Sleep in— schedule some down time	5 PM: Go over quiz questions with study partner

above. Achieving his overarching long-term goal of doing well in a course he needs for business school is the source of his motivation.

Before each week begins, remind yourself of your long-term goals and what you can accomplish over the next seven days to move you closer to them. Key 2.2 shows parts of a daily schedule and a weekly schedule.

Note daily and weekly tasks.

key 2.2

Monday, March 14

TIME	TASKS	PRIORITY
6:00 A.M.		
7:00		
8:00	Up at 8am — finish homew	
9:00		
10:00	Business Administration	
11:00	Renew driver's license @ D	
12:00 P.M.		
1:00	Lunch	
2:00	Writing Seminar (peer editi	
3:00	↓	
4:00	check on Ms. Schwartz's of	
5:00	5:30 work out	
6:00	↳6:30	
7:00	Dinner	
8:00	Read two chapters for	
9:00	Business Admin.	
10:00	↓	
11:00		
12:00		

Monday, March 28

8		Call: Mike Blair	1
9	BIO 212	Finanical Aid Office	2
10		EMS 262 *Paramedic	3
11	CHEM 203	role-play*	4
12			5
Evening	6pm yoga class		

Tuesday, March 29

8	Finish reading assignment!	Work @ library	1
9			2
10	ENG 112	(study for quiz)	3
11	↓		4
12			5
Evening		↓ until 7pm	

Wednesday, March 30

8		Meet w/advisor	1
9	BIO 212		2
10		EMS 262	3
11	CHEM 203 *Quiz		4
12		Pick up photos	5
Evening	6pm Dinner w/study group		

Indicate priority levels

On any given day, the items on your schedule have varying degrees of importance. Prioritizing these items boosts scheduling success in two ways. First, it helps you to identify your most important tasks and to focus the bulk of your energy and time on them. Second, it helps you plan when in your day to get things done. Since many top-priority items (classes, work) occur at designated times, prioritizing helps you lock in these activities and schedule less urgent items around them.

Indicate level of importance using three different categories. Identify these categories by using any code that makes sense to you. Some people use numbers, some use letters (A, B, C), and some use different-colored pens. The three categories are as follows:

- *Priority 1* items are the most crucial. They may include attending class, completing school assignments, working at a job, picking up a child from day care, and paying bills. Enter Priority 1 items on your planner first, before scheduling anything else.

- *Priority 2* items are important but more flexible parts of your routine. Examples include library study time, completing an assignment for a school club, and working out. Schedule these around Priority 1 items.

- *Priority 3* items are least important—the "it would be nice if I could get to that" items. Examples include making a social phone call, stocking up on birthday cards, and cleaning out a closet. Many people don't enter Priority 3 tasks in their planners until they know they have time for them. Others keep a separate list of these tasks so that when they have free time they can consult it and choose what they want to accomplish.

Use scheduling techniques

The following strategies will help you turn your scheduling activities into tools that move you closer to your goals:

Plan regularly. Spending time planning your schedule will reduce stress and save you from the hours of work that might result if you forget something important. At the beginning of each week, write down specific time commitments as well as your goals and priorities. Decide where to fit activities like studying and Priority 3 items. For example, if you have a test on Thursday, you can plan study sessions on the preceding days. If you have more free time on Tuesday and Friday, you can plan workouts or other low-priority tasks. Your planner only helps you when you use it—keep it with you and check it throughout the day.

Make and use to-do lists. Use a to-do list to record the things you want to accomplish on a given day or week. Write your to-do items on a separate piece of paper so you can set priorities. Then transfer the items you plan to accomplish each day to open time periods in your planner.

To-do lists are critical time-management tools during exam week and when major projects are due. They will help you rank your responsibilities so that you get things done in order of importance.

Post monthly and yearly calendars at home. Keeping track of your major commitments on a monthly wall calendar will give you the overview you need to focus on responsibilities and upcoming events. Key 2.3 shows a monthly calendar. If you live with family or friends, create a group calendar to stay aware of each other's plans and avoid scheduling conflicts.

Avoid time traps. Try to stay away from situations that eat up time unnecessarily. Say "no" graciously if you don't have time for a project; curb excess social time that interferes with academics; delegate chores if you find yourself overloaded. Pay special attention to how much time you spend surfing the Internet and chatting on-line, because these activities can waste hours.

Schedule down time. Leisure time is more than just a nice break—it's essential to your health and success. A little down time will refresh you and actually improve your productivity when you get back on task. Even half an hour a day helps. Fill the time with whatever relaxes you—reading, watching television, chatting on-line, playing a game or sport, walking, writing, or just doing nothing.

DOWN TIME

Quiet time set aside for relaxation and low-key activity.

Keep track of your time with a monthly calendar.

key 2.3

MARCH

SUNDAY	MONDAY	TUESDAY	WEDNESDAY	THURSDAY	FRIDAY	SATURDAY
	1 WORK	2 Turn in English paper topic	3 Dentist 2pm	4 WORK	5	6
7 Frank's birthday	8 Psych Test 9am WORK	9	10 6:30 pm Meeting @ Student Ctr.	11 WORK	12	13 Dinner @ Ryan's
14	15 English paper due WORK	16 Western Civ paper—Library research	17	18 Library 6 p.m. WORK	19 Western Civ makeup class	20
21	22 WORK	23 2 p.m. meeting, psych group project	20 Start running program: 2 miles	25	26 WORK Run 2 miles	27
28 Run 3 miles	29 WORK	30 Western Civ paper due	31 Run 2 miles			

get practical! MAKE A TO-DO LIST

Accomplish practical goals with a to-do list and reduce stress as a result.

Make a to-do list for what you have to do on your busiest day this week. Include all the tasks and events you know about, including attending class and study time, and the activities you would like to do (working out at the gym, watching your favorite TV show) if you have extra time. Then prioritize your list using the coding system of your choice.

Date: _____

1. _____
2. _____
3. _____
4. _____
5. _____
6. _____
7. _____
8. _____
9. _____
10. _____
11. _____
12. _____

After examining this list, record your daily schedule in your planner. Include a separate list for Priority 3 items that you can fit into empty time blocks if you finish all your higher priority commitments. At the end of the day, evaluate this system. Did the list make a difference? If you liked it, use this exercise as a guide for using to-do lists regularly.

Fight procrastination

It's human, and common for busy students, to put off difficult or undesirable tasks until later. If taken to the extreme, however, procrastination can develop into a habit that causes serious problems. This excerpt from the Study Skills Library at California Polytechnic State University at San Luis Obispo illustrates how procrastination can quickly turn into a destructive pattern.

PROCRASTINATION

The act of putting off a task until another time.

> The procrastinator is often remarkably optimistic about his ability to complete a task on a tight deadline. . . . For example, he may estimate that a paper will take only five days to write; he has fifteen days; there is plenty of time, no need to start. Lulled by a false sense of security, time passes. At some point, he crosses over an imaginary starting time and suddenly realizes, "Oh no! I am not in control! There isn't enough time!"
>
> At this point, considerable effort is directed toward completing the task, and work progresses. This sudden spurt of energy is the source of the erroneous feeling that "I work well only under pressure." Actually, at this point you are making progress only because you haven't any choice. . . . Progress is being made, but you have lost your freedom.
>
> Barely completed in time, the paper may actually earn a fairly good grade; whereupon the student experiences mixed feelings: pride of accomplishment (sort of), scorn for the professor who cannot recognize substandard work, and guilt for getting an undeserved grade. But the net result is reinforcement: The procrastinator is rewarded positively for his poor behavior ("Look what a decent grade I got after all!"). As a result, the counterproductive behavior is repeated time and time again.[11]

Among the reasons people procrastinate are:

Perfectionism. According to Jane B. Burka and Lenora M. Yuen, authors of *Procrastination: Why You Do It and What to Do About It*, habitual procrastinators often gauge their self-worth solely by their ability to achieve. In other words, "an outstanding performance means an outstanding person; a mediocre performance means a mediocre person."[12] To the perfectionist procrastinator, not trying at all is better than an attempt that falls short of perfection.

Fear of limitations. Some people procrastinate in order to avoid the truth about what they can achieve. "As long as you procrastinate, you never have to confront the real limits of your ability, whatever those limits are,"[13] say Burka and Yuen. If you procrastinate and fail, you can blame the failure on waiting too long, not on any personal shortcoming.

Being unsure of the next step. If you get stuck and don't know what to do, sometimes it seems easier to procrastinate than to make the leap to the next level of your goal.

Even if you're on the right track, you'll get run over if you just sit there.

WILL ROGERS

Facing an overwhelming task. Some projects are so big that they create immobilizing fear. If a person facing such a task fears failure, she may procrastinate in order to avoid confronting the fear.

Avoiding procrastination

Although it can bring relief in the short term, avoiding tasks almost always causes problems, such as a buildup of responsibilities and less time to complete them, work that is not up to par, the disappointment of others who are depending on your work, and stress brought on by the weight of the unfinished tasks. Particular strategies can help you avoid procrastination and the problems associated with it.

Analyze the effects of procrastinating. What may happen if you continue to put off a responsibility? Chances are you will benefit more in the long term from facing the task head-on.

Set reasonable goals. Unreasonable goals can intimidate and immobilize you. Set manageable goals and allow enough time to complete them.

Break tasks into smaller parts. If you concentrate on achieving one small step at a time, the task may become less burdensome. Setting concrete time limits for each task may help you feel more in control.

Get started whether or not you "feel like it." The motivation techniques from Chapter 1 might help you take the first step. Once you start, you may find it easier to continue.

Ask for help. You don't have to go it alone. Once you identify what's holding you up, see who can help you face the task. Another person may come up with an innovative way that you can get moving.

Don't expect perfection. No one is perfect. Most people learn by starting at the beginning, making mistakes, and learning from those mistakes. It's better to try your best than to do nothing at all.

Reward yourself. Find ways to boost your confidence when you accomplish a particular task. Remind yourself—with a break, a movie, some kind of treat—that you are making progress.

Be flexible

No matter how well you plan your time, sudden changes can upend your plans. Any change, whether minor (a room change for a class) or major (a medical emergency), can cause stress. As your stress level rises, your sense of control dwindles.

Although you can't always choose your circumstances, you have some control over how you handle them. Your ability to evaluate situations, come up with creative options, and put practical plans to work will help you manage the changes that you will inevitably encounter. Think of change as part of life, and you will be better prepared to brainstorm solutions when dilemmas arise.

Small changes—the need to work an hour overtime at your after-school job, a meeting that runs late—can result in priority shifts that jumble your schedule. For changes that occur frequently, think through a backup plan ahead of time. For surprises, the best you can do is to keep an open mind about possibilities and rely on your internal and external resources.

When change involves serious problems—your car breaks down and you have no way to get to school; you fail a class and have to consider summer school; a family member develops a medical problem and needs you more at home—use problem-solving skills to help you through. As you will see in Chapter 4, problem solving involves identifying and analyzing the problem, brainstorming and exploring possible solutions, and choosing the solution you decide is best. There are resources available at your college to help you throughout this process. Your academic advisor, counselor, dean, financial aid advisor, and instructors may have ideas and assistance.

Change is one of many factors associated with stress. In fact, stress is part of the normal college experience. If you take charge of how you manage stress, then you can keep it from taking charge of you.

How do you *cope with the stress of college life?*

If you are feeling more stress in your everyday life as a student, you are not alone.[14] Stress levels among college students have increased dramatically, according to an annual survey conducted at the University of California at Los Angeles. More than 30 percent of the freshmen polled at 683 two- and four-year colleges and universities nationwide reported that they frequently felt overwhelmed, almost double the rate in 1985. Stress factors for college students include being in a new environment; facing increased work and difficult decisions; and juggling school, work, and personal responsibilities.

Stress refers to the way in which your mind and body react to pressure. Pressure comes from situations like heavy workloads (final exam week), excitement (being a finalist for the lead in a play), change (new school, new courses), being short on time (working 20 hours a week at a job and finding time to study), or illness (having a head cold that wipes you out for a week).

The Social Readjustment Scale, developed by psychologists T. H. Holmes and R. H. Rahe, measures the intensity of people's reaction to change and the level of stress related to it (see Key 2.4). Holmes and Rahe found that people experience both positive and negative events as stressors. For example, whereas some events like the death of a relative are clearly negative, other stressors, like moving to a new house or even taking a vacation, are generally positive.

Use the Holmes-Rahe scale to find your "stress score."

To find your current "stress score," add the values of the events that you experienced in the past year. The higher the number, the greater the stress. Scoring over 300 points puts you at high risk for developing a stress-related health problem. A score between 150 and 299 reduces your risk by 30 percent, and a score under 150 means that you have only a small chance of a problem.

EVENT	VALUE	EVENT	VALUE
Death of spouse or partner	100	Son or daughter leaving home	29
Divorce	73	Trouble with in-laws	29
Marital separation	65	Outstanding personal achievement	28
Jail term	63	Spouse begins or stops work	26
Personal injury	53	Starting or finishing school	26
Marriage	50	Change in living conditions	25
Fired from work	47	Revision of personal habits	24
Marital reconciliation	45	Trouble with boss	23
Retirement	45	Change in work hours, conditions	20
Changes in family member's health	44	Change in residence	20
Pregnancy	40	Change in schools	20
Sex difficulties	39	Change in recreational habits	19
Addition to family	39	Change in religious activities	19
Business readjustment	39	Change in social activities	18
Change in financial status	38	Mortgage or loan under $10,000	17
Death of a close friend	37	Change in sleeping habits	16
Change to different line of work	36	Change in # of family gatherings	15
Change in # of marital arguments	35	Change in eating habits	15
Mortgage or loan over $10,000	31	Vacation	13
Foreclosure of mortgage or loan	30	Christmas season	12
Change in work responsibilities	29	Minor violation of the law	11

Source: Reprinted from *Journal of Psychosomatic Research, 11*(2), T. H. Holmes and R. H. Rahe, "The social readjustment rating scale," 1967, with permission from Elsevier.

Stress levels can help or hinder performance.

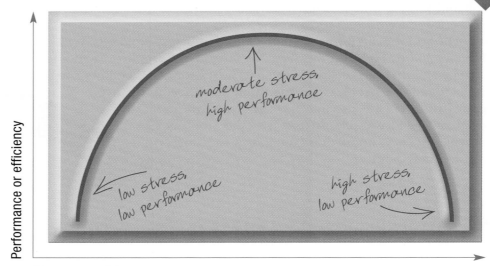

Source: From *Your Maximum Mind* by Herbert Benson, M.D., copyright © 1987 by Random House, Inc. Used by permission of Time Books, a division of Random House, Inc.

At their worst, stress reactions can make you physically ill (Chapter 10 will examine stress-related health issues—situations in which stress goes beyond normal levels, causing physical and emotional problems). But stress can also supply the heightened readiness you need to do well on tests, finish assignments on time, prepare for a class presentation, or meet new people. Your goal is to find a manageable balance. Key 2.5, based on research conducted by Drs. Robert M. Yerkes and John E. Dodson, shows that stress can be helpful or harmful, depending on how much you experience.

Successful time management and goal setting relieve stress

Dealing with the stress of college life is, and will continue to be, one of your biggest challenges. But here's a piece of good news: Every goal-achievement and time-management strategy you have read in this chapter contributes to your ability to cope with stress. Remember that stress refers to how you react to pressure. When you set up effective plans to move toward goals, you reduce pressure. When you set a schedule that works for you and stick to it, you reduce pressure. Less pressure, less stress.

Carefully analyze the relationship between stress and your time-management habits. Often, people create extra stress for themselves without realizing it. For example, say you're a night person but have a habit of scheduling early classes. You are consistently stressed about waking up in time for them. What's wrong with this picture? Reduce your stress by finding practical ways to change your scheduling. Taking later classes will help, but if that isn't possible, cope in other ways. Get to bed earlier a few nights a week, nap in the afternoon, exercise briefly before class to restore your energy. Make sure that you are not expending energy coping with stress that you can avoid with thought and planning.

Stress-management strategies

Here are some practical strategies for coping with the day-to-day stress of being a college student.

- **Eat right.** The healthier you are, the stronger you are—and the more able you will be to weather tough situations like all-nighters, illnesses, and challenging academic work. Try to eat a balanced, low-fat diet and avoid overloading on junk food. Try also to maintain a healthy weight.

- **Exercise.** Physical exercise will help you manage your stress. Find a type of exercise you like and make it a regular part of your life.

- **Get sleep.** Avoid the systemwide dysfunction that sleep deprivation can create. Figure out how much sleep you need and do your best to get it. When you pull an all-nighter, make sure you play catch-up over the next couple of days.

- **Think positively.** Try to think of all you have to do as challenges, not problems.

- **Seek balance.** A balanced life includes time by yourself—for your thoughts, hopes, and plans—and time for relaxation, in whatever form you choose.

Extracurricular activities can provide relaxation and stress relief, as these students have found in their work with the Dynamics, an a cappella group at Skidmore College.

- **Address issues.** Try not to let things lie too long. Analyze stressful situations and use problem-solving strategies (see Chapter 4) to decide on a specific plan of action.

- **Set boundaries and learn to say no.** Try to delegate. Review obligations regularly; if you evaluate that something has become a burden, then consider dropping it from your roster of activities.

- **Surround yourself with people who are good for you.** Focus on friends who are good listeners and who will support you when things get rough. Friendship and humor go a long way toward reducing stress.

Sometimes you'll be able to pull out the strategies that fit the situation, finding ways to cope with the stress you encounter. Sometimes stress will make you feel frozen, not knowing where to turn to work your way out of it. At those times, remember: *Any step toward a goal is a stress-management strategy because it reduces pressure.* In that sense, this entire book is a stress-management strategy. Every useful tool, from test-taking hints to job-hunting strategies, will help you reduce the pressure and cover the distance toward your dreams.

In Hebrew, this word, pronounced "chai," means "life," representing all aspects of life—spiritual, emotional, family, educational, and career. Individual Hebrew characters have number values. Because the characters in the word *chai* add up to 18, the number 18 has come to be associated with good luck. The word *chai* is often worn as a good luck charm. The phrase *l'chaim* means "to life" and good luck.

As you plan your goals, think about the role luck may play in your success. If you work hard and are open to new opportunities, you may find yourself in the right place at the right time to benefit from a "lucky break." Because you are prepared, you may find a teacher who is so impressed by your tenacity and focus that she offers to become your mentor. Or, after you graduate, you may meet someone with a business opportunity that is a perfect match for your skills, and you are hired on the spot. All your hard work in the direction of your goal will prepare you to take advantage of lucky breaks that come your way.

BUILDING SKILLS

FOR COLLEGE, CAREER, AND LIFE SUCCESS

SUCCESSFUL INTELLIGENCE
PRACTICAL · CREATIVE
ANALYTICAL
SUCCESSFUL INTELLIGENCE

Developing Successful Intelligence

PUTTING IT ALL TOGETHER

The Wheel of Life. This exercise uses a wheel—an image that has been used for centuries to promote understanding of the self and the world—to help you think about your strength and weakness in eight important goal areas. Assess your level of proficiency in self-knowledge, study skills, personal life goals, finances, health and stress management, relationships, career, and time management by filling out the wheel as directed in Key 2.6 on p. 54.

Let this self-assessment help you make decisions about how you approach the material in this course. If you wish to improve your career preparation, for example, pay special attention to Chapter 11. If you need work on study skills, then focus specifically on the reading, note-taking, and test-taking chapters. At the end of the book you will have a chance to revisit the Wheel. If you work hard in this course, you should sense improvement in your weaker goal areas over the course of the semester. Plus, you will have developed your ability to evaluate and manage yourself—a skill that is crucial to your success in school and at work.

Team Building

COLLABORATIVE SOLUTIONS

Multiple paths to a goal. In a group of three or four, brainstorm goals that focus on building a life skill—for example, leadership, teamwork, learning a foreign language. Write your ideas on a piece of paper. From that list, pick out one goal to explore together.

Each group member takes two minutes alone to think about this goal in terms of the first goal-achievement step on page 38—defining a strategy. In other words, answer the question: "How would I do it?" Each person writes down all of the paths they can think of.

create your future

Build self-knowledge with the Wheel of Life.

Rate yourself in each area of the wheel on a scale of 1 to 10, 1 being least developed (near the center of the wheel) and 10 being most developed (the outer edge of the wheel). In each area, at the level of the number you choose, draw a curved line and fill in the wedge below that line. Be honest—this is for your benefit only. Finally, look at what your wheel says about the balance in your life. If this were a real wheel, how well would it roll?

Albert Mejia

I need to work on my finances and my career.

Sample Wheel

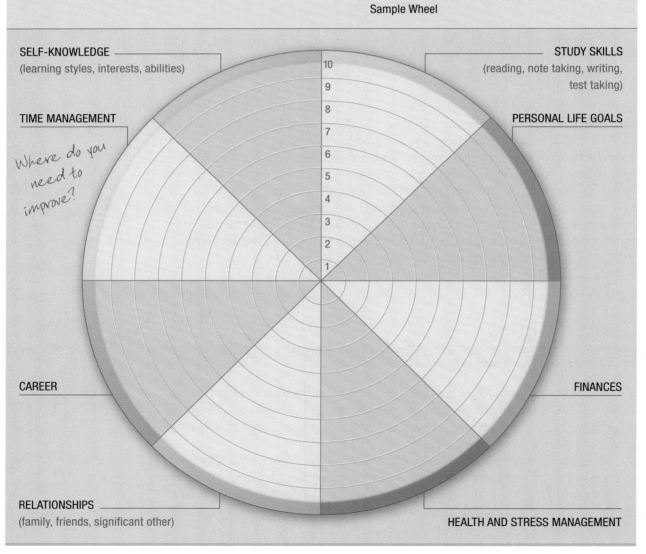

SELF-KNOWLEDGE
(learning styles, interests, abilities)

STUDY SKILLS
(reading, note taking, writing, test taking)

TIME MANAGEMENT

PERSONAL LIFE GOALS

Where do you need to improve?

CAREER

FINANCES

RELATIONSHIPS
(family, friends, significant other)

HEALTH AND STRESS MANAGEMENT

The group then gathers and everyone shares their strategies. The group evaluates strategies and chooses one that seems effective. Finally, as a group, brainstorm the rest of the goal-achievement process, based on the chosen strategy or path:

- **Set a timetable.** When do you plan to reach your goal? Discuss different time frames and how each might change the path.
- **Be accountable.** What safeguards will keep you on track? Talk about different ways to make sure you are moving ahead consistently.
- **Get unstuck.** What will you do if you hit a roadblock? Brainstorm the kinds of roadblocks that could get in the way of this particular goal. For each, come up with ways to overcome the obstacle.

At the end of the process, you should have a wealth of ideas for how to approach one particular goal—and an appreciation for how many paths you could take in order to get there.

Writing

DISCOVERY THROUGH JOURNALING

Use the tables here to record data; answer questions and write additional thoughts on a separate piece of paper or in a journal.

Discover how you spend your time. In the table below, estimate the total time you think you spend per week on each listed activity. Then, add the hours. If your number is over 168 (the number of hours in a week), rethink your estimates and recalculate so that the total is equal to 168.

Now, spend a week recording exactly how you spend your time. The chart on pages 56–57 has blocks showing half-hour increments. As you go through the week, write in what you do each hour, indicating when you started and when you stopped. Don't forget activities that don't feel like "activities" such as sleeping, relaxing, and watching TV. Finally, be sure to record your actual activities instead of how you want to have, or think you should have, spent your time. There are no wrong answers.

Activity	Estimated Time Spent	Activity	Estimated Time Spent
Class		Chores and personal business	
Work		Friends and important relationships	
Studying		Telephone time	
Sleeping		Leisure/entertainment	
Eating		Spiritual life	
Family time/child care		Other	
Commuting/traveling		**TOTAL**	

Monday		Tuesday		Wednesday		Thursday	
TIME	ACTIVITY	TIME	ACTIVITY	TIME	ACTIVITY	TIME	ACTIVITY
6:00 A.M.		6:00 A.M.		6:00 A.M.		6:00 A.M.	
6:30 A.M.		6:30 A.M.		6:30 A.M.		6:30 A.M.	
7:00 A.M.		7:00 A.M.		7:00 A.M.		7:00 A.M.	
7:30 A.M.		7:30 A.M.		7:30 A.M.		7:30 A.M.	
8:00 A.M.		8:00 A.M.		8:00 A.M.		8:00 A.M.	
8:30 A.M.		8:30 A.M.		8:30 A.M.		8:30 A.M.	
9:00 A.M.		9:00 A.M.		9:00 A.M.		9:00 A.M.	
9:30 A.M.		9:30 A.M.		9:30 A.M.		9:30 A.M.	
10:00 A.M.		10:00 A.M.		10:00 A.M.		10:00 A.M.	
10:30 A.M.		10:30 A.M.		10:30 A.M.		10:30 A.M.	
11:00 A.M.		11:00 A.M.		11:00 A.M.		11:00 A.M.	
11:30 A.M.		11:30 A.M.		11:30 A.M.		11:30 A.M.	
12:00 P.M.		12:00 P.M.		12:00 P.M.		12:00 P.M.	
12:30 P.M.		12:30 P.M.		12:30 P.M.		12:30 P.M.	
1:00 P.M.		1:00 P.M.		1:00 P.M.		1:00 P.M.	
1:30 P.M.		1:30 P.M.		1:30 P.M.		1:30 P.M.	
2:00 P.M.		2:00 P.M.		2:00 P.M.		2:00 P.M.	
2:30 P.M.		2:30 P.M.		2:30 P.M.		2:30 P.M.	
3:00 P.M.		3:00 P.M.		3:00 P.M.		3:00 P.M.	
3:30 P.M.		3:30 P.M.		3:30 P.M.		3:30 P.M.	
4:00 P.M.		4:00 P.M.		4:00 P.M.		4:00 P.M.	
4:30 P.M.		4:30 P.M.		4:30 P.M.		4:30 P.M.	
5:00 P.M.		5:00 P.M.		5:00 P.M.		5:00 P.M.	
5:30 P.M.		5:30 P.M.		5:30 P.M.		5:30 P.M.	
6:00 P.M.		6:00 P.M.		6:00 P.M.		6:00 P.M.	
6:30 P.M.		6:30 P.M.		6:30 P.M.		6:30 P.M.	
7:00 P.M.		7:00 P.M.		7:00 P.M.		7:00 P.M.	
7:30 P.M.		7:30 P.M.		7:30 P.M.		7:30 P.M.	
8:00 P.M.		8:00 P.M.		8:00 P.M.		8:00 P.M.	
8:30 P.M.		8:30 P.M.		8:30 P.M.		8:30 P.M.	
9:00 P.M.		9:00 P.M.		9:00 P.M.		9:00 P.M.	
9:30 P.M.		9:30 P.M.		9:30 P.M.		9:30 P.M.	
10:00 P.M.		10:00 P.M.		10:00 P.M.		10:00 P.M.	
10:30 P.M.		10:30 P.M.		10:30 P.M.		10:30 P.M.	
11:00 P.M.		11:00 P.M.		11:00 P.M.		11:00 P.M.	
11:30 P.M.		11:30 P.M.		11:30 P.M.		11:30 P.M.	
12–6 A.M.		12–6 A.M.		12–6 A.M.		12–6 A.M.	

Friday		Saturday		Sunday		Notes
TIME	ACTIVITY	TIME	ACTIVITY	TIME	ACTIVITY	
6:00 A.M.		6:00 A.M.		6:00 A.M.		
6:30 A.M.		6:30 A.M.		6:30 A.M.		
7:00 A.M.		7:00 A.M.		7:00 A.M.		
7:30 A.M.		7:30 A.M.		7:30 A.M.		
8:00 A.M.		8:00 A.M.		8:00 A.M.		
8:30 A.M.		8:30 A.M.		8:30 A.M.		
9:00 A.M.		9:00 A.M.		9:00 A.M.		
9:30 A.M.		9:30 A.M.		9:30 A.M.		
10:00 A.M.		10:00 A.M.		10:00 A.M.		
10:30 A.M.		10:30 A.M.		10:30 A.M.		
11:00 A.M.		11:00 A.M.		11:00 A.M.		
11:30 A.M.		11:30 A.M.		11:30 A.M.		
12:00 P.M.		12:00 P.M.		12:00 P.M.		
12:30 P.M.		12:30 P.M.		12:30 P.M.		
1:00 P.M.		1:00 P.M.		1:00 P.M.		
1:30 P.M.		1:30 P.M.		1:30 P.M.		
2:00 P.M.		2:00 P.M.		2:00 P.M.		
2:30 P.M.		2:30 P.M.		2:30 P.M.		
3:00 P.M.		3:00 P.M.		3:00 P.M.		
3:30 P.M.		3:30 P.M.		3:30 P.M.		
4:00 P.M.		4:00 P.M.		4:00 P.M.		
4:30 P.M.		4:30 P.M.		4:30 P.M.		
5:00 P.M.		5:00 P.M.		5:00 P.M.		
5:30 P.M.		5:30 P.M.		5:30 P.M.		
6:00 P.M.		6:00 P.M.		6:00 P.M.		
6:30 P.M.		6:30 P.M.		6:30 P.M.		
7:00 P.M.		7:00 P.M.		7:00 P.M.		
7:30 P.M.		7:30 P.M.		7:30 P.M.		
8:00 P.M.		8:00 P.M.		8:00 P.M.		
8:30 P.M.		8:30 P.M.		8:30 P.M.		
9:00 P.M.		9:00 P.M.		9:00 P.M.		
9:30 P.M.		9:30 P.M.		9:30 P.M.		
10:00 P.M.		10:00 P.M.		10:00 P.M.		
10:30 P.M.		10:30 P.M.		10:30 P.M.		
11:00 P.M.		11:00 P.M.		11:00 P.M.		
11:30 P.M.		11:30 P.M.		11:30 P.M.		
12–6 A.M.		12–6 A.M.		12–6 A.M.		

After a week, go through the chart below and add up how many hours you spent on the activities for which you previously estimated your hours. Tally the hours in the boxes in the following table using straight tally marks; round off to half hours and use a short tally mark for each half hour. In the third column, total the hours for each activity. Leave the "Ideal Time in Hours" column blank for now.

Activity	Time Tallied Over One-Week Period	Total Time in Hours	Ideal Time in Hours
Example: Class	IHt IHt IHt Iı	16.5	
Class			
Work			
Studying			
Sleeping			
Eating			
Family time/child care			
Commuting/traveling			
Chores and personal business			
Friends and important relationships			
Telephone time			
Leisure/entertainment			
Spiritual life			
Other			

Add the totals in the third column to find your grand total. Compare your grand total to your estimated grand total; compare your actual activity hour totals to your estimated activity hour totals. Use a separate sheet of paper to answer the following questions:

- What matches and what doesn't? Describe the most interesting similarities and differences.
- Where do you waste the most time? What do you think that is costing you?

Now evaluate what kinds of changes might improve your ability to achieve goals. Analyze what you do daily, weekly, and monthly. Go back to the chart above and fill in the "Ideal Time in Hours" column. Consider the difference between actual hours and ideal hours. Ask questions:

- On what activities do you think you should spend more or less time?
- What are you willing to do to change, and why?

Finally, write a short paragraph describing two key time-management changes in detail. Describe what goal you are aiming for, and map out how you plan to put the changes into action.

Career Portfolio

PLAN FOR SUCCESS

Complete the following in your electronic portfolio or on separate sheets of paper.

Career goals—knowledge and skills. No matter what career goals you ultimately pursue, certain knowledge and skills are useful in any career area. Consider this list of the general skills employers look for in people they hire:

Acceptance	Critical thinking	Leadership
Communication	Flexibility	Positive attitude
Continual learning	Goal setting	Teamwork
Creativity	Integrity	

Choose and circle three of these that you want to focus on developing this year.

Map out a plan for your progress by indicating a series of smaller goals—from short-term to long-term—that will lead you toward developing these skills. For each of the three skills, write what you hope to accomplish in the next year, the next six months, and the next month. For example:

Skill: Leadership

Next month: I will volunteer to lead a session with my Economics study group.

In six months: I will look into leadership positions on the college newspaper.

By the end of the year: I will have joined the newspaper team and expressed my interest in a leadership position.

SUGGESTED READINGS

Allen, David. *Getting Things Done: The Art of Stress-Free Productivity*. New York: Penguin Books, 2003.

Burka, Jane B., Ph.D. and Lenora M. Yuen, Ph.D. *Procrastination*. Reading, MA: Perseus Books, 1983.

Covey, Stephen. *The Seven Habits of Highly Effective People*. New York: Simon & Schuster, 1995.

Emmett, Rita. *The Procrastinator's Handbook: Mastering the Art of Doing It Now*. New York: Walker & Co., 2000.

Gleeson, Kerry. *The Personal Efficiency Program: How to Get Organized to Do More Work in Less Time*, 2nd ed. New York: John Wiley & Sons, 2000.

Lakein, Alan. *How to Get Control of Your Time and Your Life*. New York: New American Library, 1996.

Leyden-Rubenstein, Lori. *The Stress Management Handbook*. New York: McGraw-Hill, 1999.

Sapadin, Linda and Jack Maguire. *Beat Procrastination and Make the Grade: The Six Styles of Procrastination and How Students Can Overcome Them*. New York: Penguin USA, 1999.

Timm, Paul R. *Successful Self-Management: A Psychologically Sound Approach to Personal Effectiveness*. Los Altos, CA: Crisp Publications, 1996.

INTERNET RESOURCES

Mind Tools (section on time management): www.mind tools.com/pages/main/newMN_HTE.htm

Top Achievement—goal—setting and self-improvement resources: www.topachievement.com

About.com stress-management resources: http://stress.about.com/

Troubled With—information on stress management: www.troubledwith.com

ENDNOTES

1. Student essay submitted by the First Year Experience students of Patty Parma, Palo Alto College, San Antonio, Texas, January 2004.

2. *A Report from the Center for Academic Integrity*, Center for Academic Integrity, Kenan Institute for Ethics, Duke University, October 1999 [on-line]. Available:www.academicintegrity.org (March 2001).

3. Ibid.

4. Background information for information on cultural diversity from Afsaneh Nahavandi and Ali Malekzadeh, *Organizational Behavior: The Person-Organization Fit*. Upper Saddle River, NJ: Prentice Hall, 1999.

5. Louis E. Boone, David L. Kurtz, and Judy R. Block, *Contemporary Business Communication*, 2nd ed. Upper Saddle River, NJ: Prentice Hall, 1997, pp. 68–72.

6. Louis E. Boone and David L. Kurtz, *Contemporary Business Communication*. Englewood Cliffs, NJ: Prentice Hall, 1994, p. 643.

7. "What's an Ordinary Day Like When You're in College?" New Mexico State University Web site, June 1999 [on-line]. Available: www.nmsu.edu/aggieland/students/faq_ordinary.html (March 2004).

8. Paul Timm, *Successful Self-Management: A Psychologically Sound Approach to Personal Effectiveness*. Los Altos, CA: Crisp Publications, 1987, pp. 22–41.

9. Welch Suggs, "How Gears Turn at a Sports Factory: Running Ohio State's $79-million Athletics Program Is a Major Endeavor, with Huge Payoffs and Costs," *The Chronicle of Higher Education*, November 29, 2002 [on-line]. Available: http://chronicle.com/weekly/v49/il4/14a03201.htm (March 2004).

10. Jeffrey R. Young, "'Homework? What Homework?' Students Seem to be Spending Less Time Studying than They Used To," *The Chronicle of Higher Education*, December 6, 2002 [on-line]. Available: http://chronicle.com/weekly/v49/i15/15a03501. htm (March 2004).

11. William E. Sydnor, "Procrastination," from the California Polytechnic State University Study Skills Library [on-line]. Based on *Overcoming Procrastination* by Albert Ellis. Available: www.sas.calpoly.edu/asc/ssl/procrastination.html (May 2003). Used with permission.

12. Jane B. Burka, Ph.D. and Lenora M. Yuen, Ph.D., *Procrastination*. Reading, MA: Perseus Books, 1983, pp. 21–22.

13. Ibid.

14. The following articles were used as sources in this section: Glenn C. Altschuler, "Adapting to College Life in an Era of Heightened Stress," *New York Times*, Education Life, Section 4A, August 6, 2000, p. 12; Carol Hymowitz and Rachel Emma Silverman, "Can Workplace Stress Get Worse?" *Wall Street Journal*, January 16, 2001, p. B1; Robert M. Sapolsky, "Best Ways to Reduce Everyday Levels of Stress . . . Bad Ol' Stress," *Bottom Line Personal*, January 15, 2000, p. 13; Kate Slaboch, "Stress and the College Student: A Debate" [on-line]. Available: www.jour.unr.edu/outpost/voices/voi.slaboch.stress. htm (April 4, 2001); University of South Florida, The Counseling Center for Human Development, "Coping with Stress in College" [on-line]. Available: http://usfweb.usf.edu/counsel/self-hlp/stress.htm (April 4, 2001); Jodi Wilgoren, "Survey Shows High Stress Levels in College Freshmen," *New York Times*, January 23, 2000, p. NA.

3

Learning Styles, Majors, and Careers

KNOWING YOUR TALENTS AND FINDING YOUR DIRECTION

As a college student, you are investing valuable resources—time, effort, and money—in your education. Learning is the return on your investment. How well you learn, and therefore how good a return you receive, depends in part on knowing yourself in two ways: knowing *how* you learn and knowing what you want to *do* with what you learn.

This chapter focuses first on helping you identify your learning styles, because when you understand how you learn, you will be a more effective student. Then you will read about majors and careers, because knowing where you want your education to take you will motivate you toward a goal.

On the following page, read how student Michael Nolan is trying to find a major that reflects his talents and passions.

- How can you discover your learning styles?
- What are the benefits of knowing how you learn?
- How can you choose a major?
- How can Multiple Intelligences help you explore majors and careers?
- How can you identify and manage learning disabilities?

How can I find the right major for me?

I have loved sports as long as I can remember. I love the strategy, the thought, and the decisions involved as much as I do the athletics. In fact, to me, the creation of a winning team from a jumble of talented players is often more interesting than the game itself.

Because of this, the business of sports is fascinating to me. One problem is that it's hard to get experience in as competitive a field as sports business. Also, there aren't a lot of sports business programs in the country, particularly at schools that interest me and have strong sports programs. Ideally, I'd also like to have a major that could be used elsewhere, in case I can't find a job in sports.

How can I find a major that appeals to my interests and that leads to a good career? How can I make sure that I like my chosen occupation and test its compatibility with me at school? And how can I learn what classes I should take to learn the most about sports business and excel in my field?

Michael Nolan
Oregon State University,
Corvallis, Oregon

I encourage you to take internships in your field . . .

From early childhood, I wanted to be a scientist. I lived for the day when I'd be able to go to a real university and do real research in a real lab and contribute to the growing body of scientific knowledge. So, when one of my professors asked me to work for him on some antibiotics research at the end of my freshman year, I was ecstatic. After years of anticipation, I'd finally get to do what I'd dreamed of.

And I found that I hated it. Most of what I did was repetitive, such as reacting the product, identifying the product, purifying the product—all in long, laborious tasks for which I couldn't see the end result. Worse, even if what I was working on did turn into a lifesaving antibiotic, it would likely take decades before anyone could use it. I found I just didn't have the patience for research. I don't like long hours of repetitive lab work and I don't want to wait for decades for a theory to become useful.

So, I discovered engineering. And I found a career that seems perfect for me, even though I couldn't have imagined myself as an engineer when I began college. Yet, the irony is that I discovered that I love engineering and don't adore scientific research only because I did an internship.

Had I not decided to do research in college, I'd probably be looking for a good Ph.D. program now, rather than doing something I love. I still like research and I still love reading about what's on the cutting edge of technology, but I also realize that a life of pure research isn't for me. That's probably the most important thing that I learned from my internship. I encourage you to take internships in your field because it was a lot better for me to learn that I didn't like lab work in college than it would have been several years into my first job.

Julia Nolan
University of California,
Davis, California

How can you *discover* your learning styles?

Your style of taking in and remembering information is as unique as you are. Have you ever thought in detail about what that style is? Doing just that—working to understand your learning strengths and preferences and the primary ways in which you interact with others—will help you achieve your personal best in school and beyond.

This chapter presents two assessments designed to help you figure out how you learn and interact. The first—*Multiple Pathways to Learning*—focuses on learning strengths and preferences and is based on Professor Howard Gardner's Multiple Intelligences Theory. The second—the *Personality Spectrum*—is based on the Myers-Briggs Type Inventory® (MBTI) and helps you evaluate how you react to people and situations.

The value of learning styles assessments

Everyone has some things that they do well and other things that they find difficult. To be a successfully intelligent learner, you need to maximize your strengths and compensate for your weaknesses. The first step toward that goal is knowing what those strengths and weaknesses *are*—and that's what these assessments will help you discover. With the information you gain from the Multiple Pathways to Learning and the Personality Spectrum, you can choose your own best ways to study, manage time, remember material, and much more.

To be what we are, and to become what we are capable of becoming, is the only end of life.

ROBERT LOUIS STEVENSON

Knowing how you learn will help you set specific goals for positive change. For example, instead of saying, "I'm no good at math," you can strengthen your math skills with what you've learned from Multiple Pathways to Learning. You might draw diagrams of math problems if you are a visual learner or talk out problems with a study partner if you are an interpersonal learner. (You will learn about these and other learning styles later in the chapter.) The better you know yourself, the better you are able to handle different learning situations and challenges.

Gaining an understanding of learning style will also enhance your ability to see and appreciate how people differ, because learning style is part of the diversity that lies within. When you sit in a classroom with 30 students, you can be sure that each person is learning the material in a unique way. The more you know about how others approach learning, the more you can use that understanding to improve communication and teamwork.

LEARNING STYLE

A particular way in which the mind receives and processes information.

Putting assessment results in perspective

First, remember that any assessment is simply a snapshot, a look at who you are at a given moment. Your answers can, and will, change as you and the circumstances around you change. These assessments help you look at the present—and plan for the future—by asking questions: Who am I right now? How does this compare with who I want to be?

Second, there are no "right" answers, no "best" set of scores. Think of your responses in the same way you would if you were trying on a new set of eyeglasses to correct blurred vision. The glasses will not create new paths and possibilities, but they will help you see more clearly the ones that already exist.

Following each assessment is information about the typical traits of, and appropriate study strategies for, each intelligence or personality spectrum dimension. As you will see from your scores, you have abilities in all areas, though some are more developed than others. Therefore, you will find useful suggestions under all the headings. Try different techniques and keep what works for you.

Assess your Multiple Intelligences

In 1983, Howard Gardner, a Harvard University professor, changed the way people perceive intelligence and learning with his theory of Multiple Intelligences. Gardner believes that there are at least eight intelligences possessed by all people, and that every person has developed some intelligences more fully than others (see Key 3.1 for descriptions). According to

INTELLIGENCE

As defined by H. Gardner, an ability to solve problems or fashion products that are useful in a particular cultural setting or community.

Each intelligence is linked to specific abilities.

key 3.1

INTELLIGENCE	DESCRIPTION
Verbal–Linguistic	Ability to communicate through language (listening, reading, writing, speaking)
Logical–Mathematical	Ability to understand logical reasoning and problem solving (math, science, patterns, sequences)
Bodily–Kinesthetic	Ability to use the physical body skillfully and to take in knowledge through bodily sensation (coordination, working with hands)
Visual–Spatial	Ability to understand spatial relationships and to perceive and create images (visual art, graphic design, charts and maps)
Interpersonal	Ability to relate to others, noticing their moods, motivations, and feelings (social activity, cooperative learning, teamwork)
Intrapersonal	Ability to understand one's own behavior and feelings (self-awareness, independence, time spent alone)
Musical	Ability to comprehend and create meaningful sound and recognize patterns (music, sensitivity to sound and patterns)
Naturalistic	Ability to understand features of the environment (interest in nature, environmental balance, ecosystem, stress relief brought by natural environments)

this theory, when you find a task or subject easy, you are probably using a more fully developed intelligence. When you have trouble, you may be using a less developed intelligence.[1]

Gardner believes that the way you learn is a unique blend of intelligences, resulting from your distinctive abilities, challenges, experiences, and training. In addition, ability in the intelligences may develop or recede as your life changes. Gardner thinks that the traditional view of intelligence, based on mathematical, logical, and verbal measurements, doesn't reflect the entire spectrum of human ability:

> I believe that we should . . . look . . . at more naturalistic sources of information about how peoples around the world develop skills important to their way of life. Think, for example, of sailors in the South Seas, who find their way around hundreds, or even thousands, of islands by looking at the constellations of stars in the sky, feeling the way a boat passes over the water, and noticing a few scattered landmarks. A word for intelligence in a society of these sailors would probably refer to that kind of navigational ability.[2]

The Multiple Pathways to Learning assessment helps you determine the levels to which your eight intelligences are developed. Key 3.2, immediately following the assessment, describes specific skills associated with the eight intelligences as well as study techniques that maximize each. Finally, the Multiple Intelligence Strategies grids in Chapters 5 through 11 will demonstrate how to apply your learning styles knowledge to key college success skills.

MULTIPLE PATHWAYS TO LEARNING

Each intelligence has a set of numbered statements. Consider each statement on its own. Then, on a scale from 1 to 4, rate how closely it matches who you are right now and write that number on the line next to the statement. Finally, total each set of six questions.

rarely	sometimes	usually	always
1	**2**	**3**	**4**

1. _____ I enjoy physical activities.
2. _____ I am uncomfortable sitting still.
3. _____ I prefer to learn through doing.
4. _____ When sitting I move my legs or hands.
5. _____ I enjoy working with my hands.
6. _____ I like to pace when I'm thinking or studying.

_____ TOTAL for BODILY–KINESTHETIC

1. _____ I use maps easily.
2. _____ I draw pictures/diagrams when explaining ideas.
3. _____ I can assemble items easily from diagrams.
4. _____ I enjoy drawing or photography.
5. _____ I do not like to read long paragraphs.
6. _____ I prefer a drawn map over written directions.

_____ TOTAL for VISUAL–SPATIAL

1. _____ I listen to music.
2. _____ I move my fingers or feet when I hear music.
3. _____ I have good rhythm.
4. _____ I like to sing along with music.
5. _____ People have said I have musical talent.
6. _____ I like to express my ideas through music.

_____ TOTAL for MUSICAL

1. _____ I like doing a project with other people.
2. _____ People come to me to help settle conflicts.
3. _____ I like to spend time with friends.
4. _____ I am good at understanding people.
5. _____ I am good at making people feel comfortable.
6. _____ I enjoy helping others.

_____ TOTAL for INTERPERSONAL

1. _____ I enjoy telling stories.
2. _____ I like to write.
3. _____ I like to read.
4. _____ I express myself clearly.
5. _____ I am good at negotiating.
6. _____ I like to discuss topics that interest me.

_____ TOTAL for VERBAL–LINGUISTIC

1. _____ I like math in school.
2. _____ I like science.
3. _____ I problem-solve well.
4. _____ I question how things work.
5. _____ I enjoy planning or designing something new.
6. _____ I am able to fix things.

_____ TOTAL for LOGICAL–MATHEMATICAL

1. _____ I need quiet time to think.
2. _____ I think about issues before I want to talk.
3. _____ I am interested in self-improvement.
4. _____ I understand my thoughts and feelings.
5. _____ I know what I want out of life.
6. _____ I prefer to work on projects alone.

_____ TOTAL for INTRAPERSONAL

1. _____ I enjoy nature whenever possible.
2. _____ I think about having a career involving nature.
3. _____ I enjoy studying plants, animals, or oceans.
4. _____ I avoid being indoors except when I sleep.
5. _____ As a child I played with bugs and leaves.
6. _____ When I feel stressed I want to be out in nature.

_____ TOTAL for NATURALISTIC

Developed by Joyce Bishop, Ph.D., and based upon Howard Gardner's *Frames of Mind: The Theory of Multiple Intelligences.*[3]

SCORING GRID FOR **MULTIPLE PATHWAYS TO LEARNING**

For each intelligence, shade the box in the row that corresponds with the range where your score falls. For example, if you scored 17 in Bodily–Kinesthetic intelligence, you would shade the middle box in that row; if you scored a 13 in Visual–Spatial, you would shade the last box in that row. When you have shaded one box for each row, you will see a "map" of your range of development at a glance.

A score of 20–24 indicates a high level of development in that particular type of intelligence, 14–19 a moderate level, and below 14 an underdeveloped intelligence.

	20–24 (Highly Developed)	14–19 (Moderately Developed)	Below 14 (Underdeveloped)
Bodily–Kinesthetic			
Visual–Spatial			
Verbal–Linguistic			
Logical–Mathematical			
Musical			
Interpersonal			
Intrapersonal			
Naturalistic			

How to put your Multiple Intelligences to work for you.

ABILITIES AND SKILLS ASSOCIATED WITH EACH INTELLIGENCE

Verbal–Linguistic
- Analyzing own use of language
- Remembering terms easily
- Explaining, teaching, learning, using humor
- Understanding syntax and word meaning
- Convincing someone to do something

Musical–Rhythmic
- Sensing tonal qualities
- Creating/enjoying melodies, rhythms
- Being sensitive to sounds and rhythms
- Using "schemas" to hear music
- Understanding the structure of music

Logical–Mathematical
- Recognizing abstract patterns
- Reasoning inductively and deductively
- Discerning relationships and connections
- Performing complex calculations
- Reasoning scientifically

Visual–Spatial
- Perceiving and forming objects accurately
- Recognizing relationships between objects
- Representing something graphically
- Manipulating images
- Finding one's way in space

Bodily–Kinesthetic
- Connecting mind and body
- Controlling movement
- Improving body functions
- Expanding body awareness to all senses
- Coordinating body movement

Intrapersonal
- Evaluating own thinking
- Being aware of and expressing feelings
- Understanding self in relation to others
- Thinking and reasoning on higher levels

Interpersonal
- Seeing things from others' perspectives
- Cooperating within a group
- Communicating verbally and nonverbally
- Creating and maintaining relationships

Naturalistic
- Deep understanding of nature
- Appreciation of the delicate balance in nature

STUDY TECHNIQUES TO MAXIMIZE EACH INTELLIGENCE

Verbal–Linguistic
- Read text; highlight no more than 10%
- Rewrite notes
- Outline chapters
- Teach someone else
- Recite information or write scripts/debates

Musical–Rhythmic
- Create rhythms out of words
- Beat out rhythms with hand or stick
- Play instrumental music/write raps
- Put new material to songs you already know
- Take music breaks

Logical–Mathematical
- Organize material logically
- Explain material sequentially to someone
- Develop systems and find patterns
- Write outlines and develop charts and graphs
- Analyze information

Visual–Spatial
- Develop graphic organizers for new material
- Draw mind maps
- Develop charts and graphs
- Use color in notes to organize
- Visualize material (method of loci)

Bodily–Kinesthetic
- Move or rap while you learn; pace and recite
- Use "method of loci" or manipulatives
- Move fingers under words while reading
- Create "living sculptures"
- Act out scripts of material, design games

Intrapersonal
- Reflect on personal meaning of information
- Visualize information/keep a journal
- Study in quiet settings
- Imagine experiments

Interpersonal
- Study in a group
- Discuss information
- Use flash cards with others
- Teach someone else

Naturalistic
- Connect with nature whenever possible
- Form study groups of people with like interests

Adapted from Lazear, *Seven Pathways of Learning,* 1994.

Assess your personality with the Personality Spectrum

Personality assessments help you understand how you respond to the world around you—including information, thoughts, feelings, people, and events. The assessment used in this chapter is based on one of the most widely used personality inventories in the world—the Myers-Briggs Type Inventory, developed by Katharine Briggs and her daughter, Isabel Briggs Myers. It also relies upon the work of David Keirsey and Marilyn Bates, who combined the 16 Myers-Briggs types into four temperaments and developed an assessment called the Keirsey Sorter based on those temperaments.

The Personality Spectrum assessment adapts and simplifies their material into four personality types—Thinker, Organizer, Giver, and Adventurer—and was developed by Dr. Joyce Bishop. The Personality Spectrum helps you identify the kinds of interactions that are most, and least, comfortable for you. Key 3.3, on page 74, shows techniques that improve performance, learning strategies, and ways of relating to others for each personality type.

Three students engage verbal, bodily-kinesthetic, and interpersonal learning skills as they perform a skit about the mythological god Dionysus for a course on classic Greek mythology.

PERSONALITY SPECTRUM

STEP 1. Rank order all 4 responses to each question from most like you (4) to least like you (1) so that for each question you use the numbers 1, 2, 3, and 4 one time each. Place numbers in the boxes next to the responses.

4 most like me **3** more like me **2** less like me **1** least like me

1. I like instructors who
   a. ☐ tell me exactly what is expected of me.
   b. ☐ make learning active and exciting.
   c. ☐ maintain a safe and supportive classroom.
   d. ☐ challenge me to think at higher levels.

2. I learn best when the material is
   a. ☐ well organized.
   b. ☐ something I can do hands-on.
   c. ☐ about understanding and improving the human condition.
   d. ☐ intellectually challenging.

3. A high priority in my life is to
   a. ☐ keep my commitments.
   b. ☐ experience as much of life as possible.
   c. ☐ make a difference in the lives of others.
   d. ☐ understand how things work.

4. Other people think of me as
   a. ☐ dependable and loyal.
   b. ☐ dynamic and creative.
   c. ☐ caring and honest.
   d. ☐ intelligent and inventive.

5. When I experience stress I would most likely
   a. ☐ do something to help me feel more in control of my life.
   b. ☐ do something physical and daring.
   c. ☐ talk with a friend.
   d. ☐ go off by myself and think about my situation.

6. I would probably not be close friends with someone who is
   a. ☐ irresponsible.
   b. ☐ unwilling to try new things.
   c. ☐ selfish and unkind to others.
   d. ☐ an illogical thinker.

7. My vacations could be described as
   a. ☐ traditional.
   b. ☐ adventuresome.
   c. ☐ pleasing to others.
   d. ☐ a new learning experience.

8. One word that best describes me is
   a. ☐ sensible.
   b. ☐ spontaneous.
   c. ☐ giving.
   d. ☐ analytical.

STEP 2. Add up the total points for each letter.

TOTAL FOR **a.** ☐ Organizer **b.** ☐ Adventurer **c.** ☐ Giver **d.** ☐ Thinker

STEP 3. Plot these numbers on the brain diagram on page 73.

SCORING DIAGRAM FOR PERSONALITY SPECTRUM

Write your scores from p. 72 in the four squares just outside the brain diagram—Thinker score at top left, Giver score at top right, Organizer score at bottom left, and Adventurer score at bottom right.

Each square has a line of numbers that go from the square to the center of the diagram. For each of your four scores, place a dot on the appropriate number in the line near that square. For example, if you scored 15 in the Giver spectrum, you would place a dot between the 14 and 16 in the upper right-hand line of numbers. If you scored a 26 in the Organizer spectrum, you would place a dot on the 26 in the lower left-hand line of numbers.

Connect the four dots to make a four-sided shape. If you like, shade the four sections inside the shape using four different colors.

THINKER

- Technical
- Scientific
- Mathematical
- Dispassionate
- Rational
- Analytical
- Logical
- Problem Solving
- Theoretical
- Intellectual
- Objective
- Quantitative
- Explicit
- Realistic
- Literal
- Precise
- Formal

GIVER

- Interpersonal
- Emotional
- Caring
- Sociable
- Giving
- Spiritual
- Musical
- Romantic
- Feeling
- Peacemaker
- Trusting
- Adaptable
- Passionate
- Harmonious
- Idealistic
- Talkative
- Honest

ORGANIZER

- Tactical
- Planning
- Detailed
- Practical
- Confident
- Predictable
- Controlled
- Dependable
- Systematic
- Sequential
- Structured
- Administrative
- Procedural
- Organized
- Conservative
- Safekeeping
- Disciplined

ADVENTURER

- Active
- Visual
- Risking
- Original
- Artistic
- Spatial
- Skillful
- Impulsive
- Metaphoric
- Experimental
- Divergent
- Fast-paced
- Simultaneous
- Competitive
- Imaginative
- Open-minded
- Adventuresome

For the Personality Spectrum,
26–36 indicates a strong tendency in that dimension,
14–25 a moderate tendency,
and below 14 a minimal tendency.

Source for brain diagram: Understanding Psychology, 3/e, by Morris, © 1996.
Adapted by permission of Prentice-Hall, Inc., Upper Saddle River, NJ.

Instructors often rely on one or more teaching styles.

TEACHING STYLE	WHAT TO EXPECT IN CLASS
LECTURE, VERBAL FOCUS	Instructor speaks to the class for the entire period, with little class interaction. Lesson is taught primarily through words, either spoken or written on the board, overhead projector, handouts, or text.
GROUP DISCUSSION	Instructor presents material but encourages class discussion.
SMALL GROUPS	Instructor presents material and then breaks class into small groups for discussion or project work.
VISUAL FOCUS	Instructor uses visual elements such as diagrams, photographs, drawings, transparencies.
LOGICAL PRESENTATION	Instructor organizes material in a logical sequence, such as by time or importance.
RANDOM PRESENTATION	Instructor tackles topics in no particular order, and may jump around a lot or digress.

Play to your strengths. For example, an Organizer with an instructor who delivers material in a random way might rewrite notes in an outline format to bring structure to concepts and insert facts where they fit best. Likewise, a Giver taking a straight lecture course with no student-to-student contact might meet with a study group to go over the details and fill in factual gaps.

Work to build weaker areas. As a visual learner reviews notes from a structured lecture course, he could outline them, allot extra time to master the material, and work with a study group. A Thinker, studying for a test from notes delivered by an Adventurer instructor, could find hands-on ways to review the material (for example, for a science course, working in the lab).

Learning is not attained by chance, it must be sought for with ardor and attended to with diligence.

ABIGAIL ADAMS

Ask your instructor for additional help. If you are having trouble with coursework, communicate with your instructor through e-mail or face-to-face during office hours. This is especially important in large lectures where you are anonymous unless you speak up. The visual learner, for example, might ask the instructor to recommend graphs or figures that illustrate the lecture.

Instructors are unique. No instructor can give each of a diverse group of learners exactly what each one needs. The flexibility that you need to mesh your learning style with instructors' teaching styles is a tool for career and life success. Just as you can't hand-pick your instructors, you will rarely, if ever, be able to choose your supervisors or their work styles.

Workplace benefits

Knowing how you learn brings you these benefits in your career:

- **Better performance through self-awareness.** Since your learning styles are essentially the same as your working styles, knowing how you learn will help you identify career and work environments that suit you. Knowing your strengths will help you use and highlight them on the job. When a task involves one of your weaker skills, you can either take special care to accomplish it or suggest someone else who is a better fit.

- **Better teamwork.** The more attuned you are to abilities and personality traits, the better you will be at identifying the tasks you and others can best perform in team situations. For example, a Giver might enjoy helping new hires get used to the people and environment. Or a supervisor directing an intrapersonal learner might offer the chance to take material home to think about before a meeting.

- **Better career planning.** The more you know about how you learn and work, the more you will be able to focus on career paths that could work well for you. For the following student, strength in both logical–mathematical and interpersonal intelligence has guided him toward specific jobs and activities while in school and has helped him choose career goals:

A family joke around the Patterson household centers on the roots of eldest son Cody's love affair with mathematics. Like any young child, the story goes, Cody would grow impatient when forced to wait in line in a public place. In an attempt to distract her fidgeting son, his mother, Janalyn, would dig in her purse for her pocket calculator. Once in his hands, the calculator's blinking electronic numerals would mesmerize young Cody, and the wait was soon forgotten. . . . Patterson, 21, laughed as he recalled the hours spent punching buttons on that little gadget. "A lot of guys grew up with G.I. Joes and action figures," he said with a smile. "I grew up with calculators."[4]

Whether or not his mother's calculator did indeed encourage a life dedicated to mathematical pursuits, there is no doubt that Patterson was born with a gift for numbers. He worked as a teaching assistant for an upper-level analysis course, a "math problem" writer for math competitions, and a help session leader for advanced math courses, and has served as a Math Camp counselor and vice president of the Pi Mu Epsilon math honor society. "I'd like to be a college teacher and help students like me who have had opportunities to hit the big time," Patterson said, "and find some other students who are trying to find their place in academics, get them interested in math, and make believers out of them."

A better understanding of your learning strengths and preferences and personality traits will aid you in an upcoming educational challenge—choosing the right major.

How can you *choose a major*?

MAJOR

An academic subject area chosen as a field of specialization, requiring a specific course of study.

The major: It may not be around the corner, but it's probably not that far away. At some point in the next two years, after you complete your general education requirements, you will be asked to declare an academic major. Through this act you largely determine the courses you take, what you learn, with whom you spend your school time. Your major may also have a significant influence on your future career.

Taking a practical approach to declaring a major can help you avoid becoming overwhelmed by the task. Think of it as a long-term goal made up of multiple steps (short-term goals) that begin with knowing your learning styles, interests, and talents; exploring academic options; and establishing your academic schedule. You will be wise to start the process now, even though you probably don't need to decide right away—and even if, as is true of many students, you don't yet know what you want to study.

Short-term goal #1: Use learning styles assessments to identify interests and talents

Considering what you like and what you do well can lead to a fulfilling area of study. When you identify your interests and talents and choose a major that focuses on them, you are likely to have a positive attitude and perform at your highest level.

You may have sensed a career direction since you were young. This was the case with University of Illinois student Brian DeGraff, whose interests were mechanical: "I am amazed by how things work. The way a car can turn a tank of greasy, smelly, toxic liquid into my ride to school. People always say stop and smell the roses, but I'd rather stop and wonder why the roses smell. It was this passion that drove me to want to be an engineer; it's the best way I can imagine to spend my life figuring out how things work."[5]

> Great minds have purposes; others have wishes.
>
> **WASHINGTON IRVING**

To pinpoint the areas that spark your interest, use your Multiple Intelligences and Personality Spectrum assessment results to answer the following questions:

- What courses have I enjoyed the most in college and high school? What do these courses have in common?
- What subjects am I drawn to in my personal reading?
- What activities do I look forward to most?
- In what skills or academic areas do I perform best? Am I a "natural" in any area?
- What do people say I do well?
- What are my dominant learning styles?

Short-term goal #2:
Explore academic options

Next, find out about the academic choices available at your school. Plan to achieve the following minigoals in order to reach this short-term goal:

Learn what's possible. Consult your college catalog for guidelines on declaring (and changing) your major. Find answers to these questions:

- When do I have to declare a major? (generally at the end of the second year for four-year programs; earlier for associate or certificate programs)
- What are my options in majoring? (double majors, minors, interdisciplinary majors)
- What majors are offered at my school?

If a major looks interesting, explore it further by answering these questions:

- What minimum grade point average (GPA), if any, does the department require before it will accept me as a major?
- What GPA must I maintain in the courses included in the major?
- What preparatory courses (prerequisites) are required?
- What courses will I be required to take and in what sequence? How many credits do I need to graduate in the major?
- Will I have to write a thesis to graduate in this major?

Work closely with your advisor. Early on, begin discussing your major with your advisor; he or she can help you evaluate different options.

Visit the department. When considering a major, analyze your comfort with the academic department as well as with the material. When Ashiana Esmail decided to major in Ethnic Studies at the University of California at Berkeley, she did so in part because she wanted a close-knit department where faculty knew her and could be her advocates. Being involved like this "was better than an A+" in helping to build academic momentum, she explains.[6]

To learn more about the department, ask the department secretary for information. Then sit in on several classes to get a feel for the instructors and the work. Consider asking an instructor for an appointment to discuss the major.

Colleges offer different areas of study and types of classes. Listening to their instructor during a class on draft horses, these students learn from experiencing the horses firsthand.

Speak to people with experience in the major. Ask students who are a year or two ahead of you to describe their experiences with the courses, the workload, and the instructors.

Consider creative options for majoring. Think beyond the traditional majoring path, and investigate the possibilities at your school. One or more of the following may be open to you:

- **Double majors.** If, for example, you want to major in English and philosophy, ask your academic advisor if it is possible to meet the requirements for both departments.
- **Interdisciplinary majors.** If your preferred major isn't in the catalog, consult your advisor. Some schools allow students to design majors with guidance from advisors and instructors.
- **Minors.** A minor involves a concentration of departmental courses but has fewer requirements than a major. Many students choose a minor that is suited for a career. For example, a sociology major who wants to work in an inner-city hospital might consider a minor in Spanish.
- **Majors involving courses outside your school.** Some schools may offer study abroad programs (in which students spend a semester or a year at an affiliated college in a different country) or opportunities to take courses at nearby schools. Such courses might apply to a major that interests you.

Short-term goal #3:
Establish your academic schedule

Effective time management will enable you to fulfill the requirements of your major and complete all additional credits.

Look at your time frame. How many years do you plan to study as an undergraduate or graduate student? Do you plan to attend graduate school? If so, do you plan to go there directly after graduation or take time off?

CURRICULUM

The particular set of courses required for a degree.

Set timing for short-term goals. Within your time frame, pinpoint when to accomplish the important short-term goals that lead to graduation. What are the deadlines for completing core requirements, declaring a major, writing a thesis? Although you won't need to plan out your entire college course load at the beginning of your first semester, drafting a tentative curriculum—both within and outside your major—can help clarify where you are heading.

Identify dates connected to your goal fulfillment. Pay attention to academic dates (you will find an academic calendar in each year's college catalog and on the college's Web site). Such dates include registration dates, final date to declare a major, final date to drop a course, and so forth. Plan ahead so you don't miss a deadline.

Be flexible as you come to a decision

As with any serious challenge that involves defining your path flexibility is essential. Many students change their minds as they consider majors; some declare a major and then change it one or more times before finding a good fit. Just act on any change right away—once you have considered it carefully—by informing your advisor, completing any required paperwork, and redesigning your schedule to reflect your new choices.

LINK YOUR INTERESTS TO INTRIGUING MAJORS

Looking at a list of the majors your school offers, write down three that you want to consider.

1. _____

2. _____

3. _____

Now look at the list again. Other than what you wrote above, what majors catch your eye? Write down three intriguing majors—*without* thinking about what you would do with them or whether they are practical choices.

1. _____

2. _____

3. _____

Choose one major from the second list and explore it. Talk to your advisor about the major. Read about it in your college catalog. Consider a minor in the subject. Speak to an instructor in the department about related careers. You will have taken a casual interest and turned it into a viable academic option.

How can multiple intelligences help you *explore majors and careers*?

All that you have learned in this chapter about your learning styles and strengths has practical application as you begin thinking about your future at school and in the workplace. A strength in one or more intelligences may lead you to a major, an internship, and even a lifelong career.

Key 3.5 lists some possibilities for the eight intelligence types. This list is by no means complete. Rather, it represents only a fraction of the available opportunities. Use what you see here to inspire thought and spur investigation.

Career exploration strategies

Whatever your major, you will benefit from starting to think about careers early on. Use the following strategies to explore what's out there (later in the text, Chapter 11 will examine the topic of career exploration in depth).

Keep what you value in mind. Ask yourself what careers support the principles that guide your life. How important to you are service to others, financial security, a broad-based education, time for family?

Follow your passion. Find something you love doing more than anything else in the world, and then find a way to make money doing it. If you are sure of what you love to do but cannot pinpoint a career niche, open yourself to your instructors' advice.

MULTIPLE INTELLIGENCE	CONSIDER MAJORING IN . . .	THINK ABOUT AN INTERNSHIP AT A . . .	LOOK INTO A CAREER AS . . .
Bodily–Kinesthetic	Massage Therapy Physical Therapy Kinesiology Construction Engineering Chiropractics Sports Medicine Anatomy Dance Theater	Sports Physician's Office Athletic Club Physical Therapy Center Chiropractor's Office Construction Company Surveying Company Dance Studio Athletic Trainer Drafting Firm Theater Company	Carpenter Draftsman Recreational Therapist Physical Therapist Mechanical Engineer Massage Therapist Dancer or Acrobat Exercise Physiologist Actor
Intrapersonal	Psychology Sociology English Finance Liberal Arts Biology Computer Science Economics	Research and Development Firm Accounting Firm Computer Company Publishing House Pharmaceutical Company Engineering Firm Biology Lab	Research Scientist Motivational Speaker Engineer Physicist Sociologist Computer Scientist Economist Author Psychologist
Interpersonal	Psychology Sociology Education Real Estate Public Relations Nursing Business Hotel/Restaurant Management Rhetoric/Communications	Hotel or Restaurant Travel Agency Real Estate Agency Public Relations Firm Human Resources Customer Service Teaching Assistant Marketing/Sales Group Counseling Social Service	Social Worker PR Rep/Media Liaison Human Resources Travel Agent Sociologist Anthropologist Counselor Therapist Teacher Nurse
Naturalistic	Forestry Astronomy Geology Biology Zoology Atmospheric Sciences Oceanography Agriculture Animal Husbandry Environmental Law Physics	Museum National Park Oil Company Botanical Gardens Environmental Law Firm Outward Bound Adventure Travel Agency Zoo Camp Counselor Biological Research Firm	Forest Ranger Botanist or Herbalist Geologist Ecologist Marine Biologist Archaeologist Astronomer Adventure Travel Agent Wildlife Tour Guide Landscape Architect

(continued)

MULTIPLE INTELLIGENCE	CONSIDER MAJORING IN . . .	THINK ABOUT AN INTERNSHIP AT A . . .	LOOK INTO A CAREER AS . . .
Musical	Music Musical History Musical Theory Performing Arts Composition Voice Liberal Arts Entertainment Law	Performance Hall Radio Station Record Label Ballet or Theater Company Recording Studio Children's Music Camp Orchestra or Opera Company Musical Talent Agency Entertainment Law Firm	Lyricist or Composer Singer or Musician Voice Coach Music Teacher or Critic Record Executive Conductor Radio DJ Sound Engineer Entertainment Lawyer
Logical–Mathematical	Math Accounting Physics Economics Medicine Banking/Finance Astronomy Computer Science Systems Theory Law Chemistry Engineering	Law Firm Health Care Office Real Estate Brokerage Accounting Firm Animal Hospital Science Lab Consulting Firm Pharmaceutical Firm Bank	Doctor, Dentist, or Veterinarian Accountant Pharmacist Chemist Physicist Systems Analyst Investment Banker Financial Analyst Computer Scientist
Verbal–Linguistic	Communications Marketing English/Literature Journalism Foreign Languages Linguistic Theory Political Science Advertising/PR	Newspaper/Magazine Network TV Affiliate Publishing House Law Firm PR/Marketing Firm Speech Therapist Ad Agency Training Company Human Resources Customer Service	Author Playwright Journalist TV/Radio Producer Literature Teacher Speech Pathologist Business Executive Copywriter or Editor
Visual–Spatial	Visual Arts Architecture Interior Design Multimedia Design Film Theory Photography Art History	Art Gallery Museum Photography Studio Design Firm Advertising Agency Theatrical Set Designer Multimedia Firm Architecture Firm Film Studio	Graphic Artist Photographer Architect Cinematographer Art Therapist Designer Cartoonist/Illustrator Art Museum Curator Art Teacher

Sonia Lopez did just that when she declared a major in engineering at Rensselaer Polytechnic Institute. Sonia randomly chose aerospace engineering as her specialty until a professor told her what she could accomplish as a civil engineer. "The professor said the U. S. would be completely different if it weren't for civil engineers, and that we'd have no public transportation or sanitation system without their work." The comment changed Sonia's thinking. Suddenly, "helping build the infrastructure of towns and designing buildings seemed a lot more important than building planes and motors."[7]

Use career resources. Visit your school's career center to read current media, take an assessment, or explore the career areas that currently have good prospects. Check out careers, industries, and companies on the Internet. Talk with people who have jobs that interest you.

Explore educational requirements of careers. How much your choice of a major matters may depend on the career. For example, pursuing a career in medicine usually requires majoring in the biological sciences. In contrast, aiming for a career in law gives you more flexibility (political science, philosophy, and English are just a few possibilities for pre-law students).

Try hands-on exploration. Extracurricular activities and volunteering opportunities might provide experiences that help you decide. For example, a student interested in teaching may volunteer as a camp counselor or an after-school tutor.

Although almost everyone faces challenges in college, people with diagnosed learning disabilities have unique challenges that may interfere with college success. Focused assistance can help students who are learning disabled manage their conditions and excel in school.

How can you *identify and manage* learning disabilities?

Some learning disabilities cause reading problems, some create difficulties in math, and some make it difficult for students to process the language they hear. The following will help you understand learning disabilities and, should you be diagnosed with one, give you the tools to manage your disability successfully.

Identifying a learning disability

The National Center for Learning Disabilities (NCLD) defines learning disabilities in terms of what they are and what they are not:[8]

- They are neurological disorders that interfere with one's ability to store, process, and produce information.
- They do *not* include mental retardation, autism, behavioral disorders, impaired vision, hearing loss, or other physical disabilities.
- They do *not* include attention deficit disorder and attention deficit hyperactivity disorder (disorders involving consistent and problematic

inattention, hyperactivity, and/or impulsivity), although these problems may accompany learning disabilities.[9]

- They often run in families and are lifelong, although learning-disabled people can use specific strategies to manage and even overcome areas of weakness.
- They must be diagnosed by professionals in order for the disabled person to receive federally funded aid.

How can you determine if you should be evaluated for a learning disability? According to the NCLD, persistent problems in any of the following areas may indicate a learning disability:[10]

- reading or reading comprehension
- math calculations, understanding language and concepts
- social skills or interpreting social cues
- following a schedule, being on time, meeting deadlines
- reading or following maps
- balancing a checkbook
- following directions, especially on multistep tasks
- writing, sentence structure, spelling, and organizing written work

Details on specific learning disabilities appear in Key 3.6. For an evaluation, contact your school's learning center or student health center for a referral to a licensed professional.

Managing a learning disability

If you are diagnosed with a learning disability, focused action will help you manage it and maximize your ability to learn and succeed:

Be informed about your disability. Search the library and the Internet—try NCLD at www.ncld.org or LD Online at www.Idonline.org (other Web sites are listed at the end of the chapter). Or call NCLD at 1–888–575–7373. Make sure you understand your Individualized Education Program (IEP)— the document describing your disability and recommended strategies.

Seek assistance from your school. Speak with your advisor about specific accommodations that will help you learn. Services mandated by law for students who are learning disabled include:

- extended time on tests
- note-taking assistance (for example, having a fellow student take notes for you)
- assistive technology devices (tape recorders or laptop computers)
- modified assignments
- alternative assessments and test formats

Other services are tutoring, study skills assistance, and counseling.

Be a dedicated student. Be on time and attend class. Read assignments before class. Sit where you can avoid distractions. Review notes soon after class. Spend extra time on assignments. Ask for help.

DISABILITY/CONDITION	WHAT ARE THE SIGNS?
Dyslexia and related reading disorders	Problems with reading (including spelling, word sequencing, and comprehension) and processing (translating written language to thought or thought to written language)
Dyscalculia (developmental arithmetic disorders)	Difficulties in recognizing numbers and symbols, memorizing facts, aligning numbers, understanding abstract concepts like fractions, and applying math to life skills (time management, gauging distance, handling money, etc.)
Developmental writing disorders	Difficulties in composing complete sentences, organizing a writing assignment, or translating thoughts coherently to the page
Handwriting disorders (dysgraphia)	Disorder characterized by writing disabilities, including writing that is distorted or incorrect. Sufferers have poor handwriting that is difficult to read because of inappropriately sized and spaced letters. The use of wrong or misspelled words is also common
Speech and language disorders	Problems with producing speech sounds, using spoken language to communicate, and/or understanding what others say
LD-related social issues	Problems in recognizing facial or vocal cues from others, controlling verbal and physical impulsivity, and respecting others' personal space
LD-related organizational issues	Difficulties in scheduling and in organizing personal, academic, and work-related materials

Source: LD Online: Learning Disabilities Information and Resources, www.ldonline.org/ (accessed March 17, 2004). © 2001 WETA.

Build a positive attitude. See your accomplishments in light of how far you have come. Rely on people who support you. Know that the help you receive will give you the best possible chance to learn and grow.

Sabiduría

In Spanish, the term *sabiduría* represents the two sides of learning: knowledge and wisdom. *Knowledge* involves gaining information, understanding concepts, building what you know about how the world works. *Wisdom* is the collected meaning and significance gained from knowledge. The learning and life experiences you gain in college will build your personal *sabiduría*, which, in turn, will help you make wise personal, educational, and career choices.

Think of this concept as you acquire knowledge in your classes. Try to transform the facts and concepts you study into the building blocks of wisdom.

PERSONAL TRIUMPH

DR. JOYCE BISHOP Professor of Psychology, Golden West College, Huntington Beach, CA

Dr. Bishop, the creator of the assessments in this chapter, has a passion for learning styles that was inspired by her ordeal as a college student with a learning disability. As it did with her, knowing your learning styles can help you surmount the obstacles that come your way. Read the account; then use a separate piece of paper to answer the questions on page 88.

I have learning problems understanding words I hear, which made listening to lectures in college very hard. No one would know I had this difficulty because I learned how to compensate for it. In fact, I didn't even know it until years later. This learning disability is called auditory discrimination.

College was very confusing for me. I did well in some classes and felt totally lost in others. The hardest were the lecture-based classes. When I wasn't familiar with the information or the words, I couldn't make sense of what I was hearing.

If I read the material ahead of time, I could make visual pictures in my mind that would help me absorb the material. I could also look up words and research concepts I didn't understand. Then the lectures made more sense.

I read lips and facial expressions well, so I did well in small classes where I could consistently see the teacher's face. The disadvantage for me in small classes was the noise. Because I heard voices around me as much as I heard the speaker, I had trouble blocking the extra noise. To make my lecture classes easier to understand, I would drag a tape recorder to class so that I could play back the lecture a number of times later. I found, however, that it didn't really help when I re-listened to the tapes. After that, I bargained with my classmates to borrow their notes in exchange for typing their term papers. Typing is bodily–kinesthetic and helped me to internalize what I was learning.

The only reason I got by in college was that I am strong in logical-mathematical intelligence. School is primarily taught in the verbal-linguistic and logical-mathematical learning styles. I am also a strong visual learner. Science classes were easiest for me because they are more visual. I switched from sociology to biology my freshman year; it was easier for me to remember the visual biology material as opposed to the more verbal liberal arts classes. Without my commitment to my education and my will to succeed, I probably would not have graduated.

Twelve years after graduating, I pursued my master's in public health. Part of why I waited so long was that I needed to heal from the trauma of my own learning process. My graduate classes were much more hands-on, but there was still a great deal of reading. One day my eye doctor expressed concern about the stress my school work was causing my eyes and suggested that I get tested for a learning problem. He sent me to a center that usually tests small children for learning disabilities. The person giving the test said words and I was to spell out the words with blocks. I couldn't get some of the words right. I would consistently confuse or mistake words with close sounds. It was determined that I processed language on a fourth-grade level, a condition that has not changed in my adult life.

"How far did you go through school?" asked the therapist conducting the test.

"How far do you think I went?" I asked.

After thinking for a moment, she answered, "The tenth grade." I shared that I was just completing my master's degree. Her eyes got big and she said: "You work really hard in school, don't you?"

At that moment my head flooded with memories of report cards saying "doesn't pay attention in class" and "isn't working up to potential." I started to cry. An explanation for what had brought years of pain and struggle had finally come to the surface.

Now that I know what the problem is, I use strategies that allow me to deal with the way I learn. This is why I am so passionate about the power of learning styles. We all have our strengths and weaknesses; the way we work to manage those weaknesses while maximizing our strengths makes all the difference.

BUILDING SKILLS

FOR COLLEGE, CAREER, AND LIFE SUCCESS

Developing Successful Intelligence

PUTTING IT ALL TOGETHER

Learn from the experiences of others. Look back to Joyce Bishop's Personal Triumph on page 87. After you've read her story, relate her experience to your own life by completing the following:

Step 1. Think it through: *Analyze your experience and compare it to Joyce's.* What is a consistent challenge for you as a student, and how does this relate to Joyce's experience? How might this be explained by your learning styles? Do you have an "aha" experience story like Joyce's where you suddenly realized why you've struggled?

Step 2. Think out of the box: *Imagine ways of advising.* You are an advisor to a student identical to yourself. Be a harsh advisor—how would you criticize your performance as a student? Then be a wise advisor, focused on tapping into learning styles information—how would you identify challenges and suggest ways to handle them?

Step 3. Make it happen: *Head off your own challenges with practical strategies.* You have named a consistent challenge—and you have imagined what you would say as your own advisor. Now identify steps that will help you face your challenge (choosing particular courses, meeting with an advisor or instructor who can give you ideas, approaching work in particular ways).

Team Building

COLLABORATIVE SOLUTIONS

Ideas about personality types. Divide into groups according to the four types of the Personality Spectrum—Thinker-dominant students in one group, Organizer-dominant students in another, Giver-dominant students in a third, and Adventurer-dominant students in the fourth. If you have scored the same in more than one of these types, join whatever group is smaller. With your group, brainstorm the following lists for your type:

1. the strengths of this type
2. the struggles it brings
3. the stressors (things that cause stress) for this type
4. career areas that tend to suit this type
5. career areas that are a challenge for this type
6. people who annoy this type the most (often because they are strong in areas where this type needs to grow)

If there is time, each group can present this information to the entire class; this will boost understanding and acceptance of diverse ways of relating to information and people.

Writing

DISCOVERY THROUGH JOURNALING

Record your thoughts on a separate piece of paper or in a journal.

Strengths and weaknesses. What have the personal assessments in this chapter taught you about your strengths? Choose what you consider your greatest strength and discuss how you plan to use it to your advantage this semester. What areas of weakness did the assessments highlight? Choose a weakness that has given you difficulty in school and brainstorm ways to compensate for it this semester. Finally, brainstorm ideas for how you will deal this semester with the kinds of people who challenge you the most.

Career Portfolio

PLAN FOR SUCCESS

Complete the following in your electronic portfolio, if you can use a graphics program, or on separate sheets of paper.

Self-portrait. Because self-knowledge helps you to make the best choices about your future, a self-portrait is an important step in your career exploration. Use this exercise to synthesize everything you have been exploring about yourself into one comprehensive "self-portrait." Design your protrait in "think link" style, using words and visual shapes to describe your dominant Multiple Intelligences and Personality Spectrum dimensions, values, abilities, career interests, and anything else that is an important part of who you are.

A think link is a visual construction of related ideas, similar to a map or web, that represents your thought process. Ideas are written inside geometric shapes, often boxes or circles, and related ideas and facts are attached to those ideas by lines that connect the shapes. See the note-taking section in Chapter 6 for more about think links.

Use the style shown in the example in Key 3.7 or create your own. For example, in this exercise you may want to create a "wheel" of ideas coming off your central shape, entitled "Me." Then, spreading out from each of those ideas (interests, learning style, etc.), draw lines connecting all of the thoughts that go along with that idea. Connected to "Interests," for example, might be "singing," "stock market," and "history."

You don't have to use the wheel image. You might want to design a treelike think link or a line of boxes with connecting thoughts written below the boxes, or anything else you like. Let your design reflect who you are, just as what you write does.

One example of a self-portrait.

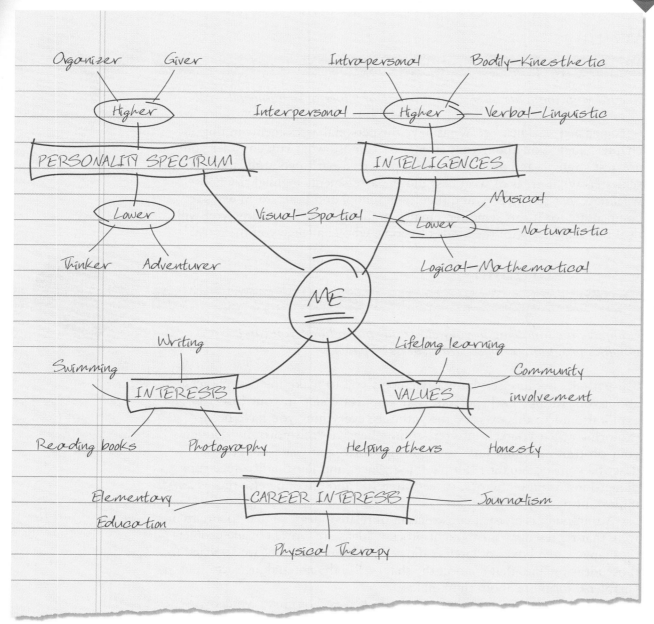

SUGGESTED READINGS

Cobb, Joyanne. *Learning How to Learn: A Guide for Getting into College with a Learning Disability, Staying in, and Staying Sane.* Washington, DC: Child Welfare League of America, 2001.

College Board, ed. *The College Board Index of Majors and Graduate Degrees 2001.* New York: College Entrance Examination Board, 2000.

Gardner, Howard. *Intelligence Reframed: Multiple Intelligences for the 21st Century.* New York: Basic Books, 2000.

Fogg, Neeta, et al. *The College Majors Handbook with Real Career Paths and Payoffs: The Actual Jobs, Earnings, and Trends for Graduates of 60 College Majors.* Indianapolis, IN: Jist Works, 2004.

Keirsey, David. *Please Understand Me II: Temperament, Character, Intelligence.* Del Mar, CA: Prometheus Nemesis Book Company, 1998.

Pearman, Roger R. and Sarah C. Albritton. *I'm Not Crazy, I'm Just Not You: The Real Meaning of the 16 Personality Types.* Palo Alto, CA: Consulting Psychologists Press, 1997.

Phifer, Paul. *College Majors and Careers: A Resource Guide for Effective Life Planning,* 4th ed. Chicago: Ferguson Publishing, 1999.

Sclafani, Annette. *College Guide for Students with Learning Disabilities.* New York: Laurel Publications, 2003.

INTERNET RESOURCES

Attention Deficit Disorder Association: www.add.org

Children and Adults with Attention Deficit/Hyperactivity Disorder: www.chadd.org

International Dyslexia Association: www.interdys.org

Keirsey Sorter and other Myers-Briggs information: www.keirsey.com

Learning Disabilities Online: www.ldonline.org/

National Center for Learning Disabilities: www.ncld.org

Prentice Hall Student Success Supersite Majors Exploration: www.prenhall.com/success/MajorExp/index.html

ENDNOTES

1. Howard Gardner, *Multiple Intelligences: The Theory in Practice.* New York: HarperCollins, 1993, pp. 5–49.

2. Ibid, p. 7.

3. Developed by Joyce Bishop, Ph.D., Golden West College, Huntington Beach, CA. Based on Howard Gardner, *Frames of Mind: The Theory of Multiple Intelligences.* New York: HarperCollins, 1993.

4. Kara Bounds Socol, "Cody Patterson '03: Math Student Benefits from Private Gifts," Texas A&M website [on-line]. Available: http://giving.tamu.edu/content/impactofgiving/studentstories/studentget.php?get=6.

5. Students Speak: Excerpts from Your Educational Experience Essays, the University of Illinois, October 2, 2001 [on-line]. Available: http://ae3.cen.uiuc.edu/stessay/StudentsSpeak (March 2004).

6. Terry Strathman, "L & S Colloquium on Undergraduate Education: What Do Students Want?," April 15, 2002 [on-line]. Available: http://ls.berkeley.edu/undergrad/colloquia/02–02.html (March 2004).

7. Elizabeth F. Farrell, "Engineering a Warmer Welcome for Female Students: The Discipline Tries to Stress Its Social Relevance, an Important Factor for Many Women," *The Chronicle of Higher Education,* February 22, 2002 [on-line]. Available: http://chronicle.com/weekly/v48/i24/24a03101.htm (March 2004).

8. National Center for Learning Disabilities. "LD at a Glance" [on-line]. Available: www.ncld.org/LDInfoZone/InfoZone_FactSheet_LD.cfm (May 2003).

9. National Center for Learning Disabilities. "Adult Learning Disabilities: A Learning Disability Isn't Something You Outgrow. It's Something You Learn to Master" (pamphlet). New York: National Center for Learning Disabilities.

10. National Center for Learning Disabilities. "LD Advocates Guide" [on-line]. Available: www.ld.org/Advocacy/tutorial_talking_about.cfm (May 2003).

4

IN THIS CHAPTER . . .

You will explore answers to the
following questions:

Critical, Creative, and Practical Thinking
SOLVING PROBLEMS AND MAKING DECISIONS

To survive and to thrive in college and beyond, you will need to use your thinking power to do more than remember formulas for a test. When problems or decisions arise on the road toward goals large and small, how can you work through them successfully? The answer lies in how you combine your analytical, creative, and practical thinking skills—in other words, how you use your successful intelligence. As you remember from Chapter 1, successful intelligence is "the kind of intelligence used to achieve important goals."[1]

Thinking, like note taking or car repair, is a skill that can be developed with practice. This chapter will help you build your ability to analyze information, come up with creative ideas, and put a practical plan into action. With these skills you can become a better thinker, problem solver, and decision maker, able to reach the goals that mean the most to you.

On the next page, read how student Parisa Malekzadeh worries about her test-taking skills.

- **What is successfully intelligent thinking?**
- **How can you improve your analytical thinking skills?**
- **How can you improve your creative thinking skills?**
- **How can you improve your practical thinking skills?**
- **How can you use your thinking skills to solve problems and make decisions?**

How can I succeed in college if I don't test well?

Although it was not always easy and I did get a few less than perfect grades, I did well in a very academic high school. My grades were good and I was also involved and successful in extracurricular activities. As a senior, I was one of four student administrators in a highly successful freshman mentor program. I am a third-degree black belt in tae kwon do, a two-time Arizona State champ, and a certified instructor. My family, my high school teachers, and my martial arts students and their parents have told me that I am so much more mature than other people my age, and they all think I will do well in college.

But I am not so sure, and there are times when I really worry. I have difficulty with multiple-choice tests and I did not do well on the SAT and ACT or several other multiple-choice tests I took for AP and other advance exams. I worry that maybe I am just not smart enough. So much of college seems to be objective tests. I can certainly express myself well in essay and when I talk with people. I rarely lose an argument!

How can I do better on these tests? How important are they really? And how can I use what I already do well to succeed in college and after?

Parisa Malekzadeh University of Arizona, Major—Undeclared

Strive to improve your skills, and know that your other strengths will lead you to success.

To accomplish goals in life one must remain focused on the objectives and maintain perseverance at all times. As Samuel Johnson said, "Great works are performed, not by strength, but perseverance." You have already demonstrated that you possess these qualities by both your academic performance and the level of expertise that you have accomplished in tae kwon do. These qualities will prove more important to your success than your test scores alone.

Don't let your past difficulties with multiple-choice tests erode your confidence. I had a similar experience. At the time of my medical education in Argentina, all the tests that I took were oral. In order to continue my postgraduate education in this country, I had to pass the Educational Commission for Foreign Medical Graduates (ECFMG) examination, which is almost entirely multiple choice.

Because I knew the medical material, I prepared myself by learning how to properly answer multiple-choice questions. I reviewed and took many sample tests. I promptly realized that the majority of my wrong answers occurred becuase I was quickly glancing at the questions instead of reading them carefully. With a more focused approach, I passed the qualifying test and was able to continue my postgraduate training that eventually led to an academic career.

A similar approach has helped me when confronted by a medical diagnostic problem. Analyzing the key signs and symptoms of a medical condition, and then correlating them to clinical and laboratory findings, has allowed me, in the majority of instances, to arrive at the proper diagnosis and treatment. However, analysis is only part of what I do. My success as a physician has come from combining analytical work with creativity—to think through situations comprehensively—and practical ability—to discuss the diagnosis with the patient, apply the appropriate treatment, and monitor the results.

Yes, your testing and analytical skills are important. Work hard to improve them, but value and build your practical and creative skills just as much, knowing that the combination will help you reach your goals. Good luck with your college career!

Benjamin E. Victorica, MD Professor Emeritus, Pediatric Cardiology, University of Florida

DOWN TO EARTH answers

What is *successfully intelligent* thinking?

Robert Sternberg uses this story to illustrate the impact of successful intelligence:

Two boys are walking in a forest. They are quite different. The first boy's teachers think he is smart, his parents think he is smart, and as a result, he thinks he is smart. He has good test scores, good grades, and other good paper credentials that will get him far in his scholastic life.

Few people consider the second boy smart. His test scores are nothing great, his grades aren't so good, and his other paper credentials are, in general, marginal. At best, people would call him shrewd or street smart.

As the two boys walk along in the forest, they encounter a problem—a huge, furious, hungry-looking grizzly bear, charging straight at them. The first boy, calculating that the grizzly bear will overtake them in 17.3 seconds, panics. In this state, he looks at the second boy, who is calmly taking off his hiking boots and putting on his jogging shoes.

The first boy says to the second boy, "You must be crazy. There is no way you are going to outrun that grizzly bear!"

The second boy replies, "That's true. But all I have to do is outrun you!"[2]

This story shows that successful problem solving and decision making require more than "book smarts." When confronted with a problem, using only analytical thinking put the first boy at a disadvantage. On the other hand, the second boy thought in different ways; he analyzed the situation, creatively considered the options, and took practical action. He asked and answered questions. He knew his purpose. And he lived to tell the tale.

Successfully intelligent thinking is balanced

Some tasks require only one thinking skill, or ability, at a time. You might use analytical thinking to complete a multiple-choice quiz, creative thinking to figure out how to get a paper done the same day you work a long shift, or practical thinking to put together a desk marked "some assembly required." However, when you need to solve a problem or make a decision, your analytical, creative, and practical thinking skills build upon one another to move you forward.[3] Envision it this way: Just as a pyramid needs three sides in order to stand, successful thinkers need all three thinking skills to develop the best solutions and decisions (see Key 4.1).

Each thinking skill adds an important dimension to accomplishing goals. Developing a balanced set of skills and knowing how and when to use each of them gives you more thinking power than having a strong aptitude in any one ability.[4] This kind of flexible thinking will help you connect your academic tasks to life goals—and show you where your hard work can take you (see Key 4.2).

Successfully intelligent thinking means asking and answering questions

What is thinking? According to experts, it is what happens when you ask questions and move toward the answers.[5] "To think through or rethink anything," says Dr. Richard Paul, director of research at the Center for Critical Thinking and Moral Critique, "one must ask questions that stimulate our thought. Questions define tasks, express problems and delineate issues. . . . only students who have questions are really thinking and learning."[6]

As you answer questions, you transform raw data into information that you can use. A *Wall Street Journal* article entitled "The Best Innovations Are Those That Come from Smart Questions" relays the story of a cell biology student, William Hunter, whose professor told him that "the difference between good science and great science is the quality of the questions posed." Later, as a doctor and the president and CEO of a pharmaceutical company, Dr. Hunter asked questions about new ways to use drugs. His questions led to the development of a revolutionary product—a drug-coated coronary stent that prevents scar tissue from forming. Through seeking answers to probing questions, Dr. Hunter reached a significant goal.[7]

You use questions in order to analyze ("How bad is my money situation?"), come up with creative ideas ("What ways could I earn money?"), and apply practical solutions ("How can I get a job on campus?"). Later in the chapter, in the sections on analytical, creative, and practical thinking, you will find examples of the kinds of questions that drive each skill.

Like any aspect of thinking, questioning is not often a straightforward process. Sometimes the answer doesn't come right away. Often the answer leads to more—and more specific—questions.

Successful intelligence helps you achieve goals in any discipline.

DISCIPLINE	ANALYTICAL THINKING	CREATIVE THINKING	PRACTICAL THINKING
Behavioral Science	Comparing one theory of child development with another	Devising a new theory of child development	Applying child development theories to help parents and teachers understand and deal with children more effectively
Literature	Analyzing the development of the main character in a novel	Writing alternative endings to the novel	Using the experience of the main character to better understand and manage one's own life situations
History	Considering similarities and differences between World War I and World War II	Imagining yourself as a German citizen, dealing with economic depression after WWI	Seeing what WWI and WWII lessons can be applied to current Middle East conflicts
Sports	Analyzing the opposing team's strategy on the soccer field	Coming up with innovative ways to move the ball downfield	Using tactics to hide your strategy from an opposing team—or a competing company

Source: Adapted from Robert J. Sternberg, *Successful Intelligence.* Plume: New York, 1997, p. 149.

Successfully intelligent thinking requires knowing your purpose

In order to ask useful questions, you need to know *why* you are questioning. In other words, you need to define your purpose. Not knowing your purpose may lead you to ask questions that take you in irrelevant directions and waste your time. For example, if an assignment asks you to analyze the effectiveness of John F. Kennedy's foreign policy during his presidency, asking questions about his personal life may lead you off the track.

A general question can be your starting point for defining your purposes: "What am I trying to accomplish, and why?" Then, within each stage of the process, you will find more specific purposes, or sub-goals, that help you generate analytical, creative, or practical questions along the way.

Successfully intelligent thinking is yours to build

You can improve, now and throughout your life, your ability to think. Studies have shown that the brain continues to develop throughout your life if you continue to learn new things.[8] Puzzle master Nob Yoshigahara has said, "As jogging is to the body, thinking is to the brain. The more we do it, the better we become."[9]

The mini-assessments within this chapter will help you to get an idea of how you perceive yourself as an analytical, creative, and practical thinker. Every other chapter's set of *Get Analytical, Get Creative*, and *Get Practical* exercises then helps you to build your skills in those areas. Finally, the *Developing Successful Intelligence: Putting It All Together* exercises at the ends of chapters encourage you to both build and combine your skills. *Your work throughout the book is geared toward building your successful intelligence.*

Begin by exploring the analytical thinking skills that you'll need in order to solve problems and make decisions effectively.

How can you improve your *analytical thinking* skills?

Analytical thinking—also known as critical thinking—is the process of gathering information, analyzing it in different ways, and evaluating it for the purposes of gaining understanding, solving a problem, or making a decision. It is as essential for real-life problems and decisions as it is for thinking through the hypothetical questions on your chemistry homework.

The first step in analytical thinking, as with all aspects of successful intelligence, is to define your purpose. What do you want to analyze, and why? Perhaps you need to analyze the plot of a novel in order to determine its structure; maybe you want to analyze your schedule in order to figure out whether you are arranging your time and responsibilities effectively.

Once you define your purpose, the rest of the analytical process involves gathering the necessary information, analyzing and clarifying the ideas, and evaluating what you've found.

Gather information

Information is the raw material for thinking. Choosing what to gather requires a careful analysis of how much information you need, how much time to spend gathering it, and whether the information is relevant. Say, for instance, that your assignment is to write a paper on one style of American jazz music. If you gathered every available resource on the topic, it might be next semester before you got to the writing stage.

Here's how you might use analysis to effectively gather information for that paper:

- Reviewing the assignment, you learn that the paper should be 10 pages and cover at least three influential musicians.
- At the library and on-line, you find lots of what appears to be relevant information.
- You choose a jazz movement, find five or six comprehensive pieces on it, and then select three in-depth sources on each of three musicians.

In this way you achieve a sub-goal—a selection of useful materials—on the way to your larger goal of writing a well-crafted paper.

Analyze and clarify information

Once you've gathered the information, the next step is to analyze it to determine whether the information is reliable and useful in helping you answer your questions.

Break information into parts

When analyzing information, you break information into parts and examine the parts so that you can see how they relate to each other and to information you already know. The following strategies help you break information down into pieces and set aside what is unclear, unrelated, or unimportant, resulting in a deeper and more reliable understanding.

Separate the ideas. If you are reading about the rise of the Bebop movement, you might name events that influenced it, key musicians, facts about the sound, and ideas behind it.

Compare and contrast. Look at how things are similar to, or different from, each other. You might explore how three Bebop musicians are similar in style. You might look at how they differ in what they want to communicate with their music.

Examine cause and effect. Look at the possible reasons why something happened (possible causes) and its consequences (effects, both positive and negative). You might examine the causes that led up to the Bebop sound as well as its effects on other non-jazz musical styles.

An important caution: Analyze carefully to seek out *true causes*—some apparent causes may not be actual causes (often called "false causes"). For example, events in the musical world and general society took place when the first musicians were developing the Bebop style. Some may have led directly to the new style; some may simply have occurred at the same time.

Look for themes, patterns, and categories. Note connections that arise out of how bits of information relate to one another. A theme of freedom vs. structure, for example, might emerge out of an examination of Bebop vs. swing jazz. A pattern of behavior might develop as you look at how different musicians broke off from the swing movement. Musicians with different styles might fall into the Bebop category based on their artistic goals.

Too often we enjoy the comfort of opinion without the discomfort of thought.

JOHN F. KENNEDY

Once the ideas are broken down, you can examine whether examples support ideas, separate fact from opinion, consider perspective, and investigate hidden assumptions.

Examine whether examples support ideas

When you encounter an idea or claim, examine how it is supported with examples or evidence (facts, expert opinion, research findings, personal experience, and so on). Ideas that aren't backed up with solid evidence or made concrete with examples are not useful. Be critical of the information you gather; don't take it at face value.

For example, an advertisement for a weight-loss pill, claiming that it allows users to drop a pound a day, quotes "Anne" who says that she lost 30 pounds in 30 days. The word of one person, who may or may not be telling the truth, is not adequate support. On the other hand, a claim that water once existed on Mars, backed up by measurements and photography from one of the Mars Exploration Rovers, may prove more reliable.

Distinguish fact from opinion

A *statement of fact* is information presented as objectively real and verifiable ("It's raining outside right now"). In constrast, a *statement of opinion* is a belief, conclusion, or judgment that is inherently difficult, and sometimes impossible, to verify ("This is the most miserable rainstorm ever"). Key 4.3 defines important characteristics of fact and opinion. Finding credible, reliable information with which to answer questions and come up with ideas enables you to separate fact from opinion. Even though facts may seem more solid, you can also make use of opinions if you determine that they are backed up with facts. However, it is important to examine opinions for their underlying perspectives and assumptions.

Examine perspectives and assumptions

Perspective is a characteristic way of thinking about people, situations, events, and ideas. Perspectives can be broad, such as a generally optimistic or pessimistic view of life. Or they can be more focused, such as an attitude about whether students should commute or live on campus.

Perspectives are associated with *assumptions*—judgments, generalizations, or biases influenced by experience and values. For example, the perspective that there are many different successful ways to be a family leads to assumptions such as "Single-parent homes can provide nurturing environments" and "Same-sex couples can rear well-adjusted children."

Shifting your perspective helps you accept and understand different ways of living and interacting. Two students communicate via sign language while walking on campus.

Having a particular experience with single-parent homes or same-sex couples can build or reinforce a perspective.

Assumptions often hide within questions and statements, blocking you from considering information in different ways. Take this classic puzzler as an example: "Which came first, the chicken or the egg?" Thinking about this question, most people assume that the egg is a chicken egg. If you think past that assumption and come up with a new idea—such as, the egg is a dinosaur egg—then the obvious answer is that the egg came first!

Examining perspectives and assumptions is important for two reasons. First, they often affect your perception of the validity of materials you read and research. Second, your own perspectives and assumptions can cloud your interpretation of the information you encounter.

Perspectives and assumptions in information

Being able to determine the perspectives that underlie materials will help you separate biased from unbiased information. For example, the conclusions in two articles on federal versus state government control of

BIASED

Leaning in a particular direction; influenced by a point of view.

Examine how fact and opinion differ.

OPINIONS INCLUDE STATEMENTS THAT . . .	FACTS INCLUDE STATEMENTS THAT . . .
. . . *show evaluation.* Any statement of value indicates an opinion. Words such as *bad, good, pointless,* and *beneficial* indicate value judgments. Example: "Jimmy Carter is the most successful peace negotiator to sit in the White House."	. . . *deal with actual people, places, objects, or events.* Example: "In 1978, Jimmy Carter's 13-day summit meeting with Egyptian President Anwar Sadat and Israeli Prime Minister Menachem Begin led to a treaty between the two countries."
. . . *use abstract words.* Words that are complicated to define, like *misery* or *success,* usually indicate a personal opinion. Example: "The charity event was a smashing success."	. . . *use concrete words or measurable statistics.* Example: "The charity event raised $5,862."
. . . *predict future events.* Statements that examine future occurrences are often opinions. Example: "Mr. Barrett's course is going to set a new enrollment record this year."	. . . *describe current events in exact terms.* Example: "Mr. Barrett's course has 378 students enrolled this semester."
. . . *use emotional words.* Emotions are by nature unverifiable. Chances are that statements using such words as *delightful* or *miserable* express an opinion. Example: "That class is a miserable experience."	. . . *avoid emotional words and focus on the verifiable.* Example: "Citing dissatisfaction with the instruction, 7 out of the 25 students in that class withdrew in September."
. . . *use absolutes.* Absolute *qualifiers,* such as *all, none, never,* and *always,* often point to an opinion. Example: "All students need to have a job while in school."	. . . *avoid absolutes.* Example: "Some students need to have a job while in school."

Source: Adapted from Ben E. Johnson, *Stirring Up Thinking.* New York: Houghton Mifflin, 1998, pp. 268–270.

education may differ radically if one appears in a politically conservative publication and one appears in a liberal publication. Comparing those articles will require that you understand and take into account the conservative and liberal perspectives on government's role in education.

Assumptions often affect the validity of materials you read and research. A historical Revolutionary War document that originated in the colonies, for example, may assume that the rebellion against the British was entirely justified and leave out information to the contrary. Clearly understanding such a document means separating the assumptions from the facts.

Personal perspectives and assumptions

Your own preferences, values, and prejudices—which influence your perspective—can affect how accurately you view information. A student who thinks that the death penalty is wrong, for example, may have a hard time analyzing the facts and arguments in an article that supports it. Or, in a research situation, he might use only materials that agree with his perspective.

Consider the perspectives and assumptions that might follow from your values. Then, when you have to analyze information, try to set them aside. "Anticipate your reactions and prejudices and then consciously resist their influence," says Colby Glass, professor of information research and philosophy at Palo Alto College.[10]

In addition to helping you analyze accurately, opening yourself to new perspectives will help you build knowledge. The more you know, the more information you have to work with as you move through life and encounter new problems and decisions. Come to school ready to hear and read new ideas, think about their merits, and make informed decisions about what you believe. Says Sternberg, "We need to . . . see issues from a variety of viewpoints and, especially, to see how other people and other cultures view issues and problems facing the world."[11]

Evaluate information

You've gathered and analyzed your information. You have examined its components, its evidence, its validity, its perspective, and any underlying assumptions. Now, based on an examination of evidence and careful analysis, you *evaluate* whether an idea or piece of information is good or bad, important or unimportant, right or wrong. You then set aside what is not useful and use the rest to form an opinion, possible solution, or decision.

For example, you're working on a group presentation on the effects of television watching on young children. You've gathered information that relates to your topic, come up with an idea, and analyzed whether the information supports this idea. Now you evaluate all of the evidence, presenting what's useful in an organized, persuasive way. Another example: In creating a résumé, you decide which information to include that will generate the most interest in potential employers and present you in the best light possible.

See Key 4.4 for some questions you can ask to build and use analytical thinking skills.

get analytical! ASSESS ANALYTICAL THINKING SKILLS

How do you perceive yourself as an analytical thinker? For each statement, circle the number that feels right to you, from 1 for "least like me" to 5 for "most like me."

1. I tend to perform well on objective tests. 1 2 3 4 5
2. People say I'm a "thinker," "brainy," "studious." 1 2 3 4 5
3. I am not comfortable with gray areas—I prefer information to be laid out in black and white. 1 2 3 4 5
4. In a group setting, I like to tackle the details of a problem. 1 2 3 4 5
5. I sometimes overthink things and miss my moment of opportunity. 1 2 3 4 5

Total your answers here: _____

If your total ranges from 5–12, you consider your analytical thinking skills to be *weak*.

If your total ranges from 13–19, you consider your analytical thinking skills to be *average*.

If your total ranges from 20–25, you consider your analytical thinking skills to be *strong*.

To gather information, ask:	• What requirements does my goal have?
	• What kinds of information do I need to meet my goal?
	• What information is available?
	• Where and when is it available? Where and when can I access it?
	• Of the sources I found, which ones will best help me achieve my goal?

To analyze, ask:	• What are the parts of this information?
	• What is similar to this information? What is different?
	• What are the reasons for this? Why did this happen?
	• What ideas or themes emerge from this material?
	• How would you categorize this information?
	• What conclusions can you make about this information?

To see if examples support an idea, ask:	• What examples, or evidence, support the idea?
	• Does the evidence make sense?
	• Does the evidence support the idea/claim?
	• Is this evidence key information that I need to answer my question?
	• Are there examples that might disprove the idea/claim?

To distinguish fact from opinion, ask:	• Do the words in this information signal fact or opinion? (See Key 4.3)
	• What is the source of this information? Is the source reliable?
	• How does this information compare to other facts or opinions?
	• If this is an opinion, is it supported by facts?
	• How can I use this fact or opinion?

To examine perspectives and assumptions, ask:	• Who is the author? What perspectives might this person have?
	• What might be emphasized or left out as a result of the perspective?
	• How could I consider this information from a different perspective?
	• What assumptions might lie behind this statement or material?
	• How could I prove, or disprove, an assumption?
	• What contradictory assumptions might be equally valid?
	• How might a personal perspective or assumption affect the way I see this material?

To evaluate, ask:	• Do I agree with this information?
	• Does this information fit what I'm trying to prove or accomplish?
	• Is this information true or false, and why?
	• How important is this information?
	• Which ideas or pieces of information would I choose to focus on?

Adapted from www.ed.fnal.gov/trc/tutorial/taxonomy.html (Richard Paul, *Critical Thinking: How to Prepare Students for a Rapidly Changing World,* 1993) and from www.kcmetro.edu/longview/ctac/blooms.htm, Barbara Fowler, Longview Community College "Bloom's Taxonomy and Critical Thinking."

Analytical thinking is only part of the picture. Pursuing your goals, in school and in the workplace, requires not just analyzing information but also thinking creatively about how to use it.

How can you improve your *creative thinking* skills?

Some researchers define creativity as combining existing elements in an innovative way to create a new purpose or result. For example, 3M researcher Spencer Silver, in 1970, created a weak adhesive; four years later, another 3M scientist, Arthur Fry, used it for a hymnal marker. Post-it Notes are now an office staple. Others see creativity as the art of generating ideas from taking a fresh look at how things are related (noting what ladybugs eat inspired organic farmers to bring them in to consume crop-destroying aphids).[12] Still others, including Sternberg, define it as the ability to make unusual connections—to view information in quirky ways that bring about unique results.

To think creatively is to generate new ideas that often go against conventional wisdom and may bring change. Consider how, in the 1940s, mathematician Grace Murray Hopper pioneered the effort to create computer languages that non-mathematicians could understand; her efforts opened the world of computers to a wide audience.

Creativity is not limited to inventions. For example, Smith College junior Meghan E. Taugher used her creative mind in two ways. First, she and her study group, as part of their class on electrical circuits, devised a

Creativity connects analytical and practical thinking.

key
4.5

solar-powered battery for a laptop computer. "We took the professor's laptop, put all the parts together, and sat outside watching it with a little device to see how much power it was saving. When it fully charged the battery, it was one of those times I felt that what I was learning was true, because I was putting it to use in real life."[13] Second, her experience led her to generate an idea of a new major and career plan—engineering.

Creativity forms a bridge between analytical and practical thinking (see Key 4.5). You need to think analytically to evaluate the quality of your creative ideas. You also need to think practically to implement them.

Where does creativity come from? Some people, through luck or natural inclination, seem to come up with inspired ideas more often than others. However, creative thinking, like analytical thinking, is a skill that can be developed. Creativity expert Roger von Oech says that mental flexibility is essential. "Like race-car drivers who shift in and out of different gears depending on where they are on the course," he says, you can enhance your creativity by learning to "shift in and out of different types of thinking depending on the needs of the situation at hand."[14]

The following strategies will help you make those shifts and build your ability to think creatively. Note that, because creative ideas often pop up at random, writing them down as they arise will help you remember them. Keep a pen and paper by your bed, your PDA in your pocket, a notepad in your car so that you can grab ideas before they fade from your mind.

These students, working through a problem for a course, demonstrate that successful problem solving often requires the input and teamwork of a group of people.

Brainstorm

Brainstorming—letting your mind free-associate to come up with different ideas or answers—is also referred to as *divergent thinking:* You start with a question and then let your mind diverge—go in many different directions—in search of solutions. Think of brainstorming as *deliberate* creative thinking—you go into it fully aware that you are attempting to create new ideas. When you brainstorm, generate ideas without thinking about how useful they are; evaluate their quality later. Brainstorming works well in groups because group members can become inspired by, and make creative use of, one another's ideas.[15]

One way to inspire ideas when brainstorming is to think of similar situations—in other words, to make analogies. For example, the discovery of Velcro is a product of analogy: When imagining how two pieces of fabric could stick to each other, the inventor thought of the similar situation of a burr sticking to clothing.

ANALOGY

A comparison based on a resemblance of things otherwise unlike.

When you are brainstorming ideas, don't get hooked on finding the one right answer. Questions may have many "right answers"—or many answers that have degrees of usefulness. The more possibilities you generate, the better your chance of finding the best one. Also, don't stop the process when you think you have the best answer—keep going until you are out of steam. You never know what may come up in those last gasps of creative energy.[16]

Shift your perspective

Just because everyone believes something doesn't make it so; just because something "has always been that way" doesn't make it good. Changing how you look at a situation or problem can inspire creative ideas. Here are some ways to do it:

Challenge assumptions. In the late 1960s, conventional wisdom said that school provided education and television provided entertainment. Jim Henson, a pioneer in children's television, asked, "Why can't we use TV to educate young children?" From that question, the characters of *Sesame Street*—and a host of other educational programs—were born.

It is better to have enough ideas for some of them to be wrong, than to be always right by having no ideas at all.

EDWARD DE BONO

Take a new and different look. Try on new perspectives by asking others for their views, reading about new ways to approach situations, or deliberately going with the opposite of your first instinct.[17] Then use those perspectives to inspire creativity. For your English Lit course, analyze a novel from the point of view of one of the main characters. For Political Science, craft a position paper for a presidential or senatorial candidate. Perception puzzles are a fun way to experience how looking at something in a new way can bring a totally different idea (see Key 4.6).

Ask "what if" questions. Set up hypothetical environments in which new ideas can grow: "What if I knew I couldn't fail?" "What if I had unlimited money or time?" Ideas will emerge from your "what if" questions. For example, the founders of Seeds of Peace, faced with generations of conflict in the Middle East, asked: What if Israeli and Palestinian teens met at a sum-

Try these perception puzzles.

key 4.6

is this a face or a musician?

lines or a letter?

a duck or a bunny?

Face puzzle: "Sara Nadar" illustration from *Mind Sights* by Roger Shepard. Copyright © 1990 by Roger Shepard. Reprinted by permission of Henry Holt & Company.

mer camp in Maine so that the next generation has greater understanding and respect than the last? And what if follow-up programs and reunions are set up to cement friendships so that relationships change the politics of the Middle East? Based on the ideas that came up, they created an organization to prepare teenagers from the Middle East with the leadership skills needed to coexist peacefully.

Set the stage for creativity

Use these strategies to give yourself the best possible chance at generating creative ideas.

Choose—or create—environments that free your mind. Find places that energize you. Play music that moves you. Paint your study walls your favorite color. Seek out people who inspire you. Sternberg agrees: "Find the environment that rewards what you have to offer," he says, "and then make the most of your creativity and of yourself in that environment."[18]

Be curious. Try something you consider new and different—take a course that is completely unlike your major, try a new sport or game, listen to a new genre of music, read a magazine or book that you've never seen before. Seeking out new experiences and ideas will broaden your knowledge, giving you more raw material with which to build creative ideas.[19]

Give yourself time to "sit" with a question. American society values speed, so much so that to say someone is "quick" is to consider that person intelligent.[20] Equating speed with intelligence can stifle creativity, because many creative ideas come when you allow time for thoughts to percolate. Take breaks when figuring out a problem. Take the pressure off by getting some exercise, napping, talking with a friend, working on something else, doing something fun. Creative ideas often come when you give your brain permission to "leave the job" for a while.[21]

Believe in yourself as a creative thinker. While it is normal to want critical approval and success for your creative efforts, you may not get it right away, especially if your ideas break new ground. When Gustav Mahler's Symphony No. 2—the Resurrection Symphony—was performed in 1910, critics walked out of the concert hall because of its innovative sound. Today, the Resurrection Symphony is considered one of the formative compositions of this era. Like Mahler, you must believe in your creative expression, no matter what others say. Critics, after all, can be wrong or simply a step or two behind.

Take risks

Creative breakthroughs can come from sensible risk taking.

Fly in the face of convention. Entrepreneur Michael Dell turned tradition on its ear when he took a "tell me what you want and I will build it for you" approach to computer marketing instead of a "build it and they will buy it" approach. The possibility of failure did not stop him from risking money, time, energy, and reputation to achieve a truly unique and creative goal.

Let mistakes be okay. Open yourself to the learning that comes from not being afraid to mess up. Sternberg reports that "in the course of their schooling . . . children learn that it's not all right to make mistakes. As a result, they become afraid to err and thus to risk the kind of independent, if sometimes flawed, thinking" that can promote creative ideas.[22] When Dr. Hunter—successful inventor of the drug-coated coronary stent—and his company failed to develop a particular treatment for multiple sclerosis, he said, "You have to celebrate the failures. If you send the message that the only road to career success is experiments that work, people won't ask risky questions, or get any dramatically new answers."[23]

As with analytical thinking, asking questions powers creative thinking. See Key 4.7 for examples of the kinds of questions you can ask to get your creative juices flowing.

When you are working to solve a problem or decision, creative thinking allows you to generate possible solutions and choices. However, choices aren't enough and potential solutions must be tried out. You need practical thinking in order to make the best solution or choice happen.

Ask these questions to jump-start creative thinking.

To brainstorm, ask:	• What do I want to accomplish?
	• What are the craziest ideas I can think of?
	• What are ten ways that I can reach my goal?
	• What ideas or strategies have worked before and how can I apply them?
	• How else can this be done?
To shift your perspective, ask:	• How has this always been done—and what would be a different way?
	• What is another way to look at this situation?
	• How can I approach this task from a completely new angle?
	• How would others do this? How would they view this?
	• What if . . . ?
To set the stage for creativity, ask:	• Where and with whom do I feel relaxed and inspired?
	• What music helps me think out of the box?
	• When in the day or night am I most likely to experience a flow of creative ideas?
	• What do I think would be new and interesting to try, to see, to read?
	• What is the most outrageous outcome of a situation that I can imagine?
To take risks, ask:	• What is the conventional way of doing this? What would be a totally different way?
	• What would be a risky approach to this problem or question?
	• What choice would people caution me about and why?
	• What is the worst that can happen if I take this risk? What is the best?
	• What have I learned from this mistake?

get creative!

How do you perceive yourself as a creative thinker? For each statement, circle the number that feels right to you, from 1 for "least like me" to 5 for "most like me."

1. I tend to resist rules and regulations.   ① ② ③ ④ ⑤
2. People say I'm "expressive," "full of ideas," "innovative."   ① ② ③ ④ ⑤
3. I break out of my routine and find new experiences.   ① ② ③ ④ ⑤
4. In a group setting, I like to toss ideas into the ring.   ① ② ③ ④ ⑤
5. If you say something is too risky, I'm all for it.   ① ② ③ ④ ⑤

Total your answers here: _____

If your total ranges from 5–12, you consider your creative thinking skills to be *weak*.

If your total ranges from 13–19, you consider your creative thinking skills to be *average*.

If your total ranges from 20–25, you consider your creative thinking skills to be *strong*.

How can you improve your *practical thinking* skills?

Practical thinking—also called "common sense" or "street smarts"—refers to how you adapt to your environment, or shape or change your environment to adapt to you, in order to pursue important goals. A basic example: Your goal is to pass your required freshman composition course. You are a visual learner in a verbally focused classroom. To achieve your goal, you can build your verbal skills (adapt to your environment) or ask the instructor and your study group to help you present information in visual terms (change your environment to adapt to you)—or both.

Why do you need to think practically? Since many academic problems can be solved with analytical thinking alone, it's easy to get the impression that strong analytical thinking skills translate into life success. However, real-world problems are different from many academic problems—they are often less clear, related closely to your life and needs, and answerable in more than one way. Plus, stakes are often higher—in other words, the way you solve a financial dilemma has a more significant impact on your life than how you work through a geometry proof. Successfully solving real-world problems demands a practical approach.[24]

Practical thinking allows you to bridge the gap between what makes a successful student and what brings real-world success. In other words, even if you ace the courses for your math and education double major, you also need to be able to apply what you learned in a specific job.

The accomplishments of David Hosei, a student at Indiana University, show how practical thinking makes things happen. As a finance and entrepreneurship major, Hosei has built extensive knowledge in business and money matters. Pursuing a goal to help others, Hosei formed HELP

(Help Educate Lots of People), a nonprofit organization, to teach peers about money management. In addition, he organizes an annual fundraiser—the IU Battle of the Bands—to raise money for Jill's House, a refuge for families seeking cancer treatments at a local medical center.[25]

Experience helps develop practical thinking skills

You gain much of your ability to think practically—your common sense—from personal experience, rather than from formal lessons. This knowledge is an important tool in achieving goals.[26]

What you learn from experience answers "how" questions—how to talk, how to behave, how to proceed.[27] For example, after completing a few papers for a particular course, you may pick up cues about how to impress that instructor. Following a couple of conflicts with a partner, you may learn how to avoid sore spots when the conversation heats up. See Key 4.8 for ways in which this kind of knowledge can be shown in "if-then" statements.

There are two keys to making practical knowledge work for you. First, make an active choice to learn from experience—to pay attention to how things work at school, in personal relationships, and at work. Second, make sure you apply what you learn, assuring that you will not have

One way to map out what you learn from experience.

key 4.8

Goal: You want to talk to the soccer coach about your status on the team.

IF the team has had a good practice and IF you've played well during the scrimmage and IF the coach isn't rushing off somewhere, THEN grab a moment with him right after practice ends.

IF the team is having a tough time and IF you've been sidelined and IF the coach is in a rush and stressed, THEN drop in on his office hours tomorrow.

to learn the same lessons over and over again. As Sternberg says, "What matters most is not how much experience you have had but rather how much you have profited from it—in other words, how well you apply what you have learned."[28]

The emotional intelligence connection

Part of what you learn from experience involves *emotional intelligence*. Based on the work of psychologist Daniel Goleman, your emotional intelligence quotient (EQ) is the set of personal and social competencies that involve knowing yourself, mastering your feelings, and developing social skills.[29] *Social competence*—involving skills such as sensing other people's feelings and needs, getting your message across to others, managing conflict, leading and bonding with people—usually is built through experience rather than by reading theory or a how-to manual.

Emotional intelligence has a significant effect on your ability to communicate and maneuver in a social environment in a way that helps you achieve your goals. It will be examined in greater detail in the section on communication in Chapter 9.

Practical thinking means action

Learning different ways to take action and stay in motion builds your practical thinking ability. Strategies you learn throughout this course will keep you moving toward your goals:[30]

- **Stay motivated.** Use techniques from Chapter 1 to persevere when you face a problem. Get started on achieving results instead of dwelling on exactly how to start. Translate thoughts into concrete actions instead of getting bogged down in "analysis paralysis."

- **Make the most of your personal strengths.** What you've learned in Chapter 2 will help you see what you do best—and use those strengths as you apply practical solutions.

- **When things go wrong, accept responsibility and reject self-pity.** You know from Chapter 1 that failure is an excellent teacher. Learn from what happened, act on what you have learned, and don't let self-pity stall your momentum.

- **Focus on the goal and avoid distractions.** Keep your eye on the big picture and complete what you've planned, rather than getting lost in the details. Don't let personal problems or other distractions take you off the track.

- **Manage time and tasks effectively.** Use what you know from Chapter 2 to plan your time in a way that promotes goal accomplishment. Avoid the pitfalls of procrastination. Accurately gauge what you can handle—don't take on too many projects, or too few.

- **Believe in yourself.** Have faith in your ability to achieve what you set out to do.

See Key 4.9 for some questions you can ask in order to apply practical thinking to your problems and decisions.

To learn from experience, ask:	• What worked well, or not so well, about my approach? My timing? My tone? My wording?
	• What did others like or not like about what I did?
	• What did I learn from that experience, conversation, event?
	• How would I change things if I had to do it over again?
	• What do I know I would do again?
To apply what you learn, ask:	• What have I learned that would work here?
	• What have I seen others do, or heard about from them, that would be helpful here?
	• What does this situation have in common with past situations I've been involved in?
	• What has worked in similar situations in the past?
To boost your ability to take action, ask:	• How can I get motivated and remove limitations?
	• How can I, in this situation, make the most of what I do well?
	• If I fail, what can I learn from it?
	• What steps will get me to my goal, and what trade-offs are involved?
	• How can I manage my time more effectively?

get practical!   ASSESS PRACTICAL THINKING SKILLS

How do you perceive yourself as a practical thinker? For each statement, circle the number that feels right to you, from 1 for "least like me" to 5 for "most like me."

1. I can find a way around any obstacle.   ① ② ③ ④ ⑤

2. People say I'm a "doer," the "go-to" person, "organized."   ① ② ③ ④ ⑤

3. When I have a vision, I translate it into steps from A to B to C.   ① ② ③ ④ ⑤

4. In a group setting, I like to set up the plan.   ① ② ③ ④ ⑤

5. I don't like to leave loose ends dangling—I'm a finisher.   ① ② ③ ④ ⑤

Total your answers here: _____

If your total ranges from 5–12, you consider your practical thinking skills to be *weak*.

If your total ranges from 13–19, you consider your practical thinking skills to be *average*.

If your total ranges from 20–25, you consider your practical thinking skills to be *strong*.

Your skills at a glance: In the sections of the triangle, write your assessment scores from *Get Analytical (p. 102); Get Creative (p. 109),* and *Get Practical (above).* Looking at the scores together will give you an idea of how you perceive your skills in all three aspects of successful intelligence, and will help you think about where you may want to build strength.

Solve problems and make decisions using successful intelligence.

PROBLEM SOLVING	THINKING SKILL	DECISION MAKING
Define the problem—recognize that something needs to change, identify what's happening, look for true causes	STEP 1 DEFINE	Define the decision—identify your goal (your need) and then construct a decision that will help you get it
Analyze the problem—gather information, break it down into pieces, verify facts, look at perspectives and assumptions, evaluate information	STEP 2 ANALYZE	Examine needs and motives—consider the layers of needs carefully, and be honest about what you really want
Generate possible solutions—use creative strategies to think of ways you could address the causes of this problem	STEP 3 CREATE	Name and/or generate different options—use creative questions to come up with choices that would fulfill your needs
Evaluate solutions—look carefully at potential pros and cons of each, and choose what seems best	STEP 4 ANALYZE (EVALUATE)	Evaluate options—look carefully at potential pros and cons of each, and choose what seems best
Put the solution to work—persevere, focus on results, and believe in yourself as you go for your goal	STEP 5 TAKE PRACTICAL ACTION	Act on your decision—go down the path and use practical strategies to stay on target
Evaluate how well the solution worked—look at the effects of what you did	STEP 6 ANALYZE (RE-EVALUATE)	Evaluate the success of your decision—look at whether it accomplished what you had hoped
In the future, apply what you've learned—use this solution, or a better one, when a similar situation comes up again	STEP 7 TAKE PRACTICAL ACTION	In the future, apply what you've learned—make this choice, or a better one, when a similar decision comes up again

How can you put *analytical, creative, and practical thinking together* to solve a problem or make a decision?

You have developed your understanding of what it means to think analytically, creatively, and practically. You have explored your perception of where your strengths and weaknesses lie. Now you will see how to put analytical, creative, and practical thinking together to solve problems and make decisions successfully—at school, in the workplace, or in your personal life.

Problem solving and decision making follow similar paths. Both require you to identify and analyze a situation, generate possibilities, choose one, follow through on it, and evaluate its success. Key 4.10 gives an overview of the paths, indicating how you think at each step.

How do you choose which path to follow? Understanding the differences will help. First of all, problem solving generally requires more focus on coming up with possible solutions; when you face a decision, your

Examine how problems and decisions differ.

SITUATION	YOU HAVE A PROBLEM IF . . .	YOU NEED TO MAKE A DECISION IF . . .
Planning summer activities	Your low GPA means you need to attend summer school—and you've already accepted a summer job.	You've been accepted into two summer abroad internship programs.
Declaring a major	It's time to declare but you don't have all the prerequisites for the major you want.	There are three majors that appeal to you and you qualify for them all.
Handling relationships with instructors	You are having trouble following the lecture style of a particular instructor.	Your psychology survey course has seven sections taught by different instructors; you have to choose one.

choices are often determined. Second, problem solving aims to remove or counteract negative effects; decision making aims to fulfill a need. See Key 4.11 for some examples. Remember, too, that whereas all problem solving requires you to make a decision—when you decide on a solution— only some decision making requires you to solve a problem.

Solving a problem

A problem exists when a situation has negative effects. Recognizing that there is a problem—being aware of those effects—is essential before you can begin to solve it. In other words, your first move is to go from the effects—"I'm unhappy/uneasy/angry"—to determining why: "My schedule is overwhelming me." "I'm over my head in this course." "My credit card debt is out of control." Then you begin the problem-solving process in earnest.

What happens if you *don't* act in a successfully intelligent way? Take, for example, a student having an issue with an instructor. He may get into an argument with the instructor during class time. He may stop showing up to class. He may not make an effort with assignments. All of these choices will most likely have bad consequences for him.

Now look at how this student might work through this problem using his analytical, creative, and practical thinking skills. Key 4.12 shows how his effort can pay off.

As you go through the problem-solving process, keep these tips in mind.

Use probing questions to define problems. Focus on causes. If you are not happy in a class, for example, you could ask questions like these:

- What do I think about when I feel unhappy?
- Do my feelings involve my instructor? My classmates?
- Is the subject matter difficult? The volume of work too much?

Chances are that how you answer one or more of these questions may lead to a clear definition—and ultimately to the right solution.

Working through a problem relating to an instructor.

DEFINE PROBLEM HERE:	ANALYZE THE PROBLEM
I don't like my Freshman Composition instructor	We have different views and personality types— I don't feel respected or heard. I'm not interested in being there and my grades are suffering from my lack of motivation.

Use boxes below to list possible solutions:

POTENTIAL POSITIVE EFFECTS	SOLUTION #1	POTENTIAL NEGATIVE EFFECTS
List for each solution: Don't have to deal with that instructor Less stress	Drop the course	*List for each solution:* Grade gets entered on my transcript I'll have to take the course eventually; it's required for my major
Getting credit for the course Feeling like I've honored a commitment	**SOLUTION #2** Put up with it until the end of the semester	Stress every time I'm there Lowered motivation Probably not such a good final grade
A chance to express myself Could get good advice An opportunity to ask direct questions of the instructor	**SOLUTION #3** Schedule meetings with advisor and instructor	Have to face instructor one-on-one Might just make things worse

Now choose the solution you think is best—circle it and make it happen.

ACTUAL POSITIVE EFFECTS	PRACTICAL ACTION	ACTUAL NEGATIVE EFFECTS
List for chosen solution: Got some helpful advice from advisor Talking in person with the instructor actually promoted a fairly honest discussion I won't have to take the course again	I scheduled and attended meetings with both advisor and instructor, and opted to stick with the course.	*List for chosen solution:* The discussion was difficult and sometimes tense I still don't know how much learning I'll retain from this course

FINAL EVALUATION: Was it a good or bad solution?

The solution has improved things. I'll finish the course, and even though the instructor and I aren't the best of friends, we have a mutual understanding now. I feel more respected and more willing to put my time into the course.

Analyze carefully. Gather all the information you can, so that you can consider the situation comprehensively. Consider what you can learn from how the problem is similar to, or different from, other problems. Clarify facts. Note your own perspective, and ask others for theirs. Make sure you are not looking at the problem through the lens of an assumption.

No problem can stand the assault of sustained thinking.

VOLTAIRE

Generate possible solutions based on causes, not effects. Addressing a cause provides a lasting solution, whereas "fixing" an effect cannot. Say your shoulder hurts when you use your computer. Getting a friend to massage it is a nice but temporary solution, because the pain returns whenever you go back to work. Changing the height of your keyboard and mouse is a better idea, because it eliminates the cause of your pain.

Making a decision

Psychologists who have studied decision making have learned that many random factors influence the choices people make. For example, you may choose a major, not because you love the subject, but because you think your parents will approve of it. The goal is to make well-considered decisions despite factors that may derail your thinking.

What happens when you make important decisions quickly, without using your analytical, creative, and practical thinking skills? Consider a student trying to decide whether to transfer schools. If she stays at her current school because a good friend says, "You can't leave me!" or transfers because she doesn't like her living situation, she may question her choice later—most likely because she didn't consider cause and effect carefully when deciding.

Now look at how this student might make a successfully intelligent decision. Key 4.13 shows how she worked through the analytical, creative, and practical parts of the process.

As you use the steps in Key 4.13 to make a decision, remember these hints.

Look at the given options—then try to think of more. Some decisions have a given set of options. For example, your school may allow you to major, double major, or major and minor. However, when you are making your decision, you may be able to brainstorm with an advisor to come up with more options—such as an interdisciplinary major you create on your own.

Think about how your decision affects others. For example, the student thinking about a transfer considers the impact on friends and family. What she concludes about that impact may inform when she transfers and even the school she chooses.

Gather perspectives. Talk with others who have made similar decisions. There are more ways of doing things than one brain can possibly imagine on its own.

Making a decision about whether to transfer schools.

DEFINE THE DECISION	EXAMINE NEEDS AND MOTIVES
Whether or not to transfer schools	I attend a small private college. My father has changed jobs and can no longer afford my tuition. My goal is to become a physical therapist, so I need a school with a full physical therapy program. My family needs to cut costs. I need to transfer credits.

Use boxes below to list possible choices:

POTENTIAL POSITIVE EFFECTS	CHOICE #1	POTENTIAL NEGATIVE EFFECTS
List for each solution:	Continue at the current college	*List for each solution:*
No need to adjust to a new place or new people		Need to finance most of my tuition and costs on my own
Ability to continue course work as planned		Difficult to find time for a job
		Might not qualify for aid
	CHOICE #2	
Opportunity to connect with some high school friends	Transfer to a state college	Need to earn some money or get financial aid
Cheaper tuition and room costs		Physical therapy program is small and not very strong
Credits will transfer		
	CHOICE #3	
Many physical therapy courses available	Transfer to the community college	No personal contacts there that I know of
School is close so I could live at home and save room costs		Less independence if I live at home
Reasonable tuition; credits will transfer		No bachelor's degree available

Now choose the one you think is best—circle it and make it happen.

ACTUAL POSITIVE EFFECTS	PRACTICAL ACTION	ACTUAL NEGATIVE EFFECTS
List for chosen solution:	Go to community college for two years; then transfer to a four-year school to get a B.A. and complete physical therapy course work.	*List for chosen solution:*
Money saved,		Loss of some independence
Opportunity to spend time on studies rather than on working to earn tuition money		Less contact with friends
Availability of classes I need		

FINAL EVALUATION: Was it a good or bad choice?
I'm satisfied with the decision. It can be hard being at home at times, but my parents are adjusting to my independence and I'm trying to respect their concerns. With fewer social distractions, I'm really getting my work done. Plus the financial aspect of the decision is ideal.

Look at the long-term effects. For important decisions, do a short-term evaluation and another evaluation after a period of time. See whether your decision has sent you down a path that has continued to bring positive effects.

Keeping your balance

No one has equal strengths in analytical, creative, and practical thinking. Adjusting your expectations to match what you can accomplish is a key principle of successful intelligence. It requires that you

- use what you've learned in this chapter and the rest of the text to maximize your analytical, creative, and practical abilities.
- reflect on what you do well, and focus on strengthening weaker skills.
- combine all three thinking skills to accomplish your goals, knowing when and how to apply your analytical, creative, and practical abilities.
- believe in your skills as a thinker.

"Successfully intelligent people," says Sternberg, "defy negative expectations, even when these expectations arise from low scores on IQ or similar tests. They do not let other people's assessments stop them from achieving their goals. They find their path and then pursue it, realizing that there will be obstacles along the way and that surmounting these obstacles is part of the challenge."[31] Let the obstacles come, as they will for everyone, in all aspects of life. You can face and overcome them with the power of your successfully intelligent thinking.

Κρινειν

The word "critical" is derived from the Greek word *krinein*, which means to separate in order to choose or select. Successful intelligence requires that you separate, evaluate, and select ideas and information as you think through problematic situations. Says Sternberg, "It is more important to know when and how to use these aspects of successful intelligence than just to have them."[32]

Think of this concept as you use your analytical, creative, and practical thinking skills to solve problems, make decisions, innovate, and question. Consider information carefully, and separate out and select the best approaches. Successful intelligence gives you the power to choose how to respond to information, people, and events in ways that help you reach your goals.

Developing Successful Intelligence

PUTTING IT ALL TOGETHER

Make an important decision. Put the decision-making process to work on something that matters to you. You will apply your analytical, creative, and practical thinking skills. Use a separate sheet of paper for steps 2 and 3.

Step 1. Analyze: *Define the decision.* Write an important long-term goal that you have, and define the decision that will help you fulfill it. Example: "My goal is to become a nurse. My decision: What to specialize in."

Step 2. Analyze: *Examine needs and concerns.* What do you want? What are your needs, and how do your values come into play? What needs of others will you need to take into account? What roadblocks might be involved? List everything you come up with. For example, the prospective nurse might list needs like: "I need to feel that I'm helping people. I intend to help with the nursing shortage. I need to make a good living."

Step 3. Be creative: *Generate options.* Ask questions to imagine what's possible. Where might you work? What might be the schedule and pace? Who might work with you? What would you see, smell, and hear on your job? What would you do every day? List, too, all of the options you know of. The prospective nurse, for example, might list ER, pediatrics, surgery, oncology, geriatrics, and so on. Brainstorm other options that might not seem so obvious.

create your future

Step 4. Analyze: *Evaluate options.* Think about how well your options will fulfill your needs. For two of your options, write potential positive and negative effects (pros and cons) of each.

Option 1: _____

Potential pros: _____

_____

Potential cons: _____

_____

Option 2: _____

Potential pros: _____

_____

Potential cons: _____

_____

Step 5. Get practical: *Imagine acting on your decision.* Describe one practical course of action, based on your thinking so far, that you might follow. List the specific steps you would take. For example, the prospective nurse might list actions that help him determine what type of nursing suits him best, such as interning, summer jobs, academic goals, and talking to working nurses.

_____

_____

_____

Finally, over time, plan to put your decision into action. Eventually you will need to complete the two final steps of the process. Step 6 is to evaluate the decision: How did it work out? Analyze whether you, and others, got what you needed. Step 7 is to practically apply what you've learned from the decision to other decisions you make in the future.

Team Building

COLLABORATIVE SOLUTIONS

Powerful group problem solving. On a 3 × 5 card or a plain sheet of paper, each student in the class writes a school-related problem—this could be a fear, a challenge, a sticky situation, or a roadblock. Students hand these in without names. The instructor writes the list up on the board.

Divide into groups of two to four. Each group chooses one problem to work on (try not to have two groups working on the same problem). Use the empty problem-solving flow chart (Key 4.14) on p. 122 to fill in your work.

Step 1. Analyze: *Define the problem.* As a group, look at the negative effects and state your problem specifically. Then, explore and write down the causes.

Step 2. Analyze: *Examine the problem.* Pick it apart to see what's happening. Gather information from all group members, verify facts, go beyond assumptions.

Step 3. Create: *Generate possible solutions.* From the most likely causes of the problem, derive possible solutions. Record all the ideas that group members offer. After 10 minutes or so, each group member should choose one possible solution to evaluate independently.

Step 4. Analyze: *Evaluate each solution.* In thinking independently through the assigned solution, each group member should (a) weigh the positive and negative effects, (b) consider similar problems, and (c) describe how the solution affects the causes of the problem. Evaluate your assigned solution. Is it a good one? Will it work?

Step 5. Get practical: *Choose a solution.* Group members then come together, share observations and recommendations, and then take a vote: Which solution is the best? You may have a tie or may want to combine two different solutions. Try to find the solution that works for most of the group. Then, together, come up with a plan for how you would put your solution to work.

Step 6. Analyze: *Evaluate your solution.* As a group, share and discuss what you had individually imagined the positive and negative effects of this solution would be. Try to come to an agreement on how you think the solution would work out.

Writing

DISCOVERY THROUGH JOURNALING

Record your thoughts on a separate piece of paper or in a journal.

Wiser choices. Think about a choice you made that, looking back, you wish you had handled differently. First, describe what the decision was, what option you chose, and what the consequences were. Then, write about what you would do if you could make the decision again. What did you learn from your experience that you can apply to other decisions? How could being analytical, creative, and practical have helped you reach a more effective outcome?

Career Portfolio

PLAN FOR SUCCESS

Generating ideas for internships. People often put more time and effort into deciding what cell phone to buy than they do with life-altering decisions like how to prepare for career success. Pursuing internships is part of a comprehensive career decision-making process. It's a practical

1. Robert J. Sternberg, *Successful Intelligence*. New York: Plume, 1997, p. 12.

2. Ibid, p. 127.

3. Matt Thomas, "What Is Higher-Order Thinking and Critical/Creative/Constructive Thinking?" The Center for Studies in Higher-Order Literacy [on-line]. Available: http://members.aol.com/MattT10574/Higher OrderLiteracy.htm#What (April 2004).

4. Sternberg, p. 128.

5. Vincent Ruggiero, *The Art of Thinking*, 2001, quoted in "Critical Thinking," Oregon State University [on-line]. Available: http//success.oregonstate.edu/study/learning.cfm (April 2004).

6. Richard Paul, "The Role of Questions in Thinking, Teaching, and Learning," The Center for Thinking and Learning, 1995 [on-line]. Available: www.criticalthinking.org/University/univclass/roleofq uest.html (April 2004).

7. "The Best Innovations Are Those That Come from Smart Questions," *Wall Street Journal*, April 12, 2004, B1.

8. Lawrence F. Lowery, "The Biological Basis of Thinking and Learning," 1998, Full Option Science System at the University of California at Berkeley [on-line]. Available: http://lhsfoss.org/newsletters/archive/pdfs/FOSS_BBT L.pdf (April 2004).

9. Ivan Moscovich, *1000 Playthinks*. New York: Workman Publishing, p. 7.

10. Colby Glass, "Strategies for Critical Thinking," March 1999 [on-line]. Available: www.accd.edu/pac/philosop/phil1301/ctstrategies.htm (April 2004).

11. Sternberg, p. 49.

12. Charles Cave, "Definitions of Creativity," August 1999 [on-line]. Available: http://members.ozemail.com.au/~caveman/Creative/B asics/definitions.htm (April 2003).

13. Elizabeth F. Farrell, "Engineering a Warmer Welcome for Female Students: The Dicipline Tries to Stress its Social Relevance, an Important Factor for Many Women," *The Chronicle of Higher Education*, February 22, 2002 [on-line]. Available: http://chronicle.com/weekly/v48/i24/24a03101.htm (March 2004).

14. Roger von Oech, *A Kick in the Seat of the Pants*. New York: Harper & Row Publishers, 1986, pp. 5–21.

15. Dennis Coon, *Introduction to Psychology: Exploration and Application*, 6th ed. St. Paul: West Publishing Company, 1992, p. 295.

16. Roger von Oech, *A Whack on the Side of the Head*. New York: Warner Books, 1990, pp. 11–168.

17. J. R. Hayes, *Cognitive Psychology: Thinking and Creating*. Homewood, IL: Dorsey, 1978.

18. Sternberg, p. 219.

19. Adapted from T. Z. Tardif and R. J. Sternberg, "What Do We Know About Creativity?" in *The Nature of Creativity*, ed. R. J. Sternberg, 1988. London: Cambridge University Press.

20. Sternberg, p. 212

21. Hayes.

22. Sternberg, p. 202.

23. "The Best Innovations Are Those That Come from Smart Questions," *Wall Street Journal*, April 12, 2004, B1.

24. Sternberg, pp. 229–230

25. "Amazing Student, David Hosei—Entrepreneur with a Heart," Indiana University Web site, 2003 [on-line]. Available: http://excellence.indiana.edu/hosei/ (March 2004).

26. Sternberg, p. 236.

27. Robert J. Sternberg and Elena L. Grigorenko, "Practical Intelligence and the Principal," Yale University: Publication Series No. 2, 2001, p. 5.

28. Sternberg, p. 241.

29. Daniel Goleman, *Emotional Intelligence: Why It Can Matter More Than IQ*. New York: Bantam, 1995.

30. Sternberg, pp. 251–269.

31. Sternberg, p. 19.

32. Sternberg, p. 128.

Because some instructors may schedule exams early and often in the semester, begin right away to develop strategies for test success. Starting off on the right foot will boost your confidence and motivate you to work even harder. The saying that "success breeds more success" couldn't be more true as you begin college.

The material in this Study Break is designed to help you organize yourself as you prepare for exams. As you learn to create a pre-test study plan and schedule, you will also build your ability to use your time efficiently.

When you reach Chapter 7, "Test Taking: Showing What You Know," you will study test taking in depth, including test preparation, test anxiety, general test taking strategies, strategies for handling different types of test questions, and learning from test mistakes.

Decide on a study plan

Start your test preparation by deciding what you will study. Go through your notes, texts, related primary sources, and handouts, and set aside materials you don't need. Then prioritize the remaining materials. Your goal is to focus on information that is most likely to be on the exam. Use the test preparation tips on pages 197 to 200 and the material on studying your text in Chapter 5 to boost your effectiveness as you prepare.

Create a study schedule and checklist

Next, use the time-management and goal-setting skills from Chapter 2 to prepare a schedule. Consider all of the relevant factors—your study materials, the number of days until the test, and the time you can study each day. If you establish your schedule ahead of time and write it in a planner, you are more likely to follow it.

Let our advance worrying become advance thinking and planning.

WINSTON CHURCHILL

A checklist like the one on the following page will help you organize and stay on track as you prepare. Use a checklist to assign specific tasks to particular study times and sessions. That way, not only do you know when you have time to study, but you also have defined goals for each study session. Make extra copies of the checklist so that you can fill out a new one each time you have an exam.

Course: _____ Instructor: _____

Date, time, and place of test: _____

Type of test (is it a midterm or a minor quiz?): _____

What the instructor said about the test, including the types of test questions, test length, and how much the test counts toward your final grade:

_____

_____

Topics to be covered on the test, in order of importance (information should also come from your instructor):

1. _____

2. _____

3. _____

4. _____

5. _____

Study schedule, including materials you plan to study (texts, class notes, homework problems, and so forth) and dates you plan to complete each:

MATERIAL   DATE OF COMPLETION

1. _____   _____

2. _____   _____

3. _____   _____

4. _____   _____

5. _____   _____

Materials you are expected to bring to the test (textbook, sourcebook, calculator, etc.):

_____

_____

_____

Special study arrangements (for example, plan study group meetings, ask the instructor for special help, get outside tutoring):

_____

_____

_____

Life-management issues (such as rearranging work hours):

_____

_____

_____

Source: Adapted from Ron Fry, "Ace" Any Test, 3rd ed. Franklin Lakes. NJ: Career Press, 1996. pp. 123–24.

Decide how well these techniques work for you

After you've used these studying and scheduling techinques to prepare for a few exams, answer the following questions:

- How did this approach help you organize your time before an exam?

  _____

  _____

  _____

- How did this approach help you organize your study material so that you remembered to cover every topic?

  _____

  _____

  _____

- Can you think of ways to change the checklist to improve your test-prep efficiency? If you can, list the ways here and incorporate them into the checklist.

  _____

  _____

  _____

5

IN THIS CHAPTER . . .

*you will explore answers
to the following questions:*

Reading and Studying
FOCUSING ON CONTENT

Your ability to read—and to understand, analyze, and use what you read—is the cornerstone of college learning. However, your background as a reader may not have prepared you for the amount and the complexity of the reading you will be assigned in college. It isn't just students with learning disabilities who face challenges. Almost all students need to adjust their habits in order to handle the increased demands of a college reading load.

Taking a step-by-step approach linked to analytical, creative, and practical thinking techniques will help you get what you need from the materials you read and study. This chapter introduces you to strategies to increase your speed, efficiency, and depth of understanding. When you use these strategies to learn more and retain more of what you learn, every hour you spend with your books will be more valuable.

On the next page, read how student Darrin Estepp is looking for ways to learn successfully while coping with learning disabilities.

- What will help you understand what you read?
- How can you set the stage for reading?
- How can SQ3R help you own what you read?
- How can you respond critically to what you read?
- How and why should you study with others?

How can I cope with learning disabilities in order to improve my reading and studying?

In elementary school I needed extra help with reading. By high school, I was having a hard time keeping up, and a test I took showed I had dyslexia. Study assistance helped, but I attended high school for an extra year to improve my record. Then I enrolled in community college and worked part-time as a nursing home cook. I transferred to Ohio State after two years. Recently I was also diagnosed with attention deficit hyperactivity disorder (ADHD).

I learn best by hearing, seeing, and doing all at once. If I just hear something, it doesn't sink in very well. It seems no matter how hard I try it's never enough. I keep hanging in there though. Eventually I would like to help others in my career—I can see myself being on the lookout for the early signs of disabilities like mine. What suggestions do you have for how I can cope with my learning disabilities?

Darrin Estepp
Ohio State University,
Columbus, Ohio

One thing I learned in college was that there is more than one way to succeed.

My reading-related disability was discovered in the fourth grade. I remember dreading to read out loud to my class; students would laugh. One thing I learned in college was that there is more than one way to succeed, even if I couldn't keep up with the reading. First, I attended every single class without exception. Second, if I got behind in my note taking (and I often did), I would borrow a friend's notes and rewrite mine, combining the two versions. Third, I made friends with my teachers, and they would help me during their office hours.

One incident showed me that anything was possible. A friend worked for a newspaper and asked me to write a story. I laughed—I said I could barely spell my name, never mind write an article. He said, "Come on, computers have spell checkers," which are a big help. I labored through it; my friend loved the writing (though he did say that I had used some very creative grammar), and it appeared as a two-part story in the travel section. I have since had 17 articles published.

It never gets easy—but one route to success is to do something you love. I write travel stories because I love traveling and sharing stories. I am now a filmmaker, and I am studying film in graduate school so I can someday teach it. Darrin, you already know the skills you need to achieve your goals, though maybe they are deep in your subconscious mind. I was 27 years old before I knew what I really wanted to do. Just keep following your passions, never give up, figure out what you need to do to achieve your goals, and know that there is more than one path to your destination.

Morgan Paar
Graduate Student, Academy of Art College
San Francisco, California

What will *help you understand* what you read?

Reading is an analytical process that requires you, the reader, to make meaning from written words. You do this by connecting what you know to what you read. Your understanding is affected by your familiarity with a subject, your cultural background and life experiences, and even the way you interpret words and phrases. Because these factors are different for every person, your reading experiences are uniquely your own.

Reading comprehension refers to your ability to understand what you read. True comprehension goes beyond parroting facts and figures to being able to apply concepts to new ideas and situations. Improving your reading comprehension is especially important in college because assignments are generally longer and more difficult, and you usually have to complete them on your own. In addition, what you learn from introductory-level texts is the foundation for your understanding of advanced course material. Following are general comprehension boosters to keep in mind as you work through this chapter and tackle early-semester reading assignments.

Read as much as you can. More than any other factor, what you already know influences comprehension by giving you a frame of reference for what you read.

Think analytically. Ask yourself questions: Do I understand the sentence, paragraph, or chapter I just read? Are the ideas and supporting examples clear? Could I explain the material to someone else? Could I apply the concepts to another topic or situation?

BE THE AUTHOR OF YOUR LIFE

get creative!

Think about a book that made a difference for you.

Henry David Thoreau, a nineteenth-century American author, poet, and philosopher, made the following observation: "How many a man has dated a new era in his life from the reading of a book." What do you think Thoreau meant by this statement?

_____

_____

Think of a book that influenced your education—or life—and describe why it is important.

_____

_____

If you could write a book that would help others succeed in college, what would be the book's message? Why do you think your book would be important for others to read?

_____

_____

_____

_____

Build vocabulary. The larger your vocabulary, the more material you will understand without checking a dictionary or guessing.

Look for order and meaning in seemingly chaotic reading materials. The information in this chapter on the SQ3R reading technique contains patterns that will help you learn new material.

Think positively. Instead of telling yourself that you cannot understand, tell yourself: *I can learn this material. I am able to complete every reading assignment.*

How can you *set the stage* for reading?

On any given day during college, you may face reading assignments like these:

- a textbook chapter on the history of South African apartheid (World History)
- an original research study on the relationship between sleep deprivation and the development of memory problems (Psychology)
- chapters 4 to 6 in John Steinbeck's classic novel *The Grapes of Wrath* (American Literature)
- a technical manual on the design of computer antivirus programs (Computer Science—Software Design)

This material is rigorous by anyone's standards. In fact, many students are surprised at how much reading there is in college, and that they may be expected to learn material that is never covered in class.

To get through it all—and master what you read—you need a systematic approach that taps into your analytic and practical thinking skills. Without one, you may face problems similar to those of this student at a large northeastern university. He explains: "I did not get off to a great start because I had never really learned to study this enormous amount of material in a systematic way. I tended to do one subject for a big span of time and then neglect it for a week. Then I moved on to another subject, and forgot about that for a week. So there was no continuity within each course. That had a lot to do with it. Finally I figured it out. This year, I'm pushing myself to spend a little bit of time every day on each subject."[1]

Take an active approach to difficult texts

Generally, the further you advance in your education, the more likely you are to encounter unfamiliar concepts and terms. This happens often when assignments involve *primary sources*—original documents rather than another writer's interpretation of these documents—or when they are from academic journals and scientific studies that don't define terms or supply examples. Primary sources include historical documents, works of literature (novels, poems, and plays), scientific studies including lab reports and accounts of experiments, and journal articles.

The following strategies may help you approach difficult material actively and positively:

● **Approach reading assignments with an open mind.** Avoid prejudging material as impossible or boring before you start.

Know that some texts require extra work and concentration. Set a goal to make your way through the material and learn. Do whatever it takes. Consult resources—instructors, students, reference materials—for help.

Own frequently used reference materials. Purchase a dictionary, a writer's style handbook, an atlas, and references in your major. "If you find yourself going to the library to look up the same reference again and again, consider purchasing that book for your personal library," advises library expert Sherwood Harris.[2]

Choose the right setting

Finding the best places and times to study will maximize your focus and discipline. Here are some suggestions:

Select the right location. Many students study at a library desk. Others prefer an easy chair or even the floor. Choose a spot that's comfortable but not so cushy that you fall asleep. Make sure you have adequate lighting and aren't too hot or cold. If you prefer to read alone, find an out-of-the-way spot at the library or an after-class hour in an empty classroom where interruptions are less likely. Even if you don't mind activity nearby, try to minimize distractions.

Reading is a means of thinking with another person's mind; it forces you to stretch your own.

CHARLES SCRIBNER JR.

Select the right time. Choose a time when you feel alert and focused. If possible, complete assignments just before or after the related class. Eventually, you will associate preferred places and times with focused reading. Recall from Chapter 2 what you learned about creating a schedule that suits your natural body rhythms—your goal is to study when your energy is high. Though night owls may be productive after ten o'clock at night, morning people will be fuzzy during late-night sessions.

Deal with internal distractions. Internal distractions—personal worries, anticipation of upcoming events, or even hunger—can get in the way of work. Try taking a break to tend to an issue that's bothering you, or use exercise, music, or silence to relax and refocus. If you're hungry, get a snack and come back to work.

● Students with young children have an added factor when deciding when, where, and how to study. Key 5.1 explores ways that these students can maximize their study efforts.

Use these tools to manage children while studying.

Keep them up to date on your schedule.

Let them know when you have a big test or project due and when you are under less pressure, and what they can expect of you in each case.

Explain what your education entails.

Tell them how it will improve your life and theirs. This applies, of course, to older children who can understand the situation and compare it with their own schooling.

Find help.

Ask a relative or friend to watch your children or arrange for a child to visit a friend. Consider trading babysitting hours with another parent, hiring a sitter to come to your home, or using a day-care center.

Keep them active while you study.

Give them games, books, or toys. If there are special activities that you like to limit, such as watching videos or TV, save them for your study time.

Offset study time with family time and rewards.

Children may let you get your work done if they have something to look forward to, such as a movie night or a trip for ice cream.

Study on the phone.

You might be able to have a study session with a fellow student over the phone while your child is sleeping or playing quietly.

SPECIAL NOTES FOR INFANTS

Study at night if your baby goes to sleep early, or in the morning if your baby sleeps late.

Study during nap times if you aren't too tired yourself.

Lay your notes out and recite information to the baby. The baby will appreciate the attention, and you will get work done.

Put baby in a safe and fun place while you study, such as a playpen, motorized swing, or jumping seat.

Define your purpose for reading

It's study time and you are about to crack open a book. Before you start, define your purpose by asking yourself: "Why am I reading this?" You might answer by completing this sentence: "In reading this material, I intend to define/learn/answer/achieve . . . "

Defining your purpose helps you choose reading strategies and decide how much time and effort to spend. You will approach each of the four following purposes in different ways. Keep in mind that you may have one or more purposes for any "reading event."

PREFIX	PRIMARY MEANING	EXAMPLE
a-, ab-	from	abstain, avert
con-, cor-, com-	with, together	convene, correlate, compare
il-	not	illegal, illegible
sub-, sup-	under	subordinate, suppose

ROOT	PRIMARY MEANING	EXAMPLE
-chron-	time	synchronize
-ann-	year	biannual
-sper-	hope	desperate
-voc-	speak, talk	convocation

SUFFIX	PRIMARY MEANING	EXAMPLE
-able	able	recyclable
-meter	measure	thermometer
-ness	state of	carelessness
-y	inclined to	sleepy

Knowing a single root can help you build different words. key 5.3

circuitous · circuit

circu (meaning. "around, on all sides")

circumvent · circumstance

circumnavigate · circumference

- Solidify your understanding by going back to sentences you previously didn't "get." For example, most children learn the Pledge of Allegiance by rote without understanding what *allegiance* means. When they finally learn the definition, the Pledge itself will help them connect "allegiance" with the concept of loyalty.
- Talk about it. If after looking up a word you still have trouble with its meaning, ask an instructor or a friend to help you figure it out.

Use a dictionary

Dictionaries provide broad information such as word origin, pronunciation, parts of speech, and multiple meanings. Get a good quality college dictionary, and consult it when you encounter unfamiliar words. Many textbooks include a *glossary* that defines terms found in the text. Electronic dictionaries are handy, although definitions are less complete. Dictionaries are also available on the Internet.

You may not always have time to use the following suggestions, but when you can, they will help you make the most of your dictionary.

- **Read every meaning of a word, not just the first.** Think critically about which meaning suits the context, then choose the one that is the best fit.
- **Use the definition.** Imagine, for example, that you read the following sentence and do not know the word *indoctrinated*:
  The cult indoctrinated its members to reject society's values.
  In the dictionary, you find several definitions, including "brainwashed" and "instructed." You decide that the one closest to the correct meaning is "brainwashed." With this term, the sentence reads:
  The cult brainwashed its members to reject society's values.

You have laid the groundwork for effective studying. You are now ready for the SQ3R process, which will give you tools for learning and mastering textbook material. As you will see next, SQ3R engages all three aspects of successful intelligence—analytical, creative, and practical.

How can SQ3R *help you own* what you read?

Even with all the time and energy you spend reading textbook chapters, there's no guarantee that you'll understand and remember what you read. The SQ3R study method will help you grasp ideas quickly, remember more, and review effectively for tests. SQ3R stands for *survey, question, read, recite*, and *review*—all steps in the studying process. Developed about 60 years ago by Francis Robinson, the technique is still used today because it works.[6]

Moving through the stages of SQ3R requires that you know how to skim and scan. Skimming involves the rapid reading of chapter elements, including introductions, conclusions, and summaries; the first and last lines of paragraphs; boldfaced or italicized terms; and pictures, charts,

SKIMMING

Rapid, superficial reading of material that involves glancing through to determine central ideas and main elements.

and diagrams. The goal of skimming is a quick construction of the main ideas. In contrast, (scanning) involves the careful search for specific ideas and facts. You might use scanning during the review phase of SQ3R to locate particular information (such as a chemistry formula).

SQ3R is a studying framework, not a rigid system. You can follow the steps exactly as they are described or adjust them according to your preferences. You may decide, for example, to survey chapter elements in a different order than your classmates or to write different questions or favor different review strategies. Explore the strategies, evaluate what works, and then make the system your own. Although SQ3R will help you as you study almost every subject, it is not suited for literature.

SCANNING

Reading material in an investigative way to search for specific information.

Survey

Surveying involves previewing, or pre-reading, material before you actually study it. Compare it to looking at a map before a trip; taking a few minutes to analyze the route may save hours when you are on the road. You are combining your analytical and practical thinking skills to assess the material as quickly as possible.

When you survey, pay attention to the following text-wide and chapter-by-chapter elements:

Front matter. Before you even get to page 1, most textbooks have a table of contents, a preface, and other materials. The table of contents tells you about coverage, topic order, and features. The preface, in particular, can point out the book's unique approach. For example, the preface for the American history text *Out of Many* states that it highlights "the experiences of diverse communities of Americans in the unfolding story of our country."[7] In other words, cultural diversity is a central theme.

Chapter elements. Chapters generally include devices that help you learn material. Among these are:

- chapter title, which establishes the topic and perhaps the author's perspective on the topic
- chapter introduction, outline, list of objectives, or list of key topics
- headings, tables and figures, quotes, marginal notes, and photographs, which help you understand the structure and identify important concepts within the chapter
- special chapter features, often presented in boxes set off from the main text, that point to text-wide themes
- particular styles or arrangements of type (boldface, italics, underline, larger fonts, bullet points, boxed text) that call attention to important words and concepts
- chapter summary, which reviews the concepts that were presented
- review questions and exercises, which help you review and think critically about the material

Skimming these elements before reading the chapter will lead you to identify what is important.

Back matter. Some texts include a glossary at the back of the book, an index to help you locate topics, and a bibliography that lists additional readings.

Key 5.4 shows the many devices that texts employ. Think about how many of these devices you already use and which you will start using to boost comprehension.

Question

Your next step in the SQ3R process is to examine the chapter headings and, on a separate page or in the book margins, to *write questions* linked to them. If your reading material has no headings, develop questions as you read. These questions help you build comprehension and relate new ideas to what you already know. You can take questions from the textbook or from your lecture notes, or come up with them when you survey, based on the ideas you think are most important.

Key 5.5 shows how this works. The column on the left contains primary- and secondary-level headings from a section of *Out of Many*. The column on the right rephrases these headings in question form.

There is no "correct" set of questions. In fact, given the same headings, you could write many different questions. As you develop the type of probing questions discussed in Chapter 4—questions that delve into the material and help you learn—you are engaging your creative and analytical abilities.

Survey with text and chapter previewing devices.

key 5.4

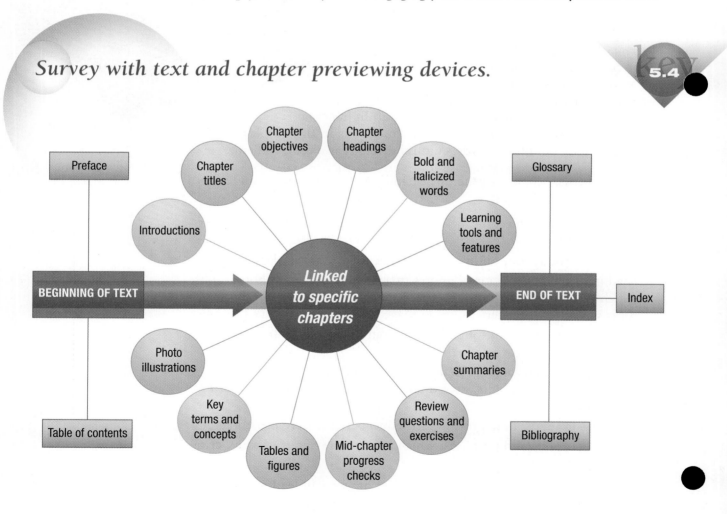

Use headings to form questions.

The Meaning of Freedom	What did freedom mean for both slaves and citizens in the United States?
Moving About	Where did African Americans go after they were freed from slavery?
The African American Family	How did freedom change the structure of the African American family?
African American Churches and Schools	What effect did freedom have on the formation of African American churches and schools?
Land and Labor after Slavery	How was land farmed and maintained after slaves were freed?
The Origins of African American Politics	How did the end of slavery bring about the beginning of African American political life?

Read

Your questions give you a starting point for *reading*, the first R in SQ3R. Learning from textbooks requires that you read actively. Active reading means engaging with the material through questioning, writing, note taking, and other activities. As you can see in Key 5.6, the activities of SQ3R promote active reading. Following are some analytical, creative, and practical strategies that encourage active involvement.

Focus on your Q-stage questions. Read the material with the purpose of answering each question. As you discover ideas and examples that relate to your question, write them down or note them in the text.

Take notes on important concepts. As you read, record keywords, phrases, and concepts in your notebook. Some students divide the notebook page into two columns, writing questions on the left and answers on the right. This method is called the Cornell note-taking system (see Chapter 6).

Mark up your textbook. Writing notes in the text margins and circling or highlighting key ideas will help you make sense of the material. Key 5.7 shows effective highlighting and marginal notes on the page of a marketing text. Owning your own texts and marking them up is an invaluable learning tool.

Selective highlighting may help you pinpoint material to review before an exam, although excessive highlighting may actually interfere with comprehension. Here are tips on striking a balance:

- Mark the text after you read the material once through. If you do it on the first reading, you may mark less important passages.

Use SQ3R to become an active reader.

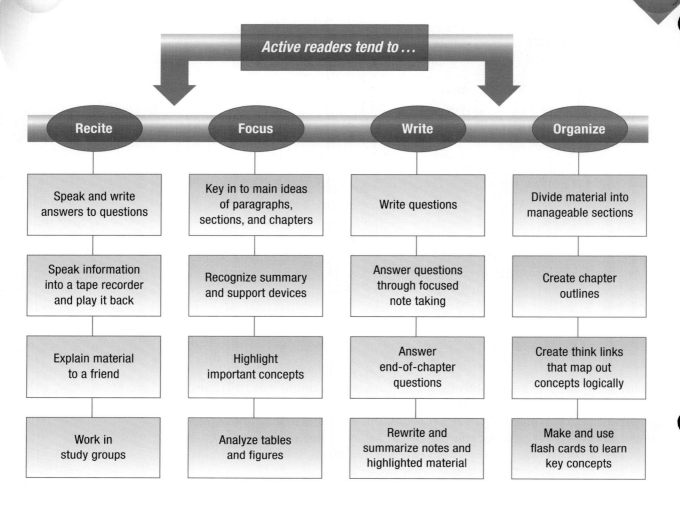

Active readers tend to ...

Recite	Focus	Write	Organize
Speak and write answers to questions	Key in to main ideas of paragraphs, sections, and chapters	Write questions	Divide material into manageable sections
Speak information into a tape recorder and play it back	Recognize summary and support devices	Answer questions through focused note taking	Create chapter outlines
Explain material to a friend	Highlight important concepts	Answer end-of-chapter questions	Create think links that map out concepts logically
Work in study groups	Analyze tables and figures	Rewrite and summarize notes and highlighted material	Make and use flash cards to learn key concepts

- **Highlight key terms and concepts.** Mark the examples that explain and support important ideas.
- **Avoid overmarking.** A phrase or two in any paragraph is usually enough, since too much underlining may overwhelm your eyes. Set off long passages with brackets rather than marking every line.
- **Don't confuse highlighting for learning.** You will not learn what you highlight unless you interact with it through careful review—questioning, writing, and reciting.

Divide your reading into digestible segments. If you are losing the thread of the ideas, try smaller segments or take a break. Try to avoid reading according to the clock—such as, "I'll read for 30 minutes and then quit"—or you may short-circuit your understanding by stopping in the middle of a key explanation.

Find the main idea. A crucial analytical skill in textbook reading is the ability to find the main idea—the thoughts that are at the heart of the writing, the ideas that create its essential meaning. Comprehension depends on your

Effective highlighting and marginal notes aid memory.

Markets

The term *market* has acquired many meanings over the years. In its original meaning, a market is a physical place where buyers and sellers gather to exchange goods and services. Medieval towns had market squares where sellers brought their goods and buyers shopped for goods. In today's cities, buying and selling occur in shopping areas rather than markets. To an economist, a market describes all the buyers and sellers who transact over some good or service. Thus, the soft-drink market consists of sellers such as Coca-Cola and PepsiCo, and of all the consumers who buy soft drinks. To a marketer, a market is the set of all actual and potential buyers of a product or service.

[Margin note: Definition of a market]

Organizations that sell to consumer and business markets recognize that they cannot appeal to all buyers in those markets, or at least not to all buyers in the same way. Buyers are too numerous, too widely scattered, and too varied in their needs and buying practices. And different companies vary widely in their abilities to serve different segments of the market. Rather than trying to compete in an entire market, sometimes against superior competitors, each company must identify the parts of the market that it can serve best.

[Margin note: Companies can't appeal to everyone]

Sellers have not always practiced this philosophy. Their thinking has passed through three stages:

- *Mass marketing.* In mass marketing, the seller mass produces, mass distributes, and mass promotes one product to all buyers. At one time, Coca-Cola produced only one drink for the whole market, hoping it would appeal to everyone. The argument for mass marketing is that it should lead to the lowest costs and prices and create the largest potential market.

[Margin note: One-size-fits-all approach]

- *Product-variety marketing.* Here, the seller produces two or more products that have different features, styles, quality, sizes, and so on. Later, Coca-Cola produced several soft drinks packaged in different sizes and containers that were designed to offer variety to buyers rather than to appeal to different market segments. The argument for product-variety marketing is that consumers have different tastes that change over time. Consumers seek variety and change.

[Margin note: Offer variety to buyers]

- *Target marketing.* Here, the seller identifies market segments, selects one or more of them, and develops products and marketing mixes tailored to each. For example, Coca-Cola now produces soft drinks for the sugared-cola segment (Coca-Cola Classic and Cherry Coke), the diet segment (Diet Coke and Tab), the no-caffeine segment (Caffeine-Free Coke), and the noncola segment (Minute Maid sodas).

[Margin note: A tailored approach to specific market segments]

Today's companies are moving away from mass marketing and product-variety marketing toward target marketing. Target marketing can better help sellers find their marketing opportunities. Sellers can develop the right product for each target market and adjust their prices, distribution channels, and advertising to reach the target market efficiently. Instead of scattering their marketing efforts (the "shotgun" approach), they can focus on the buyers who have greater purchase interest (the "rifle" approach).

[Margin note: Current approach is usually TARGET MARKETING]

87

Source: Marketing: An Introduction, 4/E by Kotler/Armstrong, © 1997. Reprinted with permission of Pearson Education, Inc., Upper Saddle River, NJ.

Reading and Studying 145

ability to recognize main ideas and to link the author's other thoughts to them. Here are places you are likely to find these core ideas:

- in a topic sentence at the beginning of the paragraph, stating the topic of the paragraph and what about that topic the author wants to communicate, followed by sentences adding support
- at the end of the paragraph, following supporting details that lead up to it
- buried in the middle of the paragraph, sandwiched between supporting details
- in a compilation of ideas from various sentences, each of which contains a critical element. It is up to the reader to piece these elements together to create the essence of meaning
- never explicitly stated, but implied by the information presented in the paragraph

How, then, do you decide just what is the main idea? Ophelia H. Hancock, a specialist in improving reading skills for college students, suggests a three-step approach:[8]

1. **Search for the topic of the paragraph.** The topic of the paragraph is not the same thing as the main idea. Rather, it is the broad subject being discussed—for example, former President John F. Kennedy, hate crimes on campus, or the Internet.

2. **Identify the aspect of the topic that is the paragraph's focus.** If the general topic is former President John F. Kennedy, the writer may choose to focus on any of thousands of aspects of that topic, such as his health problems, his civil rights policies, or his effectiveness as a public speaker.

3. **Find what the author wants you to know about the specific aspect being discussed, which is the main idea.** The main idea of a paragraph dealing with President Kennedy as a public speaker may be this: *President Kennedy was a gifted, charismatic speaker who used his humor, charm, and intelligence to make the presidency accessible to all Americans during regularly televised presidential news conferences.*

Recite

Once you finish reading a topic, stop and answer the questions you raised in the Q stage of SQ3R. Engage your practical thinking skills to choose the best way to do this. You may decide to *recite* each answer aloud, silently speak the answers to yourself, tell or teach the answers to

Knowledge is power they say. Knowledge is not only power, it is good fun.

E. M. FORSTER

another person, or write your ideas and answers in brief notes.
Writing is often the most effective way to solidify what you have read because writing from memory checks your understanding.

FIND THE MAIN IDEA

Develop your ability to analyze the parts of a paragraph.

Use the three-step approach described on page 146 to find the main idea of the following paragraph:

> Tone relates not so much to what you say as to how you say it. The tone of your writing has a major impact on what you are trying to communicate to your audience. Tone involves your choice of words interacting with your message. Have you ever reacted to someone's understanding of what you wrote with "That's not what I meant to say"? Your tone can be what has thrown your readers off track, although you can only be misunderstood if your writing is unclear or imprecise.[9]

- What is the topic of this paragraph?

  _____

  _____

- What aspect of tone is being discussed?

  _____

  _____

- What main idea is being communicated?

  _____

  _____

Now choose a meaty paragraph from one of the texts you are currently studying, and use the same questions to find the paragraph's main idea. How do these questions help you focus on the paragraph's most important points?

Keep your learning styles in mind when you explore different strategies (see Chapter 3). For example, an intrapersonal learner may prefer writing, whereas an interpersonal learner might want to recite answers aloud to a classmate. A logical–mathematical learner may benefit from organizing material into detailed outlines, whereas a musical learner might want to chant information aloud to a rhythm.

After you finish one section, read the next. *Repeat the question–read–recite cycle until you complete the entire chapter*. If you find yourself fumbling for thoughts, you may not yet "own" the ideas. Reread the section that's giving you trouble until you master its contents. Understanding each section as you go is crucial because the material in one section often forms a foundation for the next.

Review

Review soon after you finish a chapter. Reviewing immediately and periodically in the days and weeks after you read solidifies understanding. Chances are good that if you close the book after you read, you will forget most of the material. Here are reviewing techniques that engage all three components of successful intelligence. Try many, and use what works best for you.

- Skim and reread your notes. Then try summarizing them from memory.
- Answer the text's end-of-chapter review, discussion, and application questions.
- Quiz yourself, using the questions you raised in the Q stage. If you can't answer any of your own or the text's questions, scan the text for answers.
- Create a chapter outline in standard outline or think link form.
- Reread the preface, headings, tables, and (summary.)
- Recite important concepts to yourself, or record important information on a cassette tape and play it in your car or on a portable cassette player.
- Make flash cards that have an idea or word on one side and examples, a definition, or other related information on the other. Test yourself.
- Review and summarize in writing the material you have highlighted or bracketed. Your goal is to create a summary that focuses on the central ideas, setting the stage for critical thinking.
- Think critically: Break ideas down into examples, consider similar or different concepts, recall important terms, evaluate ideas, and explore causes and effects.
- Discuss the concepts with a classmate or in a study group. Trying to teach study partners what you learned will pinpoint the material you know and what still needs work.

SUMMARY

A concise restatement of the material, in your own words, that covers the main points.

If a concept is still unclear, ask your instructor for help. Pinpoint the material you wish to discuss, schedule a meeting during office hours, and bring a list of questions.

Refreshing your knowledge is easier and faster than learning it the first time. Set up regular review sessions—for example, once a week. Reviewing in different ways increases the likelihood of retention.

How can you *respond critically* to what you read?

The fundamental purpose of all college reading is understanding. Think of your reading process as an archaeological dig. The first step is to excavate a site and uncover the artifacts—that's your initial survey and reading of the material. As important as the excavation is, the process is incomplete if you stop there. The second step is to investigate each item, evaluate what they all mean, and derive knowledge from what you discover. Critical reading allows you to complete that crucial second step.

Like critical thinking, critical reading is a part of analytical thinking (see Chapter 4). Instead of simply accepting what you read, seek understanding by questioning the material as you move from idea to idea. The best critical readers question every statement for accuracy, relevance, and logic. They also extend critical analysis to all media.

Use knowledge of fact and opinion to evaluate arguments

Critical readers evaluate arguments to determine whether they are accurate and logical. In this context, *argument* refers to a persuasive case—a set of connected ideas supported by examples—that a writer makes to prove or disprove a point.

It's easy—and common—to accept or reject an argument outright, according to whether it fits with your point of view. If you ask questions, however, you can determine the argument's validity and understand it in greater depth. Evaluating an argument involves

- evaluating the quality of the evidence.
- evaluating whether support fits the concept.
- evaluating the logical connections.

When quality evidence combines with appropriate support and tight logic, the argument is solid.

What is the quality of the evidence? Ask the following questions to evaluate the evidence:

- What is the source?
- Is the source reliable and free of bias?
- Who wrote this and with what intent?
- What assumptions underlie this material?
- Is the argument based on opinion?
- How does the evidence compare with evidence from other sources?

How well does the evidence support the idea? Ask these questions to determine whether the evidence fits the concept:

- Is there enough evidence to support the central idea?
- Do examples and ideas logically connect to one another?
- Is the evidence convincing? Do the examples build a strong case?
- What different and perhaps opposing arguments seem just as valid?

Approach every argument with healthy skepticism. Have an open mind in order to assess whether you are convinced or have serious questions. Use critical thinking to make an informed decision.

If, for example, you read an article with this premise: "The dissolution of the traditional family unit (working father, stay-at-home mother, dependent children) is contributing to society's problems," you might examine the facts and examples the writer uses to support this statement, looking carefully at the cause-and-effect structure of the argument. You might question the writer's sources. You might think of examples that support the statement. You might find examples that disprove this argument, such as statistics that show strong job numbers and college degree completion in areas where nontraditional family units are common. Finally, you might think of opposing arguments, including the ideas and examples to support those arguments.

Media literacy

Use your analytical thinking skills to analyze the information you receive through the media, including television, radio, film, the Internet, newspapers, magazines, and books. By improving your *media literacy*, you will approach every media message with a healthy skepticism that leads you to ask questions, look for evidence, recognize perspectives, and challenge assumptions. This approach will help you decide which information you can trust and use.

The Center for Media Literacy explains "Five Core Concepts of Media Literacy":[10]

1. **All media are constructions.** All media are carefully constructed presentations designed for particular effect—to encourage you to feel certain emotions, to develop particular opinions, or to buy advertised products.

2. **Media use unique "languages."** Creators of media carefully choose wording, music, colors, timing, and other factors to produce a desired effect.

3. **Different audiences understand the same media message differently.** Individuals understand media in the context of their unique experiences. Someone who has climbed a mountain, for example, will experience a Mount Everest documentary differently than someone who has not.

4. **Media have commercial interests.** Creators of media are driven by the intent to sell products, services, or ideas. Advertising is chosen to appeal to the most likely audience (for example, beer and automobile ads, directed at 20 to 30 year-old men, often appear during sporting events).

5. **Media have embedded values and points of view.** Any media product reflects the values and biases of the people who created it.

Critical reading of texts and the media takes time and focus. You can learn from others by working in pairs or groups whenever you can.

Why and how should you *study with others?*

Tap your practical thinking skills to set up or find a study partner or group. When you study with others, you benefit from shared knowledge, solidified knowledge, increased motivation, and increased teamwork ability.

- **Shared knowledge.** It takes less time for study group members to pass on their knowledge to each other than for each member to learn all the material alone.

The agencies of mass communication—television, film, journalism (magazines and newspapers), books, and the Internet.

- **Solidified knowledge.** When you discuss concepts or teach them to others, you reinforce what you know and strengthen your critical thinking. Part of the benefit comes from repeating information aloud, and part comes from how you think through information before you pass it on to someone else.

> Knowledge is of two kinds. We know a subject ourselves, or we know where we can find information upon it.

SAMUEL JOHNSON

- **Increased motivation.** When you study by yourself, you are accountable to yourself alone. In a study group, however, others see your level of preparation, which may increase your motivation.
- **Increased teamwork ability.** The more experience you have with group dynamics, the more effective your teamwork will be.

A group of students taking the same course may get together once or twice a week or right before exams. Instructors sometimes initiate study groups for their students. Known as peer-assisted study sessions or supplemental instruction, these groups are common in math and science courses.

Roommates sometimes become study partners. When Lucila Crena, a freshman at Emory University and a native of Argentina, met her roommate Jolyn Taylor, she was fortunate enough to also find a partner who helped her focus. "I'm very easily distracted—she's definitely the more committed one," said Lucila. "With another student, I don't know that I would learn less, but it might be harder for me to actually do the work." The arrangement also benefited Jolyn, who turned to Lucila for help with Spanish.[11]

Group study can make a real difference if group members are dedicated. Choosing a leader, meeting at regular times, and setting goals all help groups accomplish their work.

What you learn in your textbook is often enhanced and solidified by hands-on experience. These respiratory therapy students put their knowledge to work on a medical mannequin.

Leaders and participants

Study groups and other teams rely on both leaders and participants to accomplish goals. Becoming aware of the roles each plays will increase your effectiveness.[12] Keep in mind that participants sometimes perform leadership tasks and vice versa. In addition, some teams shift leadership frequently during a project.

Being an effective participant

Some people are most comfortable when participating in a group that someone else leads. Participants are "part owners" of the team process with a responsibility for, and a stake in, the outcome. The following strategies will help you become more effective in this role.

get practical! FORM A STUDY GROUP

Form a study group for one of your courses.

Get a group together and use this form to decide on and record the details.

- Course name: _____

- Study group members (names, phone numbers, e-mail addresses):

  Member #1 _____

  Member #2 _____

  Member #3 _____

  Member #4 _____

  Member #5 _____

- Regular meeting time(s): _____

- Regular meeting place(s): _____

- Three strategies you plan to use to make the most of group time:

  Strategy #1: _____

  Strategy #2: _____

  Strategy #3: _____

- **Get involved.** Let people know your views on decisions.
- **Be organized.** The more focused your ideas, the more others will take them seriously.
- **Be willing to discuss.** Be open to different opinions. Always be respectful.
- **Keep your word.** Carry out whatever tasks you promise to do.

Being an effective leader

Some people prefer to initiate the action, make decisions, and control how things proceed. Leaders often have a "big-picture" perspective that allows them to envision and plan group projects. The following strategies help a leader succeed.

- **Define and limit projects.** The leader should define the group's purpose (Is it to brainstorm, to make decisions, or to collaborate on a project?) and limit tasks so that the effort remains focused.
- **Assign work and set a schedule.** A group functions best when everyone has an assigned task and when deadlines are clear.
- **Set meeting and project agendas.** The leader should, with advice from other members, establish and communicate goals and define how the work will proceed.

- **Focus progress.** It is the leader's job to keep everyone headed in the right direction.
- **Set the tone.** If the leader is fair, respectful, encouraging, and hard-working, group members are likely to follow the example.
- **Evaluate results.** The leader should determine whether the team is accomplishing its goals on schedule. If the team is not moving ahead, the leader should make changes.

Strategies for study group success

Every study group is unique. The way a group operates may depend on members' personalities, the subject being studied, and the group's size. No matter the particulars, the following general strategies will foster success.

- **Choose a leader for each meeting.** Rotating the leadership helps all members take ownership of the group.
- **Set long-term and short-term goals.** At your first meeting, determine what the group wants to accomplish over the semester. At the beginning of each meeting, have one person compile a list of questions to address.
- **Adjust to different personalities.** The art of getting along will serve you well no matter what you do.
- **Share the work.** The most important factor is a willingness to work, not a particular level of knowledge.
- **Set a regular meeting schedule.** Try every week, every two weeks, or whatever the group can manage.
- **Create study materials for one another.** Give each group member the task of finding a piece of information to compile, photocopy or e-mail, and review for other group members.
- **Help each other learn.** Have group members teach pieces of information, make up quizzes for each other, or go through flash cards together.
- **Pool your note-taking resources.** Compare notes with your group members and fill in any information you don't have. Try different note-taking styles (see Chapter 6 for more on note taking).
- **Be aware of cultural differences.** When members of a study group come from different countries, cultural values may impact how easily members get along. For example, whereas a student from a high-context culture such as Greece may want to begin every meeting with social talk, Americans and others from low-context cultures are likely to want to focus on assignments right away. Or students from a high-context culture like Japan may be uncomfortable talking about personal accomplishments in the way Americans do and, instead, want to emphasize what the group does together.

   Addressing the communication issues that result from these and other cultural differences requires group members to talk openly about what they observe and to work to accommodate each other's style. Making such adjustments will prepare you well for the twenty-first-century workplace. (For more on high-context and low-context cultures, see Chapter 2.)

читать

People who read Russian, Japanese, Greek, Arabic, or other languages process the symbols of their alphabets as easily as you process the letters on this page. If you read Russian, for example, you know that the word preceding this paragraph means "read." The brain's ability to process and group letters to form words, phrases, and sentences is the basis for reading and studying.

Think of the vast amounts of information your mind processes as you read and study your textbooks. Challenge yourself to raise the bar of achievement by reading often and using the strategies suggested in this chapter. You will understand more, remember more, and have more to use as you work toward goals in school and beyond.

Developing Successful Intelligence

PUTTING IT ALL TOGETHER

Studying a text page. The following page is from the chapter "Groups and Organizations" in the sixth edition of John J. Macionis's *Sociology*.[13] Apply SQ3R as you read the excerpt. Using what you learned in this chapter about study techniques, complete the questions that follow (some questions ask you to mark the page itself).

Step 1. Think it through: *Gather information and analyze it.* First gather: Skim the excerpt. Identify the headings on the page and the relationships among them. Mark primary-level headings with a #1, secondary headings with a #2, and tertiary (third-level) headings with a #3. Then analyze:

Which heading serves as an umbrella for the rest?

_____

What do the headings tell you about the content of the page?

_____

What are three concepts that seem important to remember?

1. _____

2. _____

3. _____

create your future

SOCIAL GROUPS

Virtually everyone moves through life with a sense of belonging; this is the experience of group life. A **social group** refers to *two or more people who identify and interact with one another.* Human beings continually come together to form couples, families, circles of friends, neighborhoods, churches, businesses, clubs, and numerous large organizations. Whatever the form, groups encompass people with shared experiences, loyalties, and interests. In short, while maintaining their individuality, the members of social groups also think of themselves as a special "we."

Groups, Categories, and Crowds

People often use the term "group" imprecisely. We now distinguish the group from the similar concepts of category and crowd.

Category. A *category* refers to people who have some status in common. Women, single fathers, military recruits, homeowners, and Roman Catholics are all examples of categories.

Why are categories not considered groups? Simply because, while the individuals involved are aware that they are not the only ones to hold that particular status, the vast majority are strangers to one another.

Crowd. A *crowd* refers to a temporary cluster of individuals who may or may not interact at all. Students sitting in a lecture hall do engage one another and share some common identity as college classmates; thus, such a crowd might be called a loosely formed group. By contrast, riders hurtling along on a subway train or

bathers enjoying a summer day at the beach pay little attention to one another and amount to an anonymous aggregate of people. In general, then, crowds are too transitory and impersonal to qualify as social groups.

The right circumstances, however, could turn a crowd into a group. People riding in a subway train that crashes under the city streets generally become keenly aware of their common plight and begin to help one another. Sometimes such extraordinary experiences become the basis for lasting relationships.

Primary and Secondary Groups

Acquaintances commonly greet one another with a smile and the simple phrase, "Hi! How are you?" The response is usually a well scripted, "Just fine, thanks, how about you?" This answer, of course, is often more formal than truthful. In most cases, providing a detailed account of how you are *really* doing would prompt the other person to beat a hasty and awkward exit.

Sociologists classify social groups by measuring them against two ideal types based on members' genuine level of personal concern. This variation is the key to distinguishing *primary* from *secondary* groups.

According to Charles Horton Cooley (1864–1929), a **primary group** is a *small social group whose members share personal and enduring relationships.* Bound together by primary relationships, individuals in primary groups typically spend a great deal of time together, engage in a wide range of common activities, and feel that they know one another well. Although not without periodic conflict, members of primary groups display sincere concern for each other's welfare. The family is every society's most important primary group.

Cooley characterized these personal and tightly integrated groups as *primary* because they are among the first groups we experience in life. In addition, the family and early play groups also hold primary importance in the socialization process, shaping attitudes, behavior, and social identity.

Step 2. Think out of the box: *Create useful study questions.* Based on the three concepts you pulled out, write three study questions that you can review with an instructor, a teaching assistant, or a fellow student.

1. _____

2. _____

3. _____

Step 3. Make it happen: *Read and remember.* Read the excerpt putting SQ3R to work. Using a marker pen, highlight key phrases and sentences. Write short marginal notes to help you review the material later. After reading this page thoroughly, write a short summary paragraph.

_____

_____

_____

Team Building

COLLABORATIVE SOLUTIONS

Organizing a study group. Organize a study group with three or four members of your class. At the group's first meeting:

- Set a specific goal for the group—to prepare for an upcoming test or project, for example—and create a weekly schedule. Write everything down and make sure everyone has a copy.

- Talk about the specific ways you will work together. Discuss which of the following methods you want to try in the group: pooling your notes, teaching each other difficult concepts; making up, administering, and grading quizzes for each other; creating study flash cards; using SQ3R to review required readings. Set specific guidelines for how group members will be held accountable.

As an initial group exercise, try the following:

- Review the study questions that you wrote for the *Sociology* excerpt. Each person should select one question to focus on while reading (no two people should have the same question). Group members should then reread the excerpt individually, thinking about their questions as they read and answering them in writing.

- When you finish reading critically, gather as a group. Each person should take a turn presenting the question, the response or answer that was derived through critical reading, and any other ideas that came up while reading. The other members of the group may then present any other ideas to add to the discussion. Continue until all group members have had a chance to present their concepts.

Over several weeks, try the group study methods you have chosen. Then evaluate the methods as a group, singling out the methods that most effectively helped group members master the course material. Finally, revise the group's methods if necessary, to focus on those most useful methods.

Writing

DISCOVERY THROUGH JOURNALING

Record your thoughts on a separate piece of paper or in a journal.

Reading challenges. What course this semester presents your most difficult reading challenge? What makes it tough—the type of material you have to read, the amount, the level of difficulty? Thinking about the strategies in this chapter, create and describe a plan that addresses this challenge. What techniques might help, and how will you use them? What positive effects do you think they'll have?

Career Portfolio

PLAN FOR SUCCESS

Complete the following in your electronic portfolio or on separate sheets of paper.

Reading skills on the job. American society revolves around the written word. The focus on word processing and computerized documents has increased the need for literate employees. As a recent *Condition of Education* report states, literacy is "viewed as one of the fundamental tools necessary for successful economic performance in industrialized societies. Literacy is no longer defined merely as a basic threshold of reading ability, but rather as the ability to understand and use printed information in daily activities, at home, at work, and in the community."[14]

For each of the following skill areas listed, indicate all of the ways in which you use that skill on the job or know you will need to use it in your future career. Then, also for each skill, rate your ability on a scale from 1 to 10, with 10 being highest. Finally, on the same document or sheet of paper, highlight or circle the two skills that you think will be most important for your career as well as for your success as a learner in college.

- ability to define your reading purpose
- reading speed
- reading comprehension
- vocabulary building
- identification and use of text-surveying devices
- using analytical thinking skills when reading
- evaluating reading material with others
- ability to understand and use visual aids

For the two skill areas in which you rated yourself lowest, think about how you can improve your abilities. Make a problem-solving plan for each (you may want to use a flow chart like the one on page 122). Check your progress in one month and at the end of the semester.

SUGGESTED READINGS

Armstrong, William H. and M. Willard Lampe II. *Barron's Pocket Guide to Study Tips: How to Study Effectively and Get Better Grades.* New York: Barron's Educational Series, 2004.

Chesla, Elizabeth. *Reading Comprehension Success: In 20 Minutes a Day,* 2nd ed. Florence, KY: Thomson Delmar Learning, 2002.

Frank, Steven. *The Everything Study Book.* Holbrook, MA: Adams Media, 1997.

Labunski, Richard E. *The Educated Student: Getting the Most Out of Your College Years.* Versailles, KY: Marley and Beck, 2003.

Luckie, William R., Wood Smethurst, and Sarah Beth Huntley. *Study Power Workbook: Exercises in Study Skills to Improve Your Learning and Your Grades.* Cambridge, MA: Brookline Books, 1999.

Silver, Theodore. *The Princeton Review Study Smart: Hands-on, Nuts and Bolts Techniques for Earning Higher Grades.* New York: Villard Books, 1996.

INTERNET RESOURCES

Academictips.org (study tips and links): www.academictips.org/

How to Study (study advice with valuable links): www.howtostudy.com

Prentice Hall Student Success Supersite Study Skills: www.prenhall.com/success/

ENDNOTES

1. Richard J. Light, *Making the Most of College: Students Speak Their Minds.* Cambridge, MA: Harvard University Press, 2001, pp. 23–24.

2. Sherwood Harris, *The New York Public Library Book of How and Where to Look It Up.* Englewood Cliffs, NJ: Prentice Hall, 1991, p. 13.

3. Roxanne Ruzic, CAST, "Lessons for Everyone: How Students with Reading-Related Learning Disabilities Survive and Excel in College Courses with Heavy Reading Requirements." Paper presented at the Annual Meeting of the American Educational Research Association, April 13, 2001 [on-line]. Available: www.cast.org/udl/index.cfm?i=1540 (February 2004).

4. Steve Moidel, *Speed Reading.* Hauppauge, NY: Barron's Educational Series, 1994, p. 18.

5. Ibid.

6. Francis P. Robinson, *Effective Behavior.* New York: Harper & Row, 1941.

7. John Mack Faragher, et al., *Out of Many,* 3rd ed. Upper Saddle River, NJ: Prentice Hall, p. xxxvii.

8. Ophelia H. Hancock, *Reading Skills for College Students,* 5th ed. Upper Saddle River, NJ: Prentice Hall, 2001, pp. 54–59.

9. Excerpted from Lynn Quitman Troyka, *Simon & Schuster Handbook for Writers,* 5th ed. Upper Saddle River, NJ: Prentice Hall, 1999, p. 12.

10. Center for Media Literacy, 1998.

11. Eric Hoover, "Peer Factor: Do Smart Students Improve the Performance of Others?" *The Chronicle of Higher Education,* February 7, 2003 [on-line]. Available: http://chronicle.com/weekly/v49/i22/22a02901.htm (March 2004).

12. Louis E. Boone, David L. Kurtz, and Judy R. Block, *Contemporary Business Communication.* Englewood Cliffs, NJ: Prentice Hall, 1994, pp. 489–499.

13. John J. Macionis, *Sociology,* 6th ed. Upper Saddle River, NJ: Prentice Hall, 1997, p. 174.

14. U.S. Department of Education, National Center for Education Statistics, *The Condition of Education, 1996,* NCES 96–304, by Thomas M. Smith. Washington, DC: U.S. Government Printing Office, 1996, p. 84.

6

Listening, Note Taking, and Memory

TAKING IN, RECORDING, AND REMEMBERING INFORMATION

College exposes you daily to all kinds of information—and your job as a student is to take it in, sort through it, and keep what is important. This chapter shows you how to do just that by building your listening (taking in information), note-taking (recording what's important), and memory skills (remembering information).

Compare these skills to using a camera: You start by locating an image through the viewfinder, then you carefully focus the lens (listening), record the image on film or a digital card (note taking), and produce a print (remembering). The whole process engages your analytical, creative, and practical abilities and helps you build knowledge you can use.

On the following page, read how student Shyama Parikh is working to improve her memory skills.

- **How can you become a better listener?**
- **How can you make the most of note taking?**
- **Which note-taking system should you use?**
- **How can you write faster when taking notes?**
- **How does memory work?**
- **What memory strategies can improve recall?**

How can I improve my memory?

Recently I took a memory test in one of my psychology classes. I discovered that I'm better at remembering a full definition to a word rather than reading the definition and remembering the word. Most of my classmates had the same results. This surprised all of us; it seems like it would be easier to recall a word than an entire definition, but that was not the case.

Sometimes I find memorization work difficult, even though I know I have the ability. For instance, I know I have the material written down in my notes, down to the exact page, but then on the test, I sometimes can't remember the answers. I find Biology especially hard for that reason; there's a lot more memorization because of all the diagrams and classification systems.

I'm aware of mnemonic devices and I try to incorporate those into my study time, but that doesn't always work. I know rereading and repetition probably reinforce what I've studied, but I don't always have enough time. I am involved in so many other activities on campus that it's hard to find the time to devote to retaining information for five classes. I think memorization for me is the first step in learning, so I need to learn more effective ways to memorize.

I've just been accepted to law school, and I'm concerned because it seems that law requires learning a lot of technical terms. Can you suggest ways for me to improve my memory?

Shyama Parikh
DePaul University, Chicago, Illinois

A combination of organization, reading comprehension, and reinforcement will help with your memory concerns.

First, an important point: The definitions exercise you took in your psychology class illustrates how meaning enhances memory. The reason you are more likely to remember a sentence of 30 words than a list of 15 random words is because the sentence is organized in such a way that it has meaning for you. Keep this point in mind.

When you study, understand how the material is organized. For example, if a chapter outline makes sense to you, then the material is more likely to make sense. Organization improves recall (that's why mnemonics help when memorizing unrelated items). Because understanding is just as important, though, you need to both organize *and* understand. For instance, if a system of categorizing biology terms makes sense to you, then you are more likely to understand and recall the terms. Mentally placing information in logical categories enhances memory. How do you know if you have memorized a list? Write it down to find out exactly what you do and do not know.

Reading comprehension is similar. To enhance your reading comprehension, preview the entire textbook or chapter before reading it. Read the table of contents, chapter titles, sections, and subsections. By understanding the organization of the textbook you can more actively make meaningful connections and, therefore, learn the details more efficiently.

The final technique is reinforcement. As you read a text, continually ask yourself whether the information makes sense. If not, try to figure out why you're stuck. For reinforcement of reading comprehension, pause at good stopping points and try taking notes from memory. Your notes are proof that you can recall and understand the material. This pause-and-reflect technique is critical for learning new material. Good luck!

Stephen Beck
Director, Learn-to-Learn Company
Winston-Salem, North Carolina

How can you become a better *listener?*

The act of hearing isn't the same as the act of (listening.) Hearing refers to sensing spoken messages from their source. Listening, however, involves a complex process of communication. Successful listening occurs when the listener understands the speaker's intended message. The good news is that listening is a teachable—and learnable—skill that engages analytical and practical abilities.

> ➤ LISTENING —
>
> A process that involves sensing, interpreting, evaluating, and reacting to spoken messages.

Know the stages of listening

Listening is made up of four stages that happen instantaneously and build on one another: sensing, interpreting, evaluating, and reacting. You move through these stages without being aware as they take the message from the speaker to the listener and back to the speaker (see Key 6.1).

During the *sensation* stage, your ears pick up sound waves and transmit them to the brain. For example, you are sitting in class and hear your instructor say, "The only opportunity to make up last week's test is Tuesday at 5:00 P.M."

In the *interpretation* stage, listeners attach meaning to a message. This involves understanding what is being said and relating it to what you already know. You relate this message to your knowledge of the test, whether you need to make it up, and what you are doing on Tuesday at 5:00 P.M.

Understand the stages of listening.

key 6.1

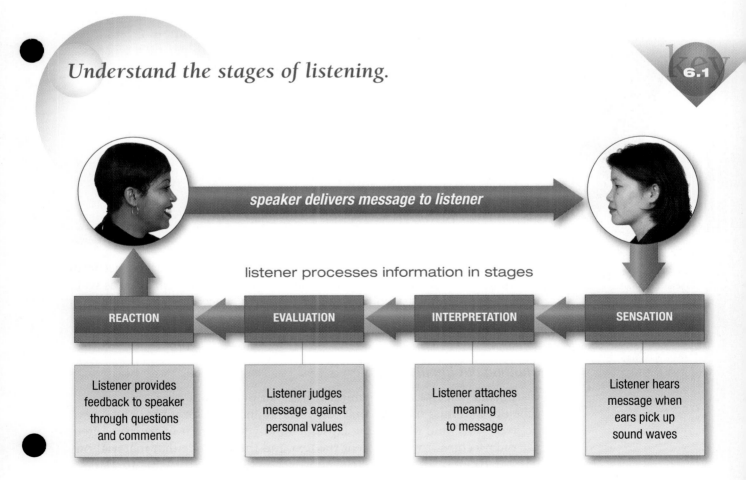

speaker delivers message to listener

listener processes information in stages

REACTION	EVALUATION	INTERPRETATION	SENSATION
Listener provides feedback to speaker through questions and comments	Listener judges message against personal values	Listener attaches meaning to message	Listener hears message when ears pick up sound waves

In the *evaluation* stage, you decide how you feel about the message, whether, for example, you like it or agree with it and how it relates to your needs and values. If the message goes against your values or does not fulfill your needs, you may reject it, stop listening, or argue in your mind with the speaker. In this example, if you do need to make up the test but have to work on Tuesday at 5:00 P.M., you may evaluate the message as less than satisfactory.

The final stage of listening is a *reaction* to the message in the form of direct feedback. In a classroom, direct feedback comes in the form of questions and comments. Your reaction, in this case, may be to ask the instructor if she can schedule another test time.

Improving your listening skills involves two primary goals: managing listening challenges (maximizing the sensation stage) and becoming an active listener (maximizing the interpretation and evaluation stages).

Manage listening challenges

Classic studies have shown that immediately after listening, students are likely to recall only half of what was said. This is partly due to such listening challenges as divided attention and distractions, the tendency to shut out the message, the inclination to rush to judgment, and partial hearing loss or learning disabilities.[1] Fortunately, you can minimize these challenges. Here are some ways to do it.

Divided attention and distractions

Internal and external distractions often divide your attention. *Internal distractions* include anything from hunger to headache to personal worries. Something the speaker says may also trigger a reaction that causes your mind to drift. In contrast, *external distractions* include anything from noises (whispering, police sirens) to excessive heat or cold to a wobbly seat. It is hard to listen when you are sweating, uncomfortable, or distracted by talkers.

Opportunities are often missed because we are broadcasting when we should be listening.

AUTHOR UNKNOWN

Use practical strategies to reduce distractions so that you can concentrate on what you're hearing. Sitting near the front of the room will help, as will moving away from chatting classmates. Work to concentrate when you're in class and save worrying about personal problems for later. Get enough sleep to stay alert, eat enough to avoid hunger, and dress comfortably.

Shutting out the message

If students perceive that a subject is difficult or uninteresting, they may tune out and miss material that forms the foundation for what comes next. To avoid this kind of listening lapse, remind yourself that instructors often use their lectures to supplement the text and then include that material on tests. If you pay attention to the entire lecture, you will be able to read over your notes later, compare your notes to the textbook, and use your analytical thinking skills to figure out how everything fits together.

If you experience a listening lapse, refocus your concentration quickly, instead of worrying about what you missed. Later, connect with a classmate to fill in the gaps in your notes.

The rush to judgment

It is common for people to stop listening when they hear something they don't like. Their focus turns to their personal reactions and away from the message. Students who disagree during a lecture often spend valuable class time figuring out how to word a question or comment in response.

Judgments may also involve reactions to the speakers themselves. If you do not like your instructors or if you have preconceived notions about their ideas or background, you may decide that you don't value what they have to say. Anyone whose words have ever been ignored because of race, ethnicity, gender, physical characteristics, or disability understands how prejudice can interfere with listening. Although it is human nature to stop listening, at times, in reaction to a speaker or message, this tendency can get in the way of your education.

Partial hearing loss and learning disabilities

If you have a hearing loss, seek out special services, including tutoring and equipment that can help you listen in class. For example, listening to a taped lecture at a higher-than-normal volume can help you hear things you missed in the classroom. Meeting with your instructor outside of class to clarify your notes may also help. It is also smart to sit near the front of the room.

Other disabilities, such as attention deficit disorder (ADD) or a problem with processing spoken language, can add to listening difficulties. People with these problems may have trouble paying attention or understanding what they hear. If you have a disability that creates a listening challenge, seek help through the counseling or student health center, an advisor, or an instructor.

Become an active listener

On the surface, listening seems like a passive activity: you sit back and take in information as someone else speaks. Effective listening, however, is an active process that involves setting a listening purpose, asking questions, paying attention to verbal signposts, and expecting the unexpected.

Set purposes for listening. Begin by establishing what you want to achieve, such as understanding the material better or mastering a specific task. Many instructors state their purpose at the beginning of the class. Writing it down will help you focus on the message.

Ask questions. A willingness to ask questions shows a desire to learn and is the mark of an active, analytical thinker and listener. Among the most important types of questions you will ask are *clarifying questions*, which state your understanding of what you heard and ask whether that understanding is correct.

Although questions and comments turn you into an active, analytical participant, they may sometimes distract you from the speaker. One practical way to avoid this is to jot down your questions quickly and come back to them during a discussion period. This strategy helps you relax and continue to listen.

Students from different cultures may take different approaches to questioning. American students are more likely to actively question instructors than students from Japan and other high-context cultures who tend to avoid confronting someone in authority. In addition, because students from high-context cultures are accustomed to hearing vague, indirect language designed to move them to form their own conclusions, they may be less likely to ask for clarification. (For more on high-context and low-context cultures, see Chapter 2.)

Pay attention to verbal signposts. Speakers' choice of words may tell you a lot about the information they consider important and help you predict test questions. For example, an idea described as "new and exciting" or "classic" is more likely to be on a test than one described as "interesting." Verbal signposts often involve transition words and phrases that help organize information, connect ideas, and indicate what is important and what is not. Listen for phrases like those in Key 6.2 and pay attention to the material that follows.

Expect the unexpected. Active listening requires opening your mind to diverse points of view and to the heated classroom debates that may result. When the literature students in the following example listened actively, they were surprised where the discussion led:

> The professor said she had attended a symposium where the author Ward Just said: "In my books, I always make sure readers know by about page 35 how each of the key characters earns their living. I just think this is critical to help each reader put all the characters in my writing in a context."

Verbal signposts point out important information.

SIGNALS POINTING TO KEY CONCEPTS	SIGNALS OF SUPPORT
There are two reasons for this . . .	For example, . . .
A critical point in the process involves . . .	Specifically, . . .
Most important, . . .	For instance, . . .
The result is . . .	Similarly, . . .

SIGNALS POINTING TO DIFFERENCES	SIGNALS THAT SUMMARIZE
On the contrary, . . .	Finally, . . .
On the other hand, . . .	Recapping this idea, . . .
In contrast, . . .	In conclusion, . . .
However, . . .	As a result, . . .

Take a look at your personal listening habits.

Complete the following:

- Analyze how present you are as a listener. Are you easily distracted, or can you focus well? Do you prefer to listen, or do you tend to talk?

  _____

  _____

- When you are listening, what tends to distract you?

  _____

  _____

- What happens to your listening skills when you become confused?

  _____

  _____

- How do you react when you strongly disagree with something your instructor says—when you are convinced that you are "right" and your instructor is "wrong"?

  _____

  _____

- Thinking about your answers and about your listening challenges, list two strategies from the chapter that can help you focus and improve your listening skills.

1. _____

2. _____

My instructor then assigned two books for us to read. One was by Ward Just, and it was organized exactly as promised. The other was by a different writer, who . . . obviously couldn't care less whether readers ever learned how characters earned their living. Each of us was asked to come prepared to either agree or disagree with Mr. Just's idea. . . . It was clear the professor was hoping for some disagreement.

Well, she got it. Three of us took the same position as Mr. Just. The other five strongly disagreed. And about a half-hour into the discussion, which was as spirited as we had all semester, one of the women said she couldn't help noticing that the three who shared Mr. Just's view just happened to be the three men in the class, while the five who disagreed happened to be the five women. "Does that imply anything?" she wondered. Which, as you can easily imagine, quickly led to an even more spirited discussion about how gender of both author and reader might influence the way we think about the structure of writing.[2]

Effective listening skills prepare you to take effective notes—a necessary and powerful study tool.

How can you make the most of *note taking?*

By encouraging you to decide what is worth remembering, the act of note taking gets you thinking analytically and practically. Note taking involves you in the learning process in many important ways:

- Having notes to read after class can help you process and learn information for tests.
- When you take notes, you listen better and become more involved in class.
- Notes help you think critically and organize ideas.
- When a lecture includes information not found in your text, you will have no way to study it without writing it down.
- Note taking is a lifetime skill that you will use at work and in your personal life.

He listens well who takes notes.

DANTE ALIGHIERI

Record information in class

Taking useful notes involves effort before class (preparation), during class (focus and note-taking strategies), and after class (reviewing and revising notes).

Preparing to take class notes

There are a number of ways to prepare for note-taking sessions:

Preview your reading material. *More than anything else you do, reading the assigned materials before class prepares you to understand the lecture and class discussion.* It also gives you the background to take effective notes. The class syllabus should tell you when specific reading assignments are due. If you have any questions, ask your instructor.

Gather your supplies. Use separate pieces of notebook paper for each class. Punch holes in handouts and insert them immediately into your binder following your notes for that day. If you take notes on a laptop, open the file containing your class notes right away.

Location, location, location. Find a seat where you can see and hear. Sitting near the front will minimize distractions. Be ready to write when the instructor begins speaking.

Choose the best note-taking system. Later in the chapter, you will learn about different note-taking systems. Take the following factors into account when choosing an appropriate system for any situation:

- The instructor's style (you'll be able to identify it after a few classes). Whereas one instructor may deliver organized lectures at a normal speaking rate, another may jump from topic to topic or talk very quickly.

- The course material. You may decide that an informal outline works best for a highly structured philosophy course, but that a think link is better for a looser sociology course. Try a note-taking system for a few classes, then make adjustments.

- Your learning style. Choose strategies that make the most of your strong points and help boost weaker areas. A visual–spatial learner might prefer think links or the Cornell system; a thinker type might stick to outlines; an interpersonal learner might use the Cornell system and fill in the cue column in a study group setting (see Chapter 3 for a complete discussion of learning styles). You might even find that one system is best in class and another works best for review sessions.

Writing down important information helps to keep you involved. As they take notes, these community college students are staying connected to what's happening in class.

Gather support. Set up a support system with two students in each class. Then, when you are absent, you can ask either one for the notes you missed.

Record information effectively during class

Because no one has time to write everything down, the following practical strategies will help you record what you consider important for later study. This is not a list of "musts." Rather, it is a list of ideas to try as you work to find the right note-taking strategy for you.

- Date and identify each page. When you take several pages of notes, add an identifying letter or number to the date on each page: 11/27A, 11/27B, 11/27C, for example, or 11/27—1 of 3, 11/27—2 of 3, 11/27—3 of 3. This will help you keep track of page order. Add the specific lecture topic at the top of the page so you can gather all your notes on that topic.

- If your instructor jumps from topic to topic during a single class, it may help to start a new page for each new topic.

- Record whatever an instructor emphasizes—key terms, definitions, ideas, and examples. (Key 6.3 shows methods an instructor might use to call attention to information.)

- Write down all questions raised by the instructor; these questions may appear on a test.

- Leave one or more blank spaces between points. This "white space" will help you review your notes, which will be in segments. (This suggestion does not apply to a think link.)

Note Taking

Note taking is a critical learning tool. The tips below will help you retain information for both the short and long term.

INTELLIGENCE	SUGGESTED STRATEGIES	WHAT WORKS FOR YOU? WRITE NEW IDEAS HERE
Verbal–Linguistic	• Rewrite important ideas and concepts in class notes from memory. • Write summaries of your notes in your own words.	
Logical–Mathematical	• Organize the main points of a lecture or reading using outline form. • Make charts and diagrams to clarify ideas and examples.	
Bodily–Kinesthetic	• Make note taking as physical as possible—use large pieces of paper and different colored pens. • When in class, choose a comfortable spot where you have room to spread out your materials and shift body position when you need to.	
Visual–Spatial	• Take notes using colored markers. • Rewrite lecture notes in think link format, focusing on the most important and difficult points from the lecture.	
Interpersonal	• Whenever possible, schedule a study group right after a lecture to discuss class notes. • Review class notes with a study buddy. See what you wrote that he or she missed and vice versa.	
Intrapersonal	• Schedule some quiet time as soon as possible after a lecture to reread and think about your notes. If no class is meeting in the same room after yours and you have free time, stay in the room and review there.	
Musical	• Play music while you read your notes. • Write a song that incorporates material from one class period's notes or one particular topic. Use the refrain to emphasize the most important concepts.	
Naturalistic	• Read or rewrite your notes outside. • Review notes while listening to a nature CD—running water, rain, forest sounds.	

Plan a review schedule

Review within a day of the lecture. You don't have to spend hours memorizing every word. Just set some time aside to reread your notes and perhaps write questions and comments on them. An hour between classes, for example, would be an ideal time for a quick review.

Review regularly. Try to schedule times during the week for reviewing notes from that week's class meetings. For example, if you know you are free from 2 P.M. to 5 P.M. every Tuesday and Thursday, plan to review notes from two courses on Tuesday and from two others on Thursday. Having a routine helps assure that you will look at material regularly.

Review with an eye toward tests. Step up your efforts before a test. Schedule longer review sessions, call a study group meeting, and review more frequently. Shorter sessions of intense review work interspersed with breaks may get more results than long hours of continuous studying. Some students find that recopying their notes, before an exam or earlier in the study process, helps them remember key concepts.

Revise using other sources and critical thinking

Adding text material, other required course readings, and Internet material to your notes is one of the best ways to link and apply new information to what you already know. Try using the following analytical, creative, and practical strategies to build understanding as you revise:

- Brainstorm and record examples from other sources that illustrate ideas in your notes.
- Pay attention to similarities between your text materials and class notes (ideas that appear in both are probably important to remember).
- Think of material from the readings that supports and clarifies ideas in your notes.
- Consider what in your class notes differs from your readings and why.
- Write down new ideas that occur to you as you review.
- Extend and apply the concepts from your notes and other sources to new situations.

When you use your notes to inspire successfully intelligent thinking, your grades may reflect your efforts. The student in the following example learned this lesson after doing poorly on some tests. He explains:

> All four of us in my rooming group are taking Economics. I would say we are all about equally smart. . . . Yet they are getting A's and I kept getting C's. I just couldn't figure out why.
>
> Finally, it was driving me nuts, so I went for help. My resident advisor asked if she could see my notes from that class. She looked them over carefully, and then asked me a few questions based on those notes. She helped me realize that I was great on "giving back the facts," but not so good at all at extending those facts to new situations. Yet here at college, all the questions on exams are about new situations. . . .

It took someone here to help me refocus how I study. . . . I still am not getting A's, but at least solid B+'s. I don't know what would have happened if I hadn't asked for help and had just continued using that old high school style.[3]

Summarize

Summarizing your notes involves critically evaluating which ideas and examples are most important and then rewriting the material in a shortened form. You may prefer to summarize as you review, with the notes in front of you. If you are using the Cornell system (see page 175), you would summarize in space at the bottom of the page.

Some students summarize from memory after review, to see how much they have retained. Others summarize as they read, then summarize from memory, and compare the two.

Work with study groups

When you work with a study group, you have the opportunity to review both your personal notes and those of your classmates. This can be an enormous help if, for example, you lost concentration during part of a lecture and your notes don't make sense. You and another student may even have notes that have radically different information. When this happens, try to reconstruct what the instructor said and, if necessary, bring in a third person to clear up the confusion. See Chapter 5 for more on effective studying in groups.

Which *note-taking system* should you use?

The most common note-taking systems include outlines, the Cornell system, and think links. Consider two factors when choosing which to use—what feels comfortable to you and what works best with course content. For example, someone who prefers the Cornell system might use it for European History but will switch to a think link for French.

Take notes in outline form

When a reading assignment or lecture seems well organized, you may choose to take notes in outline form. Outlining means constructing a line-by-line representation, with certain phrases set off by varying indentations, showing how concepts, facts, and examples are related.

Formal outlines indicate ideas and examples with Roman numerals, uppercase and lowercase letters, and numbers. In contrast, *informal outlines* show the same associations but replace the formality with a system of consistent indenting and dashes. Key 6.4 shows the difference between the two outline forms. Many students find informal outlines easier for in-class note taking. Key 6.5 shows how a student has used

Choose between different outline structures.

FORMAL OUTLINE	INFORMAL OUTLINE
Topic	Topic
I. First Main Idea	First Main Idea
A. Major supporting fact	—Major supporting fact
B. Major supporting fact	—Major supporting fact
1. First reason or example	—First reason or example
2. Second reason or example	—Second reason or example
a. First supporting fact	—First supporting fact
b. Second supporting fact	—Second supporting fact
II. Second Main Idea	Second Main Idea
A. Major supporting fact	—Major supporting fact
1. First reason or example	—First reason or example
2. Second reason or example	—Second reason or example
B. Major supporting fact	—Major supporting fact

the structure of a formal outline to write notes on the topic of civil rights legislation.

From time to time, an instructor may give you a guide, usually in outline form, to help you take notes in class. This outline may be on the board, on an overhead projector, or on a handout that you receive at the beginning of class. Because these *guided notes* are usually general and sketchy, they require that you fill in the details.

Use the Cornell note-taking system

The Cornell note-taking system, also known as the T-note system, developed by Walter Pauk at Cornell University, consists of three sections on ordinary notepaper.[4]

- Section 1, the largest section on the right, is the *note-taking column*. Record your notes here in whatever form is most comfortable for you.
- Section 2, to the left of your notes, is the *cue column*. Leave it blank while you read or listen, then fill it in later as you review. You might fill it with comments that highlight main ideas, clarify meaning, suggest examples, or link ideas and examples. You can even draw diagrams. Many students use this column to raise questions that they will ask themselves when they study. By placing specific questions in the cue column, you can help yourself focus on critical details.
- Section 3, at the bottom of the page, is known as the *summary area*. Here you briefly summarize the notes on the page. Use this section during the review process to reinforce concepts and provide an overview of what the notes say.

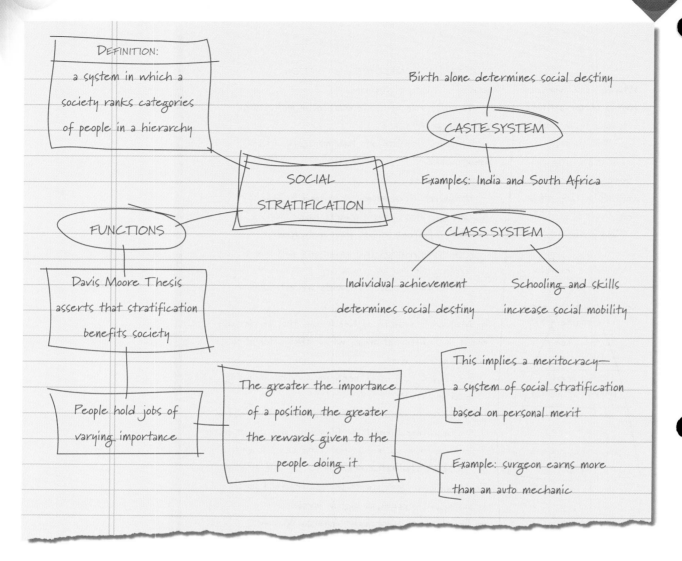

DEFINITION:
a system in which a society ranks categories of people in a hierarchy

Birth alone determines social destiny

CASTE SYSTEM

Examples: India and South Africa

SOCIAL STRATIFICATION

FUNCTIONS

CLASS SYSTEM

Individual achievement determines social destiny

Schooling and skills increase social mobility

Davis Moore Thesis asserts that stratification benefits society

People hold jobs of varying importance

The greater the importance of a position, the greater the rewards given to the people doing it

This implies a meritocracy— a system of social stratification based on personal merit

Example: surgeon earns more than an auto mechanic

specific facts related to the idea, linking them to the idea with lines. Continue the process, connecting thoughts to one another by using circles, lines, and words. Key 6.7 shows how a student used this particular think link structure to map out the sociology concept of social stratification. Other think link designs include stair steps showing connected ideas that build toward a conclusion or a tree shape with roots as causes and branches as effects.

A think link may be difficult to construct in class, especially if your instructor talks quickly. In this case, use another note-taking system during class. Then, create a think link as part of the review process.

Use other visual note-taking strategies

Several other note-taking strategies will help you organize information and are especially useful to visual learners. These strategies may be too involved to complete during class, so you may want to use them when taking notes on a text chapter or when rewriting your notes for review.

Time lines. A time line can help you organize information—such as dates in the French Revolution—into chronological order. Draw a vertical or horizontal line on the page and connect each item to the line, in order, noting the dates.

Tables. Tables throughout this text display information in vertical or horizontal columns. Use tables to arrange information according to categories.

Hierarchy charts. Charts showing the (hierarchy) of information can help you visualize how each piece fits into the hierarchy. A hierarchy chart could show levels of government, for example, or levels of scientific classification of animals and plants.

> HIERARCHY
> A graded or ranked series.

No matter what note-taking system you choose, your success will depend on how well you use it. Mastering the practical skill of personal shorthand will help you make the most of your choice.

How can you *write faster* when taking notes?

Using some form of personal (shorthand,) you can push your pen faster. Because you alone are the intended reader, you can misspell and abbreviate words in ways that only you understand.

To avoid forgetting what shorthand notations mean, review your notes while they are fresh in your mind. If anything confuses you, spell out words as you review.

Here are some suggestions that will help you master this important practical skill:

> SHORTHAND
> A system of rapid hand-writing that employs symbols, abbreviations, and shortened words to represent words and phrases.

1. Use standard abbreviations in place of complete words.

w/	with	cf	compare, in comparison to
w/o	without	ff	following
→	means; resulting in	Q	question
←	as a result of	p.	page
↑	increasing	*	most important
↓	decreasing	<	less than
∴	therefore	>	more than
∵ or b/c	because	=	equals
≈	approximately	%	percent
+ or &	and	△	change
−	minus; negative	2	to; two; too
no. or #	number	vs	versus; against
i.e.	that is,	eg	for example
etc.	and so forth	c/o	care of
ng	no good	lb	pound

2. Shorten words by removing vowels from the middle of words.

prps	=	purpose
lwyr	=	lawyer
cmptr	=	computer

3. Substitute word beginnings for entire words.

assoc	=	associate; association
info	=	information
subj	=	subject

4. Form plurals by adding s to shortened words.

prblms	=	problems
drctrys	=	directories
prntrs	=	printers

5. Make up your own symbols and use them consistently.

b/4	=	before
4tn	=	fortune
2thake	=	toothache

6. Use standard or informal abbreviations for proper nouns such as places, people, companies, scientific substances, events, and so on.

DC	=	Washington, D.C.
H_2O	=	water
Moz.	=	Wolfgang Amadeus Mozart

7. If you are repeatedly writing a word or phrase throughout a class, write it out once and then create an abbreviation. For example, if you are taking notes on Argentina's former first lady Eva Perón, you might start by writing *Eva Perón (EP)* and then use *EP* through the rest of your notes for that class.

Finally, throughout your note taking, remember that the primary goal is to generate materials that help you learn and remember information. No matter how sensible any note-taking strategy might be, it won't do you any good if it doesn't help you reach that goal. Keep a close eye on what works for you and stick to it.

If you find that your notes aren't comprehensible, legible, or focused, analyze the problem. Can't read your notes? You might have been sleepy. Confusing gaps in information? You might be distracted in class, have an instructor who jumps around in the lecture, or lack an understanding of the course material. Put your problem-solving skills to work and brainstorm solutions from the variety of strategies in this chapter. With effort, your notes will become a helpful learning tool in school and beyond.

Learning listening skills and finding a system for taking effective notes prepare you for one of the most important challenges you face in school—developing your memory so you can remember what you hear in class, study in your texts, and record in your notes.

How does *memory* work?

Your Accounting instructor is giving a test tomorrow on the double-entry accounting system. You feel confident because you spent hours last week memorizing your notes. Unfortunately, by the time you take the test, you remember very little. This is not surprising, since most forgetting occurs within minutes after memorization.

In a classic study conducted in 1885, researcher Herman Ebbinghaus memorized a list of meaningless three-letter words such as CEF and LAZ. He then examined how quickly he forgot them. Within one hour he forgot more than 50 percent of what he had learned; after two days, he knew fewer than 30 percent of the material. Although Ebbinghaus's recall of the nonsense syllables remained fairly stable after that, his experiment shows how fragile memory can be—even when you take the time and expend the energy to memorize information.[5]

How your brain remembers: Short-term and long-term memory

Memories are stored in three different "storage banks" in your brain. The first, called sensory memory, is an exact copy of what you see and hear and lasts for a second or less. Certain information is then selected from sensory memory and moved into short-term memory, a temporary information storehouse that lasts no more than 10 to 20 seconds. You are consciously aware of material in short-term memory. Unimportant information is quickly dumped. Important information is transferred to long-term memory—the mind's more permanent storehouse.

Although all three stages are important, targeting long-term memory will solidify learning the most. "Short-term—or working—memory is useful when we want to remember a phone number until we can dial," says biologist James Zull. "We use short-term memory for these momentary challenges, all the time, every day, but it is limited in capacity, tenacity, and time."[6] Zull explains that short-term memory can hold only small amounts of information for brief periods. In addition, it is unstable—a distraction can easily dislodge information.

Retaining information in long-term memory

In order to retain information in long-term memory, your brain moves through a four-stage process, which relates directly to the stages of the listening process described on pages 163–164. Key 6.8 illustrates the process.

1. **Experiencing the material** (concrete experience). Your brain takes in the information through one or more of your senses.

2. **Relating the material to what you already know** (reflexive observation). You reflect on the new information and connect it to previous knowledge.

3. **Forming new ideas** (abstract hypothesis). You come up with new insights from the combination of what you knew before and what you are learning now.

Long-term memory involves four stages.

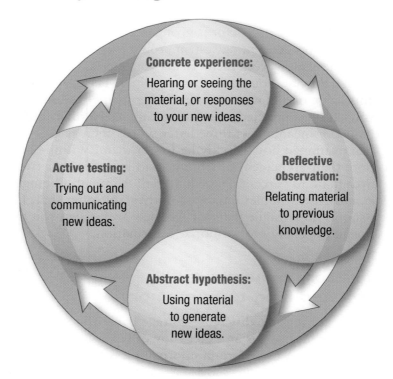

Concrete experience:
Hearing or seeing the material, or responses to your new ideas.

Active testing:
Trying out and communicating new ideas.

Reflective observation:
Relating material to previous knowledge.

Abstract hypothesis:
Using material to generate new ideas.

4. **Trying out and communicating new ideas** (active testing). You explore your ideas to see if they make sense and work.

Here's an example to illustrate the process.

1. In your Introduction to Business course, you hear the following information during the lecture: "During the economic bubble of the 1990s, ethical lapses were frequent at the highest levels of business. Among the corporations involved in ethical abuses were Enron and Tyco. Corporate executives at these companies bent the rules and ignored the law to maximize personal gain."

We rarely forget that which has made a deep impression on our minds.

TRYON EDWARDS

2. You think about the material in relation to what you know. First, you remember reading about the unethical practices of the billionaires of the 1930s, including J. P. Morgan and Andrew Carnegie, who built corporate empires—and amassed personal fortunes—through unethical business practices. Second, you think about ethical and unethical behavior you have seen in people you know personally.

3. You form a new idea: Government regulations are necessary to curb the all-too-human tendency to bend rules for personal gain.

4. You try out your idea by talking to classmates and thinking further.

Result: Information about business ethics is solidly anchored in long-term memory.

What memory strategies can improve *recall?*

If forgetting is so common, why do some people have better memories than others? Some may have an inborn talent for remembering. More often, though, they succeed because they have practiced and mastered analytical, creative, and practical techniques for improving recall.

Develop helpful strategies

The following practical and analytical strategies will help improve your recall.

Have purpose and intention. Why can you remember the lyrics to dozens of popular songs but not the functions of the pancreas? Perhaps this is because you want to remember the lyrics or you have an emotional tie to them. To strengthen your intention to remember academic information, focus on why the information is important and how you can use it.

Understand what you memorize. The best way to guarantee that concepts become part of your long-term memory is to use your analytical ability to understand them inside and out. With a depth of learning comes the framework on which to place related concepts. Thus, if you are having trouble remembering something new, think about how the idea fits into what you already know. A simple example: If a new vocabulary word puzzles you, try to identify the word's root, prefix, or suffix. Knowing that the root *bellum* means "war" and the prefix *ante* means "before" will help you recognize and remember that *antebellum* means "before the war."

Recite, rehearse, and write. When you *recite* material, you repeat key concepts aloud, in your own words, to help you memorize them. *Rehearsing* is similar to reciting but is done silently. It is the process of mentally repeating, summarizing, and associating information with other information. *Writing* is reciting on paper. Organizational tools, such as an outline or a think link, will help you record material in ways that show the logical connections within its structure.

Attending class with a clear, focused mind can help you retain what you hear. This professor begins and ends each class with a short meditation, with the goal of improving how he and his students perform.

Study during short, frequent sessions. Research has shown that you can improve your chances of remembering material if you learn it more than once. To get the most out of study sessions, spread them over time and rest in between. You may feel as though you accomplish a lot by studying for an hour without a break; however, you'll probably remember more from three 20-minute sessions.

Sleep can actually aid memory because it reduces interference from new information. Since you can't always go to sleep immediately after studying for an exam, try postponing the study of other subjects until your exam is over. When studying for several tests at once, avoid studying two similar subjects back to back. Your memory is likely to be more accurate when you study History right after Biology rather than, for example, Chemistry after Biology.

Limit and organize material. This involves two key activities:

- Separate main points from unimportant details. Ask yourself: What is the most important information? Highlight only the key points in your texts, and write notes in the margins about central ideas. See the example in Key 5.7 on page 145.

- Divide material into manageable sections. Generally, when material is short and easy to understand, studying it from start to finish improves recall. With longer material, however, you may benefit from dividing it into logical sections, mastering each section, putting all the sections together, and then testing your memory of all the material. Actors take this approach when learning the lines of a play, and it can work just as well for students trying to learn new concepts.

Practice the middle. When you are trying to learn something, you usually study some material first, attack other material in the middle of the session, and approach still other topics at the end. The weak link in your recall is likely to be the material you study midway. It pays to give this material special attention.

Create groupings. When items do not have to be remembered in any particular order, the act of grouping can help you recall them better. Say, for example, that you have to memorize these four 10-digit numbers:

9806875087   9876535703   7636983561   6724472879

It may look impossible. If you group the numbers to look like telephone numbers, however, the job may become more manageable:

(980) 687–5087   (987) 653–5703   (763) 698–3561   (672) 447–2879

In general, try to limit groups to 10 items or fewer. It's hard to memorize more at one time.

Use flash cards. Flash cards are a great visual memory tool. They give you short, repeated review sessions that provide immediate feedback, and they are portable, which gives you the flexibility to use them wherever you go. Use the front of a 3-by-5-inch index card to write a word, idea, or phrase you want to remember. Use the back for a definition, an explanation, and other key facts. Key 6.9 shows two flash cards used to study for a Psychology exam.

Here are some suggestions for making the most of your flash cards:

- Carry the cards with you and review them frequently.
- Shuffle the cards and learn the information in various orders.

- Test yourself in both directions. First, look at the terms and provide the definitions or explanations. Then turn the cards over and reverse the process.

Use a tape recorder. Use a tape recorder as an immediate feedback "audio flash card." Record short-answer study questions on tape, leave 10 to 15 seconds between questions to answer out loud, then record the correct answer after each pause. For example, a question for a writing class might be, "What are the three elements of effective writing? . . . (10–15 second pause) . . . topic, audience, and purpose."

Use mnemonic devices

Certain performers entertain their audiences by remembering the names of 100 strangers or flawlessly repeating 30 ten-digit phone numbers. Although these performers probably have superior memories, they also rely on memory techniques, known as mnemonic devices (pronounced neh-MAHN-ick), for assistance.

> MNEMONIC DEVICES
>
> Memory techniques that involve associating new information with information you already know.

Mnemonic devices depend on vivid associations (relating new information to other information). Instead of learning new facts by rote (repetitive practice), associations give you a "hook" on which to hang these facts and retrieve them later. Mnemonic devices make information familiar and meaningful through unusual, unforgettable mental associations and visual pictures. Forming mnemonics depends on activating your creative ability.

There are different kinds of mnemonic devices, including visual images and associations, acronyms, and songs and rhymes. Study how these devices work, then use your creative thinking skills to apply them to your own memory challenges.

Create visual images and associations

You are more likely to remember a piece of information if you link it to a visual image. The best mental images often involve bright colors, three dimensions, action scenes, inanimate objects with human traits, ridiculousness, and humor.

Turning information into mental pictures helps improve memory, especially for visual learners. To remember that the Spanish artist Picasso painted *The Three Women*, you might imagine the women in a circle dancing to a Spanish song with a pig and a donkey (pig-asso). The more outlandish the image the better, since these images are the most memorable.

Memory is the stepping-stone to thinking, because without remembering facts, you cannot think, conceptualize, reason, make decisions, create, or contribute.

HARRY LORAYNE

Use the mental walk strategy to remember items in a list

Using the mental walk strategy, you imagine that you store new ideas in familiar locations. Say, for example, that for Biology you have to remember the major endocrine glands. To do this, you can think of the route you take to the library. You pass the college theater, the science center, the bookstore, the cafeteria, the athletic center, and the social science building before reaching the library. At each spot along the route, you "place" the idea or concept you wish to learn. You then link the concept with a similar-sounding word that brings to mind a vivid image:

- At the campus theater, you imagine bumping into the actor Brad Pitt, who is holding two terriers (pituitary gland).
- At the science center, you visualize Mr. Universe with bulging thighs. When you are introduced, you learn that his name is Roy (thyroid gland).
- At the campus bookstore, you envision a second Mr. Universe with his thighs covered in mustard (thymus gland).
- In the cafeteria, you see an ad for Dean Al for president (adrenal gland).
- At the athletic center, you visualize a student throwing a ball into a pan and creatures applauding from the bleachers (pancreas).
- At the social science building, you imagine receiving a standing ovation (ovaries).
- And at the library, you visualize sitting at a table taking a test that is easy (testes).

Create acronyms

ACRONYM
A word formed from the first letters of a series of words, created in order to help you remember the series.

Another helpful association method involves the use of **acronyms.** In History class, you can remember the World War II Allies—Britain, the United States, and Russia—with the acronym BAR. This is an example of a word acronym, because the first letters of the items you wish to remember spell a word. The word (or words) spelled don't necessarily have to be real words. As you see in Key 6.10, the acronym Roy G. Biv will help you remember the colors of the spectrum.

An acronym will help you recall the colors of the spectrum.

red

orange

yellow

green

blue

indigo

violet

R O Y G. B I V

Other acronyms take the form of an entire sentence in which the first letter of each word in each sentence stands for the first letter of the memorized term. This is called a *list order acronym*. For example, when science students want to remember the list of planets in order of their distance from the sun (Mercury, Venus, Earth, Mars, Jupiter, Saturn, Uranus, Neptune, and Pluto), they can learn the sentence:

My very elegant mother just served us nine pickles.

Use songs or rhymes

Some of the classic mnemonic devices are rhyming poems that tend to stick in your mind. One you may have heard is the rule about the order of "i" and "e" in spelling:

I before E, except after C, or when sounded like "A" as in "neighbor" and "weigh." Four exceptions if you please: either, neither, seizure, seize.

Make up your own poems or songs, linking tunes or rhymes that are familiar to you with information you want to remember. When Susan W. Fisher teaches Introductory Biology at Ohio State University, she uses this "biorap," performed by class members, to help everyone remember part of DNA replication (the rap includes references to the football coach and student-government president):

A pairs with T and G pairs with C
It works 'cause the code's complementary
It lets you be you and me be me
From Coach Tressel to Eddie Pauline.

The chorus "*DNA makes protein*" is then repeated four times. Said junior David S. Waterman of this musical mnemonic, "Because the performances are entertaining, students are more apt to pay attention and remember what we see or hear."[7]

Improving your memory requires energy, time, and work. In school, it also helps to master SQ3R, the textbook study technique that was introduced in Chapter 5. By going through the steps in SQ3R and using

Make a mnemonic device to help you remember something important to you.

● As you study your texts in the next few weeks, identify a group of connected facts that you have to memorize—for example, for a Political Science course, the names of every presidential candidate after World War II; for an English Literature course, the names of all the characters in Shakespeare's *Romeo and Juliet*. Indicate your choice here:

_____

_____

● Now create a mnemonic that will help you memorize the group. Use any of the mnemonic devices presented in this chapter including visual images and associations, acronyms, and songs and rhymes. Write the mnemonic here (use additional paper if necessary).

_____

_____

_____

the specific memory techniques described in this chapter, you will be able to learn more in less time—and remember what you learn long after exams are over.

ཤེས་ར་མ་ཡེང་ཤེན

In Sanskrit, the classical written language of India and other Hindu countries, these characters—pronounced as *sem ma yeng chik*—mean "do not be distracted." Think of this concept as you strive to improve your concentration for listening, note taking, and remembering. Focus on the ideas at hand. Try not to be distracted by other thoughts, other people's notions of what is "correct," or negativity as you take in and record information and commit it to memory. Be present in the moment so you can apply your skills to learning as much as you can.

PERSONAL TRIUMPH

CAROL COMLISH Graduate of the University of Alabama, Tuscaloosa, Alabama

Life's twists and turns can put stubborn roadblocks in your path. With perseverance, and with a focus on hard work and memory that kept her coming back to school over a span of 29 years, Carol Comlish kept clearing the road that led to her goal of a college degree. Read the account, then use a separate piece of paper to answer the questions on page 190.

The author Jack London once said, "You can't wait for inspiration. You have to go after it with a club." After pursuing my bachelor's degree for 29 years, London's statement keeps reminding me that, indeed, there were many times I had to flog myself for inspiration to persevere.

When I was in high school, I chose a business curriculum because I knew I had no means to attend college. My mother, a single parent of six, was left ill-equipped to provide the encouragement or the funds to help steer me toward a college education. After high school, I worked as a government secretary in Washington, D.C., and later as a flight attendant. Every penny I earned paid for much-needed dental work and for shoes and clothing my mother was unable to provide. There was no money left for schooling.

During those years, I married and had four children. I had much of what I had always wanted, but I still felt the drive to get an education. So, when my youngest child was two years old, I enrolled in my first college course—15 years after high school. I had not taken college prep courses to prepare me, and it was tough. Soon another baby appeared on the scene, and I quit school. Two years later, I had yet another baby. School and studying were out of the question. I could barely hold my head above water.

Then, when my youngest child began kindergarten, I tried school again. But it was so difficult to maintain a balance between the constant demands of the family and the demands of schoolwork that, after a couple of years of that grueling routine, I dropped out again.

Over the next 10 years, my desire for learning was exceptionally intense. Everything interested me. I learned to speak French, I read Shakespeare, and I devoured history. I was fairly self-educated but wanted the satisfaction of a formal education.

When my sixth child was in junior high, I began working to help pay for college expenses for my brood. But, in time, my personal desire to get a degree led me to the University of Alabama External Degree program. The program was difficult because it required that I complete assignments without the benefit of classroom lectures and the help of professors. For six years, I toiled in the program while working full-time and trying to maintain equilibrium in a household with two remaining children whose needs still had to be met.

The most difficult aspect of the program was cramming assignments into every single weekend. There was no time for leisure—not if I wanted to achieve my goal. However, with all my other responsibilities, I have to admit that I was not always as motivated as I might have been. I would burn out periodically and not open a book for months.

When the end was finally in sight, I was unable to continue my studies due to a particularly discouraging experience with one of my courses. I was ready to quit for good. But I soon realized that, since so much was invested, I had to go on. I pushed harder than ever. At last, on May 19, 2001, at the University of Alabama in Tuscaloosa, I received my B.A. degree in Humanities, with high honors.

SUCCESSFUL INTELLIGENCE

PRACTICAL CREATIVE

ANALYTICAL

SUCCESSFUL INTELLIGENCE

Developing Successful Intelligence

PUTTING IT ALL TOGETHER

Learn from the experiences of others. Look back to Carol Comlish's Personal Triumph on p. 189. After you've read her story, relate her experience to your own life by completing the following:

Think it through: *Analyze your experience and compare it to Carol's.* What academic goal are you trying to reach now that will take you a long time, and how does this relate to Carol's experience? Why is this goal important to you? From your memory of reaching other important goals, what strategies will help you achieve it?

Think out of the box: *Let others inspire ideas.* Choose two people whom you respect. Put your listening skills to work: Spend a few minutes talking with each of them about your goal. Ask them about similar experiences they have had, and listen to the ideas that they used. From what you've heard, begin brainstorming ideas about how you will achieve your goal.

Make it happen: *Put a practical plan together.* Map out how you will achieve your goal. Create a mnemonic device that will help you remember your plan. Envision your success as you put your plan into action.

Team Building

COLLABORATIVE SOLUTIONS

Create a note-taking team. Although students often focus much more on taking notes in class than on taking notes while reading, reading notes are just as important to your understanding of the course material. In

create your future

your most demanding course, form a study group with two other people and choose a reading assignment—a text chapter, an article, or any other assigned reading—to work on together. Agree to read it and take notes independently before your next meeting. Each student should make photocopies of his or her notes for the other group members.

When you meet again, compare your notes, focusing on the following characteristics:

- Legibility (Can everyone read what is written?)
- Completeness (Did you all record the same information? If not, why not?)
- Organizational effectiveness (Does everyone get an idea of how ideas flow?)
- Value of the notes as a study aid (Will this help everyone remember the material?)

Based on what you've discussed with your group, come up with specific ways to improve your personal note-taking skills. You can also work with your study group to compare notes taken in a particular class period and work on improving in-class note-taking techniques.

Writing

DISCOVERY THROUGH JOURNALING

Record your thoughts on a separate piece of paper or in a journal.

How people retain information. How do you react to the following statement? "We retain 10 percent of what we read, 20 percent of what we hear, 30 percent of what we see, 50 percent of what we hear and see, 70 percent of what we say, 90 percent of what we say and do." How can you use this insight to improve your ability to retain information? What will you do differently as a result of this insight?

Career Portfolio

PLAN FOR SUCCESS

Matching career to curriculum. Your success in most career areas depends in part on your academic preparation. Some careers, such as medicine, require very specific curriculum choices (for example, specific biology and chemistry courses are required for medical school). Some careers require certain courses that teach basic competencies; for example, to be an accountant, you have to take accounting and bookkeeping. Other career areas, such as many business careers, don't have specific requirements, but employers often look for certain curriculum choices that indicate the mastery of particular skills and knowledge.

Put your listening and note-taking skills to work as you investigate your options. Choose a career area that interests you. Interview two people in that area—one from an academic setting (such as an instructor in a related subject area or an academic advisor) and one from the working world (such as a person working in that career or a career planning and placement office counselor). Choose a setting where you can listen well and take effective notes.

Ask your interviewees two questions: First, ask them about curriculum—what courses are required for this area, and what courses are beneficial but not required. Then ask them how you can stretch yourself outside of class in ways that will help you stand out—extracurricular activities, internships, leadership roles, part-time work, and any other helpful pursuits.

When you have completed your interviews, create two lists—one of recommended courses, marking the required ones with a star, and one of activities, internships, and any other recommendations.

SUGGESTED READINGS

Burley-Allen, Madelyn. *Listening: The Forgotten Skill: A Self-Teaching Guide.* New York: John Wiley & Sons, 1995.

DePorter, Bobbi and Mike Hernacki. *Quantum Notes: Whole-Brain Approaches to Note-Taking.* Chicago: Learning Forum, 2000.

Dunkel, Patricia A., Frank Pialorsi, and Joane Kozyrez. *Advanced Listening Comprehension: Developing Aural & Note-Taking Skills,* 3rd ed. Boston: Heinle & Heinle, 2004.

Higbee, Kenneth L. *Your Memory: How It Works and How to Improve It.* New York: Marlowe & Co., 2001.

Lebauer, R. Susan. *Learn to Listen, Listen to Learn: Academic Listening and Note-Taking.* Upper Saddle River, NJ: Prentice Hall, 2000.

Levin, Leonard. *Easy Script Express: Unique Speed Writing Methods to Take Fast Notes and Dictation.* Chicago: Legend Publishing, 2000.

Lorayne, Harry. *Super Memory—Super Student: How to Raise Your Grades in 30 Days.* Boston: Little, Brown & Company, 1990.

Lorayne, Harry. *The Memory Book: The Classic Guide to Improving Your Memory at Work, at School, and at Play.* New York: Ballantine Books, 1996.

Robbins, Harvey A. *How to Speak and Listen Effectively.* New York: AMACOM, 1992.

Roberts, Billy. *Working Memory: Improving Your Memory for the Workplace.* London: Bridge Trade, 1999.

Roberts, Billy. *Educate Your Memory: Improvement Techniques for Students of All Ages.* London: Allison & Busby, 2000.

INTERNET RESOURCES

ForgetKnot: A Source for Mnemonic Devices:
http://members.tripod.com/~ForgetKnot/

Prentice Hall Student Success Supersite—Study Skills:
www.prenhall.com/success/StudySkl/index.html

Helpful advice on listening from the Kishwaukee College Learning Skills Center:
kish.cc.il.us/lsc/ssh/listening.shtml

1. Ralph G. Nichols, "Do We Know How to Listen? Practical Helps in a Modern Age," *Speech Teacher* (March 1961): 118–124.

2. Richard J. Light, *Making the Most of College: Students Speak Their Minds*. Cambridge, MA: Harvard University Press, 2001, pp. 48–49.

3. Ibid, p. 38.

4. Walter Pauk, *How to Study in College*, 7th ed. Boston: Houghton Mifflin, 2001, pp. 236–241.

5. Herman Ebbinghaus, *Memory: A Contribution to Experimental Psychology*, trans. H. A. Ruger and C. E. Bussenius. New York: New York Teacher's College, Columbia University, 1885.

6. James Zull, *The Art of Changing the Brain: Enriching Teaching by Exploring the Biology of Learning*. Sterling, VA: Stylus Publishing, 2002.

7. Vyacheslav Kandyba, "Professor Uses Music to Bring Biology to Life," *The Chronicle of Higher Education*. March 30, 2003 [on-line]. Available: http://chronicle.com/weekly/v49/i38/38a01002.htm (March 2004).

Test Taking
SHOWING WHAT YOU KNOW

For a runner, a race is equivalent to a test because it measures ability at a given moment. Doing well in a race requires training similar to the studying you do for exams. The best runners—and test takers—understand that they train not just for the race or test, but to achieve a level of competence that they will use elsewhere.

When you successfully show what you know on tests, you achieve educational goals and develop confidence that you can perform well again and again. Exams also help you gauge your progress and, if necessary, improve your efforts. Most important, smart test preparation results in real learning that you take with you from course to course and into your career and life.

As you will see in this chapter, test taking is about preparation, persistence, and strategy—all of which tap into your analytical, creative, and practical abilities. It is also about conquering fears, paying attention to details, and learning from mistakes.

On the following page, read about student Peter Changsak's experience with test anxiety and his desire to overcome it.

- How can preparation improve test performance?
- How can you work through test anxiety?
- What general strategies can help you succeed on tests?
- How can you master different types of test questions?
- How can you learn from test mistakes?

How can I combat test anxiety?

I am a Yu'pik Eskimo from a village on the Yukon River. Before attending college, I worked for six years as a clerk at the Native Corporation, a gas station and general store. When the manager passed away, the business offered to make me a manager. Even though I knew how to do much of the work, I didn't feel I was ready, so I decided to go to school for more training.

College life is different from what I am accustomed to. The hardest part has been taking tests. I study hard, but then when I get in class and the test begins, my mind goes blank. When I read, I understand what I'm reading—ing, but as soon as I close the book, I can't remember what I just read. My favorite class is Biology Lab—probably because we can walk around.

I love mechanics and construction. When I worked at the Native Corporation, we built a new building. I felt like I was a success at work, but I don't feel success-ful as a student. Sometimes I feel like quitting, but I also think it can help me have more choices if I stick with it. I'm learning how to be a serious student, but it isn't easy. Can you give suggestions about how I can get over my test anxiety?

Peter Changsak
Sheldon-Jackson College,
Sitka, Alaska

Focus on preparation and work to change your attitude toward tests.

Many students experience test anxiety, especially students who are new to the educational setting. Often, anxiety is a result of feeling uncomfortable or distressed when charting unfamiliar waters. The first test administered in a class can bring about a great deal of anxiety.

First, it is important to adequately prepare for class exams:

- Attend class regularly.
- Pay attention in class and take *good notes*.
- Join a *study group* with fellow classmates.
- Spend three hours outside of the classroom studying for every hour you spend in class. Start studying early (don't wait until the week of the exam to study).
- Communicate with your instructor to make sure you understand course expectations, lecture information, and special projects that are due.
- Before the exam, get plenty of rest and eat a light breakfast or snack.

Second, when taking an exam:

- Close your eyes, take a deep breath, then review the test.
- Begin by responding to the questions you are most comfortable/familiar with.
- Continue reviewing the test to look for clues to answer those questions that you are not sure about.

Third, after taking the exam:

- After each test/exam, review your test/exam to learn about the areas you need to improve.
- Continue studying the information from the last exam along with new course information.

Finally, remember not all anxiety is bad—test anxiety, believe it or not, can encourage us to rise to an occasion. The stress of an upcoming test can help you work very hard and be prepared for the exam. Once the prepara-tion is done, it is important for you to remind yourself that an exam is your opportunity to show off your knowledge. Changing your attitude toward the exam and looking forward to the opportunity to share your knowledge will help you think more positively about tests.

Tonjua Williams, M.Ed.
Associate Provost, Health Programs, St. Petersburg College

How can preparation improve *test performance?*

You prepare for exams every day of the semester. By attending class, staying on top of assignments, completing readings and projects, and participating in class discussions, you are actively learning and retaining what you need to know in order to do well on exams. This knowledge is the most important test-preparation tool you have.

The following additional measures will help you to be as prepared as possible for exam day because they will help you put your analytical, creative, and practical thinking skills into action.

Ninety percent of life is just showing up.

WOODY ALLEN

Identify test type and material covered

Before you begin studying, find out as much as you can about the test, including:

- **Topics that will be covered.** Will it cover everything since the semester began or will it be limited to a narrow topic?
- **Types of questions.** Objective (multiple choice, true/false, sentence completion), subjective (essay), or a combination?
- **Material you will be tested on.** Will the test cover only what you learned in class and in the text, or will it also cover outside readings?

Your instructors may answer many of these questions. They may tell you the question format and the topics that will be on the test. Some instructors may even drop hints about possible questions, either directly ("I might ask a question on this subject on your next exam") or more subtly ("One of my favorite theories is . . . ").

Here are other practical strategies for predicting what may be on a test.

Use SQ3R to identify what's important. Often, the questions you write and ask yourself when you read assigned materials may be part of the test. Textbook study questions are also good candidates.

Talk to people who already took the course. Try to get a sense of test difficulty, whether tests focus primarily on assigned readings or class notes, what materials are usually covered, and what types of questions are asked. Also ask about instructors' preferences. If you learn that the instructor pays close attention to specific facts, for example, use flash cards to drill yourself on details. If the instructor emphasizes a global overview, focus on concepts.

Examine old tests, if the instructor makes them available. You may find old tests in class, on-line, or on reserve in the library. Make sure you have the instructor's permission to consult them. Old tests will help you answer questions like:

- Do tests focus on examples and details, general ideas and themes, or a combination?

get creative!

WRITE YOUR OWN TEST

Prepare for an upcoming exam using a pretest you create yourself.

Use the tips in this chapter to predict the material that will be covered, the types of questions that will be asked (multiple choice, essay, etc.), and the nature of the questions (a broad overview of the material or specific details).

Then be creative. Your goal is to write questions that your instructor is likely to ask—interesting questions that tap what you have learned and make you think about the material in different ways. Go through the following steps:

1. Write the questions you come up with on a separate sheet of paper.

2. Use what you created as a pretest. Set up test-like conditions—a quiet, timed environment— and see how well you do. Avoid looking at your text or notes unless the test is open book.

3. Evaluate your pretest answers against your notes and the text. How did you do?

_____

_____

4. Finally, after you take your instructor's exam, evaluate whether you think this exercise improved your performance on the actual exam. Would you use this technique again when you study for another exam? Why or why not?

_____

_____

_____

- Are the questions straightforward or confusing and sometimes tricky?
- Will you be asked to integrate facts from different areas in order to draw conclusions?

After taking the first exam in the course, you will have a better idea of what to expect.

Create a study plan and schedule

Use the guidelines presented on page 125 to create a study plan and schedule. Make copies of the checklist on page 126 and complete it for every exam. It is an invaluable tool for organizing your pre-exam studying.

Studying for final exams, which usually take place the last week of the semester, is a big commitment that requires careful time management. Your college may schedule study days, sometimes known as "reading period" or "dead days," between the end of classes and the beginning of finals. Lasting from a day or two to several weeks, these days give you uninterrupted hours to prepare for exams and finish papers.

End-of-year studying often requires flexibility. For example, instead of working at the library during this period, students at the University of Texas at Austin are often seen at Baron Springs, a spring-fed pool near campus. Anna Leeker and Jillian Adams chose this site to study Biology because of the beautiful surroundings—and because they had little choice. "We heard that the libraries are packed, and that students are waiting in line for tables," said Jillian. Both realize that they have to be vigilant about maintaining their focus, no matter where they study.[1]

Prepare through careful review

A thorough review, using analytical and practical strategies like the following, will give you the best shot at remembering the material you study:

Use SQ3R. The reading method you studied in Chapter 5 provides an excellent structure for reviewing your reading materials.

- *Surveying* gives you an overview of topics.
- *Questioning* helps you focus on important ideas and determine the meaning.
- *Reading* (or, in this case, rereading) reminds you of concepts and supporting information.
- *Reciting* helps to anchor the concepts in your head.
- *Reviewing*, such as quizzing yourself on the Q-stage questions, summarizing highlighted sections, making key-concept flash cards, and outlining chapters, helps solidify learning.

Review your notes. Use the following techniques to review your notes before an exam:

- Time your reviews carefully. Review notes for the first time within a day of the lecture, if you can, and then review again closer to the test day.
- Mark up. Reread your notes, filling in missing information, clarifying points, writing out abbreviations, and highlighting key ideas.

Learning is what most adults will do for a living in the 21st century.

BOB PERELMAN

- Organize. Consider adding headings and subheadings to your notes to clarify the structure of the information. Rewrite your notes using a different organizing structure— for example, an outline if you originally used a think link.
- Summarize. Evaluate which ideas and examples are most important, then rewrite your notes in shortened form. Summarize your notes in writing or with a summary think link. Try summarizing from memory as a self-test.

Take a pretest

Use end-of-chapter text questions to create your own pretest. If your course doesn't have an assigned text, develop questions from your notes and assigned outside readings. Old homework problems will also help target areas you need to work on. Choose questions that are likely to be covered, then answer them under test-like conditions—in a quiet place, with no books or notes to help you (unless the exam is open book), and with a clock to tell you when to quit.

The same test-preparation skills you learn in college will help you do well on standardized tests for graduate school. Sharon Smith describes how students in her preparatory program used practice tests and other techniques to help boost their scores on the Medical College Admission Test (MCAT). They "started with un-timed practices in order to work on accuracy, and timed practices were incorporated as the semester progressed. Everyone tried to finish the tests/passages in the allotted time, and, at the end of each practice session, go over answer choices to understand why they are correct or incorrect." During spring semester they were "given mock exams, and it was important to treat the mock MCAT as if it were the real exam. This gave the best assessment of performance on test day."[2]

Prepare physically

Most tests ask you to work at your best under pressure. A good night's sleep will leave you rested and alert and improve your ability to remember the material you studied the night before. Eating a light, well-balanced meal is also important. When time is short, grab a quick-energy snack such as a banana, orange juice, or a granola bar. For more ideas on getting adequate sleep and eating a balanced diet, look ahead to the chapter on Personal Wellness (Chapter 10).

Make the most of last-minute studying

Cramming—studying intensively and around the clock right before an exam—often results in information going into your head and popping right back out shortly after the exam is over. If learning is your goal, cramming is not a good idea. The reality, however, is that nearly every student crams during college, especially during midterms and finals. Use these hints to make the most of this intensive study time:

- **Review your flash cards.** If you use flash cards, review them one last time.
- **Focus on crucial concepts.** Resist reviewing notes or texts page by page.
- **Create a last-minute study sheet.** On a single sheet of paper, write down key facts, definitions, formulas, and so on. If you prefer visual notes, use think links to map out ideas and supporting examples.
- **Arrive early.** Study the sheet or your flash cards until you are asked to clear your desk.

After your exam, evaluate how cramming affected your recall. Within a few days, you will probably remember very little—a reality that will work against you in advanced courses that build on this knowledge and in careers that require it. Think ahead about how you can start studying earlier to prepare for your next exam.

Whether you cram or not, you may experience anxiety on test day. Many students do. Following are some ideas for how to handle test anxiety when it strikes.

How can you work through *test anxiety?*

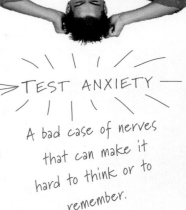

A certain amount of stress can be a good thing. Your body is alert, and your energy motivates you to do your best. Some students, however, experience incapacitating stress before and during exams, especially midterms and finals.

Test anxiety can cause sweating, nausea, dizziness, headaches, and fatigue. It can reduce your ability to concentrate, make you feel overwhelmed, and cause you to "blank out." As a result, test anxiety often results in lower grades that may not reflect what you really know. Take two steps to minimize your anxiety: Prepare thoroughly and build a positive attitude.

> TEST ANXIETY
>
> A bad case of nerves that can make it hard to think or to remember.

Preparation

The more confident you feel about the material, the better you will perform on test day. In this sense, consider all the preparation and study information in *Keys to Success* as test-anxiety assistance. Also, finding out what to expect on the exam will help you feel more in control. Seek out information about the material that will be covered, the question format, the length of the exam, and the points assigned to each question.

Creating a detailed study plan builds your knowledge as it combats anxiety. Divide the plan into small tasks. As you finish each, you gain an increased sense of accomplishment, confidence, and control.

Attitude

Here are ways to maintain an attitude that will help you succeed.

- **See the test as an opportunity to learn.** Instead of thinking of tests as contests that you either "win" or "lose," think of them as signposts along the way to mastering the material. Learning is far more important than "winning."

- **Understand that tests measure performance, not personal value.** Your grade does not reflect your ability to succeed. Whether you get an A or an F, you are the same person.

- **Appreciate your instructor's purpose.** Your instructors want to help you succeed. Don't hesitate to visit them during office hours and send e-mail questions to clarify material.

- **Seek study partners who challenge you.** Find study partners who can inspire you to do your best. Try to avoid people who are also anxious, because you both may pick up on each other's fears and negativity. (For more on study groups, see Chapter 5.)

- **Set yourself up for success.** Expect progress and success—not failure. Take responsibility for creating success through your work and attitude.

- **Practice relaxation.** When you feel test anxiety mounting, breathe deeply, close your eyes, and visualize positive mental images such as getting a good grade and finishing with time to spare. Try to ease muscle tension—stretch your neck, tighten and then release your muscles.

- **Practice positive self-talk.** Tell yourself that you can do well and that it is normal to feel anxious, particularly before an important exam. As you walk into the testing room, give yourself a pep talk that builds confidence—something like, "I know this stuff, and I'm going to show everyone what I know." Also, slay your perfection monster by telling yourself, "I don't have to get a perfect score."

When you study in a group, you can compare your information, gain from what others know, and solidify your learning through teaching others.

Students from other cultures may not experience test anxiety in the same way as Americans. Because of cultural differences, U. S. students may experience more anxiety than students from countries, such as England, where group achievement tends to be emphasized more than individual achievement.

Math exams are a special problem for many students. Dealing with the anxieties associated with these exams will be examined on pages 257–259, where you will find stress-management, studying, and exam-taking techniques.

Test anxiety and the returning student

If you're returning to school after years away, you may wonder how well you will handle exams. To deal with these feelings, focus on what you have learned through life experience, including the ability to handle work and family pressures. Without even knowing it, you have developed the time-management, planning, and communication skills necessary for college success.

In addition, your life experiences will give real meaning to abstract classroom ideas. For example, workplace relationships may help you understand Social Psychology concepts, and refinancing your home mortgage may help you grasp the importance of interest-rate swings—a key concept in economics.

Parents who have to juggle child care with study time can find the challenge especially difficult before a test. Here are some suggestions that might help:

- **Find help.** This is especially important with younger children.
- **Plan activities.** If you have younger children, have a supply of games, books, and videos on hand to use while you study.
- **Explain the time frame.** Tell school-aged children your study schedule and the test date. Plan a reward after your test.

Preparing for an exam sets the stage for taking the exam. You are now ready to focus on methods to help you succeed when the test begins.

If the topic or format of a test challenges your stronger or weaker intelligences, these tips will help you make the most of your time and abilities.

INTELLIGENCE	SUGGESTED STRATEGIES	WHAT WORKS FOR YOU? WRITE NEW IDEAS HERE
Verbal–Linguistic	• Think of and write out questions your instructor may ask on a test. Answer the questions and then try rewriting them in a different format (essay, true/false, and so on). • Underline important words in review questions or practice questions.	
Logical–Mathematical	• Make diagrams of review or practice questions. • Outline the key steps involved in topics on which you may be tested.	
Bodily–Kinesthetic	• Use your voice to review out loud. Recite concepts, terms and definitions, important lists, dates, and so on. • Create a sculpture, model, or skit to depict a tough concept that will be on your test.	
Visual–Spatial	• Create a think link to map out an important topic and its connections to other topics in the material. Study it and redraw it from memory a day before the test. • Make drawings related to possible test topics.	
Interpersonal	• Develop a study group and encourage each other. • In your group, come up with as many possible test questions as you can. Ask each other these questions in an oral exam–type format.	
Intrapersonal	• Brainstorm test questions. Then, come back to them after a break or even a day's time. On your own, take the sample "test" you developed. • Make time to review in a solitary setting.	
Musical	• Play music while you read if it does not distract you. • Study concepts by reciting them to rhythms you create or to music.	
Naturalistic	• Bring your text, lecture notes, and other pertinent information to an outdoor spot that inspires you and helps you to feel confident, and review your material there.	

What *general strategies* can help you succeed on tests?

Even though every test is different, there are general strategies that will help you handle almost all tests, including short-answer and essay exams.

Write down key facts

Before you even look at the test, write down key information—including formulas, rules, and definitions—that you studied recently and that you don't want to forget. Use the back of the question sheet or some scrap paper for your notes. (Be sure your instructor knows that you made these notes after the test began.)

Begin with an overview

Although exam time is precious, spend a few minutes at the start of the test gathering information about the questions—how many there are in each section, what types, and their point values. Then, analyze the situation and think practically to schedule your time. For example, if a two-hour test is divided into two sections of equal point value—an essay section with four questions and a short-answer section with 60 questions—you might spend an hour on the essays (15 minutes per question) and an hour on the short answers (one minute per question).

You may need to take level of difficulty into account as you come up with options for how to parcel out your time. For example, if you think you can get through the short-answer questions in 45 minutes and sense that you'll have a tougher time with the writing section, you can budget an hour and a quarter for the essays.

Read test directions

Reading test directions carefully can save you trouble. For example, although a History test of 100 true/false questions and one essay may look straightforward, the directions may tell you to answer 80 of the 100 questions or that the essay is optional. If the directions indicate that you are penalized for incorrect answers—meaning that you lose points instead of simply not gaining points—avoid guessing unless you're fairly certain.

When you read the directions, you may learn that some questions or sections are weighted more heavily than others. For example, the short-answer questions may be worth 30 points, whereas the essays are worth 70. In this case, it's smart to spend more time on the essays than the short answers. To stay aware of the specifics of the directions, use the practical strategy of circling or underlining key information.

Mark up the questions

Highlight instructions and keywords to avoid careless errors. As you read each question, circle qualifiers such as *always, never, all, none,* and *every,* verbs that communicate specific test instructions, and concepts that are tricky or need special attention.

Take special care on machine-scored tests

Use the correct pencil (usually a number 2) on machine-scored tests, and mark your answer in the proper space, filling the space completely. Periodically, use your practical thinking skills to check the answer number against the question number to make sure they match. If you mark the answer to question 4 in the space for question 5, not only will your response to question 4 be wrong, but your responses to all subsequent questions will be off by a line. To avoid this problem, put a small dot next to any number you skip and plan to return to later.

Neatness counts on these tests because the computer can misread stray pencil marks or partially erased answers. If you mark two answers to a question and partially erase one, the computer will read both responses and charge you with a wrong answer.

Work from easy to hard

Begin with the easiest questions, and answer them as quickly as you can without sacrificing accuracy. This will boost your confidence and leave more time for questions that require more focus and effort. Mark tough questions as you reach them, and return to them after answering the questions you know.

Watch the clock

Keep track of how much time is left and how you are progressing. Some students are so concerned about time that they rush through the test and have time left over. If this happens to you, spend the remaining time refining and checking your work instead of leaving early. You may be able to correct mistakes, change answers, or add more information to an essay.

While it's tempting to rush through a test to get it over with, taking time to think when you need to will help you be more sure of your answers and may even help you stay calm.

Master the art of intelligent guessing

When you are unsure of an answer on a short-answer test, you can leave it blank or guess. As long as you are not penalized for incorrect answers, guessing helps you. "Intelligent guessing," writes Steven Frank, an authority on student studying and test taking, "means taking advantage of what you do know in order to try to figure out what you don't. If you guess intelligently, you have a decent shot at getting the answer right."[3]

When you check your work at the end of the test, use your analytical ability to decide whether you would make the same guesses again. Chances are that you will leave your answers alone, but you may notice something that changes your mind—a qualifier that affects meaning, a miscalculation in a math problem. Or you may recall information that you drew a blank on the first time around.

Maintain academic integrity

Cheating as a strategy to pass a test or get a better grade robs you of the opportunity to learn the material, which, ultimately, is your loss. Cheating also jeopardizes your future if you are caught. You may be seriously reprimanded—or even expelled—if you violate your school's code of academic integrity.

Now that you have explored these general strategies, you can use what you've learned to address specific types of test questions.

How can you master *different types* of test questions?

Every type of test question has a different way of finding out how much you know about a subject. For **objective questions,** you choose or write a short answer, often making a selection from a limited number of choices. Multiple-choice, fill-in-the-blank, matching, and true/false questions fall into this category. **Subjective questions** require you to plan, organize, draft, and refine a response. All essay questions are subjective. In general, subjective questions tap your creative abilities more than short-answer questions do.

Key 7.1 shows samples of real test questions from Western Civilization, Macroeconomics, Spanish, and Biology college texts published by Pearson Education. Included are multiple-choice, true/false, fill-in-the-blank, matching, and essay questions, including a short-answer essay. Seeing these questions firsthand will help you feel more comfortable with testing formats and question types when you take your first exams.

OBJECTIVE QUESTIONS

Short-answer questions that test your ability to recall, compare, and contrast information and to choose the right answer from a limited number of choices.

SUBJECTIVE QUESTIONS

Essay questions that require you to express your answer in terms of your own personal knowledge and perspective.

Multiple-choice questions

Multiple-choice questions are the most popular type of question on standardized tests. The following analytical and practical strategies can help you answer them:

Carefully read the directions. Directions can be tricky. For example, whereas most test items ask for a single correct answer, some give you the option of marking several choices that are correct. For some tests, you might be required to answer only a certain number of questions.

Read each question thoroughly. Then look at the choices, and try to choose an answer. This strategy makes it less likely that you'll get confused.

Real test questions from real college texts.

From Chapter 29, "The End of Imperialism," in *Western Civilization: A Social and Cultural History*, 2nd edition.[4]

■ MULTIPLE-CHOICE QUESTION

India's first leader after independence was:

A. Gandhi   B. Bose   C. Nehru   D. Sukharno   *(answer: C)*

■ FILL-IN-THE-BLANK QUESTION

East Pakistan became the country of _____ in 1971.

A. Burma   B. East India   C. Sukharno   D. Bangladesh   *(answer: D)*

■ TRUE/FALSE QUESTION

The United States initially supported Vietnamese independence.   T   F   *(answer: false)*

■ ESSAY QUESTION

Answer one of the following:

1. What led to Irish independence? What conflicts continued to exist after independence?

2. How did Gandhi work to rid India of British control? What methods did he use?

From Chapter 6, "Unemployment and Inflation," in *Macroeconomics: Principles and Tools*, 3rd edition.[5]

■ MULTIPLE-CHOICE QUESTION

If the labor force is 250,000 and the total population 16 years of age or older is 300,000, the labor-force participation rate is

A. 79.5%   B. 83.3%   C. 75.6%   D. 80.9%   *(answer: B)*

■ FILL-IN-THE-BLANK QUESTION

Mike has just graduated from college and is now looking for a job, but has not yet found one. This causes the employment rate to _____ and the labor-force participation rate to _____.

A. increase; decrease   C. stay the same; stay the same

B. increase; increase   D. increase; stay the same   *(answer: C)*

■ TRUE/FALSE QUESTION

The Consumer Price Index somewhat overstates changes in the cost of living because it does not allow for substitutions that consumers might make in response to price changes.   T   F   *(answer: true)*

■ SHORT-ANSWER ESSAY QUESTION

During a press conference, the Secretary of Employment notes that the unemployment rate is 7.0%. As a political opponent, how might you criticize this figure as an underestimate? In rebuttal, how might the Secretary argue that the reported rate is an overestimate of unemployment?

(Possible answer: The unemployment rate given by the secretary might be considered an underestimate because discouraged workers, who have given up the job search in frustration, are not counted as unemployed. In addition, full-time workers may have been forced to work part-time. In rebuttal, the secretary might note that a portion of the unemployed have voluntarily left their jobs. Most workers are unemployed only briefly and leave the ranks of the unemployed by gaining better jobs than they had previously held.)

Continued.

From *Mosaicos: Spanish as a World Language,* 3rd edition.[6]

- **MATCHING QUESTION**

You are learning new words and your teacher asks you to think of an object similar to or related to the words he says. His words are listed below. Next to each word, write a related word from the list below.

el reloj   el cuaderno   el pupitre   una computadora
el televisor   la tiza   el lápis   la mochila

1. el escritorio _____   4. la pizarra _____

2. el bolígrafo _____   5. el libro _____

3. la videocasetera _____

(answers: 1. el pupitre; 2. el lápis; 3. el televisor; 4. la tiza; 5. el cuaderno)

- **ESSAY QUESTION**

Your mother always worries about you and wants to know what you are doing with your time in Granada. Write a short letter to her describing your experience in Spain. In your letter, you should address the following points:

1. What classes you take   4. What you do with your time (mention three activities)

2. When and where you study   5. Where you go during your free time (mention two places)

3. How long you study every day

From Chapter 13, "DNA Structure and Replication," in *Biology: A Guide to the Natural World,* 2nd edition.[7]

- **MULTIPLE-CHOICE QUESTION**

What units are bonded together to make a strand of DNA?

A. chromatids   B. cells   C. enzymes   D. nucleotides   E. proteins   *(answer: D)*

- **TRUE/FALSE QUESTION**

Errors never occur in DNA replication, because the DNA polymerases edit out mistakes.   T   F

(answer: false)

- **FILL-IN-THE-BLANK QUESTION**

In a normal DNA molecule, adenine always pairs with _____ and cytosine always pairs with _____.

(answers: thymine; guanine)

- **MATCHING QUESTION**

Match the scientist and the approximate time frames (decades of their work) with their achievements.

Column 1	Column 2
____ 1. Modeled the molecular structure of DNA	A. George Beadle and Edward Tatum, 1930s and 1940s
____ 2. Generated X-ray crystallography images of DNA	B. James Watson and Francis Crick, 1950s
____ 3. Correlated the production of one enzyme with one gene	C. Rosalind Franklin and Maurice Wilkins, 1950s

(answers: 1–B; 2–C; 3–A)

Underline keywords and phrases. If the question is complicated, try to break it down into small sections that are easy to understand.

Pay attention to words that could throw you off. For example, it is easy to overlook negatives in a question ("Which of the following is not . . . ").

If you don't know the answer, eliminate answers that you know or suspect are wrong. If you can leave yourself with two possible answers, you will have a 50–50 chance of making the right choice. To narrow down, ask questions about each of the choices:

- **Is the choice accurate on its own terms?** If there's an error in the choice— for example, a term that is incorrectly defined—the answer is wrong.

- **Is the choice relevant?** An answer may be accurate, but unrelated to the question.

- **Are there any qualifiers?** Absolute qualifiers, like *always, never, all, none*, or *every*, often signal an exception that makes a choice incorrect. For example, the statement "Normal children always begin talking before the age of two" is untrue (most normal children begin talking before age two, but some start later). Analysis has shown that choices containing conservative qualifiers like *often, most, rarely*, or *may sometimes be* are often correct.

- **Do the choices give clues?** Does a puzzling word remind you of a word you know? Does any part of an unfamiliar word—its prefix, suffix, or root—ring a bell?

Make an educated guess by looking for patterns. Certain patterns tend to appear in multiple-choice questions and may help you make smart guesses. Although these patterns may not apply to the specific test questions you encounter, they're important to keep in mind. Experts advise you to:

- consider the possibility that a choice that is *more general* than the others is the right answer.

- consider the possibility that a choice that is *longer* than the others is the right answer.

- look for a choice that has a *middle value in a range* (the range can be from small to large or from old to recent). It is likely to be the right answer.

- look for two choices that have *similar meanings*. One of these answers is probably correct.

- look for answers that *agree grammatically* with the question. For example, a fill-in-the-blank question that has an *a* or *an* before the blank gives you a clue to the correct answer.

Make sure you read every word of every answer. Instructors have been known to include answers that are almost right, except for a single word. Focus especially on qualifying words such as *always, never, tend to, most, often*, and *frequently*.

When questions are linked to a reading passage, read the questions first. This will help you focus on the information you need to answer the questions.

Here are some examples of the kinds of multiple-choice questions you might encounter in an Introduction to Psychology course[8] (the correct answer follows each question):

1. Arnold is at the company party and has had too much to drink. He releases all of his pent-up aggression by yelling at his boss, who promptly fires him. Arnold normally would not have yelled at his boss, but after drinking heavily he yelled because_____.

    A. parties are places where employees are supposed to be able to "loosen up"

    B. alcohol is a stimulant

    C. alcohol makes people less concerned with the negative consequences of their behavior

    D. alcohol inhibits brain centers that control the perception of loudness

(The correct answer is C)

2. Which of the following has not been shown to be a probable cause of or influence in the development of alcoholism in our society?

    A. intelligence   C. personality

    B. culture   D. genetic vulnerability

(The correct answer is A)

3. Geraldine is a heavy coffee drinker who has become addicted to caffeine. If she completely ceases her intake of caffeine over the next few days, she is likely to experience each of the following EXCEPT_____.

    A. depression   C. insomnia

    B. lethargy   D. headaches

(The correct answer is C)

True/false questions

Read true/false questions carefully to evaluate what they are asking. If you're stumped, guess (unless you're penalized for wrong answers).

Look for qualifiers in true/false questions—such as *all, only,* and *always* (the absolutes that often make a statement false) and *generally, often, usually,* and *sometimes* (the conservatives that often make a statement true)—that can turn a statement that would otherwise be true into one that is false or vice versa. For example, "The grammar rule 'I before E except after C' is *always* true" is false, whereas "The grammar rule 'I before E except after C' is *usually* true" is true. The qualifier makes the difference.

Matching questions

Matching questions ask you to match the terms in one list with the terms in another list, according to the directions. For example, the directions

> Here are some examples of the kinds of true/false questions you might encounter in an Introduction to Psychology course.[9] The correct answer follows each question:
>
> Are the following questions true or false?
>
> 1. Alcohol use is clearly related to increases in hostility, aggression, violence, and abusive behavior. *(True)*
>
> 2. Marijuana is harmless. *(False)*
>
> 3. Simply expecting a drug to produce an effect is often enough to produce the effect. *(True)*
>
> 4. Alcohol is a stimulant. *(False)*

may tell you to match a communicable disease with the germ that usually causes it. The following practical strategies will help you handle these questions.

Make sure you understand the directions. The directions tell you whether each answer can be used only once or more than once.

Work from the column with the longest entries. The left-hand column usually contains terms to be defined or questions to be answered, whereas the right-hand column contains definitions or answers. As a result, entries in the right-hand column are usually longer than those on the left. Reading the items on the right only once each will save time as you work to match them with the shorter phrases on the left.

Start with the matches you know. On your first run-through, mark these matches with a penciled line, waiting to finalize your choices after you've completed all the items. Keep in mind that if you can use an answer only once, you may have to change answers if you reconsider any of your original choices.

Finally, tackle the matches you're not sure of. On your next run-through, focus on the more difficult matches. Look for clues and relationships you might not have considered.

If one or more phrases seem to have no correct answer, look back at your easy matches to be sure that you did not jump too quickly. Consider the possibility that one of your sure-thing answers is wrong.

Fill-in-the-blank questions

Fill-in-the-blank questions, also known as sentence completion questions, ask you to supply one or more words or phrases with missing information that completes the sentence. These strategies will help you make successful choices.

Be logical. Insert your answer, then reread the sentence from beginning to end to be sure it is factually and grammatically correct and makes sense.

Note the length and number of the blanks. These are important clues but not absolute guideposts. If two blanks appear right after one another, the instructor is probably looking for a two-word answer. If a blank is longer than usual, the correct response may require additional space. However, if you are certain of an answer that doesn't seem to fit the blanks, trust your knowledge and instincts.

Pay attention to how blanks are separated. If there is more than one blank in a sentence and the blanks are widely separated, treat each one separately. Answering each as if it were a separate sentence-completion question increases the likelihood that you will get at least one answer correct. Here is an example:

> When Toni Morrison was awarded the _____ Prize for Literature, she was a professor at _____ University.
> (*Answer: Morrison received the Nobel Prize and is a professor at Princeton University.*)

Think out of the box. If you can think of more than one correct answer, put them both down. Your instructor may be impressed by your assertiveness and creativity.

If you are uncertain of an answer, make an educated guess. Have faith that after hours of studying, the correct answer is somewhere in your subconscious mind and that your guess is not completely random.

Here are examples of fill-in-the-blank questions you might encounter in an Introduction to Astronomy course[10] (correct answers follow questions):

1. A _____ is a collection of hundreds of billions of stars. *(galaxy)*

2. Rotation is the term used to describe the motion of a body around some _____. *(axis)*

3. The solar day is measured relative to the Sun; the sidereal day is measured relative to the _____. *(stars)*

4. On December 21, known as the _____ _____, the Sun is at its _____ _____. *(winter solstice; southernmost point)*

Essay questions

An essay question allows you to express your knowledge and views more extensively than a short-answer question. With this freedom comes the challenge to organize and express that knowledge clearly.

The following steps will help improve your responses to essay questions. The process is basically a less extensive version of the writing process—you plan, draft, revise, and edit your response (see Chapter 8). The primary differences here are that you are writing under time pressure and that you are working from memory.

1. **Start by reading the questions.** Decide which to tackle (if there's a choice). Use your analytical ability to focus on what each question is asking. Then engage practical strategies as you read the directions carefully and do everything asked.

Some essay questions may contain more than one part, so it is important to budget your time. For example, if you have one hour to answer three question sections, you might budget 20 minutes for each section, and break that down into writing stages (3 minutes for planning, 15 minutes for drafting, 2 minutes for revising and editing).

2. **Watch for action verbs.** Certain verbs can help you figure out how to think. Key 7.2 explains some words commonly used in essay questions. Underline these words as you read and use them to guide your writing.

3. **Plan.** Use your creative thinking skills to brainstorm ideas and examples. Create an informal outline or a think link to map your ideas and list supporting examples.

Focus on action verbs on essay tests.

key 7.2

Analyze—Break into parts and discuss each part separately.

Compare—Explain similarities and differences.

Contrast—Distinguish between items being compared by focusing on differences.

Criticize—Evaluate the positive and negative effects of what is being discussed.

Define—State the essential quality or meaning. Give the common idea.

Describe—Visualize and give information that paints a complete picture.

Discuss—Examine in a complete and detailed way, usually by connecting ideas to examples.

Enumerate/List/Identify—Recall and specify items in the form of a list.

Evaluate—Give your opinion about the value or worth of something, usually by weighing positive and negative effects, and justify your conclusion.

Explain—Make the meaning of something clear, often by making analogies or giving examples.

Illustrate—Supply examples.

Interpret—Explain your personal view of facts and ideas and how they relate to one another.

Outline—Organize and present the main examples of an idea or sub-ideas.

Prove—Use evidence and argument to show that something is true, usually by showing cause and effect or giving examples that fit the idea to be proven.

Review—Provide an overview of ideas and establish their merits and features.

State—Explain clearly, simply, and concisely, being sure that each word gives the image you want.

Summarize—Give the important ideas in brief.

Trace—Present a history of the way something developed, often by showing cause and effect.

4. **Draft.** Start with a thesis statement that states clearly what your essay will say. Then, devote one or more paragraphs to the main points in your outline. Back up the general statement that starts each paragraph with evidence in the form of examples, statistics, and so on. Use simple, clear language, and look back at your outline to make sure you cover everything. Wrap it up with a short, pointed conclusion. Since you probably won't have time for redrafting, try to be as complete and organized as possible.

5. **Revise.** Make sure you answer the question completely and include all of your points. Look for ideas you left out, general statements that need more support, paragraphs that don't hold together well, unnecessary material, and confusing sentences. Fix problems by adding new material in the margins and crossing out what you don't need. When adding material, you can indicate with an arrow where it fits or note that inserts can

get analytical! WRITE TO THE VERB

Hone your ability to read and follow essay instructions accurately.

Focusing on the action verbs in essay test instructions can mean the difference between giving instructors what they want and answering off the mark.

● Start by choosing a topic you learned about in this text—for example, the concept of successful intelligence or internal and external barriers to listening. Write your topic here:

_____

_____

● Put yourself in the role of instructor. Write an essay question on this topic, using one of the action verbs in Key 7.2 to frame the question. For example, "List the three aspects of successful intelligence," or "Analyze the classroom-based challenges associated with internal barriers to listening."

_____

_____

● Now choose three other action verbs from Key 7.2. Use each one to rewrite your original question.

1. _____

2. _____

3. _____

● Finally, analyze how each new verb changes the focus of the essay.

1. _____

_____

2. _____

_____

3. _____

_____

be found on separate pages. If you have more than one insert, label each to avoid confusion (e.g., Insert #1, Insert #2, etc.).

6. **Edit.** Check for mistakes in grammar, spelling, punctuation, and usage. No matter your topic, being technically correct in your writing makes your work more impressive.

Neatness is a crucial factor in essay writing. No matter how good your ideas are, if your instructor can't read them, your grade will suffer. If your handwriting is a problem, try printing your answers, skipping every other line, and writing on only one side of the paper. Students with illegible handwriting might ask to take the test on a laptop computer.

To answer the third essay question from the box below, one student created the planning outline shown in Key 7.3. Notice how abbreviations and shorthand help the student write quickly. It is much faster to write "Role of BL in IC" than "Role of Body Language in Interpersonal Communication" (see Chapter 6 for shorthand strategies). Key 7.4 shows the student's essay, including the word changes and inserts she made while revising the draft.

Here are some examples of essay questions you might encounter in an Interpersonal Communication course. In each case, notice the action verbs from Key 7.2.

1. Summarize the role of the self-concept as a key to interpersonal relationships and communication.

2. Explain how internal and external noise affects the ability to listen effectively.

3. Describe three ways that body language affects interpersonal communication.

Create an informal outline during essay tests.

Roles of BL in IC

1. To contradict or reinforce words

    —e.g., friend says "I'm fine"

2. To add shades of meaning

    —saying the same sentence in 3 diff. ways

3. To make lasting 1st impression

    —impact of nv cues and voice tone greater than words

    —we assume things abt person based on posture, eye contact, etc.

Response to an essay question with revision marks.

QUESTION: Describe three ways that body language affects interpersonal communication.

Body language plays an important role in interpersonal communication and helps

, especially when ∧
you meet someone
for the first time

shape the impression you make. Two of the most important functions of body

language are to contradict and reinforce verbal statements. When body

~~delivered~~

language contradicts verbal language, the message ~~conveyed~~ by the body is

dominant. For example, if a friend tells you that she is feeling "fine," but her

her eye contact
minimal,

posture is slumped, and her facial expression troubled, you have every reason to

wonder whether she is telling the truth. If the same friend tells you that

she is feeling fine and is smiling, walking with a bounce in her step, and has

accurately reflecting
and reinforcing her
words.

direct eye contact, her body language is ~~telling the truth.~~
                                        ∧

The nonverbal cues that make up body language also have the power to add

shades of meaning. Consider this statement: "This is the best idea I've heard

all day." If you were to say this three different ways—in a loud voice while

standing up; quietly while sitting with arms and legs crossed and

maintaining

looking away; and while ~~maintening~~ eye contact and taking the receiver's

hand—you might send three different messages.

Although first
impressions emerge
from a combination
of nonverbal cues,
tone of voice, and
choice of words,
nonverbal elements
(~~cues and tone~~)
usually come across
first and strongest.

Finally, the impact of nonverbal cues can be greatest when you meet

someone for the first time. When you meet someone, you tend to make

assumptions based on nonverbal behavior such as posture, eye contact, gestures,

and speed and style of movement.

crucial

In summary, nonverbal communication plays a ~~crucial~~ role in interpersonal

relationships. It has the power to send an accurate message that may

belie

~~destroy~~ the speaker's words, offer shades of meaning, and set the tone

of a first meeting.

How can you learn from *test mistakes?*

he purpose of a test is to see how much you know, not merely to get a grade. Use the following strategies to analyze and learn from your mistakes so that you avoid repeating them.

Try to identify patterns in your mistakes. Look for the following:

- Careless errors. In your rush to finish, did you misread the question or directions, blacken the wrong box on the answer sheet, skip a question, write illegibly?
- Conceptual or factual errors. Did you misunderstand a concept? Did you fail to master facts or concepts? Did you skip part of the text or miss classes in which ideas were covered?

Rework the questions you got wrong. Based on instructor feedback, try to rewrite an essay, recalculate a math problem from the original question, or redo questions following a reading selection. If you discover a pattern of careless errors, redouble your efforts to be more careful and save time to double-check your work.

Our greatest glory is not in never falling, but in rising every time we fall.

CONFUCIUS

After reviewing your mistakes, fill in your knowledge gaps. If you made mistakes because of a lack of understanding, develop a plan to learn the material. Solidifying your knowledge can help you on future exams and in life situations that involve the subject you're studying.

Talk to your instructors. Talk with your instructor about your specific mistakes on short-answer questions or about a weak essay. If you are not sure why you were marked down on an essay, ask what you could have done to improve your grade. Take advantage of this opportunity to determine how to do better on the next exam.

If you fail a test, don't throw it away. Use it as a way to review material that you had trouble with or didn't know as well as you should have. You might also want to keep it as a reminder that you can improve if you have the will to succeed. When you compare a failure to later successes, you'll see how far you've come.

The willingness to learn from test mistakes is critical for all students, including those with reading-related learning disabilities. When CAST researcher Roxanne Ruzic examined how students who are learning disabled prepare for tests, she found that successful students took advantage of instructor feedback; they applied what they learned from their mistakes on one test to their preparation for others. Students who dismissed this feedback did not excel.

Jack is a case in point, as Ruzic explains: "When Jack received his graded midterm exam [in Introduction to International Business], he discounted some of what the instructor wrote in his blue book, claiming she was wrong, rather than trying to figure out how to ensure that he knew

LEARN FROM YOUR MISTAKES

Examine what went wrong on a recent exam to build knowledge for next time.

Look at an exam on which your performance fell short of expectations. If possible, choose one that contains different types of objective and subjective questions. With the test and answer sheet in hand, use your analytical and practical thinking skills to answer the following questions:

- Identify the types of questions on which you got the most correct answers (for example, matching, essay, multiple choice).

  _____

- Identify the types of questions on which you made the greatest number of errors.

  _____

- Analyze your errors to identify patterns—for example, did you misread test instructions, or did you ignore qualifiers that changed the questions' meanings? What did you find?

  _____

  _____

- Finally, what are two practical actions you are committed to take during your next exam to avoid the same problems?

  Action 1: _____

  Action 2: _____

the material and she knew that he knew it. While Jack did not do as well on the midterm as he would have liked, he used the same study techniques to prepare for the final exam as he had used for the midterm. Had Jack talked more to other people (including instructors) regularly to assess his understanding of content and expectations and worked in study-groups, he would have been much more successful in his courses." Jack's final course grade was a C+—not where he could have been had he made the effort to learn from earlier setbacks.[11]

Sine qua non

Although Latin is no longer spoken and is considered a "dead" language, it plays an important role in modern English, since many English words and phrases have Latin roots. The Latin phrase *sine qua non* (pronounced sihn-ay kwa nahn) means, literally, "without which not." In other words, a sine qua non is "an absolutely indispensable or essential thing."

Think of learning as the sine qua non of test taking. When you have worked hard to learn, review, and retain information, you will be well prepared for tests, no matter what form they take. Focus on knowledge to transform test taking from an intimidating challenge into an opportunity to demonstrate what you know.

BUILDING SKILLS

FOR COLLEGE, CAREER, AND LIFE SUCCESS

Developing Successful Intelligence

PUTTING IT ALL TOGETHER

Prepare effectively for tests. Take a detailed look at your performance on and preparation for a recent test.

Step 1. Think it through: *Analyze how you did.* Were you pleased or disappointed with your performance and grade? Why?

_____

_____

Thinking about your performance, look at the potential problems listed below. Circle any that you feel were a factor in this exam. Fill in the empty spaces with any key problems not listed.

- Incomplete preparation
- Fatigue
- Feeling rushed during the test
- Shaky understanding of concepts
- Poor guessing techniques

- Feeling confused about directions
- Test anxiety
- _____
- _____
- _____

If you circled any problems, think about why you made mistakes (if it was an objective exam) or why you didn't score well (if it was an essay exam).

Step 2. Think out of the box: *Be creative about test-preparation strategies.* If you had absolutely no restrictions on time or on access to materials, how would you have prepared for this test?

create your future

Describe briefly what your plan would be and how it would minimize any problems you encountered.

_____

_____

Now think back to your actual preparation for this test. Describe techniques you used and note time spent.

_____

_____

How does what you would like to do differ from what you actually did?

_____

_____

Step 3. Make it happen: *Improve preparation for the future.* Think about the practical actions you will take the next time you face a similar test.

Actions I took this time, but do not intend to take next time:

_____

_____

Actions I did not take this time, but intend to take next time:

_____

_____

Team Building

COLLABORATIVE SOLUTIONS

Test study group. Form a study group with two or three other students. When your instructor announces the next exam, ask each study group member to record everything he or she does to prepare for the exam, including:

- learning what to expect on the test (topics and material that will be covered, types of questions that will be asked)
- examining old tests
- creating and following a study schedule and checklist
- using SQ3R to review material
- taking a pretest
- getting a good night's sleep before the exam
- doing last-minute cramming
- mastering general test-taking strategies
- mastering test-taking strategies for specific types of test questions (multiple choice, true/false, matching, fill in the blank, essay)

After the exam, come together to compare preparation strategies. What important differences can you identify in the routines followed by group members? How did learning styles play a role in those differences? How do you suspect that different routines affected test performance and outcome? On a separate piece of paper, for your own reference, write down what you learned from the test-preparation habits of your study mates that may help you as you prepare for upcoming exams.

Writing

DISCOVERY THROUGH JOURNALING

Record your thoughts on a separate piece of paper or in a journal.

Test anxiety. Do you experience test anxiety? Describe how tests generally make you feel (you might include an example of a specific test situation and what happened). Identify your specific test-taking fears, and brainstorm ideas for how to overcome fears and self-defeating behaviors.

Career Portfolio

PLAN FOR SUCCESS

Complete the following in your electronic portfolio or on separate sheets of paper.

On-the-job testing. Depending on what careers you are considering, you may encounter one or more tests throughout your career. Some are for entry into the field (e.g., medical boards); some test your proficiency on particular equipment (e.g., a proficiency test on Microsoft Word); some move you to the next level of employment (e.g., a technical certification test to become a certified actuary). Choose one career you are thinking about and investigate what tests are involved as you advance through different stages of the field. Be sure to look for tests in any of the areas described above. Write down everything you find out about each test involved. For example:

- what it tests you on
- when, in the course of pursuing this career, you would need to take the test
- what preparation is necessary for the test (including course work)
- whether the test needs to be retaken at any time (e.g., airline pilots usually need to be recertified every few years)

Finally, see if you can review any of the tests you will face if you pursue this career. For example, if your career choice requires proficiency on a specific computer program, your college's career or computer center may have the test available.

SUGGESTED READINGS

Browning, William G., Ph.D. *Cliffs Memory Power for Exams.* Lincoln, NE: CliffsNotes Inc., 1990.

Frank, Steven. *Test Taking Secrets: Study Better, Test Smarter, and Get Great Grades.* Holbrook, MA: Adams Media Corporation, 1998.

Fry, Ron. *"Ace" Any Test,* 5th ed. Florence, KY: Thomson Delmar Learning, 2004.

Hamilton, Dawn. *Passing Exams: A Guide for Maximum Success and Minimum Stress.* New York: Continuum International, 2003.

Kesselman-Turkel, Judy and Franklynn Peterson. *Test Taking Strategies.* Madison, WI: University of Wisconsin Press, 2004.

Luckie, William R. and Wood Smethurst. *Study Power: Study Skills to Improve Your Learning and Your Grades.* Cambridge, MA: Brookline Books, 1997.

Meyers, Judith N. *Secrets of Taking Any Test: Learn the Techniques Successful Test-Takers Know.* New York: Learning Express, July 2000.

INTERNET RESOURCES

Prentice Hall Student Success SuperSite (testing tips in study skills section): www.prenhall.com/success

Florida State University (list of sites offering information on test-taking skills): http://osi.fsu.edu/hot/testtaking/skills.htm

Test Taking Tips.com (test taking and study skills): www.testtakingtips.com

University of North Dakota (study strategies home page): www.d.umn.edu/student/loon/acad/strat/

ENDNOTES

1. Ben Gose, "Notes from Academe: Living It Up on the Dead Days," *The Chronicle of Higher Education,* June 7, 2002 [on-line]. Available: http://chronicle.com/weekly/v48/i39/39a04801.htm (April 2004).

2. "Students Speak," MEDPREP: Medical/Dental Education Preparatory Program, Southern Illinois University School of Medicine [on-line]. Available: www.som.siu.edu/medprep/students_speak.html (March 2004).

3. Steven Frank, *The Everything Study Book.* Holbrook, MA: Adams Media Corporation, 1996, p. 208.

4. King, Margaret L., *Instructor's Manual with Tests for Western Civilization: A Social & Cultural History,* 2nd Edition, ©2003. Reprinted by permission of Pearson Education, Inc., Upper Saddle River, NJ.

5. O'Sullivan, Arthur, *Test Item File #2 for Macroeconomics: Principles & Tools,* 3rd Edition, ©2003.

Reprinted by permission of Pearson Education, Inc., Upper Saddle River, NJ.

6. Castells, Matilde Olivella, *Testing Program for Mosaics: Spanish as a World Language,* 3rd Edition, ©2002. Reprinted by permission of Pearson Education, Inc., Upper Saddle River, NJ.

7. Krogh, David, *Test Item File for Biology: A Guide to the Natural World,* 2nd Edition, ©2002. Reprinted by permission of Pearson Education, Inc., Upper Saddle River, NJ.

8. Piggrem, Gary W.; Morris, Charles G., *Test Item File for Understanding Psychology,* 3rd Edition, ©1996. Reprinted by permission of Pearson Education, Inc., Upper Saddle River, NJ.

9. Ibid.

10. Chaisson, Eric; McMillan, Steve, *Astronomy Today,* 3rd Edition, ©1999. Reprinted by permission of Pearson Education, Inc., Upper Saddle River, NJ.

IN THIS CHAPTER. . .

you will explore answers
to the following questions:

Researching and Writing
GATHERING AND COMMUNICATING IDEAS

Research and writing, powerful tools that engage your successful intelligence, are at the heart of your education. Through library and Internet research, you gather and analyze information from sources all over the world. Through writing, you analyze ideas, think creatively about what they mean, and communicate information and perspectives to others. Whether you write an essay in English or a summary of a scientific study for Biology, the writing process helps sharpen your thinking and your practical communication skills.

This chapter has two goals: to help you improve your skill in finding information at your college library and on the Internet, and to reinforce some of the writing basics that most students study in an English composition course. In school and in your career, researching and writing are essential to success.

On the following page, read about student Beverly Andre's search for tools that can help her improve both her writing and her confidence as a writer.

- **How can you make the most of your library?**
- **How can you do research on the Internet?**
- **What is the writing process?**

How can I become more confident about my writing?

The best thing I ever wrote was in the sixth grade. My teacher let us pick a topic, and I chose to write about riding horses because I loved it and knew a lot about it. In high school, writing was okay because my teacher was helpful. College papers, on the other hand, have been a real challenge. I don't think my topic ideas are very original, and I feel that my vocabulary is not that advanced. If a professor assigns a topic I know nothing about, I usually don't have as much interest as with something familiar.

One of the reasons I don't like to write is because I don't like researching. Knowing how to begin gets confusing because there's so much to choose from. Once I do pull the information together, I can't seem to expand on an idea without being redundant. I also go off on all sorts of tangents. The bottom line is that I find it difficult to put my thoughts to paper. How can I become a better writer?

Beverly Andre
Triton College, Continuing Education Program, River Grove, Illinois

Concentrate on trying to improve your skills instead of worrying about getting a good grade.

No matter your writing goal, in most cases the person you are writing for, your instructor, wants you to improve. Keeping this in mind may help you concentrate on trying to improve your skills instead of worrying about getting a good grade.

I suggest a two-pronged approach to better writing. The first step is to read. Read novels, the newspaper, and nonfiction articles. Reading helps you learn to organize your thoughts, and it increases your vocabulary. If you want to focus on a specific area of study, read publications in that area. Create file folders for pieces of writing that you like. For example, make a copy of a business letter that you think is well written, and refer to it when you need to write a similar correspondence.

Second, bridge the gap between what you should know and what an instructor can tell you. Ask your instructor what he or she thinks you need to work on. Focus your energy on understanding the assignment and strengthening technical skills such as sentence structure and grammar. Another tip is to read what you've written, sentence by sentence, and think about how you could say it better.

If you don't know where to begin your research, start with what feels comfortable. If you are at ease with computers, use the Internet. If you prefer libraries, start by asking the reference librarian for assistance. The main point with research is to jump right in. Once you read something that relates to your topic, it will refer you to something else.

Finally, don't get frustrated by setbacks. Writing is a process that you learn as you would a type of exercise. Set goals you can attain. Finishing something builds confidence.

Raymond Montolvo Jr.
Writers Program, University of Southern California, Los Angeles, California

How can you *make the most* of your library?

A library is a home for information; consider it the "brain" of your college. Your practical thinking skills will help you to find what you need quickly and efficiently.

Start with a road map

Make your life easier right off the bat by learning how your library is organized:

Circulation desk. All publications are checked out at the circulation desk, which is usually near the library entrance.

Reference area. Here you'll find reference books, including encyclopedias, directories, dictionaries, almanacs, and atlases. You'll also find librarians and other library employees who can direct you to information. Computer terminals, containing the library's catalog of holdings as well as on-line bibliographic and full-text databases, are usually part of the reference area.

Book area. Books—and, in many libraries, magazines and journals in bound or boxed volumes—are stored in the stacks. A library with *open stacks* allows you to search for materials on your own. In a *closed-stack* system, a staff member retrieves materials for you.

Periodicals area. Here you'll find recent issues of popular and scholarly magazines, journals, and newspapers. Because you usually cannot check out unbound periodicals, you may find photocopy machines nearby where you can copy pages.

PERIODICALS

Magazines, journals, and newspapers that are published on a regular basis throughout the year.

Audiovisual materials areas. Many libraries have special areas for video, art and photography, and recorded music collections.

Computer areas. Computer terminals, linked to college databases and the Internet, may be scattered throughout the building or set off in particular areas. You may be able to access these databases and the Internet from computer labs and writing centers. Many college dorm rooms are also wired for computer access, enabling students to connect via personal computers.

Microform areas. Most libraries have microform reading areas. *Microforms* are materials printed in reduced size on film, either *microfilm* (a reel of film) or *microfiche* (a sheet or card of film), that is viewed through special machines.

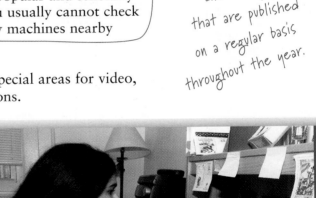

While the library is still a major resource center, on-line research has become a significant source of information for many students.

Almost all college libraries offer orientation sessions on how to find what you need. In addition, library Web pages usually contain on-line catalogs from your college and associated colleges, on-line databases, and phone numbers and e-mail addresses for reference librarians. If you need help, take a real or virtual tour and sign up for training.

My library
Was dukedom large enough.

WILLIAM SHAKESPEARE

Learn how to conduct an information search

The most successful and time-saving search for information involves a specific *search strategy*—a practical, step-by-step method that takes you from general to specific sources. Starting with general sources provides an overview of your topic and can lead to more specific information and sources.

get practical!

DISCOVER YOUR COLLEGE LIBRARY

Learn the nuts and bolts of your college's library system.

Identify the following:

- Name and location of the college library. (If your college has more than one library, identify the branch you are most likely to use.)

  _____

  _____

- Hours of operation: _____

- Library Web site address: _____

- Important e-mail addresses and phone numbers, including those of the reference and circulation desks:

  _____

  _____

- Stack locations of the books and other publications you may need in this semester's courses:

  _____

  _____

- Names and URLs of computer databases you are likely to use:

  _____

  _____

- Location of a library nook or chair that is ideal for studying:

  _____

For example, an encyclopedia article on the archaeological discovery of the Dead Sea Scrolls—manuscripts written between 250 B.C.E. and 68 C.E. that trace the roots of Judaism and Christianity—may mention that one of the most important books on the subject is *Understanding the Dead Sea Scrolls,* edited by Hershel Shanks. This book, in turn, leads you to 13 experts who wrote specialized text chapters.

It's important to narrow your topic, because broad topics yield too much data. Instead of using the topic "Dead Sea Scrolls" in your search, for example, consider narrowing it to any of the following:

- how the Dead Sea Scrolls were discovered by Bedouin shepherds in 1947
- the historical origins of the scrolls
- the process archaeologists used to reconstruct scroll fragments

Conducting a keyword search

To find materials related to your topic, conduct a *keyword search* of the library database—a method for locating sources through the use of topic-related words and phrases. To narrow your topic and reduce the number of "hits," add more keywords. For example, instead of searching through the broad category *art,* focus on *nineteenth-century French impressionist art.*

Keyword searches use natural language, rather than specialized classification vocabulary. Key 8.1 provides tips to help you use the keyword system.

As you search, keep in mind that

- double quotes around a word or phrase will locate the exact term you entered ("financial aid").
- using uppercase or lowercase does not affect the search (*Scholarships* will find *scholarships*).
- singular terms will find the plural (*scholarship* will find *scholarships*).

How to perform an effective keyword search.

KEY 8.1

IF YOU ARE SEARCHING FOR ...	DO THIS	EXAMPLE
A word	Type the word normally	aid
A phrase	Type the phrase in its normal word order (use regular word spacing) or surround the phrase with double quotation marks	financial aid *or* "financial aid"
Two or more keywords without regard to word order	Type the words in any order, surrounding the words with quotation marks (use *and* to separate the words)	"financial aid" and "scholarships"
Topic A or topic B	Type the words in any order, surrounding the words with quotation marks (use *or* to separate the words)	"financial aid" or "scholarships"
Topic A but not topic B	Type topic A first within quotation marks, and then topic B within quotation marks (use *not* to separate the words)	"financial aid" not "scholarships"

Conduct research using a search strategy

Knowing where to look during each phase of your search helps you find information quickly and efficiently. A successful search strategy often begins with general references and moves to more specific references (see Key 8.2).

Use general reference works

CD-ROM

A compact disc, containing words and images in electronic form, that can be read by a computer (CD-ROM stands for "compact disc read-only memory").

Begin your research with general reference works. These works cover many different topics in a broad, nondetailed way. General reference guides are often available on-line or on CD-ROM. Works that fall into the general reference category include the following:

- encyclopedias such as the multivolume *Encyclopedia Americana* and the single-volume *New Columbia Encyclopedia*
- almanacs such as the *World Almanac* and *Book of Facts*
- yearbooks such as the *McGraw-Hill Yearbook of Science and Technology* and the *Statistical Abstract of the United States*
- dictionaries such as *Webster's New World College Dictionary*
- biographical reference works such as the *New York Times Biographical Service, Webster's Biographical Dictionary,* and various editions of *Who's Who*
- bibliographies such as *Books in Print* (especially the *Subject Guide to Books in Print*)

Scan these sources for an overview of your topic. Bibliographies at the end of encyclopedia articles may also lead to important sources.

Search specialized reference works

Turn next to specialized reference works for more specific facts. Specialized reference works include encyclopedias and dictionaries that focus on a narrow field. Although the entries in these volumes are short, they focus

A library search strategy will help you find information.

key 8.2

Check general and specific reference works	→	Read appropriate sections
Check the book catalog for authors and book titles	→	Read books
Check periodical indexes for author and article titles	→	Read articles
Check the Internet, on-line services, and CD-ROM databases for complete articles and other data	→	Read computer screen and print information

on critical ideas and on the keywords you need to conduct additional research. Bibliographies that accompany the articles point to the works of recognized experts. Examples of specialized reference works, organized by subject, include the following:

- history (*Encyclopedia of American History*)
- science and technology (*Encyclopedia of Biological Sciences*)
- social sciences (*Dictionary of Education*)
- current affairs (*Social Issues Resources Series [SIRS]*)

Browse through books on your subject

Use the computerized *library catalog* to find books and other materials on your topic. The catalog, searchable by author, title, and subject, tells you which publications the library owns. Each catalog listing refers to the library's classification system, which in turn tells you exactly where the publication can be found.

Use periodical indexes to search for periodicals

Periodicals, a valuable source of current information, include journals, magazines, and newspapers. *Journals* are written for readers with specialized knowledge. Whereas *Newsweek* magazine may run a general-interest article on AIDS research, the *Journal of the American Medical Association* may print the original scientific study for an audience of scientists. Many libraries display periodicals that are up to a year or two old and convert older copies to microform. Many full-text articles are also available on computer databases and via the Internet.

> The outcome of any serious research can only be to make two questions grow where only one grew before.

THORSTEIN VEBLEN

Periodical indexes lead you to specific articles. *The Reader's Guide to Periodical Literature*, available in print and on CD-ROM, indexes general information sources including articles in hundreds of general-interest publications. Look in the Infotrac family of databases (available on-line or on CD-ROM) for other periodical indexes such as *Health Reference Center* and *General Business File*.

Indexing information is listed in the *Standard Periodical Directory*, *Ulrich's International Periodicals Directory*, and *Magazines for Libraries*. Each database lists the magazines and periodicals it indexes. Because there is no all-inclusive index for technical, medical, and scholarly journal articles, you'll have to search indexes that specialize in narrow subject areas. Such indexes also include abstracts (article summaries). Among the available indexes are *ERIC (Educational Resources Information Center)*, *The Humanities Index*, *Index Medicus*, and *Psychological Abstracts*. You'll also find separate newspaper indexes in print, in microform, on CD-ROM, or on-line.

Almost no library owns all of the publications listed in these and other specialized indexes. However, journals that are not part of your library's collection or that are not available in full-text form on-line may be available through an interlibrary loan, which allows patrons to request materials from other libraries. The librarian will help you arrange the loan.

Ask the librarian

Librarians can assist you in solving research problems. They can help you locate sources, navigate catalogs and databases, and uncover research shortcuts. Say, for example, you are researching recent federal gun-control legislation, and you want to contact groups on both sides of the issue. Using Google to conduct a keyword Internet search, you come up with nearly 17,000 hits—and you have no way of knowing which organizational Web sites are the best. To help you make a decision, the librarian may lead you to the *Encyclopedia of Associations,* which lists the National Rifle Association, a pro-gun organization, and Handgun Control Inc., a gun-control group.

Librarians are not the only helpful people in the library. For simplicity's sake, this book uses the term *librarian* to refer to both librarians and other staff members who are trained to help. Here are some tips that will help you get the advice you are seeking from the librarian.

- **Be prepared and be specific.** Instead of asking for information on the American presidency, focus on the topic you expect to write about in your American History paper—for example, President Franklin D. Roosevelt's leadership during World War II.

- **Ask for help when you can't find a specific source.** For example, when a specific book is not on the shelf, the librarian may direct you to another source that works as well.

- **Ask for help with computers and other equipment.** Librarians are experts in using the computers and other equipment, so turn to them for help with technical problems.

Following are typical inquiries reference librarians received at Moraine Valley Community College in Illinois, along with where the information was found and how long each search took. The librarians successfully located information using analytical, creative, and practical thinking. Note that the Internet did not always yield the answer; librarians often used traditional reference works.[1]

- "I want to find information about holistic medicine and nursing in nursing journals." Search time: 9 minutes. The librarian introduced the student to a specialized health care database and showed her how to narrow the search range.

- "We need movie advertising costs per week and box-office receipts to make a comparison of return on investment for a business class." Search time: 45 minutes. The librarian and student scanned business and general databases and searched the Web. They found what they needed for some movies, but not others.

- "I need literary criticism about the poetry of Adrienne Rich." Search time: 15 minutes. The librarian used on-line databases and reference books to find several articles.

- "What Cajun restaurant in Blue Island, Illinois, is supposed to be haunted?" Search time: 45 minutes. A Web search was fruitless, so the librarian led the student to several books about haunted buildings in suburban Chicago.

The library an indispensable tool in your efforts to gather information—the foundation of knowledge. Chad Clunie, a political science major at Indiana University's Southeast Campus, is driven to use the library by what he describes as the "quest for knowledge." As an officer in the local student branch of the American Civil Liberties Union, Chad uses library resources to formulate debates on current topics, such as same-sex marriage and the Patriot Act. "There's so much to learn," said Chad. "There's no way of knowing it all."[2]

Internet research supplements library research as it connects you almost instantaneously to billions of information sources. A miracle of technology, the Internet allows you to search for information at lightning speed.

How can you do *research* on the Internet?

The *Internet* is a computer network that links organizations and people around the world. To get what you need from it, you need to think analytically about what you want to know, conduct creative searches in which you explore topics from different perspectives, and use practical tools to locate information.

According to Bob Kieft, library director at Pennsylvania's Haverford College, students must "think critically and independently about the sources they use, be curious and imaginative about the projects they are working on, be open to the topic in ways that lead them to ask good questions, and bring their analytical powers to bear. . . . What students know about technology is less important than how they think about their work"[3] and the steps they take to find answers.

The basics

With a basic knowledge of the Internet, you can access facts and figures, read articles and reports, purchase products, download files, send messages electronically via e-mail, and even "talk" to people in real time. Following is some information that you should know:

- Access. Users access the Internet through Internet Service Providers (ISPs). Some ISPs are commercial, such as America Online or Internet Explorer. Others are linked to companies, colleges, and other organizations.

- Information locations. Most information is displayed on *Web sites,* cyberspace locations developed by companies, government agencies, organizations, and individuals. Together, these sites make up the *World Wide Web.*

- Finding locations. The string of text and numbers that identifies an Internet site is called a *URL* (Universal Resource Locator). You can type in a URL to access a specific site. Many Web sites include *hyperlinks*—URLs, usually underlined and highlighted in color—that when clicked on will take you directly to another Web location.

Use search directories and search engines

Commercial search engines and directories are your portal to the World Wide Web. Among the most powerful and popular search sites are Google (www.google.com), Yahoo! (www.yahoo.com), MSN Search (www.msnsearch.com), Overture (www.overture.com), Excite (www.excite.com), Alta Vista (http://altavista.com), HotBot (www.hotbot.com), Ask (www.ask.com), and Lycos (www.lycos.com). Information is accessible through keyword searches.

> The flood of unedited information on Google demands that users sharpen critical thinking skills, to filter the results. Google forces us to ask, "What do we really want to know?"
>
> **ESTHER DYSON**

The academic publications that you may need in higher level courses are generally inaccessible through Google and other popular search tools even though these publications are available on-line, free of charge, through university libraries. For example, although the University of Michigan includes the full texts of 22,000 scholarly volumes in its digital collection, these collections are all but invisible to search engines. This is changing as Google, Yahoo!, and other search engines are working with librarians and colleges to make digitized academic archives available to everyone.[4]

Internet search strategy

The World Wide Web has been called "the world's greatest library, with all its books on the floor." *Your goal is to find enough information without being overwhelmed by too much information.* With no librarian in sight, engage successful intelligence to use this basic search strategy:

1. **Think carefully about what you want to locate.** Professor Eliot Soloway recommends phrasing your search in the form of a question. For example, *What vaccines are given to children before age five?* Then he advises identifying the important words in the question (*vaccines, children, before age five*) as well as other related words (*chicken pox, tetanus, polio, shot, pediatrics,* and so on). This will give you a collection of terms to use in different combinations as you search.[5]

2. Use a search engine or directory to isolate sites under your desired topic or category. Save the sites that look useful. Most Internet software has a "bookmark" or "favorites" feature for recording sites you want to find again.

3. Explore these sites to get a general idea of what's out there. If the search engine or directory takes you where you need to go, you're in luck. More often, in academic research, you will need to dig deeper. Use what you find to notice useful keywords and information locations.

GOOGLE (YES, IT'S A VERB)

get creative!

Explore ways to use Google and other search engines effectively.

Google accesses 6 billion documents and has the capacity to return 750,000 Internet links in a third of a second. Despite this, Leon Botstein, president of Bard College, warns of Google's pitfalls: "In general, Google overwhelms you with too much information, much of which is hopelessly unreliable or beside the point. It's like looking for a lost ring in a vacuum bag. What you end up with mostly are bagel crumbs and dirt."[6]

With this warning in mind, use your creativity and analysis to complete the following:

- Choose a common topic—for example, apples, kitchen sinks, snowflakes. Google the topic to see how many Web sites you access. Write that number here. _____
  Now spend 10 minutes scanning the Web listings. How many different topics did your search uncover other than the topic you intended?

  _____

- Pick three of the off-the-topic links you found and write a thesis statement to a paper that would require you to use these leads in your research. Be creative.

  _____

  _____

  _____

- In all likelihood, your thesis statement makes little sense. What does this tell you about the need for critical thinking when using Google and other search directories and engines in your research?

  _____

  _____

  _____

- Finally, open your mind to the creative possibilities your research uncovered. Did any of the Web sites spark ideas about your topic that you had never considered? Write down two ideas you never thought of before.

  1. _____

  2. _____

4. **Use your keywords in a variety of ways to uncover different possibilities.** Make sure to spell keywords correctly.
   - Vary word order if you are using more than one keyword (for example, search under "*education, college, statistics*" and "*statistics, education, college*").
   - Use the words "and," "not," and "or" in ways that limit your search (see Key 8.1 for tips for using keywords in library searches).

5. **Evaluate the list of links that appears.** If there are too many, narrow your search by using more keywords or more specific keywords (Broadway

could become Broadway AND "fall season" AND 2005). If there are too few, broaden your search by using fewer or different keywords.

6. **When you think you are done, start over.** Choose another search engine or directory and perform your search again. Why? Because different systems access different sites and sources.

Use analytical thinking to evaluate every source

It is up to you to evaluate the truth and usefulness of Internet information. Since the Internet is largely uncensored and unmonitored—a kind of "information free-for-all"—you must decide which sources to value and which to ignore. Use the following strategies to analyze the validity and usefulness of each source.[7]

- **Ask questions about the source.** Is the author a recognized expert? Does he or she write from a particular perspective that may bias the presentation? Is the source recent enough for your purposes? Where did the author get the information?

  Note also the Web site's name and the organization that creates and maintains the site. Is the organization reputable? Is it known as an authority on the topic you are researching? If you are not sure of the source, the URL may give you a clue. For example, URLs ending in .edu originate at an educational institution, and .gov sites originate at government agencies.

- **Evaluate the material.** Evaluate Internet sources the way you would other material. Is the source a published document (newspaper article, professional journal article, etc.), or is it simply one person's views? Can you verify the data by comparing it to other material? Pay attention, also, to writing quality. Texts with grammatical and spelling errors, poor organization, or factual errors are likely to be unreliable.

Take advantage of the wealth of material the Internet offers—but be picky. Always remember that your research will only be as strong as your thinking. If you work hard to ensure that your research is solid and comprehensive, the product of your efforts will speak for itself.

Library and Internet research is often done as a step in writing a research paper. The success of your paper depends on the quality of your research and on your ability to write.

What is the *writing process?*

Knowing how to write well is so important for success—academic and otherwise—that most schools require students to pass a semester- or yearlong writing course. Many schools also have self-directed writing labs where students can practice and hone specific skills. This overview is intended to reinforce some of the basics you will learn in these settings.

The writing process for research papers and essays allows you to get your thoughts down on paper and rework them until you express yourself clearly. The four main parts of the process are planning, drafting, revising, and editing. Analytical, creative, and practical thinking play important roles throughout.

Planning

Planning gives you a chance to think about what to write and how to write it. Planning involves brainstorming for topic ideas, using (prewriting strategies) to define and narrow your topic, conducting research, writing a thesis statement, and writing a working outline. Although these steps are listed in sequence, in real life they overlap one another as you plan your document.

Open your mind through brainstorming

Brainstorming is a creative technique that involves generating ideas about a subject without making judgments (see Chapter 4). To begin brainstorming, write down anything on the assigned subject that comes to mind, in no particular order. Then, organize that list into an outline or think link that helps you see the possibilities more clearly. To make the outline or think link, separate the items you've listed into general ideas or categories and sub-ideas or examples. Then, associate the sub-ideas or examples with the ideas they support or fit.

Key 8.3 shows a portion of an outline that student Michael B. Jackson constructed from a brainstorming list. The assignment is a five-paragraph essay on a life-changing event. Here Michael brainstorms the topic of "boot camp"; then he organizes his ideas into categories.

PREWRITING STRATEGIES

Techniques for generating ideas about a topic and finding out how much you already know before you start your research and writing.

Brainstorm your topic and organize ideas in an outline.

key 8.3

A LIFE CHANGING EVENT
— family
— childhood
→ military
    — travel
    → boot camp
        — physical conditioning
            • swim tests
            • intensive training
            • ENDLESS push-ups!
        — Chief who was our commander
        — mental discipline
            • military lifestyle
            • perfecting our appearance
        — self-confidence
            • walk like you're in control
            • don't blindly accept anything

Narrow your topic through prewriting strategies

Next, use one or more of the following prewriting strategies to narrow your topic, focusing on the specific sub-ideas and examples from your brainstorming session.[8] As you prewrite, keep paper length, due date, and other requirements (such as topic area or purpose) in mind. These requirements influence your choice of a final topic.

Brainstorming. The same process you used to generate ideas also helps you narrow your topic. Write down your thoughts about the possibility you have chosen, and then organize them into categories. See if any of the sub-ideas or examples might make good topics.

Freewriting. When you freewrite, you use your creative ability to write whatever comes to mind without censoring ideas or worrying about language or organization. Creative freewriting enables you to begin integrating what you know. Here is a sample of freewriting:

> Boot camp for the Coast Guard really changed my life. First of all, I really got in shape. We had to get up every morning at 5 A.M., eat breakfast, and go right into training. We had to do endless military-style push-ups—but we later found out that these have a purpose, to prepare us to hit the deck in the event of enemy fire. We had a lot of aquatic tests, once we were awakened at 3 A.M. to do one in full uniform! Boot camp also helped me to feel confident about myself and be disciplined. Chief Marzloff was the main person who made that happen. He was tough but there was always a reason. He got angry when I used to nod my head whenever he would speak to me, he said that made it seem like I was blindly accepting whatever he said, which was a weakness. From him I have learned to keep an eye on my body's movements when I communicate. I learned a lot more from him too.

Asking journalists' questions. Who? What? Where? When? Why? How? Ask these journalists' questions about any sub-idea or example to discover what you may want to discuss.

Prewriting helps you develop a topic broad enough to give you something with which to work but narrow enough to be manageable. Prewriting also helps you see what you know and what you don't know and where more research is required.

Who?	Who was at boot camp? Who influenced me the most?	
What?	What about boot camp changed my life? What did we do?	
When?	When in my life did I go to boot camp and for how long?	
Where?	Where was camp located? Where did we spend our day-to-day time?	
Why?	Why did I decide to go there? Why was it such an important experience?	
How?	How did we train in the camp? How were we treated? How did we achieve success?	

Conduct research and make notes

Try doing your research in stages. In the first stage, look for a basic overview that can lead to a thesis statement. In the second stage, go into more depth, tracking down information that helps you fill in gaps.

As you research, create source notes and content notes on index cards. These help you organize your work, keep track of your sources, and avoid plagiarism.

Source notes are the preliminary notes you take as you review research. Each source note should include the author's full name; the title of the work; the edition (if any); the publisher, year, and city of publication; issue and/or volume number when applicable (such as for a magazine); and the page numbers you consulted. After this bibliographic information, write a short summary and a critical evaluation of the work. Key 8.4 shows an example of how you can write source notes on index cards.

Create source note cards as you review research.

key
8.4

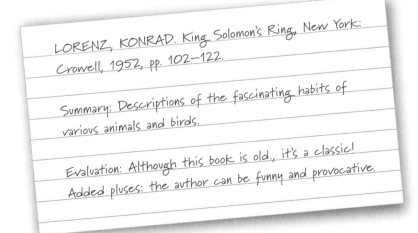

LORENZ, KONRAD. *King Solomon's Ring*, New York: Crowell, 1952, pp. 102–122.

Summary: Descriptions of the fascinating habits of various animals and birds.

Evaluation: Although this book is old, it's a classic! Added pluses: the author can be funny and provocative.

Content notes,* written on large index cards, in a notebook, or on your computer are taken during a thorough reading and provide an in-depth look at sources. Use them to record the information you need to write your draft. To supplement your content notes, make notations—marginal notes, highlighting, and underlining—directly on photocopies of sources.

When research-based writing projects involve teamwork, you may need to adjust to the differences in how team members work. If you are collaborating with a student from a high-context culture such as Indonesia or the Philippines, for example, the student may hesitate to express an opinion in writing that differs from the instructor's. Since these cultures value respect to people in authority, disagreeing with the instructor is often considered rude. (For more on high-and low-context cultures, see Chapter 2.)

Write a thesis statement

Your work has prepared you to write a *thesis statement,* the central message you want to communicate. The thesis statement states your subject and point of view, reflects your **writing purpose** and **audience,** and acts as the organizing principle of your paper. Here is an example from Michael's paper:

WRITING PURPOSE

The point of a paper, which is usually to inform or persuade readers.

AUDIENCE

The readers of your work for whom your purpose and content must be clear.

Topic:	Coast Guard boot camp
Purpose:	To inform
Audience:	Instructor who probably knows little about the topic
Thesis statement:	Chief Marzloff, our Basic Training Company Commander at the U.S. Coast Guard Basic Training Facility, shaped my life through physical conditioning, developing self-confidence, and instilling strong mental discipline.

Write a working outline

The final step in the preparation process is writing a working outline or think link. Use this outline as a loose guide instead of a final structure. Only by allowing changes to occur do you get closer to what you really want to say.

Create a checklist

Use the checklist in Key 8.5 to make sure your preparation is complete. Under Date Due, create your own writing schedule, giving each task an intended completion date. Work backward from the date the assignment is due and estimate how long it will take to complete each step. Keep in mind that you'll probably move back and forth among the tasks on the schedule.

Use a preparation checklist to complete tasks and stay on schedule.

DATE DUE	TASK	IS IT COMPLETE?
	Brainstorm	
	Define and narrow	
	Use prewriting strategies	
	Conduct research if necessary	
	Write thesis statement	
	Write working outline	
	Complete research	

Drafting

A first draft involves putting ideas down on paper for the first time—but not the last. You may write many versions of the assignment until you are satisfied. Each version moves you closer to saying exactly what you want in the way you want to say it.

When you think of drafting, it might help to imagine that you are creating a kind of "writing sandwich." The bottom slice of bread is the introduction, the top slice is the conclusion, and the sandwich stuffing is made of central ideas and supporting evidence (see Key 8.6).

Think of the parts of your draft as a "writing sandwich."

Conclusion

Main Points and Supporting Evidence

Introduction

Freewriting your rough draft

Take everything that you have developed in the planning stages and freewrite a rough draft. For now, don't consciously think about your introduction, conclusion, or the structure within the paper's body. Simply focus on getting your ideas out onto paper. When you have something written, you can start to give it a more definite form. First, work on how you want to begin.

Writing an introduction

The introduction tells readers what the rest of the paper contains and includes a thesis statement. Take a look at this draft of an introduction for Michael's paper about the Coast Guard. The thesis statement is underlined at the end of the paragraph.

> Chief Marzloff took on the task of shaping the lives and careers of the youngest, newest members of the U.S. Coast Guard. During my eight weeks in training, he was my father, my instructor, my leader, and my worst enemy. He took his job very seriously and demanded that we <u>do the same. The Chief was instrumental in conditioning our bodies, developing our self-confidence, and instilling mental discipline within us.</u>

Creating the body of a paper

The body of the paper contains your central ideas and supporting evidence. *Evidence* consists of facts, statistics, examples, and expert opinions. Think about how you might group the evidence with the particular ideas it supports. Then, try to find a structure that helps you organize your ideas and evidence into a clear pattern. Key 8.7 presents several organizational options.

Writing the conclusion

A conclusion summarizes the information that is in the body of your paper and critically evaluates what is important about it. Think about using one of the following strategies to conclude a paper:

- Summarize main points (if material is longer than three pages).
- Relate a provocative story, statistic, quote, or question.
- Call the reader to action.
- Look to the future.

Find the best way to organize the body of the paper.

ORGANIZATIONAL STRUCTURE	WHAT TO DO
Arrange ideas by time	Describe events in order or in reverse order.
Arrange ideas according to importance	Start with the idea that carries the most weight and move to less important ideas. Or move from the least to the most important ideas.
Arrange ideas by problem and solution	Start with a problem and then discuss solutions.
Arrange ideas to present an argument	Present one or both sides of an issue.
Arrange ideas in list form	Group a series of items.
Arrange ideas according to cause and effect	Show how events, situations, or ideas cause subsequent events, situations, or ideas.
Arrange ideas through the use of comparisons	Compare and contrast the characteristics of events, people, situations, ideas.

Avoid introducing new facts or restating what you've already proved. Let your ideas in the body of the paper speak for themselves. Readers should feel that they have reached a natural point of completion.

Avoiding plagiarism: Crediting authors and sources

When you incorporate ideas from other sources into your work, you are using other writers' *intellectual property*. Using another writer's words, content, unique approach, or illustrations without crediting the author is called plagiarism and is illegal and unethical. The following techniques will help you properly credit sources and avoid plagiarism:

> **PLAGIARISM**
> The act of using someone else's exact words, figures, unique approach, or specific reasoning without giving appropriate credit.

- **Make source notes as you go.** Plagiarism often begins accidentally during research. You may forget to include quotation marks around a quotation, or you may intend to cite or paraphrase a source but never do. To avoid forgetting, write detailed source and content notes as you research. Try writing something like "Quotation from original, rewrite later" next to quoted material you copy into notes, and add bibliographic information (title, author, source, page number, etc.) so you don't spend hours trying to locate it later.

- **Learn the difference between a quotation and a paraphrase.** A *quotation* repeats a source's exact words, which are set off from the rest of the text by quotation marks. A *paraphrase* is a restatement of the quotation in your own words. A restatement requires that you completely rewrite the idea, not just remove or replace a few words. As Key 8.8 illustrates, a paraphrase may not be acceptable if it is too close to the original.

Avoid plagiarism by learning how to paraphrase.

QUOTATION

"The most common assumption that is made by persons who are communicating with one another is . . . that the other perceives, judges, thinks, and reasons the way he does. Identical twins communicate with ease. Persons from the same culture but with a different education, age, background, and experience often find communication difficult. American managers communicating with managers from other cultures experience greater difficulties in communication than with managers from their own culture."*

UNACCEPTABLE PARAPHRASE (THE UNDERLINED WORDS ARE TAKEN DIRECTLY FROM THE QUOTED SOURCE.)

When we communicate, we assume that the person to whom we are speaking perceives, judges, thinks, and reasons the way we do. This is not always the case. Although identical twins communicate with ease, persons from the same culture but with a different education, age, background, and experience often encounter communication problems. Communication problems are common among American managers as they attempt to communicate with managers from other cultures. They experience greater communication problems than when they communicate with managers from their own culture.

ACCEPTABLE PARAPHRASE

Many people fall into the trap of believing that everyone sees the world exactly as they do and that all people communicate according to the same assumptions. This belief is difficult to support even within our own culture as African-Americans, Hispanic-Americans, Asian-Americans, and others often attempt unsuccessfully to find common ground. When intercultural differences are thrown into the mix, such as when American managers working abroad attempt to communicate with managers from other cultures, clear communication becomes even harder.

*Source of quotation: Lynn Quitman Troyka, *Simon & Schuster Handbook for Writers* (Upper Saddle River, NJ: Prentice Hall, 1996).

- **Use a citation even for an acceptable paraphrase.** Take care to credit any source that you quote, paraphrase, or use as evidence. To credit a source, write a footnote or endnote that describes it, using the format preferred by your instructor. Writing handbooks explain the two standard documentation styles from the American Psychological Association (APA) and the Modern Language Association (MLA).

- **Understand that lifting material off the Internet is plagiarism.** Words in electronic form belong to the writer just as words in print form do. If you cut and paste sections from a source document onto your draft, you are committing plagiarism.

Instructors consider work to be plagiarized when a student

- submits a paper from a Web site that sells or gives away research papers.
- buys a paper from a non-Internet service.
- hands in a paper written by a fellow student or a family member.
- copies material in a paper directly from a source without proper quotation marks or source citation.
- paraphrases material in a paper from a source without proper source citation.

Students who plagiarize place their academic careers at risk, in part because the cheating is easy to discover. Increasingly, instructors are using *get analytical!*

Think about plagiarism and explore your views on this growing problem.

Complete the following:

- Why is plagiarism considered an offense that involves both stealing and lying? Describe how you look at it.

  _____

  _____

- Citing sources indicates that you respect the ideas of others. List two additional ways that accurate source citation strengthens your writing and makes you a better student.

  1. _____

  2. _____

- What specific penalties for plagiarism are described in your college handbook? Explain whether you feel that these penalties are reasonable or excessive and whether they will keep students from plagiarizing.

  _____

  _____

  _____

- Many experts believe that researching on the Internet is behind many acts of plagiarism. Do you agree? Why or why not?

  _____

  _____

anti-plagiarism software to investigate whether strings of words in student papers match those in a database.

Make a commitment to hand in your own work and to uphold the highest standards of academic integrity. The potential consequences of cheating are not worth the risk.

Continue your checklist

Create a checklist for your first draft (see Key 8.9). The elements of a first draft do not have to be written in order. In fact, many writers prefer to write the introduction after the body of the paper, so the introduction reflects the paper's content and tone. Whatever order you choose, make sure your schedule gives you enough time for revisions.

Revising

When you revise, you critically evaluate the word choice, paragraph structure, and style of your first draft. Be thorough as you add, delete, replace, and reorganize words, sentences, and paragraphs. If your instructor evaluates

Update your checklist for the first draft.

DATE DUE	TASK	IS IT COMPLETE?
	Freewrite a draft	
	Plan and write the introduction	
	Organize the body of the paper	
	Include research evidence in the body	
	Plan and write the conclusion	
	Check for plagiarism and rewrite passages to avoid it	
	Credit your sources	
	Solicit feedback	

an early draft of your paper, incorporate his or her ideas into the final product. If you disagree with a point, schedule a conference to talk it over.

Some classes include a peer review process in which students critique each other's work. Many schools also have tutors in writing or learning centers who can act as peer readers of a draft. Key 8.10 shows a paragraph from Michael's first draft, with revision comments added.

During the revision process, you assess what you have done and revisit any part of your work that is off the mark. The best time to critically evaluate your writing is after you let it sit for a while, says Dr. Mel Levine, author of *The Myth of Laziness*. "The writing experience needs time to incubate. It is preferable to check something several days later or the night after it came to be. With time, it is much easier to evaluate your own work, to detect and correct its flaws with some objectivity, and to deftly surmount the impasses that felt insurmountable while you were immersed in the act of writing."[9]

Using analytical abilities as you revise

Engage your analytical thinking to evaluate the content and form of your paper. Ask yourself these questions as you revise:

- Does the paper fulfill the requirements of the assignment?
- Will my audience understand my thesis and how I've supported it?
- Does the introduction prepare the reader and capture attention?
- Is the body of the paper organized effectively?
- Is each idea fully developed, explained, and supported by examples?
- Are my ideas connected to one another through logical transitions?
- Do I have a clear, concise, simple writing style?
- Does the conclusion provide a natural ending to the paper?

Sample first draft with revision comments.

Of the changes that ~~happened to us,~~ the physical transformation is the ~~biggest.~~ ~~When~~
military recruits undergo, *most evident*

~~we arrived at the training facility, it was January, cold and cloudy. At the time,~~ I was a
Too much *Maybe— upon my January arrival at the training facility,*

little thin, but I had been working out and thought that I could physically do anything.

Oh boy, was I wrong! The Chief said to us right away: "Get down, maggots!" Upon this
his trademark phrase

command, we all to drop to the ground and do military-style push-ups. Water survival
were *endless*

tactics were also part of the training ~~that we had to complete.~~ Occasionally, my dreams of
unnecessary

home were interrupted at 3 a.m. when we had a surprise aquatic test. Although we ~~didn't~~

~~feel too happy about~~ this sub-human treatment at the time, we learned to appreciate how
resented *mention how chief was involved*

the conditioning was turning our bodies into fine-tuned machines.
say more about this (swimming in uniform incident?)

Evaluating paragraph structure

Make sure that each paragraph has a *topic sentence* that states the paragraph's main idea (a topic sentence does for a paragraph what a thesis statement does for an entire paper). The remainder of the paragraph should support the idea with evidence. Most topic sentences are at the beginning of the paragraph, although sometimes topic sentences appear elsewhere. The topic sentence in the paragraph below is underlined.

In addition, examine how paragraphs flow into one another by evaluating transitions—the words, phrases, or sentences that connect ideas.

Chief Marzloff played an integral role in the development of our self-confidence.
He taught us that anything less than direct eye contact was disrespectful to both him and ourselves. He encouraged us to be confident about our own beliefs and to think about what was said to us before we decided whether to accept it. Furthermore, the Chief reinforced self-confidence through his own example. He walked with his chin up and chest out, like the proud parent of a newborn baby. He always gave the appearance that he had something to do and that he was in complete control.

Writing

The techniques below can help you to uncover valuable research sources and clearly communicate what you want to say.

INTELLIGENCE	SUGGESTED STRATEGIES	WHAT WORKS FOR YOU? WRITE NEW IDEAS HERE
Verbal–Linguistic	• Read many resources and take comprehensive notes on them. Summarize the main points from your resources. • Interview someone about the topic and take notes.	
Logical–Mathematical	• Take notes on 3x5 cards and organize them according to topics and subtopics. • Create a detailed, sequential outline of your writing, project. If your assignment requires persuasive writing, make sure that your argument is logical.	
Bodily–Kinesthetic	• Visit places/sites that hold resources you need or that are related to your topic—businesses, libraries, etc. • After brainstorming ideas for an assignment, take a break involving physical activity. During the break, think about your top three ideas and see what insight occurs to you.	
Visual–Spatial	• Create full-color charts as you read each resource or interview someone. • Use think link format or another visual organizer to map out your main topic, subtopics, and related ideas and examples. Use different colors for different subtopics.	
Interpersonal	• As you gather resource material, discuss it with a fellow student. • Pair up with a classmate and become each other's peer editors. Read each other's first drafts and next-to-final drafts, offering constructive feedback.	
Intrapersonal	• Take time to mull over any assigned paper topic. Think about what emotions it raises in you, and why. Let your inner instincts guide you as you begin to write. • Schedule as much research time as possible.	
Musical	• Play your favorite relaxing music while you brainstorm topics for a writing assignment.	
Naturalistic	• Pick a research topic that relates to nature. • Build confidence by envisioning your writing process as a successful climb to the top of a mountain.	

Checking for clarity and conciseness

Rewrite wordy phrases in a more straightforward, conversational way. For example, write "if" instead of "in the event that," and "now" instead of "at this point in time."

Editing

Editing involves correcting technical mistakes in spelling, grammar, and punctuation, as well as checking for consistency in such elements as abbreviations and capitalization. Editing comes last, after you are satisfied with your ideas, organization, and writing style. If you use a computer, start with the grammar check and spell check to find mistakes, realizing that you still need to check your work manually. Although a spell checker won't pick up the mistake in the sentence, "They are not hear on Tuesdays," someone who is reading for sense will.

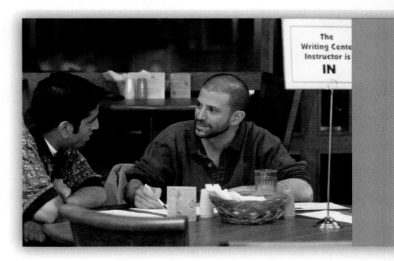

Help is available for writers struggling through assignments. Here a writing center tutor helps a student move forward with his work on a paper.

Peer-editing can sharpen your writing. Kristina Torres, a senior at Susquehanna University in Selinsgrove, Pennsylvania, is convinced that her relationship with Adam Cole helped make her a better writer. A senior, she has worked with Adam for more than three years to fine-tune her work. In one case, Adam helped Kristina cut a 40-page paper in half. "It's hard to do that on your own," she said, "because you get really attached to a line or a section. You need to have someone who can help you step back and take another look at it."[10]

Proofreading is the last editing stage and happens once your paper reaches its final form. Proofreading means reading every word and sentence for accuracy. Look for technical mistakes, run-on sentences, and sentence fragments. Look for incorrect word usage and unclear references.

A final checklist

You are now ready to complete your revising and editing checklist. All the tasks listed in Key 8.11 should be complete before you submit your paper. Key 8.12 shows the final version of Michael's paper.

Writing is rewriting.

ERNEST HEMINGWAY

Your final paper reflects your efforts. Ideally, you have a piece of work that shows how you used your analytical, creative, and practical thinking to communicate ideas.

Use a revising and editing checklist to finalize your paper.

DATE DUE	TASK	IS IT COMPLETE?
	Check the body of the paper for clear thinking and adequate support of ideas	
	Finalize introduction and conclusion	
	Check word spelling, usage, and grammar	
	Check paragraph structure	
	Make sure language is familiar and concise	
	Check punctuation and capitalization	
	Check transitions	
	Eliminate sexist language	
	Get feedback from peers and/or instructor	

Suà

Suà is a Shoshone Indian word, derived from the Uto-Aztecna language, that means "to think." Use your thinking skills to evaluate research sources as the basis for your positions and communicate your conclusions effectively through writing and speaking. Through the power of thought, you will choose sources that support your thesis and express your insights.

Michael B. Jackson   March 19, 2006

BOYS TO MEN

His stature was one of confidence, often misinterpreted by others as cockiness. His small frame was lean and agile, yet stiff and upright, as though every move were a calculated formula. For the longest eight weeks of my life, he was my father, my instructor, my leader, and my worst enemy. His name is Chief Marzloff, and he had the task of shaping the lives and careers of the youngest, newest members of the U.S. Coast Guard. As our Basic Training Company Commander, he took his job very seriously and demanded that we do the same. Within a limited time span, he conditioned our bodies, developed our self-confidence, and instilled within us a strong mental discipline.

Of the changes that recruits in military basic training undergo, the physical transformation is the most immediately evident. On my January arrival at the training facility, I was a little thin, but I had been working out and thought that I could physically do anything. Oh boy, was I wrong! The Chief wasted no time in introducing me to one of his trademark phrases: "Get down, maggots!" Upon this command, we were all to drop to the ground and produce endless counts of military-style push-ups. Later, we found out that exercise prepared us for hitting the deck in the event of enemy fire. Water survival tactics were also part of the training. Occasionally, my dreams of home were interrupted at about 3 A.M. when our company was selected for a surprise aquatic test. I recall one such test that required us to swim laps around the perimeter of a pool while in full uniform. I felt like a salmon swimming upstream, fueled only by natural instinct. Although we resented this subhuman treatment at the time, we learned to appreciate how the strict guidance of the Chief was turning our bodies into fine-tuned machines.

Beyond physical ability, Chief Marzloff also played an integral role in the development of our self-confidence. He would often declare in his raspy voice, "Look me in the eyes when you speak to me! Show me that you believe what you're saying!" He taught us that anything less was an expression of disrespect. Furthermore, he appeared to attack a personal habit of my own. It seemed that whenever he would speak to me individually, I would nervously nod my head in response. I was trying to demonstrate that I understood, but to him, I was blindly accepting anything that he said. He would roar, "That is a sign of weakness!" Needless to say, I am now conscious of all bodily motions when communicating with others. The Chief also reinforced self-confidence through his own example. He walked with his square chin up and chest out, like the proud parent of a newborn baby. He always gave the appearance that he had something to do, and that he was in complete control. Collectively, the methods that the Chief used were all successful in developing our self-confidence.

Perhaps the Chief's greatest contribution was the mental discipline that he instilled in his recruits. He taught us that physical ability and self-confidence were nothing without the mental discipline required to obtain any worthwhile goal. For us, this discipline began with adapting to the military lifestyle. Our day began promptly at 0500 hours, early enough to awaken the oversleeping roosters. By 0515 hours, we had to have showered, shaved, and perfectly donned our uniforms. At that point, we were marched to the galley for chow, where we learned to take only what is necessary, rather than indulging. Before each meal, the Chief would warn, "Get what you want, but you will eat all that you get!" After he made good on his threat a few times, we all got the point. Throughout our stay, the Chief repeatedly stressed the significance of self-discipline. He would calmly utter, "Give a little now, get a lot later." I guess that meant different things to all of us. For me, it was a simple phrase that would later become my personal philosophy on life. The Chief went to great lengths to ensure that everyone under his direction possessed the mental discipline required to be successful in boot camp or in any of life's challenges.

Chief Marzloff was a remarkable role model and a positive influence on many lives. I never saw him smile, but it was evident that he genuinely cared a great deal about his job and all the lives that he touched. This man single-handedly conditioned our bodies, developed our self-confidence, and instilled a strong mental discipline that remains in me to this day. I have not seen the Chief since March 28, 1995, graduation day. Over the years, however, I have incorporated many of his ideals into my life. Above all, he taught us the true meaning of the U.S. Coast Guard slogan, "Semper Peratus" (Always Ready).

Developing Successful Intelligence

PUTTING IT ALL TOGETHER

Be a planner. Engage analytical, creative, and practical skills as you work through the planning stage of writing.

Step 1. Think it through: *Analyze your writing goal.* Imagine that you have been asked to write an essay on a time when you turned a difficulty into an opportunity. First, write a brief description of your topic:

_____

_____

Next, think about your purpose and audience. How might you frame your purpose if you were writing to a person who is going through a tough time and needs inspiration? How would your purpose change if you were writing to an instructor who wanted to know what you learned from a difficult experience? Write your purpose and intended audience here.

_____

_____

_____

_____

Step 2. Think out of the box: *Prewrite to create ideas.* On a separate sheet of paper, use prewriting strategies to start the flow of ideas.

- Brainstorm your ideas.
- Freewrite.
- Ask journalists' questions.

create your future

Step 3. Make it happen: *Write a thesis statement.* With the thesis statement, you make your topic as specific as possible and you clearly define your purpose. Write your thesis statement here:

_____

_____

_____

Team Building

COLLABORATIVE SOLUTIONS

Team research. Join with three other classmates and decide on two relatively narrow research topics that interest all of you and that you can investigate by spending no more than an hour in the library. The first topic should be current and in the news—for example, safety problems in sport utility vehicles (SUVs), body piercing, or the changing U. S. family. The second topic should be more academic and historical—for example, the polio epidemic in the 1950s, the Irish potato famine, or South African apartheid.

Working alone, team members will use the college library and the Internet to research both topics. Set a research time limit of no more than one hour per topic. The goal should be to collect a list of sources for later investigation. When everyone is through, the group should come together to discuss the research process. Ask each other questions such as:

- How did you "attack" and organize your research for each topic?
- What research tools did you use to investigate each topic?
- How did your research differ from topic to topic? Why do you think this was the case?
- How did your use of library and Internet resources differ from topic to topic?
- Which research techniques yielded the best results? Which techniques led to dead ends?

Next, compare the specific results of everyone's research. Analyze each source for what it is likely to yield in the form of useful information. Finally, come together as a group and discuss what you learned that might improve your approach to library and Internet research.

Writing

DISCOVERY THROUGH JOURNALING

Record your thoughts on a separate piece of paper or in a journal.

Learning from other writers. Identify a piece of powerful writing that you have recently read. (It could be a work of literature, a biography, a magazine or newspaper article, or even a section from one of your college texts.) Describe, in detail, why it was powerful. Did it make you feel something, think something, or take action? Why? What can you learn about writing from this piece that you can apply to your own writing?

A cover letter should express your job interest and summarize why you are a strong candidate.

First name Last name
1234 Your Street
City, ST 12345

November 1, 2005

Ms. Prospective Employer
Prospective Company
5432 Their Street
City, ST 54321

Dear Ms. Employer:

On the advice of Mr. X, career center advisor at Y College, I am writing to inquire about the position of production assistant at KWKW Radio. I read the description of the job and your company on the career center's employment-opportunity bulletin board, and I would like to apply for the position.

I am a senior at Y College and will graduate this spring with a degree in communications. Since my junior year when I declared my major, I have wanted to pursue a career in radio. For the last year I have worked as a production intern at KCOL Radio, the college's station, and have occasionally filled in as a disc jockey on the evening news show. I enjoy being on the air, but my primary interest is production and programming. My enclosed résumé will tell you more about my background and experience.

I would be pleased to talk with you in person about the position. You can reach me anytime at 555/555-5555 or by e-mail at xxxx@xx.com. Thank you for your consideration, and I look forward to meeting you.

Sincerely,

Sign Your Name Here

First name Last name

Enclosure(s) *(use this notation if you have included a résumé or other item with your letter)*

Career Portfolio

Writing sample: A job interview cover letter. To secure a job interview, you will, at some point, have to write a letter describing your background and explaining your value to the company. For your portfolio, write a one-page, three-paragraph cover letter to a prospective employer. (The letter will accompany your résumé.) Be creative—you may use fictitious names, but select a career and industry that interest you. Use the format shown in the sample letter in Key 8.13 on the following page.

- **Introductory paragraph:** Start with an attention getter—a statement that convinces the employer to read on. For example, name a person the employer knows who told you to write, or refer to something positive about the company that you read in the paper. Identify the position for which you are applying, and tell the employer that you are interested in working for the company.

- **Middle paragraph:** Sell your value. Try to convince the employer that hiring you will help the company in some way. Center your "sales effort" on your experience in school and the workplace. If possible, tie your qualifications to the needs of the company. Refer indirectly to your enclosed résumé.

- **Final paragraph:** Close with a call to action. Ask the employer to call you, or tell the employer to expect your call to arrange an interview.

Exchange your first draft with a classmate. Read each other's letter and make notes in the margins that try to improve the letter's impact and persuasiveness, as well as its writing style, grammar, punctuation, and spelling. Discuss each letter and make whatever corrections are necessary to produce a well-written, persuasive letter. Create a final draft for your portfolio.

SUGGESTED READINGS

Becker, Howard S. *Tricks of the Trade: How to Think About Your Research While You're Doing It.* Chicago: University of Chicago Press, 1998.

Booth, Wayne C., Gregory G. Columb, and Joseph M. Williams. *The Craft of Research.* 2nd ed. Chicago: University of Chicago Press, 2003.

Cameron, Julia. *The Right to Write: An Invitation into the Writing Life.* New York: Putnam, 2000.

Gibaldi, Joseph and Phyllis Franklin. *MLA Handbook for Writers of Research Papers,* 6th ed. New York: Modern Language Association of America, 2003.

LaRocque, Paula. *Championship Writing: 50 Ways to Improve Your Writing.* Oak Park, IL: Marion Street Press, 2000.

Markman, Peter T. and Roberta H. Markman. *10 Steps in Writing the Research Paper,* 6th ed. New York: Barron's Educational Series, 2001.

Strunk, William, Jr. and E. B. White. *The Elements of Style,* 4th ed. New York: Allyn & Bacon, 2000.

Troyka, Lynn Quitman. *Simon & Schuster Handbook for Writers,* 7th ed. Upper Saddle River, NJ: Prentice Hall, 2004.

Walsch, Bill. *Lapsing into a Comma: A Curmudgeon's Guide to the Many Things That Can Go Wrong in Print—and How to Avoid Them.* New York: Contemporary Books, 2000.

Williams, Joseph M. *Style: Ten Lessons in Clarity and Grace.* Chicago: University of Chicago Press, 2003.

INTERNET RESOURCES

Prentice Hall Student Success SuperSite—study skills section (valuable information on writing and research): www.prenhall.com/success

National Writing Centers Association (a collection of writing labs and writing centers on the web): http://iwca.syr.edu

Online Writing Lab—Purdue University: http://owl.english.purdue.edu

How to Organize a Research Paper and Document It with MLA Citations (specific citation rules from the Modern Language Association): www.geocities.com/Athens/Oracle/4184

A Student's Guide to WWW Research: Web Searching, Web Page Evaluation, and Research Strategies (a comprehensive site developed at St. Louis University): www.slu.edu/departments/english/research

ENDNOTES

1. Scott Carlson, "The Deserted Library: As Students Work Online, Reading Rooms Empty Out—Leading Some Campuses to Add Starbucks," *The Chronicle of Higher Education,* November 16, 2001 [on-line]. Available: http://chronicle.com/weekly/v48/i12/12a03501.htm (March 2004).

2. Indiana University Web Site, "Amazing Student, Chad Clunie: On a Knowledge Quest," [on-line] http://excellence.indiana.edu/clunie/.

3. Joyce Kasman Valenza, "Skills That College Freshmen Need," *Philadelphia Inquirer,* April 26, 2001, p. NA.

4. Jeffrey R. Young, "Libraries Try to Widen Google's Eyes," *The Chronicle of Higher Education,* May 21, 2004, p. A1.

5. Lori Leibovich, "Choosing Quick Hits Over the Card Catalog," *New York Times,* August 10, 2000, p. 1.

6. David Hochman, "In Searching We Trust," *New York Times,* March 14, 2004, Section 9, p. 1.

7. Floyd H. Johnson (May 1996), "The Internet and Research: Proceed with Caution" [on-line]. Available: www.lanl.gov/SFC/96/posters.html#johnson (August 2000).

8. Analysis based on Lynn Quitman Troyka, *Simon & Schuster Handbook for Writers.* Upper Saddle River, NJ: Prentice Hall, 1996, pp. 22–23.

9. Mel Levine, *The Myth of Laziness.* New York: Simon & Schuster, 2003, p. 183.

10. Thomas Bartlett, "Undergraduates Heed the Writer's Muse: English Departments Add Programs as More Students Push to Write Fiction and Poetry," *The Chronicle of Higher Education,* March 15, 2002 [on-line]. Available: http://chronicle.com/weekly/v48/i27/2703901.htm (March 2004).

SUCCESSFUL INTELLIGENCE

**Slay the Math
Anxiety Dragon**

A special form of test anxiety, math anxiety is based on common misconceptions about math, such as the notion that people are born with or without an ability to think quantitatively or that men are better at math than women. Students who feel they can't do math may give up without asking for help. On exams, these students may experience a range of physical symptoms—including sweating, nausea, dizziness, headaches, and fatigue—that reduce their ability to concentrate and leave them feeling defeated.

The material in this Study Break is designed to help you deal with the kind of math-related anxiety that affects your grades on exams. As you learn concrete ways to calm your nerves and discover special techniques for math tests, you will feel more confident in your ability to succeed.

These test-taking tips supplement what you learned in Chapter 7, "Test Taking: Showing What You Know," in which you studied test taking in depth and generalized test anxiety. Chapter 7 also includes valuable information on test preparation, general test-taking strategies, strategies for handling different types of test questions, and learning from test mistakes.

Use special techniques for math tests

Use the general test-taking strategies presented in Chapter 7 as well as the techniques below to achieve better results on math exams.

- **Read through the exam first.** When you first get an exam, read through every problem quickly and make notes on how you might attempt to solve the problems.

Do not worry about your difficulties in mathematics,
I assure you that mine are greater.

ALBERT EINSTEIN

- **Analyze problems carefully.** Categorize problems according to type. Take the "givens" into account, and write down any formulas, theorems, or definitions that apply before you begin. Focus on what you want to find or prove.
- **Estimate before you begin** to come up with a "ballpark" solution. Work the problem and check the solution against your estimate. The two answers should be close. If they're not, recheck your calculations. You may have made a calculation error.

Gauge your level of math anxiety

Use the questionnaire on the next page to get an idea of your math anxiety level.

ARE YOU ANXIOUS ABOUT MATH?

Rate each of the following statements on a scale of 1 (Strongly Disagree) to 5 (Strongly Agree).

1. _____ I cringe when I have to go to math class.

2. _____ I am uneasy when asked to go to the board in a math class.

3. _____ I am afraid to ask questions in math class.

4. _____ I am always worried about being called on in math class.

5. _____ I understand math now, but I worry that it's going to get really difficult soon.

6. _____ I tend to zone out in math class.

7. _____ I fear math tests more than any other kind.

8. _____ I don't know how to study for math tests.

9. _____ Math is clear to me in math class, but when I go home it's like I was never there.

10. _____ I'm afraid I won't be able to keep up with the rest of the class.

SCORING KEY

40–50   Sure thing, you have math anxiety.

30–39   No doubt! You're still fearful about math.

20–29   On the fence.

10–19   Wow! Loose as a goose!

Source: Freedman, Ellen. (March 1997). *Test Your Math Anxiety* [on-line]. Available: www.mathpower.com/anxtest.htm (May 2004).

The best way to overcome math-related anxiety is through practice. Keeping up with your homework, attending class, preparing well for tests, and doing extra problems will help you learn the material and boost your confidence.

Following are ten additional ways to reduce math anxiety and do well on tests.

1. Overcome your negative self-image about math by remembering that even Albert Einstein wasn't perfect.

2. Ask questions of your teachers and your friends, and seek outside assistance when needed.

3. Math is a foreign language—practice it often.

4. Don't study mathematics by trying to memorize information and formulas.

5. READ your math textbook.

6. Study math according to your personal learning style.

7. Get help the same day you don't understand something.

8. Be relaxed and comfortable while studying math.

9. "TALK" mathematics. Discuss it with people in your class. Form a study group.

10. Develop a sense of responsibility for your own successes and failures.

Source: Adapted from Freedman, Ellen. *Ten Ways to Reduce Math Anxiety* [on-line]. Available: www.mathpower.com/reduce.htm (May 2004).

- Break the calculation into the smallest possible pieces. Go step-by-step and don't move on to the next step until you are clear about what you've done so far.
- Recall how you solved similar problems. Past experience can provide valuable clues.
- Draw a picture to help you see the problem. Visual images such as a diagram, chart, probability tree, or geometric figure may help clarify your thinking.
- Be neat. Sloppy numbers can mean the difference between a right and a wrong answer. A 4 that looks like a 9 will be marked wrong.
- Use the opposite operation to check your work. Work backward from your answer to see if you are right.
- Look back at the question to be sure you did everything. Did you answer every part of the question? Did you show all required work?

Decide how well these techniques work for you

Use what you just learned about yourself and math to answer the following questions:

- What did you learn from the math anxiety questionnaire? Describe your current level of math anxiety.

_____
_____
_____

- What effect do you think your attitude toward math will have on your future?

_____
_____
_____

- Which suggestions for reducing math anxiety are you likely to use? How do you think they will help you feel more comfortable with math?

_____
_____
_____

- Which suggestions for improving your performance on math tests are you likely to use?

_____
_____
_____

- What other ways can you think of to improve your math performance?

_____
_____
_____

Relating to Others
COMMUNICATING IN A DIVERSE WORLD

Among your most meaningful, life-changing experiences at college will be those that take you out of your "comfort zone" and force you to question your thinking and even your basic beliefs. Encountering the diversity of the people around you can inspire this kind of questioning. As you read this chapter, you will explore how accepting differences and rejecting prejudice can lead to respect for others and strong teamwork skills, both of which are key ingredients for success in school and beyond.

In this chapter, you will investigate how analytical, creative, and practical abilities can help you build the cultural competence that will allow you to relate successfully to others. You will explore how to communicate effectively, investigating different communication styles and methods for handling conflict. Finally, you will look at how your personal relationships can inspire you and enhance your college and life experience.

On the following page, read how student Nisar Nikzad is seeking to connect to a new community while staying in touch with his own culture.

- ● **How do you experience diversity?**
- ● **How can you develop cultural competence?**
- ● **How can minority students make the most of college?**

- ● **How can you communicate effectively?**
- ● **How do you make the most of personal relationships?**

How can I adjust to a new society and connect to my college fellows and people of my community?

I came to the United States a little over two and a half years ago from Afghanistan. I am a Biology student aiming to go to medical school. My goal is to join the team of doctors called "Doctors Without Borders" and travel to underdeveloped countries where I can help people in need of medical services.

I am sociable and like hanging out with friends from a variety of different backgrounds. However, I often feel that in order to connect with American students on my campus, I need to do what they do— even when it comes to partying. I learn better when I am connecting to people, but I want to be myself and not to have to change to meet others' expectations. I like learning new cultures but still want to keep mine and this makes it tougher for me to adjust well.

How can I connect to my community without losing myself and my culture?

Nisar Nikzad
Community College of Denver
Denver, Colorado

Find a way to incorporate both your home country culture and U. S. culture into who you are.

The challenge you are facing—to adapt and to integrate—is called *acculturation* and it is common, not only for students, but for all those who come to a new country. I faced a similar situation when I came to the United States from Iran to go to college. You already possess three characteristics essential to successful acculturation. First, you are aware of cultural differences and you are able to approach them without negative judgment. Second, you are also aware of your own culture and have a desire to preserve it. Third, you have recognized that adaptation does not happen overnight, and you are willing to put in the work and resolve conflicts.

Given that your home country culture and your new U. S. culture are both important to you, your goal is to bring the two together and create a new culture of sorts for yourself. The first step is to continue learning about the United States. Although it may appear that there is a uniform culture among American college students, there actually are considerable differences and diversity in beliefs, values, and behaviors. Because Americans are used to seeing different people around us, we tend to be more open to other cultures. Additionally, although we each may have a dominant culture, we are all part of many different cultures that make up who we are. You are Afghani, American, male, part of the medical profession (or planning to be), and so forth.

The other thing you can do to help your acculturation is to be an ambassador about your values and your way of life. Talk to your friends here about your country, religion, language, school, family, and so forth. You are likely to find them eager to learn, although sometimes their early stereotypes and assumptions may be simplistic. Learning about your culture will increase the richness of everyone's cultural context.

Don't give up your identity. You will change as a result of your experiences; you are likely to feel more "American," but you will also change those around you and they will become a little more "Afghani." This give-and-take will enrich both you and those around you and allow you to be successful.

Afsaneh Nahavandi Professor of Management and Director of Freshman Programs Arizona State University West

How do you experience *diversity*?

A century ago it was possible to live an entire lifetime knowing no one from a culture different from your own. Not so today. With waves of new immigrants continually arriving, just as they have done throughout U.S. history, American society consists of people from a multitude of countries and cultural backgrounds.

The speed of cultural change is dramatic: In the 2000 census, American citizens described themselves in terms of 63 different racial categories, compared with only 5 in 1990.[1] Technology and economic interdependence add to our growing cultural awareness. Cable television, the Internet, and the global marketplace link people from all over the world in ways that were unimaginable less than a decade ago. You have unprecedented access to information about what people do and how they live in nearly every corner of the globe.

Diversity affects everyone

As you read in Chapter 1, diversity exists both within each person and among all people:

- **The diversity within each person.** Your physical being, personality, learning style, talents and skills, and analytical, creative, and practical abilities set you apart from everyone else. *No one else has been or will ever be exactly like you.*

- **The diversity among people.** Differences in skin color, gender, ethnicity and national origin, age, physical characteristics and abilities, and sexual orientation are among the major differences that exist among people. Differences in cultural and religious beliefs and practices, education and socioeconomic status, family background, and marital and parental status add to our country's cultural mosaic.

You may work with people from different backgrounds. You may encounter all kinds of people as you attend religious services, buy groceries and stamps, swim at a pool, or socialize. You may experience diversity within your family—often the kind of diversity that is not visible. Even if friends or family members have the same racial and ethnic background as you do, they might be completely different in how they learn, the way they communicate, what they value, and what they do well.

Workplaces and college campuses are filled with people of every age and stage of life. On track to receive her bachelor's degree, this 85-year-old student is determined to achieve her goal.

Diversity on campus

In college you are likely to meet classmates or instructors who reflect America's growing diversity, including

- bi- or multiracial individuals or those who come from families with more than one religious tradition.

- non-native English speakers who may have immigrated from countries outside the United States.
- people older than "traditional" 18- to 22-year-old students.
- persons living with various kinds of disabilities.
- persons practicing different lifestyles—often expressed in the way they dress, their interests, their sexual orientation, and their leisure activities.

Being able to appreciate and adjust to differences among people is crucial to your success at school, at work, and in your personal relationships. You can accomplish this goal by using your analytical, creative, and practical abilities to develop cultural competence.

How can you develop *cultural competence?*

As you learned in Chapter 2, *cultural competence* refers to the ability to understand and appreciate differences among people and change your behavior in a way that enhances, rather than detracts from, relationships and communication. According to the National Center for Cultural Competence, to develop cultural competence you must act upon the following five steps:[2]

1. Value diversity.
2. Identify and evaluate personal perceptions and attitudes.
3. Be aware of what happens when different cultures interact.
4. Build knowledge about other cultures.
5. Use what you learn to adapt to diverse cultures as you encounter them.

As you develop cultural competence, you heighten your ability to analyze how people relate to one another. Most important, you develop practical skills that enable you to connect to others by bridging the gap between who you are and who they are.[3]

Value diversity

Valuing diversity means having a basic respect for, and acceptance of, the differences among people. Every time you meet someone new, you have a choice about how to relate. If you value diversity, you will choose to treat people with tolerance and respect, granting them the right to think, feel, and believe without being judged.

Being open-minded in this way will help your relationships thrive, as shown in Key 9.1. Even though you won't like every person you meet, you can make an effort to show respect while focusing on the person as an individual.

Approaching diversity with an open mind builds relationships.

YOUR ROLE	SITUATION	CLOSED-MINDED ACTIONS	OPEN-MINDED ACTIONS
Fellow student	For an assignment, you are paired with a student old enough to be your mother.	You assume the student will be clueless about the modern world. You think she might preach to you about how to do the assignment.	You get to know the student as an individual. You stay open to what you can learn from her experiences and knowledge.
Friend	You are invited to dinner at a friend's house. When he introduces you to his partner, you realize that he is gay.	You are turned off by the idea of two men in a relationship. You make an excuse to leave early. You avoid your friend after that.	You have dinner with the two men and make an effort to get to know more about them, individually and as a couple.
Employee	Your new boss is of a different racial and cultural background than yours.	You assume that you and your new boss don't have much in common. You think he will be distant and uninterested in you.	You rein in your stereotypes. You pay close attention to how your new boss communicates and leads. You adapt to his style and make an effort to get to know him better.

Identify and evaluate personal perceptions and attitudes

Whereas people may value the *concept* of diversity, attitudes and emotional responses may influence how they act when they confront the *reality* of diversity in their own lives. As a result, many people have prejudices that lead to damaging stereotypes.

Prejudice

Almost everyone has some level of prejudice, meaning that they prejudge others, usually on the basis of characteristics such as gender, race, sexual orientation, and religion. People judge others without knowing anything about them because of . . .

- **influence of family and culture.** Children learn attitudes, including intolerance, superiority, and hate, from their parents, peers, and community.
- **fear of differences.** It is human to fear, and to make assumptions about, the unfamiliar.
- **experience.** One bad experience with a person of a particular race or religion may lead someone to condemn all people with the same background.

Stereotypes

Prejudice is usually based on stereotypes—assumptions made, without proof or critical thinking, about the characteristics of a person or group of people. Stereotyping emerges from . . .

- **a desire for patterns and logic.** People often try to make sense of the world by using the labels, categories, and generalizations that stereotypes provide.

PREJUDICE

A preconceived judgment or opinion, formed without just grounds or sufficient knowledge.

STEREOTYPE

A standardized mental picture that represents an oversimplified opinion or uncritical judgment.

- **media influences.** The more people see stereotypical images—the air-head beautiful blonde, the jolly fat man—the easier it is to believe that stereotypes are universal.
- **laziness.** Labeling group members according to a characteristic they seem to have in common takes less energy than exploring the qualities of individuals.

Stereotypes stall the growth of relationships, because pasting a label on a person makes it hard for you to see the real person underneath. Even stereotypes that seem "positive" may not be true and may get in the way of perceiving people as individuals. Key 9.2 shows some "positive" and "negative" stereotypes.

Use your analytical abilities to question your own ideas and beliefs and to weed out the narrowing influence of prejudice and stereotyping. Giving honest answers to questions like the following is an essential step in the development of cultural competence:

- How do I react to differences?
- What prejudices or stereotypes come to mind when I see people, in real life or the media, who are a different color than I am? From a different culture? Making different choices?
- Where did my prejudices and stereotypes come from?
- Are these prejudices fair? Are these stereotypes accurate?
- What harm can having these prejudices and believing these stereotypes cause?

With the knowledge you build as you answer these questions, move on to the next stage: Looking carefully at what happens when people from different cultures interact.

Stereotypes involve generalizations that may not be accurate.

POSITIVE STEREOTYPE	NEGATIVE STEREOTYPE
Women are nurturing.	Women are too emotional for business.
African Americans are great athletes.	African Americans struggle in school.
Hispanic Americans are family oriented.	Hispanic Americans have too many kids.
White people are successful in business.	White people are cold and power hungry.
Gay men have a great sense of style.	Gay men are sissies.
People with disabilities have strength of will.	People with disabilities are bitter.
Older people are wise.	Older people are set in their ways.
Asian Americans are good at math and science.	Asian Americans are poor leaders.

EXPAND YOUR PERCEPTION OF DIVERSITY

Heighten your awareness of diversity by examining your own uniqueness.

Being able to respond to people as individuals requires that you become more aware of the diversity that is not always on the surface. Brainstorm 10 words or phrases that describe you. The challenge: Keep references to your ethnicity or appearance (brunette, Cuban American, wheelchair dependent, and so on) to a minimum, and fill the rest of the list with characteristics others can't see at a glance (laid-back, only child, 24 years old, drummer, marathoner, interpersonal learner, and so on).

1. _____
2. _____
3. _____
4. _____
5. _____
6. _____
7. _____
8. _____
9. _____
10. _____

Use a separate piece of paper to make a similar list for someone you know well—a friend or family member. Again, stay away from the most obvious visible characteristics. See if anything surprises you about the different image you create of this familiar person.

Be aware of what happens when cultures interact

As history has shown, when people from different cultures interact, they often experience problems caused by lack of understanding, prejudice, and stereotypic thinking. At their mildest, these problems create roadblocks that obstruct relationships and communication. At their worst, they set the stage for acts of discrimination and hate crimes.

Discrimination

Discrimination refers to actions that deny people equal employment, educational, and housing opportunities, or treat people as second-class citizens. Federal law says that you cannot be

Minds are like parachutes. They only function when they are open.

SIR JAMES DEWAR

denied basic opportunities and rights because of your race, creed, color, age, gender, national or ethnic origin, religion, marital status, potential or actual pregnancy, or potential or actual illness or disability (unless the illness or disability prevents you from performing required tasks and unless accommodations are not possible).

Despite these legal protections, discrimination is common and often appears on college campuses. Students may not want to work with students of other races. Members of campus clubs may reject prospective members because of religious differences. Outsiders may harass students attending gay and lesbian alliance meetings. Instructors may judge students according to their weight, accent, or body piercings.

Hate crimes

HATE CRIME

A crime motivated by a hatred of a specific characteristic thought to be possessed by the victim.

When prejudice turns violent, it often manifests itself in hate crimes directed at racial, ethnic, and religious minorities and homosexuals:

- In Wyoming in 1998, Matthew Shepard, a gay college student, was kidnapped and tied to a fence where his captors beat and abandoned him. He died of his injuries.
- In California in 1999, Buford O. Furrow Jr. entered a community center and shot five people because they were Jewish. He then shot and killed a Filipino-American letter carrier.

The increase in hate crimes in recent years is alarming. According to FBI statistics, reported hate crimes more than doubled from 1991 to 2001.[4] Incidents categorized as hate crimes include simple assault (the most common hate crime), aggravated assault, forcible sex offenses, arson, manslaughter, and murder. Because the statistics include only reported incidents, they tell only a part of the story—many more crimes likely go unreported by victims fearful of what might happen if they contact authorities.

Build cultural knowledge

The successfully intelligent response to discrimination and hate, and the next step in your path toward cultural competence, is to gather knowledge. You have a personal responsibility to learn about people who are different from you, including those you are likely to meet on campus.

What are some practical ways to begin?

- *Read* newspapers, books, magazines, and Web sites.
- *Ask questions* of all kinds of people, about themselves and their traditions.
- *Observe* how people behave, what they eat and wear, how they interact with others.
- *Travel internationally* to unfamiliar places where you can experience different ways of living firsthand.
- *Travel locally* to equally unfamiliar, but close-by, places where you will encounter a variety of people.
- *Build friendships* with fellow students or coworkers you would not ordinarily approach.

Some colleges have international exchange students who can help you appreciate the world's cultural diversity. When Yiting Liu left China to study mathematics and economics at a U.S. college, she knew little about the United States. Dorothy Smith, her African American roommate, helped her adjust. "Yiting didn't know much about race relations when she first got to America," explained Dorothy, "but from hanging around us, she's been able to get an interpretive experience." Also, said Dorothy, when Yiting "first came here, she was an outsider. She didn't know what the taboos were. Now she's able to cross into different groups."[5]

Building knowledge also means exploring yourself. Talk with family, read, seek experiences that educate you about your own cultural heritage. Then share what you know with others.

Adapt to diverse cultures

Here's where you take everything you have gathered—your value of diversity, your self-knowledge, your understanding of how cultures interact, your information about different cultures—and put it to work with practical actions. With these actions you can improve how you relate to others, and perhaps even change how people relate to one another on a larger scale. Think carefully, and creatively, about what kinds of actions feel right to you. Make choices that you feel comfortable with, that cause no harm, and that may make a difference, however small.

Dr. Martin Luther King Jr. believed that careful thinking could change attitudes. He said:

> The tough-minded person always examines the facts before he reaches conclusions: in short, he postjudges. The tender-minded person reaches conclusions before he has examined the first fact; in short, he prejudges and is prejudiced. . . . There is little hope for us until we become tough minded enough to break loose from the shackles of prejudice, half-truths, and down-right ignorance.[6]

Try the following suggestions. In addition, let them inspire your own creative ideas about what else you can do in your daily life to improve how you relate to others.

Look past external characteristics. If you meet a woman with a disability, get to know her. She may be an accounting major, a daughter, and a mother. She may love baseball, politics, and science fiction novels. These characteristics—not just her physical person—describe who she is.

Put yourself in other people's shoes. Shift your perspective and try to understand what other people feel, especially if there's a conflict. If you make a comment that someone interprets as offensive, for example, think about why what you said was hurtful. If you can talk about it with the person, you may learn even more about how he or she heard what you said and why.

Adjust to cultural differences. When you understand someone's way of being and put it into practice, you show respect and encourage communication. If a friend's family is formal at home, dress appropriately and behave formally when you visit. If an instructor maintains a lot of personal space, keep a respectful distance when you visit during office hours. If a study group member takes offense at a particular kind of language, avoid it when you meet.

When you meet different people, you discover many ways of being and learning. After having a stroke, this student learned how to write with her feet using a special device.

Help others in need. Newspaper columnist Sheryl McCarthy wrote about an African American who, in the midst of the 1992 Los Angeles riots, saw an Asian American man being beaten and helped him to safety: "When asked why he risked grievous harm to save an Asian man he didn't even know, the African-American man said, 'Because if I'm not there to help someone else, when the mob comes for me, will there be someone there to save me?'"[7]

Stand up against prejudice, discrimination, and hate. When you hear a prejudiced remark or notice discrimination taking place, think about what you can do to encourage a move in the right direction. You may choose to make a comment, or to get help by approaching an authority such as an instructor or dean. Sound the alarm on hate crimes—let authorities know if you suspect that a crime is about to occur, join campus protests, support organizations that encourage tolerance.

Recognize that people everywhere have the same basic needs. Everyone loves, thinks, hurts, hopes, fears, and plans. When you are trying to find common ground with diverse people, remember that you are united first through your essential humanity.

When people use successful intelligence to work through problems, changes can happen. After a gay tutor left a job at a university rather than face harassment, his friends organized an intercollegiate meeting on intolerance. Chandra J. Johnson, assistant to the president at the University of Notre Dame, asked participants to start by examining themselves: "This is an opportunity to see how our own biases have been formed," she said. "We are not born with notions of racism. These kinds of social ills have been projected onto us. . . . These things are very, very real and people's spirits are destroyed every day as a result of a bias or a misconception."

Ada Maxwell, a student attendee, believes that talking about intolerance is the key to eliminating it. "It doesn't have to be taboo," she said. "Half of the education . . . is the classes and the professors, but the other half—and it's a really important half—is what you can learn from other people. Your thinking can change and other people's thinking can change."[8]

Many minority students experience a dimension to college life unknown to majority students. Examining their experiences and choices will help *all* students understand the complexity of what it means to be a minority in America.

How can *minority students* make the most of college?

Who fits into the category of "minority student" at your school? The term *minority* includes students of color; students who are not part of the majority Christian sects; and gay, lesbian, and bisexual students. However, even for members of these groups, there is no universal "minority" experience. Each person's experiences are unique.

If you are a minority student, two actions will help you make the most of college: Defining your perspective and defining your experience.

Define your perspective

You have a choice about what perspective to bring to your new relationships. Do you expect others to stereotype you right away, or do you expect that they will be open to getting to know you as an individual? What might be the consequences of each perspective? For your part, do you plan to try to approach each person as an individual rather than to type them according to their ethnic or cultural status, age or gender, values or choices?

Part of getting off to a positive and productive start at college means being open-minded and avoiding assumptions as you get to know people. Yes, everyone will have their own ideas, values, and ways of living. It is possible, however—as well as productive—to get to know these ideas and values in the people you encounter without immediately making assumptions or placing judgments. Working toward understanding is the key. As Paul Barrett Jr., political science major at Earlham College, says,

> As a black male, I am faced with situations very different from that of a white male, a white female, a black female, an Asian-American male, and so on. We must have the ability to approach situations with a panoramic perspective rather than the narrow scope of our own worlds. Is that not the very essence of diversity? Is it not the ability to at least try to understand differences in culture and understand what makes a person act or think the way that he or she does?[9]

University of Michigan student Fiona Rose describes the benefits of a positive approach to diversity this way:

> My years at U-M have been enhanced by relationships with men and women from all cultures, classes, races, and ethnicities. Such interactions are essential to an education. While courses teach us the history and academic value of diversity, friendships prepare us to survive and thrive in our global community. Good institutions consider not only what a potential student will gain from classes and course work, but what he or she will bring to the campus community.[10]

Consider the mind-set you want to take as you begin college. Adopt the perspective that will open you to new friendships and horizon-broadening experiences.

Define your experience

When you start school, it's natural to want to live with, sit next to, or socialize with people similar to you. However, if you define your entire college experience by these ties, you may limit your understanding of others and your opportunities for growth.

Along with activities that appeal to the general student population, most colleges have organizations and services that support minority groups. Among these are specialized student associations, cultural centers, arts groups with a minority focus, minority fraternities and sororities, and political-action groups. Many minority students look for a balance, involving themselves in activities with members of their group as well as with the college mainstream. For example, a student may join the African-American Students Association as well as clubs for all students such as the campus newspaper or an athletic team.

To make choices as a minority student on campus, ask yourself these questions:

- How much time do I want to spend pursuing minority-related activities? Do I want to focus my studies on a minority-related field, such as African American studies?
- Do I want to minimize my ties with my minority group? Will I care if other minority students criticize my choices?
- Do I want to spend part of my time among people who share my background and part with students from other groups?

The attitudes and habits you develop now may have implications for the rest of your life—in your choice of friends, where you decide to live, your work, and even your family. Think carefully about the path you take, and follow your head and heart.

> I have a dream that one day on the red hills of Georgia the sons of former slaves and the sons of former slave owners will be able to sit down together at the table of brotherhood.
>
> **MARTIN LUTHER KING JR.**

So far, the chapter has focused on the need to accept and adapt to diversity in its many forms. Just as there is diversity in skin color and ethnicity, there is also diversity in the way people communicate. Effective communication helps people of all cultures understand one another and make connections.

get practical!

MAKE A DIFFERENCE

Find personal ways to connect with other cultures.

Rewrite three strategies in the "Adapt to Diverse Cultures" section on pages 269–270 as specific actions to which you commit. For example, "Help others in need" might become "Sign up to tutor in the Writing Center." Circle or check the number when you have completed each task or, if it is ongoing, when you have begun the change.

1. _____

_____

_____

2. _____

_____

_____

3. _____

_____

_____

How can you *communicate effectively?*

Clear-spoken communication promotes success at school, at work, and in personal relationships. Successfully intelligent communicators analyze and adjust to communication styles, learn to give and receive criticism, analyze and make practical use of body language, and work through communication problems.

Adjust to communication styles

When you speak, your goal is for listeners to receive the message as you intended. Problems arise when one person has trouble "translating" a message coming from someone using a different communication style. Your knowledge of the Personality Spectrum (see Chapter 3) will help you understand and analyze the ways diverse people communicate.

Identifying your styles

Following are some communication styles that tend to be associated with the four dimensions in the Personality Spectrum. No one style is better than another. Successful communication depends on understanding your personal style and becoming attuned to the styles of others.

Thinker-dominant communicators focus on facts and logic. As speakers, they tend to rely on logical analysis to communicate ideas and prefer quantitative concepts to those that are conceptual or emotional. As listeners, they often do best with logical messages. Thinkers may also need time to process what they have heard before responding. Written messages—on paper or via e-mail—are often useful for these individuals because writing can allow for time to put ideas together logically.

Organizer-dominant communicators focus on structure and completeness. As speakers, they tend to deliver well-thought-out, structured messages that fit into an organized plan. As listeners, they often appreciate a well-organized message that defines practical tasks in concrete terms. As with Thinkers, a written format is often an effective form of communication to or from an Organizer.

Giver-dominant communicators focus on concern for others. As speakers, they tend to cultivate harmony, analyzing what will promote closeness in relationships. As listeners, they often appreciate messages that emphasize personal connection and address the emotional side of an issue. Whether speaking or listening, Givers often favor in-person talks over written messages.

Adventurer-dominant communicators focus on the present. As speakers, they focus on creative ideas, tending to convey a message as soon as the idea arises and move on to the next activity. As listeners, they appreciate up-front, short, direct messages that don't get sidetracked. Like Givers, Adventurers tend to communicate and listen more effectively in person.

Use this information as a jumping-off point for your self-exploration. Just as people tend to demonstrate characteristics from more than one Personality Spectrum dimension, communicators may demonstrate different styles. Analyze your style by thinking about the communication styles associated with your dominant Personality Spectrum dimensions. Compare them to how you tend to communicate and how others seem to respond to you. Then, use creative and practical thinking skills to decide what works best for you as a communicator.

Speakers adjust to listeners

Listeners may interpret messages in ways you never intended. Think about practical solutions to this kind of problem as you read the following example involving a Giver-dominant instructor and a Thinker-dominant student (the listener):

Instructor: "Your essay didn't communicate any sense of your personal voice."

Student: "What do you mean? I spent hours writing it. I thought it was on the mark."

- **Without adjustment:** The instructor ignores the student's need for detail and continues to generalize. Comments like, "You need to elaborate. Try writing from the heart. You're not considering your audience," might confuse or discourage the student.

- **With adjustment:** Greater logic and detail will help. For example, the instructor might say: "You've supported your central idea clearly, but you didn't move beyond the facts into your interpretation of what they mean. Your essay reads like a research paper. The language doesn't sound like it is coming directly from you."

Listeners adjust to speakers

As a listener, improve understanding by being aware of stylistic differences and translating the message into one that makes sense to you. The following example of an Adventurer-dominant employee speaking to an Organizer-dominant supervisor shows how adjusting can pay off.

Employee: "I'm upset about the e-mail you sent me. You never talked to me directly and you let the problem build into a crisis. I haven't had a chance to defend myself."

- **Without adjustment:** If the supervisor is annoyed by the employee's insistence on direct personal contact, he or she may become defensive: "I told you clearly what needs to be done. I don't know what else there is to discuss."

- **With adjustment:** In an effort to improve communication, the supervisor responds by encouraging the in-person exchange that is best for the employee. "Let's meet after lunch so you can explain to me how you believe we can improve the situation."

Although adjusting to communication styles helps you speak and listen more effectively, you also need to understand, and learn how to effectively give and receive, criticism.

Communication

Using techniques corresponding to your stronger intelligences boosts your communication skills both as a speaker and as a listener.

INTELLIGENCE	SUGGESTED STRATEGIES	WHAT WORKS FOR YOU? WRITE NEW IDEAS HERE
Verbal–Linguistic	• Find opportunities to express your thoughts and feelings to others—either in writing or in person. • Remind yourself that you have two ears and only one mouth. Listening is more important than talking.	
Logical–Mathematical	• Allow yourself time to think through solutions before discussing them—try writing out a logical argument on paper and then rehearsing it orally. • Accept the fact that others may have communication styles that vary from yours and that may not seem logical.	
Bodily–Kinesthetic	• Have an important talk while walking or performing a task that does not involve concentration. • Work out physically to burn off excess energy before having an important discussion.	
Visual–Spatial	• Make a drawing or diagram of points you want to communicate during an important discussion. • If your communication is in a formal classroom or work setting, use visual aids to explain your main points.	
Interpersonal	• Observe how you communicate with friends. If you tend to dominate the conversation, brainstorm ideas about how to communicate more effectively. • Remember to balance speaking with listening.	
Intrapersonal	• When you have a difficult encounter, take time alone to evaluate what happened and to decide how you can communicate more effectively next time. • Remember that, in order for others to understand clearly, you may need to communicate more than you expect to.	
Musical	• Play soft music during an important discussion if it helps you, making sure it isn't distracting to the others involved.	
Naturalistic	• Communicate outdoors if that is agreeable to all parties. • If you have a difficult exchange, imagine how you might have responded differently had it taken place outdoors.	

Know how to give and receive criticism

CONSTRUCTIVE

Promoting improvement or development.

Criticism can be either constructive or nonconstructive. Constructive criticism is a practical problem-solving strategy, involving goodwill suggestions for improving a situation. In contrast, nonconstructive criticism focuses on what went wrong, doesn't offer alternatives or help that might help solve the problem, and is often delivered negatively, creating bad feelings.

When offered constructively and carefully, criticism can help bring about important changes. Consider a case in which someone has continually been late to study group sessions. The group leader can comment in one of two ways. Which comment would encourage you to change your behavior?

- **Constructive.** The group leader talks privately with the student: "I've noticed that you've been late a lot. We count on you, because our success depends on what each of us contributes. Is there a problem that is keeping you from being on time? Can we help?"

- **Nonconstructive.** The leader watches the student arrive late and says, in front of everyone, "If you can't start getting here on time, there's really no point in your coming."

While at school, your instructors will criticize your class work, papers, and exams. On the job, criticism may come from supervisors, coworkers, or customers. No matter the source, constructive comments can help you grow as a person. Be open to what you hear, and always remember that most people want to help you succeed.

Offering constructive criticism

When offering constructive criticism, use the following strategies to be effective:

- **Criticize the behavior rather than the person.** Avoid personal attacks. "You've been late to five group meetings" is much preferable to "You're lazy."

- **Define the problematic behavior specifically.** Try to focus on the facts, substantiating with specific examples and minimizing emotions. Avoid additional complaints—people can hear criticisms better if they are discussed one at a time.

- **Suggest new approaches and offer help.** Talk about practical ways of handling the situation. Work with the person to develop creative options. Help the person feel supported.

- **Use a positive approach and hopeful language.** Express the conviction that changes will occur and that the person can turn the situation around.

Receiving criticism

When you find yourself on criticism's receiving end, use the following techniques:

- **Analyze the comments.** Listen carefully, then evaluate what you heard. What does it mean? What is the intent? Try to let nonconstructive comments go without responding.

GIVE CONSTRUCTIVE CRITICISM

get analytical!

Imagine how you would offer constructive criticism.

Briefly describe a situation in your life that could be improved if you were able to offer constructive criticism to a friend or family member. Describe the improvement you want:

_____

_____

Imagine that you have a chance to speak to this person. First describe the setting—time, place, atmosphere—where you think you would be most successful:

_____

_____

Now develop your "script." Keeping in mind what you know about constructive criticism, analyze the situation and decide on what you think would be the best approach. Freewrite what you would say. Keep in mind the goal you want your communication to achieve.

_____

_____

_____

_____

_____

Finally, if you can, make your plan a reality. Will you do it?   Yes   No

If you do have the conversation, note here: Was it worth it?   Yes   No

---

- Request suggestions on how to change your behavior. Ask, "How would you like me to handle this in the future?"
- Summarize the criticism and your response to it. Make sure everyone understands the situation.
- Use a specific strategy. Use problem-solving skills to analyze the problem, brainstorm ways to change, choose a strategy, and take practical action to make it happen.

Criticism, as well as other thoughts and feelings, may be communicated nonverbally. You will become a more effective communicator if you understand body language.

Understand body language

Body language has an extraordinary capacity to express people's real feelings through gestures, eye movements, facial expressions, body positioning and posture, touching behaviors, vocal tone, and use of personal space. Why is it important to know how to analyze body language?

Nonverbal cues shade meaning. What you say can mean different things depending on body positioning or vocal tone. The statement "That's a great idea" sounds positive. However, said while sitting with your arms and legs crossed and looking away, it may communicate that you dislike the idea. Said sarcastically, the tone may reveal that you consider the idea a joke.

Culture influences how body language is interpreted. For example, in the United States, looking away from someone may be a sign of anger or distress; in Japan, the same behavior is usually a sign of respect.

Nonverbal communication strongly influences first impressions. First impressions emerge from a combination of verbal and nonverbal cues. Nonverbal elements, including tone of voice, posture, eye contact, and speed and style of movement, usually come across first and strongest.

Although reading body language is not an exact science, the following practical strategies will help you use it to improve communication.

- **Pay attention to what is said through nonverbal cues.** Focus on your tone, your body position, whether your cues reinforce or contradict your words. Then do the same for those with whom you are speaking. Look for the level of meaning in the physical.
- **Note cultural differences.** Cultural factors influence how an individual interprets nonverbal cues. In cross-cultural conversation, discover what seems appropriate by paying attention to what the other person does on a consistent basis, and by noting how others react to what you do.
- **Adjust body language to the person or situation.** What body language might you use when making a presentation in class? Meeting with your advisor? Confronting an angry coworker? Think through how to use your physicality to communicate successfully.

Communicate across cultures

As you meet people from other countries and try to form relationships with them, you may encounter communication issues that are linked to cultural differences.[11] As you recall from Chapter 2, these problems often stem from the different communication styles that are found in high-context and low-context cultures.

You cannot shake hands with a clenched fist.

INDIRA GANDHI

In the United States and other low-context cultures, communication is linked primarily to words and to the explicit messages sent through these words. In contrast, in high-context cultures, such as those in the Middle and Far East, words are often considered less important than such factors as context, situation, time, formality, personal relationships, and nonverbal behavior.

Key 9.3 will help you see how 12 world cultures fit on the continuum of high- to low-context communication styles. Key 9.4 summarizes some major communication differences you should be aware of when talking with someone from a different culture. Being attuned to culture-

The continuum of high- and low-context cultures.

LOW-CONTEXT CULTURES   **HIGH-CONTEXT CULTURES**

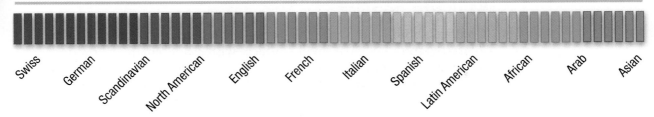

Swiss   German   Scandinavian   North American   English   French   Italian   Spanish   Latin American   African   Arab   Asian

based communication differences will help you interact comfortably with people who come from different parts of the world.

Language barriers may also arise when communicating cross-culturally. When speaking with someone who is struggling with your language, make the conversation easier by choosing words the person is likely to know, avoiding slang expressions, being patient, and using body language to fill in what words can't say. Also, invite questions—and ask them yourself—so that you both can be as clear as possible.

Some ways communication differs in high- and low-context cultures.

FACTORS AFFECTING COMMUNICATION	LOW-CONTEXT CULTURES	HIGH-CONTEXT CULTURES
Personal Relationships	The specific details of the conversation are more important than what people know about each other.	Personal trust is the basis for communication, so sharing personal information forms a basis for strong, long-lasting relationships.
Time	People expect others to be punctual and to meet schedules.	Time is seen as a force beyond the person's control. Therefore lateness is common, and not considered rude.
Formality	A certain degree of civility is expected when people meet, including hand-shakes and introductions.	People often require formal introductions that emphasize status differences. As a result, a student will speak with great respect to an instructor.
Eye Contact	Expect little direct eye contact.	• Arab natives may use prolonged, direct eye contact. • Students from Japan and other Far Eastern countries are likely to turn their eyes away from instructors as a sign of respect.
Personal Space	In the United States, people converse while remaining between 4 and 12 feet apart.	People from Latin America and the Middle East may sit or stand between 18 inches and 4 feet away from you.

Source: Adapted from Louis E. Boone, David L. Kurtz, and Judy R. Block. *Contemporary Business Communication,* 2nd ed. Upper Saddle River, NJ: Prentice Hall, 1997, p. 72.

One of the biggest barriers to successful communication is conflict, which can result in anger and even violence. With effort, you can successfully manage conflict and stay away from those who cannot.

Manage conflict

Conflicts, both large and small, arise when there is a clash of ideas or interests. You may have small conflicts with a housemate over a door left unlocked. You may have major conflicts with your partner about finances or with an instructor about a failing grade. Conflict, as unpleasant as it can be, is a natural element in the dynamic of getting along with others. Prevent it when you can—and when you can't, use problem-solving strategies to resolve it.

Conflict prevention strategies

These two strategies can help you to prevent conflict from starting in the first place.

ASSERTIVE

Able to declare and affirm one's own opinions while respecting the rights of others to do the same.

Being assertive. No matter what your dominant learning styles, you tend to express yourself in one of three ways—aggressively, assertively, or passively. Aggressive communicators focus primarily on their own needs and can become impatient when needs are not satisfied. Assertive communicators are likely both to get their message across and to give listeners the opportunity to speak, without attacking others or sacrificing their own needs. Passive communicators focus primarily on the needs of others and often deny themselves power, causing frustration.

Key 9.5 contrasts the characteristics of these three. Assertive behavior strikes a balance between aggression and passivity and promotes the most productive communication. Aggressive and passive communicators can use practical strategies to move toward a more assertive style of communication.

- Aggressive communicators might take time before speaking, use "I" statements, listen to others, and avoid giving orders.
- Passive communicators might acknowledge anger, express opinions, exercise the right to make requests, and know that their ideas and feelings are important.

Send "I" messages. "I" messages help you communicate your needs rather than attacking someone else. Creating these messages involves some simple rephrasing: "You didn't lock the door!" becomes "I felt uneasy when I came to work and the door was unlocked." Similarly, "You never called last night" becomes "I was worried when I didn't hear from you last night."

"I" statements soften the conflict by highlighting the effects that the other person's actions have on you, rather than focusing on the person or the actions themselves. These statements help the receiver feel freer to respond, perhaps offering help and even acknowledging mistakes.

Conflict resolution

All too often, people deal with conflict through avoidance (a passive tactic that shuts down communication) or escalation (an aggressive tactic that often leads to fighting). Conflict resolution demands calm communication,

Assertiveness fosters successful communication.

AGGRESSIVE	ASSERTIVE	PASSIVE
Loud, heated arguing	Expressing feelings without being nasty or overbearing	Concealing one's own feelings
Blaming, name-calling, and verbal insults	Expressing oneself and giving others the chance to express themselves	Feeling that one has no right to express anger
Walking out of arguments before they are resolved	Using "I" statements to defuse arguments	Avoiding arguments
Being demanding: "Do this"	Asking and giving reasons: "I would appreciate it if you would do this, and here's why . . ."	Being noncommittal: "You don't have to do this unless you really want to . . ."

motivation, and careful thinking. Use your analytical, creative, and practical thinking skills to apply the problem-solving plan (Chapter 4):

- Define and analyze the problem.
- Brainstorm possible solutions.
- Analyze potential solutions.
- Choose a solution and make it happen with practical action.

Trying to calm anger is an important part of resolving conflict. All people get angry at times—at people, events, and themselves. However, excessive anger can contaminate relationships, stifle communication, and turn friends and family away.

Manage anger

Strong emotions can get in the way of happiness and success. It is hard to concentrate on American History when you are raging over being cut off in traffic or can't let go of your anger with a friend. Psychologists report that angry outbursts may actually make things worse. When you feel yourself losing control, try some of these practical anger-management techniques.

- **Relax.** Breathe deeply. Slowly repeat a calming phrase or word like "Take it easy" or "Relax."
- **Change your environment.** Take a break from what's upsetting you. Go for a walk, go to the gym, see a movie. Come up with some creative ideas about what might calm you down.
- **Think before you speak.** When angry, most people tend to say the first thing that comes to mind, even if it's hurtful. Inevitably, this escalates the hard feelings and the intensity of the argument. Instead, wait to say something until you are in control.
- **Do your best to solve a problem,** but remember that not all problems can be solved. Instead of blowing up, think about how you can handle

what's happening. Analyze a challenging situation, make a plan, resolve to do your best, and begin. If you fall short, you will know you made an effort and be less likely to turn your frustration into anger.

- **Get help if you can't keep your anger in check.** If you consistently lash out, you may need the help of a counselor. Many schools have mental health professionals available to students.

Your ability to communicate and manage conflict has a major impact on your relationships with friends and family. Successful relationships are built on self-knowledge, good communication, and hard work.

How do you make the most of *personal relationships?*

Personal relationships with friends, classmates, spouses and partners, and parents can be sources of great satisfaction and inner peace. Good relationships can motivate you to do your best in school, on the job, and in life. When relationships fall apart, however, nothing may seem right. You may be unable to eat, sleep, or concentrate. Relationships have enormous power.

Use positive relationship strategies

Here are some strategies for improving personal relationships.

Make personal relationships a high priority. Life is meant to be shared. In some marriage ceremonies, the bride and groom share a cup of wine, symbolizing that the sweetness of life is doubled by tasting it together and the bitterness is cut in half when shared by two.

Invest time. You devote time to education, work, and sports. Relationships benefit from the same investment. In addition, spending time with people you like can relieve stress.

Spend time with people you respect and admire. Life is too short to hang out with people who bring you down or encourage you to ignore your values. "Try to nurture at least one friendship in each class," advises a Palo Alto College student. "If you know negative people who will try to discourage you and crush your spirit, avoid them. . . . You need nurturing and positivity."[12]

If you want a friend, be a friend. If you treat others with the kind of loyalty and support that you appreciate yourself, you are likely to receive the same in return.

Work through tensions. Negative feelings can fester when left unspoken. Get to the root of a problem by discussing it, compromising, forgiving, and moving on.

Take risks. It can be frightening to reveal your deepest dreams and frustrations, to devote yourself to a friend, or to fall in love. However, if you open yourself up, you stand to gain the incredible benefits of companionship, which for most people outweigh the risks.

Find a pattern that suits you. Some students date exclusively and commit early. Some students prefer to socialize in groups. Some students date casually. Be honest with yourself—and others—about what you want in a relationship.

If a relationship fails, find ways to cope. When an important relationship becomes strained or breaks up, analyze the situation and choose practical strategies to help you move on. Some people need time alone; others need to be with friends and family. Some seek counseling. Some throw their energy into school or exercise. Some cry. Whatever you do, believe that in time you will emerge from the experience stronger.

Avoid destructive relationships

On the far end of the spectrum are relationships that turn destructive. College campuses see their share of violent incidents. The more informed you are, the less likely you are to add to the sobering statistics.

Sexual harassment

Both men and women can be victims, although the most common targets are women. Sexual harassment basically consists of these two types:

- *Quid pro quo harassment* refers to a request for a sexual favor or activity in exchange for something else. "If you don't do X for me, I will fail you/fire you/make your life miserable."

- *Hostile environment harassment* indicates any situation where sexually charged remarks, behavior, or items cause discomfort. Examples include lewd jokes and pornography.

How to cope. If you feel degraded by anything that goes on at school or work, address the person whom you believe is harassing you, or speak to a dean or supervisor.

Violence in relationships

Statistics indicate that violent relationships among students are increasing.[13]

- One in five college students has experienced and reported at least one violent incident while dating, from being slapped to more serious violence.

- In three of four violent relationships, problems surface after the couple has dated for a while.

- In six of ten cases, drinking and drugs are associated with the violence.

Women in their teens and twenties are more likely to be victims of domestic violence than older women. Here's why: First, when trouble occurs, students are likely to turn to friends rather than counselors or the law. Second, peer pressure makes them uneasy about leaving the relationship. And finally, some inexperienced women may believe that the violence is normal.[14]

How to cope. Analyze your situation and use problem-solving skills to come up with options. If you see warning signs such as controlling behavior, unpredictable mood swings, personality changes associated with alcohol and drugs, and outbursts of anger, consider ending the relationship. If you are being abused, call a shelter or abuse hotline or seek counseling at school or at a community center. If you need medical attention, go to a clinic or hospital emergency room. If you believe that your life is in danger, get out and obtain a restraining order that requires your abuser to stay away from you.

Rape and date rape

Any intercourse or anal or oral penetration by a person against another person's will is defined as rape. Rape is primarily an act of rage and control, not a sexual act. Acquaintance rape, or date rape, refers to sexual activity during a date that is against one partner's will, including situations where one partner is too drunk or drugged to give consent. A drug called Rohypnol, known as roofies, is sometimes used by date rapists to sedate victims and is difficult to detect in a drink.

Campus Advocates for Rape Education (C.A.R.E.), an organization at Wheaton College, MA, describes date rape's particular damage. "One's trust in a friend, date, or acquaintance is violated . . . fear, self-blame, guilt, and shame are magnified because the assailant is known."[15]

DATE RAPE

Sexual assault perpetrated by the victim's escort during an arranged social encounter.

How to cope. Communicate—clearly and early—what you want and don't want to do. When on a date with someone who seems unstable or angry, stick to safe, public places. Keep a cell phone handy. Avoid alcohol or drugs that might make it difficult for you to stay in control.

If you are raped, whether by an acquaintance or a stranger, seek medical attention immediately. Next, talk to a close friend or counselor. Consider reporting the incident to the police or to campus officials. Whether or not you take legal action, continue to get help through counseling, a rape survivor group, or a hotline.

Choose communities that enhance your life

Personal relationships often take place within communities, or groups, that include people who share your interests—for example, sororities and fraternities, athletic clubs, and political groups. So much of what you accomplish in life is linked to your network of personal contacts.

If you affiliate with communities that are involved in positive activities, you are more likely to surround yourself with responsible and character-rich people who may become your friends and colleagues. You may find among them your future spouse or partner, your best friend, a person who helps you land a job, your doctor, accountant, real estate agent, and so on.

PERSONAL TRIUMPH

GUSTAVO MINAYA Student at Essex Community College, Baltimore, Maryland

Connecting with others can be difficult, especially if you start out feeling exceptionally different. Gustavo Minaya spoke no English when he came to the United States as a child. Through learning and getting involved in activities, he has found his niche. Read the account, then use a separate piece of paper to answer the questions on page 287.

I am a native of Peru. When I was six years old, my mother told me that we were going to America for a better life. My father was already living in the United States so my mother went to the embassy to apply for a visa, but our visa was denied. In desperation, she decided to hire "coyotes." These are people who know secret routes to the United States. Their job was to help us cross the border.

Our journey began at night with cold train rides. At different points, we stopped to eat or to get on a different train. Along the way other families joined us. At the Mexico–Texas border, the coyotes instructed us to walk under a highway. Once we were out again in the open, everyone began running for the U. S. border. Helicopters were circling overhead with their search lights on, and people were shouting. It was pandemonium.

Exhausted, we made it across the border and into a van, where people were stacked on top of each other. At another border check, my mother and I were arrested and taken into custody by immigration officers who took our fingerprints. They arranged to have us transported to an emergency shelter run by the American Red Cross. Meanwhile, my dad completed the paperwork for legal immigration, and we joined him a few months later.

Of course, I didn't know English. When I started school in the second grade I looked different from the other kids, and I sounded different because of my accent. Some of the kids picked on me. I cried a lot back then. The next year I took English as a Second Language (ESL) classes. Gradually, I learned English and began to feel like I fit in.

When I look back over my experiences, I believe the one thing that has helped me adjust to the changes is friendliness. I like to make people laugh, and I go into things with a positive attitude. Being friendly with other students, and people in general, has helped me gain a sense of belonging.

My main advice to international students who want to make the most of their education is to participate in campus activities. You can join a club or work on campus, maybe at the school store or library. This way you meet new people, and you'll learn English faster. You can't fit in if you isolate yourself.

Participation is also important for developing leadership skills. I look at clubs and other campus activities as opportunities to enhance my education. For example, I joined the International Student Association (ISA) and am now the president. During the meetings, I give my ideas and show my support by volunteering for projects. I've discovered that one of my strengths is bringing people together for a good cause.

I'm very proud of my parents for how hard they worked to make a better life for me and my brothers and sisters. In my native country of Peru, you can work as hard as you want, but it gets you nowhere. Some of the smartest people there are taxicab drivers because they can't find jobs doing anything else. Here, if you are willing to work, you can have a profession and achieve what you want. I plan to achieve as much as I can.

Finding and working with a community of people with similar interests can have positive effects in personal relationships and in workplace readiness, as Eastern Kentucky University student Kasey Doyle explains:

During my sophomore year, a friend persuaded me to join a service sorority on campus. I was hesitant at first, but once I began to get involved, I realized that I had missed out on many opportunities. Not only have I made many friends, I have also become more outgoing and personable. . . . I found a place where I fit in.

Joining this organization also prepared me for my major and my job at [the campus newspaper] The Progress.

As a reporter, you are expected to be outgoing and personable, and before joining an organization, I was extremely shy. I'm definitely not timid anymore, and I have matured and become more self-confident.[16]

If you find yourself drawn toward communities that encourage negative and even harmful behavior, such as gangs or groups that haze pledges, stop and think. Analyze why you are drawn to these groups. Resist the temptation to join. If you are already involved and want out, stand up for yourself and be determined.

Kente

The African word *kente* means "that which will not tear under any condition." Kente cloth is worn by men and women in African countries such as Ghana, Ivory Coast, and Togo. There are many brightly colored patterns of kente, each beautiful, unique, and special.

Think of how this concept applies to people. Like the cloth, all people are unique, with brilliant and subdued aspects. Despite mistreatment or misunderstanding by others, you need to remain strong so that you don't tear, allowing the weaker fibers of your character to show through. The kente of your character can help you endure, stand up against injustice, and fight peacefully, but relentlessly, for the rights of all people.

Developing Successful Intelligence

PUTTING IT ALL TOGETHER

Learn from the experiences of others. Look back to Gustavo Minaya's Personal Triumph on page 285. After you've read his story, relate his experience to your own life by completing the following:

Step 1. Think it through: *Analyze your experience and compare it to Gustavo's.* When in your life have you felt like an outsider, and how does this relate to Gustavo's experience? What was his key to finding his place in his new world? What was yours?

Step 2. Think out of the box: *Create a challenge.* Think about the activities and organizations at your school with which you would most feel "at home." Then imagine that none of those are available—and that you are required to get involved with three organizations or activities that you would never naturally choose. How would you challenge yourself? Name the three choices and describe what you think you could gain from your experiences. Consider trying one—for real!

Step 3. Make it happen: *Use practical strategies to connect with others.* Choose one of those organizations or activities that feel natural to you. Then choose one from your list of those that would be your challenges. Now try them both. Contact a person involved with each organization or activity and ask them for details—when the group meets, what they do, what the time commitment would likely be, what the benefit would be. Then join both in the coming semester, making an effort to get to know others who are involved.

create your future

Writing

Record your thoughts on a separate piece of paper or in a journal.

Opening your mind. On what topic is it most difficult for you to be accepting? Describe your difficulty with race, culture, ethnic origin, weight, gender, sexual orientation, or any other human characteristic. What do you think is the source of your uneasiness—parents, peers, experience, any other source? Describe what you can do now to think more openly, and think about why it may help you to combat your prejudices.

Team Building

Problem solving close to home. Divide into groups of two to five students. Assign one group member to take notes. Discuss the following questions, one at a time:

1. What are the three largest problems the world faces with regard to how people get along with and accept others?

2. What could we do to deal with these three problems?

3. What can each individual student do to make improvements? (Talk about what you specifically feel that you can do.)

When all groups have finished, gather as a class and hear each group's responses. Observe the variety of problems and solutions. Notice whether more than one group came up with one or more of the same problems. If there is time, one person in the class, together with your instructor, could gather the responses to question 3 into an organized document that you can send to your school or local paper.

Career Portfolio

Complete the following in your electronic portfolio or on separate sheets of paper.

Compiling a résumé. What you have accomplished in various work and school situations will be important for you to emphasize as you strive to land a job that is right for you. Your roles—on the job, in school, at home, or in the community—help you gain knowledge and experience.

On one electronic page or sheet of paper, list your education and skills information. On the other, list job experience. For each job, record job title, the dates of employment, and the tasks that this job entailed (if the job had no particular title, come up with one yourself). Be as detailed as possible—it's best to write down everything you remember. When you

Désirée Williams

237 Custer Street, San Francisco, CA 94101 • 650/555-5252 (w) or 415/555-7865 (h) • fax: 707/555-2735 • e-mail: desiree@zzz.com

EDUCATION

2001 to present

San Francisco State University, San Francisco, CA

Pursuing a B.A. in the Spanish BCLAD (Bilingual, Cross-Cultural Language Acquisition Development) Education and Multiple Subject Credential Program. Expected graduation: June, 2005

PROFESSIONAL EMPLOYMENT

10/02 to present

Research Assistant, Knowledge Media Lab

Developing ways for teachers to exhibit their inquiry into their practice of teaching in an on-line, collaborative, multimedia environment.

5/01 to present

Webmaster/Web Designer

Work in various capacities at QuakeNet, an Internet Service Provider and Web Commerce Specialist in San Mateo, CA. Designed several sites for the University of California, Berkeley, Graduate School of Education, as well as private clients such as A Body of Work and Yoga Forever.

9/01 to 6/02

Literacy Coordinator

Coordinated, advised, and created literacy curriculum for an America Reads literacy project at Prescott School in West Oakland. Worked with non-reader 4th graders on writing and publishing, incorporating digital photography, Internet resources, and graphic design.

8/01

Bilingual Educational Consultant

Consulted for Children's Television Workshop, field-testing bilingual materials. With a research team, designed bilingual educational materials for an ecotourism project run by an indigenous rain forest community in Ecuador.

1/01 to 6/01

Technology Consultant

Worked with 24 Hours in Cyberspace, an on-line worldwide photojournalism event. Coordinated participation of schools, translated documents, and facilitated public relations.

SKILLS

Languages:

Fluent in Spanish.

Proficient in Italian and Shona (majority language of Zimbabwe).

Computer:

Programming ability in HTML, Javascript, Pascal, and Lisp. Multimedia design expertise in Adobe Photoshop, Netobjects Fusion, Adobe Premiere, Macromedia Flash, and many other visual design programs.

Personal:

Perform professionally in Mary Schmary, a women's a cappella quartet. Have climbed Mt. Kilimanjaro.

compile your résumé, you can make this material more concise. Keep this list current by adding experiences and accomplishments as you go along.

Using the information you have gathered and Key 9.6 as your guide, draft a résumé for yourself. Remember that there are many ways to construct a résumé; consult other resources, such as those listed in the bibliography, for different styles. You may want to reformat your résumé according to a style that your career counselor or instructor recommends, that best suits the career area you plan to enter, or that you like best.

Keep your résumé draft on hand—and on a computer disk. When you need to submit a résumé with a job application, update the draft and print it out on high-quality paper.

Here are some general tips for writing a résumé:

- Always put your name and contact information at the top. Make it stand out.

- State an objective if it is appropriate—if your focus is specific or you are designing this résumé for a particular interview or career area.

- List your post-secondary education, starting from the latest and working backward. This may include summer school, night school, seminars, and accreditations.

- List jobs in reverse chronological order (most recent job first). Include all types of work experience (full-time, part-time, volunteer, internship, and so on).

- When you describe your work experience, use action verbs and focus on what you have accomplished, rather than on the description of assigned tasks.

- Include keywords that are linked to the description of the jobs for which you will be applying (see page 229 for more on keywords).

- List references on a separate sheet. You may want to put "References upon request" at the bottom of your résumé.

- Use formatting (larger font sizes, different fonts, italics, bold, and so on) and indents selectively to help the important information stand out.

- Get several people to look at your résumé before you send it out. Other readers will have ideas that you haven't thought of and may find errors that you have missed.

SUGGESTED READINGS

Dublin, Thomas, ed. *Becoming American, Becoming Ethnic: College Students Explore Their Roots.* Philadelphia: Temple University Press, 1996.

Feagin, Joe R., Hernan Vera, and Nikitah O. Imani. *The Agony of Education: Black Students at White Colleges and Universities.* New York: Routledge, 1996.

Gonzales, Juan L., Jr. *The Lives of Ethnic Americans*, 2nd ed. Dubuque, IA: Kendall/Hunt, 1994.

Hockenberry, John. *Moving Violations.* New York: Hyperion, 1996.

Levey, Marc, Michael Blanco, and W. Terrell Jones. *How to Succeed on a Majority Campus: A Guide for Minority Students.* Belmont, CA: Wadsworth Publishing Co., 1997.

Qubein, Nido R. *How to Be a Great Communicator: In Person, on Paper, and at the Podium.* New York: John Wiley & Sons, 1996.

Schuman, David. *Diversity on Campus.* Dubuque, IA: Kendall/Hunt, 2001.

Suskind, Ron. *A Hope in the Unseen: An American Odyssey from the Inner City to the Ivy League.* New York: Broadway Books, 1999.

Takaki, Ronald. *A Different Mirror: A History of Multicultural America.* Boston: Little, Brown & Company, 1994.

Tannen, Deborah. *You Just Don't Understand: Women and Men in Conversation.* New York: Perennial Currents, 2001.

Tatum, Beverly Daniel. *"Why Are All the Black Kids Sitting Together in the Cafeteria?" and Other*

Conversations About Race: A Psychologist Explains the Development of Racial Identity. Philadelphia: Basic Books, 2003.

Terkel, Studs. *Race: How Blacks and Whites Think and Feel About the American Obsession.* New York: Free Press, 1995.

Trotter, Tamera and Joycelyn Allen. *Talking Justice: 602 Ways to Build and Promote Racial Harmony.* Saratoga, FL: R & E Publishers, 1993.

INTERNET RESOURCES

Prentice Hall Student Success Supersite (success stories from students from a diversity of backgrounds): www.prenhall.com/success

Asian-American Resources: www.ar.mit.edu/people/irie/aar/

Britannica Guide to Black History: http://blackhistory.eb.com

Latino USA: www.latinousa.org

The Sociology of Race and Ethnicity (with multiple links to other resources): www.trinity.edu/~mkear/race.html

ENDNOTES

1. "For 7 Million, One Census Race Category Wasn't Enough," *New York Times*, March 13, 2001, pp. A1 and A14.

2. "Conceptual Frameworks/Models, Guiding Values and Principles," National Center for Cultural Competence, 2002 [on-line]. Available: http://gucchd.georgetown.edu//nccc/framework.html (May 2004).

3. Information in the sections on the five stages of building competency is based on Mark A. King, Anthony Sims, and David Osher, "How Is Cultural Competence Integrated in Education?" Cultural Competence [on-line]. Available: www.air.org/cecp/cultural/Q_integrated.htm#def (May 2004).

4. FBI Hate Crime statistics, from a grid created by the Anti-Defamation League, 2001 [on-line]. Available: www.adl.org/combating_hate/ (May 2004).

5. Jen Lin-Liu, "China's 'Harvard Girl': A College Student Has Become an Example for a New Style of Raising Children," *The Chronicle of Higher Education*, May 30, 2003 [on-line]. Available: http://chronicle.com/weekly/v49/i38/38a04001.htm (March 2004).

6. Martin Luther King Jr., from his sermon "A Tough Mind and a Tender Heart," *Strength in Love*. Philadelphia: Fortress Press, 1986, p. 14.

7. Sheryl McCarthy, *Why Are the Heroes Always White?* Kansas City, MO: Andrews and McMeel, 1995, p. 137.

8. Doug Gavel, "Students Speak Out at Hate Crime Forum," *Harvard University Gazette*, www.news.harvard.edu/gazette/2001/02.15/01-hatecrime.html.

9. Paul Barrett Jr., "Solutions Offered to Address Racism On Campus," *Earlham Word Online*, Volume XIII, Issue 11, November 20, 1998. Available: http://word.cs.earlham.edu/issues/XIII/112098/opin91.html (November 2004).

10. Media Watch, *Diversity Web*, Fall 1997. Available: www.diversityweb.org/Digest/F97/mediawatch.html#top (November 2004).

11. Information for this section from Philip R. Harris and Robert T. Moran. *Managing Cultural Differences*, 3rd ed. Houston, TX: Gulf Publishing Company, 1991 and Lennie Copeland and Lewis Griggs, *Going International: How to Make Friends and Deal Effectively in the Global Marketplace.* New York: Random House, 1985.

12. Student essay submitted by the First Year Experience students of Patty Parma, Palo Alto College, San Antonio, Texas, January 2004.

13. Tina Kelley, "On Campuses, Warnings About Violence in Relationships," *New York Times*, February 13, 2000, p. 40.

14. Ibid.

15. U.S. Department of Justice, Bureau of Justice Statistics, "Sex Offenses and Offenders," 1997, and "Criminal Victimization," 1994.

16. Kasey Doyle, "Getting Involved on Campus Important," *The Eastern Progress*, November 4, 2004 [on-line]. Available: www.easternprogress.com/news/2004/11/04/Perspective/Getting.Involved.On.Campus.Important-792180.shtml.

10

IN THIS CHAPTER . . .

*you will explore answers
to the following questions:*

Personal Wellness
TAKING CARE OF YOURSELF

Focusing on personal wellness means targeting preventative actions you can take to stay healthy. Most likely, you have learned from personal experience that how well you do in school is directly related to your physical and mental health. Among the most important wellness strategies are those that deal with stress management. This chapter expands on the coverage of stress in Chapter 2 as it examines ways to manage stress through health maintenance and presents ideas for how to handle stress-related health issues.

Your personal wellness also depends on your decisions about drugs, alcohol, tobacco, and sex. Nearly every college student faces important choices on these issues. Your goal is to make decisions that are in your best interest and that keep you healthy.

Approach all the topics in this chapter with successful intelligence. Analyze your situations and choices, brainstorm creative options, and take practical actions that work for you.

On the following page, read how student Randy Ust is wondering how to manage the stress he feels about making friends and finding a place in the college community.

● **How can you maintain a healthy body and mind?**

● **How can you make successfully intelligent decisions about alcohol, tobacco, and drugs?**

● **How can you make successfully intelligent decisions about sex?**

How can I fit in at college?

I started high school with my best friend since seventh grade, and our big plan was to star on the freshman basketball team. The after-school workouts paid off, and when we made the final cuts, we envisioned future NBA contracts. We started our sophomore year with the same dreams, ready for the next step toward stardom. After weeks of conditioning sessions, we felt like invincible heroes.

Our mortality hit me when in October of that year my friend went into cardiac arrest and passed away. For a while I isolated myself and didn't let friends get close, fearing that they, too, would leave me. After more than two years, I've opened up to people again, and my two best friends and I are like brothers. Now that we've graduated, though, the fear is back. It scares me to think that when we get to new places in life, we could grow apart. I know I will soon be in a new place meeting new friends. How do I adapt to the stress of being away from old friends and fitting into my college community?

Randy Ust
University of Mary, Bismarck, North Dakota

Get involved . . . broaden your horizons and talk to people.

Weeks before students move into their new residence hall rooms, a group of individuals (the Resident Advisors, or RAs) gather for comprehensive training. I am an RA. In training, we learn how to deal with any situation that may arise in the residence halls: fire alarms, alcohol and drug situations, roommate conflicts, and most important, making college feel like home for the residents. One of my first duties as an RA is to hold a floor meeting where I meet my residents, and they meet each other. I share with them these tips to help them reduce the stress of being in a new situation.

The most important thing I tell them is to get involved. Most colleges have hundreds of clubs and sports that anyone can join. Look for the clubs that interest you most. Playing a sport, whether at the intramural, club, or collegiate level, helps you meet people and get active. Try a couple of different things to see what you like most, but try not to overload yourself with activities and let your studies slack.

Another way to begin to fit in is to reach out to the people with whom you live. Keep your room doors open, go to planned activities together, and be friendly—others will be friendly back! You can also meet great people on campus. Talk to people while you are in line at the cafeteria, get to know your chemistry lab partners, sit next to someone new in the student union and introduce yourself. Broaden your horizons and talk to people different from yourself.

There are new things all around you in college—give them a try. Remember that your old friends are no more than a mouse click or a phone call away. They'll be there for you any time of the day—or night! Make sure you all make the effort to continue to be friends—it'll pay off. Finally, you can always ask your RA or other older students for advice. They will help you find ways to reduce stress and to feel a part of your new community, while you still keep in touch with friends from home.

Tracy Ust St. Cloud State University, St. Cloud, Minnesota

How can you maintain a healthy *body and mind?*

The healthier you are, the more you'll be able to reach your potential. Make your physical health a priority by eating right, exercising, getting enough sleep, reviewing your vaccinations, and taking steps to stay safe. Make your mental health a priority by recognizing mental health problems, related to stress or other causes, and understanding ways to get help.

Eat right

Making healthier choices about what you eat can lead to more energy, better general health, and an improved quality of life. Medical and nutritional experts in the federal government publish *Dietary Guidelines for Americans,* which lists seven practical, basic rules of healthy eating:

1. Eat a variety of foods.
2. Maintain a healthy weight.
3. Choose a diet low in fat and cholesterol.
4. Choose a diet with plenty of vegetables, fruits, and grain products.
5. Use sugars in moderation.
6. Use salt and sodium only in moderation.
7. If you drink alcoholic beverages, do so in moderation.

You can sum up this list with two words: *balance* and *moderation.* For balance, try to vary your diet by targeting different food groups—meats, fish, poultry, and other protein sources; dairy; breads and grains; and fruits and vegetables. For moderation, eat reasonable amounts. Just because you are served a supersized portion doesn't mean you have to eat it all. Decide how much food is enough and stop when you are full.

Take steps to avoid obesity

Obesity is a serious problem in the United States.[1] Government statistics indicate how widespread obesity is:[2]

- The overweight and the obese make up the majority of the population, with 61 percent of women and 67 percent of men currently falling into these two groups.[3]
- Between 1960 and 2000, the number of obese people in the United States more than doubled, to 30 percent of Americans now considered obese.

Obesity is a major risk factor in the development of adult-onset diabetes, coronary heart disease, high blood pressure, stroke, cancer, and other illnesses. In fact, after smoking, obesity is the second leading cause of preventable death. In addition, obese people often suffer social and employment discrimination and may find daily life difficult.

College life can make it tough to eat right. Students spend hours sitting in class or studying and tend to eat on the run, build social events around food, and eat as a reaction to stress. Many new students find

> **OBESE**
> Having excessive body fat in relation to lean body mass.

> **OVERWEIGHT**
> Having increased body weight in relation to height, whereby the weight can come from either fat or muscle mass.

that the "freshman 15"—referring to 15 pounds that people say freshmen tend to gain in the first year of school—is much more than a myth.

These practical tips will help you pay attention to how you eat, and make changes when you need to, so that you can lose weight or avoid gaining.

Target your ideal weight. Your college health clinic has charts of ideal weight ranges for men and women with different body builds and heights. You can also find this information on Internet sites such as the Centers for Disease Control, which has a calculator for body mass index (BMI) at www.cdc.gov/nccdphp/dnpa/bmi/calc-bmi.htm.

Make small but effective changes. Pledge to stop drinking sugar-filled soda and to give up fried foods. Record your goals on paper so they become real.

Reduce portion size. A serving of cooked pasta is about one-half cup, for example, and cheese about 1.2 ounces. At restaurants, ask for a half portion or take home what you don't finish.

Make smart choices. Avoid high-fat, high-sugar foods. If you eat out, order a low-fat and balanced meal and limit your portions. Choose snacks with fewer than 200 calories such as a frozen fruit juice bar or a container of low-fat fruit yogurt.

Plan your meals. Try to eat at regular times and in a regular location. Attempt to minimize late-night eating sprees during study sessions. Avoid skipping meals since it may make you more likely to overeat later.

Identify "emotional triggers" for your eating. If you eat to relieve stress or handle disappointment, try substituting a positive activity. If you are upset about a course, spend more time studying, talk with your instructor, or write in your journal.

Get help. If you need to lose weight, find a support group, such as Weight Watchers or an on-campus organization, that can help you stay on target.

Set reasonable goals. Losing weight and keeping it off take time and patience. Start by aiming to lose 5 to 10 percent of your current weight; for example, if you weigh 200 pounds, your weight-loss goal is 10 to 20 pounds. Work toward your goal at a pace of approximately 1 to 2 pounds a week. When you reach it, set a new goal if you need to lose more, or begin a maintenance program.

Exercise

Being physically fit enhances your general health, increases your energy, and helps you cope with stress. During physical activity, the brain releases endorphins, chemical compounds that have a positive and calming effect on the body.

College athletes use daily exercise as a stress reliever. Larisa Kindell, a senior and co-captain of Wesleyan University's swimming team, credits her athletic routine with helping her balance her life. "If I didn't have swimming, a place to release my academic stress, I don't think I'd be as effective in the classroom or studying at night," she said. Swimming has taught her "discipline, time management, and motivation" and has contributed to her academic success.[4]

Always check with a physician before beginning an exercise program, and adjust your program to your physical needs and fitness level. If you don't currently exercise, walking daily is a good way to begin. If you exercise frequently and are already in good shape, you may prefer an intense workout.

Types of exercise

There are three general categories of exercises. The type you choose depends on your exercise goals, available equipment, your time and fitness level, and other factors.

Finding a physical activity you enjoy will improve the health of both your body and your mind. This brother-and-sister team suits up for a college fencing competition.

- *Cardiovascular training* strengthens your heart and lung capacity. Examples include running, swimming, in-line skating, aerobic dancing, and biking.

- *Strength training* strengthens different muscle groups. Examples include using weight machines and free weights and doing push-ups and abdominal crunches.

- *Flexibility training* increases muscle flexibility. Examples include stretching and yoga.

Some exercises, such as lifting weights or biking, fall primarily into one category. Others, like power yoga, combine elements of two or all three. For maximum benefit, try alternating exercise methods through cross-training. For example, if you lift weights, use a stationary bike for cardiovascular work and build stretching into your workout.

CROSS-TRAINING
Alternating types of exercise and combining elements from different types of exercise.

Making exercise a priority

Busy students often have trouble getting to the gym, even when there is a fully equipped athletic center on campus. Use these ideas to help make exercise a priority, even in the busiest weeks:

- Walk to classes and meetings. When you reach your building, use the stairs.

- Use your school's fitness facilities.

- Play team recreational sports at school or in your community.

- Use home exercise equipment such as weights, a treadmill, or an elliptical trainer.

- Find activities you can do outside of a club, such as running or pick-up basketball.

- Work out with friends or family to combine socializing and exercise.

Get enough sleep

College students are infamous for being sleep deprived. While research indicates that students need eight to nine hours of sleep a night to function well, recent studies show that students average six to seven hours—and often get much less.[5]

During sleep your body repairs itself while your mind sorts through problems and questions. Inadequate sleep hinders your ability to concentrate, raises stress levels, increases irritability, and makes you more susceptible to illness. It can also have more serious effects such as an increased risk of auto accidents. According to Dr. Tracy Kuo, a clinical psychologist at the Stanford Sleep Disorders Clinic, "A sleepy driver is just as dangerous as a drunk driver."[6]

Students, overwhelmed with responsibilities, often feel that they have no choice but to prioritize schoolwork over sleep. Michelle Feldman, a sophomore at Syracuse University, stays up regularly until 4:00 A.M. getting her reading and studying done. Fellow Syracuse student Brian Nelson, a junior aiming to complete a triple major, only manages two hours a night as he works to keep up with the 24 credits he's taking in one semester.[7]

> The groundwork of all happiness is health.
>
> **LEIGH HUNT**

For the sake of both your health and your GPA, find a way to get the sleep you need. Gauge your needs by first analyzing how you feel. If you are groggy in the morning, doze off during the day, or regularly need caffeine to make it through your classes, you may be sleep deprived. Sleep expert Gregg D. Jacobs, Ph.D., recommends the following practical suggestions for improving sleep habits:[8]

- **Reduce consumption of alcohol and caffeine.** Caffeine may keep you awake, especially if you drink it late in the day. Alcohol causes you to sleep lightly, making you feel less rested when you awaken.
- **Exercise regularly.** Regular exercise, especially in the afternoon or early evening, promotes sleep.
- **Take naps.** Studies have shown that taking short afternoon naps can reduce the effects of sleep deprivation.
- **Be consistent.** Try to establish somewhat regular times to wake up and go to bed.
- **Complete tasks an hour or so before sleep.** Give yourself a chance to wind down.
- **Establish a comfortable sleeping environment.** Wear something comfortable, turn down the lights and noise, find a blanket and pillow that you like, and keep the room cool. Use earplugs, soft music, or a white noise machine if you're dealing with outside distractions.

Review your immunizations

Immunizations are not just for kids. Adults often need them to prevent diseases in particular circumstances or because they didn't receive a full course of shots as children. Following is immunization information that may prevent major illness or literally save your life. If you think you need these vaccines, check with your doctor or the college health service:

- Many colleges recommend that freshmen receive the *meningococcal meningitis vaccine* to prevent the spread of bacteria that can lead to permanent, serious disability and even death. Meningococcal bacteria are spread through direct contact (such as sharing a glass) or indirect contact (such as sneezing) with infected individuals. Outbreaks are linked to close living situations common in college.

- A *tetanus booster* is recommended every 10 years to protect you from bacterial infections related to certain wounds.

- Three shots to prevent *hepatitis B* are recommended in childhood. Vaccinations are advised in college if you have not been immunized. Homosexuals and intravenous drug users are at increased risk.

- The *chicken pox vaccine* is recommended for any adult who did not have this illness as a child and who risks exposure. Chicken pox can be severe in adults.

- Although it used to be given only to adults who are over 65 or who have weak immune systems, the *influenza* vaccine is now recommended for many adults. It is available each fall from around mid-October through the end of November.

- The *measles-mumps-rubella (MMR)* vaccine is recommended for unvaccinated adults born after 1956 as well as adults who received vaccinations between 1963 and 1967.

A common illness, not protected by immunization, is mononucleosis. "Mono" is caused by a virus passed in saliva and is related to kissing and sharing drinking cups. Major symptoms, which can last for a few days or a few months, are fever, sore throat, swollen lymph glands, and fatigue. The only treatment is rest, fluids, and a balanced diet. Protect yourself by being careful in your relationships with friends, family, and roommates.

Stay safe

Staying safe is another part of staying well. Take these practical measures to prevent incidents that jeopardize your well-being.

Avoid situations that present clear dangers. Don't walk or exercise alone at night, especially in isolated areas. Don't work or study alone in a building. If a person looks suspicious, contact someone who can help.

Avoid drugs or overuse of alcohol. Anything that impairs judgment makes you vulnerable to assault. Avoid driving while impaired or riding with someone who has taken drugs or alcohol.

Avoid people who make you uneasy. If a fellow student gives you bad feelings, avoid situations that place you alone together. Speak to an instructor if you feel threatened.

It is not enough to have a healthy body. Your well-being also depends on a healthy mind.

get practical!

IMPROVE YOUR PHYSICAL HEALTH

Make a change in how you eat, exercise, or sleep.

First, decide what you most need to change. What's most important to your health right now—to eat better, exercise more, or get more sleep? Name it: _____

    Now, considering your individual situation and looking at the strategies in this chapter, list five practical actions you can take right away to improve in this area. Word them as action statements. *Examples:* "I will leave earlier so that I can walk to my first class." "I will stop keeping candy bars in my room." "I will take a nap whenever I'm dragging in the afternoon."

1. _____

2. _____

3. _____

4. _____

5. _____

The final step: Just do it!

Recognize mental health problems

With life's ups and downs, no one is happy all the time. However, you can target positive mental health by finding ways to feel good about who you are and what you are doing right now, to have hope for the future, and to build the resilience to cope with life's setbacks.

    College students who feel overwhelmed by stress are susceptible to developing mental health problems or to having existing problems grow worse. Use the following information to analyze your situation and, if necessary, to take practical steps to improve your health.

Depression

Almost everyone has experienced sadness after the death of a friend or relative, the end of a relationship, or a setback such as failing a course. However, as many as 10 percent of Americans will experience a major depression, going beyond temporary blues, at some point in their lives. A depressive disorder is an illness, not a sign of weakness or a mental state that can be escaped by trying to "snap out of it." This illness requires a medical evaluation and is treatable.

    A depressive disorder is "a 'whole-body' illness, involving your body, mood, and thoughts."[9] Among the symptoms of depression are the following:

- feeling constantly sad, worried, or anxious
- difficulty with decisions or concentration
- no interest in classes, people, or activities
- frequent crying
- hopeless feelings and thoughts of suicide
- constant fatigue
- sleeping too much or too little

- low self-esteem
- eating too much or too little
- physical aches and pains
- low motivation

Depression can have a genetic, psychological, physiological, or environmental cause, or a combination. Key 10.1 describes these causes along with strategies for fighting depression.

If you recognize any of these feelings in yourself, seek help. Start with your school's counseling office or student health service, which may also post information on the school Web site. You may be referred to a specialist who will help you sort through your symptoms and determine treatment. For some people, adequate sleep, a regular exercise program, a healthy diet, and the passage of time are enough to lessen stress and ease the disorder. For others, medication is important. If you are diagnosed with depression, know that your condition is common, even among college students. Be proud that you have taken a step toward recovery.

At its worst, depression can lead to suicide. SA\VE (Suicide Awareness\Voices of Education) lists these suicide warning signs:[10]

- Statements about hopelessness or worthlessness: "The world would be better off without me."
- Loss of interest in people, things, or activities.
- Preoccupation with suicide or death.
- Making final arrangements such as visiting or calling family and friends and giving things away.
- Sudden sense of happiness or calm. (A decision to commit suicide often brings a sense of relief that convinces others that the person "seemed to be on an upswing.")

What causes depression and what can help.

POSSIBLE CAUSES OF DEPRESSION	HELPFUL STRATEGIES IF YOU FEEL DEPRESSED
A genetic trait that makes depression more likely	Do the best you can and don't have unreasonable expectations of yourself.
A chemical imbalance in the brain	Try to be with others rather than alone.
Seasonal Affective Disorder, which occurs when a person becomes depressed in reaction to reduced daylight during autumn and winter	Don't expect your mood to change right away; feeling better takes time.
Highly stressful situations such as financial trouble, school failure, a death in the family	Try to avoid making major life decisions until your condition improves.
Illnesses, injuries, lack of exercise, poor diet, reaction to medication	Remember not to blame yourself for your condition.

Source: National Institutes of Health Publication No. 94-3561, National Institutes of Health, 1994.

Stress Management

Everyone handles stress differently—the strategies linked to your stronger intelligences help you improve your coping skills

INTELLIGENCE	SUGGESTED STRATEGIES	WHAT WORKS FOR YOU? WRITE NEW IDEAS HERE
Verbal–Linguistic	• Keep a journal of what makes you stressed. • Make time to write letters or e-mail friends or talk with them.	
Logical–Mathematical	• Think through problems critically using a problem-solving process and devise a plan. • Analyze possible positive effects that may result from the stress.	
Bodily–Kinesthetic	• Choose a physical activity that helps you release tension—running, yoga, team sports—and do it regularly. • Plan fun physical activities for your free time—go for a hike, take a bike ride, go dancing with friends.	
Visual–Spatial	• Take as much time as you can to enjoy beautiful things—art, nature, etc. Visit an exhibit, see an art film, shoot a roll of film with your camera. • Use a visual organizer to plan out a solution to a stressful problem.	
Interpersonal	• Spend time with people who care about you and are very supportive. • Practice being a good listener to others who are stressed.	
Intrapersonal	• Schedule down time when you can think through what is stressing you. • Allow yourself five minutes a day for visualizing a positive way in which you want a stressful situation to evolve.	
Musical	• Play music that "feeds your soul." • Write a song about what stresses you out—or about anything that transports your mind.	
Naturalistic	• Spend as much time as possible in your most soothing places in nature. • Listen to tapes of outdoor sounds to help you relax.	

If you recognize these symptoms in someone you know, begin talking with the person about his or her feelings. Then do everything you can to convince the individual to see a doctor or mental health professional. Don't keep your concerns a secret; sound an alarm that may save a life. If you recognize these symptoms in yourself, know that you can find help if you reach out.

Eating disorders

Millions of people develop serious and sometimes life-threatening eating disorders every year, including anorexia nervosa, bulimia, and binge eating. Because these disorders are common on college campuses, student health and counseling centers generally offer medical and psychological help, including referrals to trained specialists.

One ceases to recognize the significance of mountain peaks if they are not viewed occasionally from the deepest valleys.

DR. AL LORIN

Anorexia nervosa. People with anorexia become dangerously thin through restricted food intake, constant exercise, and use of laxatives, all the time believing they are overweight. An estimated 5 to 7 percent of college undergraduates, most of whom are women, suffer from anorexia.[11] The desire to emulate an "ideal" body type is one cause of the disease. In addition, eating disorders tend to run in families. Effects of anorexia-induced starvation include loss of menstrual periods in women, impotence in men, organ and bone damage, heart failure, and death.

Bulimia. People who binge on excessive amounts of food, usually sweets and fattening foods, and then purge through self-induced vomiting have bulimia. They may also use laxatives or exercise obsessively. Bulimia can be hard to notice because bulimics are often able to maintain a normal appearance. The causes of bulimia, like those of anorexia, can be rooted in a desire to fulfill a body-type ideal or can come from a chemical imbalance. Bulimics often suffer from depression or other psychiatric illnesses. Effects of bulimia include damage to the digestive tract and even heart failure due to the loss of important minerals.

Binge eating. Like bulimics, people with binge eating disorder eat large amounts of food and have a hard time stopping. However, they do not purge afterward. Binge eaters are often overweight and feel that they cannot control their eating. As with bulimia, depression and other psychiatric illnesses may contribute to the problem. Binge eaters may suffer from all of the health problems associated with obesity.

The stresses of college lead some students to experiment with alcohol, tobacco, and other potentially addictive substances. Although these substances may be quick, temporary fixes that alleviate stress, they have potentially serious consequences that can do long-term damage.

How can you make successfully *intelligent decisions* about alcohol, tobacco, and drugs?

Abusing alcohol, tobacco, and drugs can cause financial struggles, emotional traumas, family and financial upheaval, health problems, and even death. As you read, think about the effects of your actions on yourself and others, and consider how to make positive, life-affirming choices.

Alcohol

Alcohol is a depressant that slows vital body functions and is the most frequently abused drug on campus. Even a few drinks affect thinking and muscle coordination. Heavy drinking can damage the liver, the digestive system, and brain cells and can impair the central nervous system. Prolonged use also leads to addiction, making it seem impossible to quit. In addition, alcohol contributes to the deaths of 100,000 people every year through both alcohol-related illnesses and accidents involving drunk drivers.[12]

ADDICTION
Compulsive physiological need for a habit-forming substance.

The National Institute on Alcohol Abuse and Alcoholism (NIAAA) offers these statistics about college students and alcohol:[13]

- Nearly nine out of ten students have used alcohol.

- Among heavy drinkers, there is an increased incidence of sexual assault and unwanted sexual advances as a result of drinking.

- Drinking with a group and serving one's own drinks may contribute to greater alcohol consumption. Both situations are common at large gatherings such as fraternity parties.

BINGE DRINKING

Having five or more drinks at one sitting.

Of all alcohol consumption, binge drinking is associated with the greatest problems. Here are statistics from a recent survey:[14]

- Forty-three percent of the students surveyed labeled themselves as binge drinkers, and 21 percent said that they binge drink frequently.

- Eight out of ten of the students who do not binge drink reported experiencing such "secondhand effects" as vandalism, sexual assault or unwanted sexual advances, or interrupted sleep or study.[15]

- Students who binge drink are more likely to miss classes, be less able to work, have hangovers, become depressed, and engage in unplanned or unsafe sexual activity.[16]

From what Darra Clark, a freshman at a large university in the Southwest, has seen, it is not possible to be a successful student if you drink too much. You can't do well in school and have friends if you "get drunk and stoned out of your gourd every night," she explains. "I think that the whole drinking scene is probably the thing I've found most appalling about college (our student handbook specifically outlaws beer funnels, for example). The problem, of course, is that drinking becomes a really hard behavior to regulate. . . . Drinking and drugs have done some awful things to some of the kids I've seen around here."[17]

The Get Analytical exercise on page 308, a self-test, will help you analyze your drinking habits. If you think you have a problem, use your creative and practical thinking skills to come up with a viable solution. The information on addiction on pages 307 and 309 introduces possible options.

Tobacco

The National Institute on Drug Abuse (NIDA) found that nearly 40 percent of college students reported smoking at least once in the year before they were surveyed, and 25 percent had smoked once within the previous month. Nationally, about 60 million people are habitual smokers.[18]

There are many ways to have a good time in college. Many students take entertaining short courses such as ballroom dancing, which is a social event as well as an educational experience.

When people smoke they inhale nicotine, a highly addictive drug found in all tobacco products. Nicotine's immediate effects may include an increase in blood pressure and heart rate, sweating, and throat irritation. Long-term effects may include high blood pressure, bronchitis, emphysema, stomach ulcers, and heart disease. Pregnant women who smoke increase their risk of having infants with low birth weight, premature births, or stillbirths.

Inhaling tobacco smoke damages the cells that line the air sacs of the lungs and can cause lung cancer. Lung cancer causes more deaths in the United States than any other type of cancer. Smoking also increases the risk of mouth, throat, and other cancers.[19] Over time, smoking will wrinkle your skin, cause chronic coughing, and even change the sound of your voice.

In recent years, the health dangers of secondhand smoke have been recognized. Simply being around smokers on a regular basis causes about 3,000 lung cancer deaths per year in nonsmokers.[20] This awareness has led many colleges (and local jurisdictions) to ban smoking in classrooms and other public spaces and even in many dorm rooms. If you smoke regularly, you can quit by being motivated, persevering, and seeking help. Practical suggestions for quitting include:[21]

- Try a nicotine patch or nicotine gum, and be sure to use them consistently.
- Get support and encouragement from a health care provider, a "quit smoking" program, a support group, and friends and family.
- Avoid situations that increase your desire to smoke, such as being around other smokers and drinking heavily.
- Find other ways to lower stress, such as exercise or other activities you enjoy.
- Set goals. Set a quit date and tell friends and family. Make and keep medical appointments.

The positive effects of quitting—increased life expectancy, greater lung capacity, and more energy—may inspire any smoker to consider making a lifestyle change. Quitting provides financial benefits as well. In fact, one study reports that if a one-pack-a-day smoker who paid $1.75 a pack for 50 years had put that money in the bank instead, he or she would have $169,325. A three-pack-a-day smoker would have saved $507,976.[22]

In order to assess the level of your potential addiction, you may want to take the self-test in the exercise on page 308, replacing the words "alcohol" or "drugs" with "cigarettes" or "smoking." Think about your results, weigh your options, and make a responsible choice.

Drugs

The NIDA reports that nearly 32 percent of college students have used illicit drugs at least once in the year prior to being surveyed, and 16 percent in the month before.[23] College students may use drugs to relieve stress, be accepted by peers, or just to try something new.

In most cases, the negative consequences of drug use outweigh any temporary high. Drug use violates federal, state, and local laws, and you may be arrested, tried, and imprisoned for possessing even a small amount of drugs. You can jeopardize your reputation, your student status, and your ability to get a job if you are caught using drugs or if drug use impairs your performance. Finally, long-term drug use can damage your body and mind. Key 10.2 shows commonly used drugs and their potential effects.

> A habit is no damn private hell. . . . A habit is hell for those you love.
>
> **BILLIE HOLIDAY**

One drug that doesn't fit cleanly into a particular category is methylenedioxymethamphetamine (MDMA), better known as Ecstasy. The use of this drug, a combination stimulant and hallucinogen, is on the rise at college parties, raves, and concerts. Its immediate effects include diminished anxiety and relaxation. When the drug wears off, nausea, hallucinations, shaking, vision problems, anxiety, and depression replace these highs. Long-term users risk permanent brain damage in the form of memory loss, chronic depression, and other disorders.[24]

You are responsible for analyzing the potential consequences of what you introduce into your body. Ask questions like the following: Why do I want to do this? What positive and negative effects might my behavior have? Why do others want me to take drugs? What do I really think of these people? How would my drug use affect the people in my life?

Use the self-test to assess your relationship with drugs. If you believe you have a problem, read the following section on steps that can help you get your life back on track.

Identifying and overcoming addiction

People with addictions have lost control. Many addicts hide their addictions well and continue to function, but their lives are severely impaired. If you think you may be addicted, take the initiative to change. Those suffering from addiction have to help themselves in order for others to help them.

Facing addiction

Because substances often cause physical and chemical changes and psychological dependence, habits are tough to break and quitting may involve a painful withdrawal. Asking for help isn't an admission of failure but a courageous move to reclaim your life.

The ways in which drugs affect body and mind.

DRUG CATEGORY	DRUG TYPES	HOW THEY MAKE YOU FEEL	PHYSICAL EFFECTS	DANGER OF PHYSICAL DEPENDENCE	DANGER OF PSYCHOLOGICAL DEPENDENCE
Stimulants	Cocaine, amphetamines	Alert, stimulated, excited	Nervousness, mood swings, stroke or convulsions, psychoses, paranoia, coma at large doses	Relatively strong	Strong
Depressants	Alcohol, Valium, Xanax, Rohypnol	Sedated, tired, high	Cirrhosis; impaired blood production; greater risk of cancer, heart attack, and stroke; impaired brain function	Strong	Strong
Opiates	Heroin, codeine, other pain pills	Drowsy, floating, without pain	Infection of organs, inflammation of the heart, hepatitis	Yes, with high dosage	Yes, with high dosage
Cannabinols	Marijuana, hashish	Euphoria, mellowness, little sensation of time	Impairment of judgment and coordination, bronchitis and asthma, lung and throat cancers, anxiety, lack of energy and motivation, reduced ability to produce hormones	Moderate	Relatively strong
Hallucinogens	LSD (acid), mushrooms	Heightened sensual perception, hallucinations, confusion	Impairment of brain function, circulatory problems, agitation and confusion, flashbacks	Insubstantial	Insubstantial
Inhalants	Glue, aerosols	Giddiness, lightheadedness	Damage to brain, heart, liver, and kidneys	Insubstantial	Insubstantial

Source: Adapted from *Educating Yourself about Alcohol and Drugs: A People's Primer* by Marc Alan Schuckit, M.D. New York: HarperCollins, 1998.

Even one "yes" answer on the self-test on the next page may indicate that you need to evaluate your alcohol or drug use and to monitor it more carefully. If you answered yes to three or more questions, you may benefit from talking to a professional about your use and the problems it may be causing you.

Working through addiction

The following resources can help you generate options and develop practical plans for recovery.

Counseling and medical care. You can find help from school-based, private, government-sponsored, or workplace-sponsored resources. Ask your school's counseling or health center, your personal physician, or a local hospital for a referral.

get analytical!

EVALUATE YOUR SUBSTANCE USE

Even one "yes" answer may indicate a need to look carefully at your habits. Three or more "yes" answers indicates that you may benefit from discussing your use with a counselor.

WITHIN THE LAST YEAR:

Y N 1. Have you tried to stop drinking or taking drugs but found that you couldn't do so for long?

Y N 2. Do you get tired of people telling you they're concerned about your drinking or drug use?

Y N 3. Have you felt guilty about your drinking or drug use?

Y N 4. Have you felt that you needed a drink or drugs in the morning—as an "eye-opener"—in order to cope with a hangover?

Y N 5. Do you drink or use drugs alone?

Y N 6. Do you drink or use drugs every day?

Y N 7. Have you found yourself regularly thinking or saying, "I need" a drink or any type of drug?

Y N 8. Have you lied about or concealed your drinking or drug use?

Y N 9. Do you drink or use drugs to escape worries, problems, mistakes, or shyness?

Y N 10. Do you find you need increasingly larger amounts of drugs or alcohol in order to achieve a desired effect?

Y N 11. Have you forgotten what happened while drinking or using drugs because you had a blackout?

Y N 12. Have you been surprised by how much you were using alcohol or drugs?

Y N 13. Have you spent a lot of time, energy, and/or money getting alcohol or drugs?

Y N 14. Has your drinking or drug use caused you to neglect friends, your partner, your children, or other family members, or caused other problems at home?

Y N 15. Have you gotten into an argument or a fight that was alcohol- or drug-related?

Y N 16. Has your drinking or drug use caused you to miss class, fail a test, or ignore schoolwork?

Y N 17. Have you rejected planned social events in favor of drinking or using drugs?

Y N 18. Have you been choosing to drink or use drugs instead of performing other activities or hobbies you used to enjoy?

Y N 19. Has your drinking or drug use affected your efficiency on the job or caused you to fail to show up at work?

Y N 20. Have you continued to drink or use drugs despite any physical problems or health risks that your use has caused or made worse?

Y N 21. Have you driven a car or performed any other potentially dangerous tasks while under the influence of alcohol or drugs?

Y N 22. Have you had a drug- or alcohol-related legal problem or arrest (possession, use, disorderly conduct, driving while intoxicated, etc.)?

Source: Adapted from the Criteria for Substance Dependence and Criteria for Substance Abuse in the *Diagnositc and Statistical Manual of Mental Disorders,* Fourth Edition, published by the American Psychiatric Association, Washington, DC, and from materials entitled "Are You an Alcoholic?" developed by Johns Hopkins University.

Detoxification ("detox") centers. If you have a severe addiction, you may need a controlled environment where you can separate yourself completely from drugs or alcohol. Some are outpatient facilities. Other programs provide a 24-hour environment through the withdrawal period.

Support groups. Alcoholics Anonymous (AA) is the premier support group for alcoholics. Based on a 12-step recovery program, AA membership costs little or nothing. AA has led to other support groups for addicts such as Overeaters Anonymous (OA) and Narcotics Anonymous (NA). Many schools have AA, NA, or other group sessions on campus.

When people address their problems directly instead of avoiding them through substance abuse, they can begin to grow and improve. Working through substance-abuse problems can lead to a restoration of health and self-respect.

Another important aspect of both physical and mental health involves being comfortable with your sexuality and making wise sexual decisions. Choosing birth control and knowing how to avoid sexually transmitted infections have short- and long-term consequences for the rest of your life.

How can you make successfully intelligent decisions *about sex*?

What sexuality means to you and the role it plays in your life are your own business. However, the physical act of sex goes beyond the private realm. Individual sexual conduct can result in an unexpected pregnancy and in contracting or passing a sexually transmitted infection (STI). These consequences affect everyone involved in the sexual act and, often, their families.

Your self-respect depends on making choices that maintain health and safety—yours as well as those of the person with whom you are involved. Analyze sexual issues carefully, weighing the positive and negative effects of your choices. Ask questions like the following:

- Is this what I really want? Does it fit with my values?
- Do I feel ready or do I feel pressured?
- Is this the right person/moment/situation? Does my partner truly care for me and not just for what we might be doing? Will this enhance or damage our emotional relationship?
- Do I have what I need to prevent pregnancy and exposure to STIs? If not, is having unprotected sex worth the risk?

Birth control

Using birth control is a choice, and it is not for everyone. For some, using any kind of birth control goes against religious or personal

FIND MORE FUN

Broaden your repertoire of fun things to do.

Sometimes, college students get involved in potentially unsafe activities because it seems like there isn't anything else to do. Use your creativity to make sure you have a variety of enjoyable activities to choose from when you hang out with friends. Check out your resources: What possibilities can you find at your student union, student activities center, college or local arts organizations, athletic organizations, various clubs, nature groups? Could you go hiking? Paint pottery? Check out a baseball game? Run a 5K? Try a new kind of cuisine? Volunteer at a children's hospital ward? See a play?

   Expand your horizons. List here 10 specific activities available to you.

1. _____   6. _____
2. _____   7. _____
3. _____   8. _____
4. _____   9. _____
5. _____   10. _____

beliefs. Others may want to have children. Many sexually active people, however, choose one or more methods of birth control.

   In addition to preventing pregnancy, some birth control methods also protect against STIs. Key 10.3 describes established methods, with effectiveness percentages and STI prevention based on proper and regular use.

   Evaluate the pros and cons of each option for yourself as well as for your partner. Consider cost, ease of use, reliability, comfort, and protection against STIs. Communicate with your partner and together make a choice that is comfortable for both of you. For more information, check your library, the Internet, or a bookstore; talk to your doctor; or ask a counselor at the student health center.

Sexually transmitted infections

STIs spread through sexual contact (intercourse or other sexual activity that involves contact with the genitals). All are highly contagious. The only birth control methods that offer protection are the male and female condoms (latex or polyurethane only), which prevent skin-to-skin contact. Most STIs can also spread to infants of infected mothers during birth. Have a doctor examine any irregularity or discomfort as soon as you detect it. Key 10.4 describes common STIs.

AIDS and HIV

The most serious of the STIs is AIDS (acquired immune deficiency syndrome), which is caused by the human immunodeficiency virus (HIV). Not everyone who tests positive for HIV will develop AIDS, but AIDS has

Make an educated decision about birth control.

METHOD	APPROXIMATE EFFECTIVENESS	PREVENTS STIs?	DESCRIPTION
Abstinence	100%	Only if no sexual activity occurs	Just saying no. No intercourse means no risk of pregnancy. However, alternative modes of sexual activity can still spread STIs.
Condom (male)	94%	Yes, if made of latex	A sheath that fits over the penis and prevents sperm from entering the vagina.
Condom (female)	90%	Yes	A sheath that fits inside the vagina, held in place by two rings, one of which hangs outside. Made of polyurethane.
Diaphragm or cervical cap	85%	No	A bendable rubber cap that fits over the cervix and pelvic bone inside the vagina (the cervical cap is smaller and fits over the cervix only). Both must be fitted initially by a gynecologist and used with a spermicide.
Oral contra-ceptives (the pill)	97%	No	A dosage of hormones taken daily by a woman, preventing the ovaries from releasing eggs. Side effects can include headaches, weight gain, and increased chances of blood clotting. Various brands and dosages; must be prescribed by a gynecologist.
Spermicidal foams, jellies, inserts	84% if used alone	No	Usually used with diaphragms or condoms to enhance effectiveness, they have an ingredient that kills sperm cells (but not STIs). They stay effective for a limited period of time after insertion.
Intrauterine device (IUD)	94%	No	A small coil of wire inserted into the uterus by a gynecologist (who must also remove it). Prevents fertilized eggs from implanting in the uterine wall. Possible side effects include bleeding.
Depo-Provera (the shot)	Nearly 100%	No	An injection that a woman must receive from a doctor every few months. Possible side effects may resemble those of oral contraceptives.
Tubal ligation	Nearly 100%	No	Surgery for women that cuts and ties the fallopian tubes, preventing eggs from traveling to the uterus. Difficult and expensive to reverse. Recommended for those who do not want any, or any more, children.
Vasectomy	Nearly 100%	No	Surgery for men that blocks the tube that delivers sperm to the penis. Like tubal ligation, difficult to reverse and recommended only for those who don't want any, or any more, children.
Rhythm method	Variable	No	Abstaining from intercourse during the ovulation segment of the woman's menstrual cycle. Can be difficult to time and may not account for cycle irregularities.
Withdrawal	Variable	No	Pulling the penis out of the vagina before ejaculation. Unreliable, because some sperm can escape in the fluid released prior to ejaculation. Dependent on a controlled partner.

DISEASE	SYMPTOMS	HEALTH PROBLEMS IF UNTREATED	TREATMENTS
Chlamydia	Discharge, painful urination, swollen or painful joints, change in menstrual periods for women	Can cause pelvic inflammatory disease (PID) in women, which can lead to sterility or ectopic pregnancies; infection; miscarriage or premature birth.	Curable with full course of antibiotics; avoid sex until treatment is complete.
Gonorrhea	Discharge, burning while urinating	Can cause PID, swelling of testicles and penis, arthritis, skin problems, infections.	Usually curable with antibiotics; however, certain strains are becoming resistant to medication.
Genital herpes	Blisterlike itchy sores in the genital area, headache, fever, chills	Symptoms may subside and then reoccur, often in response to high stress levels; carriers can transmit the virus even when it is dormant.	No cure; some medications, such as Acyclovir, reduce and help heal the sores and may shorten recurring outbreaks.
Syphilis	A genital sore lasting one to five weeks, followed by a rash, fatigue, fever, sore throat, headaches, swollen glands	If it lasts over four years, it can cause blindness, destruction of bone, insanity, or heart failure; can cause death or deformity of a child born to an infected woman.	Curable with full course of antibiotics.
Human Papilloma Virus (HPV, or genital warts)	Genital itching and irritation, small clusters of warts	Can increase risk of cervical cancer in women; virus may remain in body and cause recurrences even when warts are removed.	Treatable with drugs applied to warts or various kinds of wart removal surgery.
Hepatitis B	Fatigue, poor appetite, vomiting, jaundice, hives	Some carriers will have few symptoms; others may develop chronic liver disease that may lead to other diseases of the liver.	No cure; some will recover, some will not. Bed rest may help ease symptoms. Vaccine is available.

no cure and results in eventual death. Key 10.5 shows some alarming statistics on AIDS.

HIV can lie undetected in the body for up to 10 years before surfacing, and a carrier can spread it during that time. Medical science continues to develop drugs to combat AIDS and its related illnesses. The drugs can cause severe side effects, however, and none are cures.

HIV is transmitted through two types of bodily fluids: fluids associated with sex (semen and vaginal fluids) and blood. People have acquired HIV through sexual relations, by sharing hypodermic needles for drug use, and by receiving infected blood transfusions. You cannot become infected unless one of those fluids is involved. Therefore, it is unlikely you can contract HIV from toilet seats, hugging, kissing, or sharing a glass.

- Since the AIDS epidemic began in the United States, an estimated 886,575 people have been diagnosed, and approximately 501,669 have died of AIDS.

- Since the epidemic began, well over one million Americans have been infected with HIV.

- It is estimated that between 850,000 and 950,000 people in the United States are currently HIV-positive.

- The year 2002 brought over 40,000 newly diagnosed AIDS patients. Over half of these were people under the age of 25.

- As of the end of 2002, 384,906 Americans were living with AIDS.

- Approximately 60 percent of newly infected men contracted HIV from homosexual sex, 25 percent through injection drug use, and 15 percent through heterosexual sex.

- Approximately 75 percent of newly infected women contracted HIV through heterosexual sex and 25 percent through injection drug use.

Source: National Institute of Allergy and Infectious Diseases, "HIV/AIDS Statistics," January 2004 [on-line]. Available: www.niaid.nih.gov/factsheets/aidsstat.htm#2 (May 2004).

Protecting yourself

The best defense against AIDS is not having sex or being in a long-term monogamous relationship. Condoms are the next best choice. The U.S. Department of Health and Human Services reports: "THERE'S ABSOLUTELY NO GUARANTEE EVEN WHEN YOU USE A CONDOM. But most experts believe that the risk of getting AIDS and other sexually transmitted diseases can be greatly reduced if a condom is used properly. . . . Sex with condoms ISN'T totally 'safe sex,' but it IS 'less risky' sex."[25] Always use a latex condom, because natural skin condoms may let the virus pass through. Avoid petroleum jelly, which can destroy the latex in condoms.

Keep in mind that your emotional defenses can cloud your thinking about safe sex. If you are young and healthy, you may believe, incorrectly, that nothing bad can happen to you. This sense of invulnerability is leading an increasing number of gay students to engage in unprotected sex. For example, John, a gay student at Tufts University, tries to be safe, but often rationalizes his failure to use condoms during all sexual encounters. When Benjamin, a student at Hunter College of the City University of New York, complains of "safe sex fatigue," he is also admitting that he isn't always willing to assess his risks.[26]

To be safe, have an HIV test done at your doctor's office or at a government-sponsored clinic. Your school's health department may also administer HIV tests, and home HIV tests are available over the counter. If you are infected, first inform all sexual partners and seek medical assistance. Then, contact support organizations in your area or call the National AIDS Hotline at 1-800-342-AIDS.

Joie de vivre

The French have a phrase that is commonly used in the English language as well: *joie de vivre,* which literally means "joy of living." A person with joie de vivre finds joy and optimism in all parts of life, is able to enjoy life's pleasures, and can find something positive in its struggles. Without experiencing challenges, people might have a hard time recognizing and appreciating happiness and satisfaction.

Think of this concept as you examine your personal wellness. If you focus on the positive, your attitude can enhance all areas of your life.

FOR COLLEGE, CAREER, AND LIFE SUCCESS

Developing Successful Intelligence

PUTTING IT ALL TOGETHER

Take steps toward better health. Put your successful intelligence to work in improving your physical health.

Step 1. Think it through: *Analyze your habits.* Pick a topic—eating, drinking, sleeping, sexual activity—that is an issue for you. To examine why it is a problem, identify behaviors and attitudes and note their positive and negative effects.

Example: *Issue: binge drinking*

Behavior: I binge drink probably three times a week.

Attitude: I don't think it's any big deal. I like using it to escape.

Positive effects: I have fun with my friends. I feel confident, accepted, social.

Negative effects: I feel hung over and foggy the next day. I miss class. I'm irritable.

Your turn: *Issue:*

Behavior:

Attitude:

Positive effects:

_____

Negative effects:

_____

Question to think about: Is it worth it?

create your future

Step 2. Think out of the box: *Brainstorm ways to change.* First think about what you want to be different, and why. Then come up with changes you could make. Be creative!

How you might change your behavior: _____

_____

How you might change your attitude: _____

_____

Positive effects you think these changes would have: _____

_____

Step 3. Make it happen: *Put a practical health improvement plan into action.* Choose two actions to take—one that would improve your attitude and one that would improve your behavior—that you think would have the most positive effect for you. Commit to these actions with specific plans and watch the positive change happen.

Attitude improvement plan: _____

_____

Behavior improvement plan: _____

_____

Team Building

COLLABORATIVE SOLUTIONS

Actively dealing with stress. By yourself, make a list of stressors—whatever events or factors cause you stress. As a class, discuss the stressors you have listed. Choose the five most common. Divide into five groups according to who would choose what stressor as his or her most important (redistribute some people if the group sizes are unbalanced). Each group should discuss its assigned stressor, brainstorming solutions and strategies. List your best coping strategies and present them to the class. Groups may want to make extra copies of the lists so that every member of the class has five, one for each stressor.

Writing

DISCOVERY THROUGH JOURNALING

Record your thoughts on a separate piece of paper or in a journal.

Addiction. Many people have, at one time or another, had to cope with some kind of addiction. Describe how you feel about addiction in any form—to alcohol, drugs, food, sex, the Internet, gambling. How has addiction ensnared you, if at all? How did you deal with it? If you have never faced an addiction nor been close to someone who did, describe how you think you would work through the problem it if it ever happened to you.

Career Portfolio

Complete the following in your electronic portfolio or on separate sheets of paper.

Setting effective boundaries at work. In the current working world, many companies are putting pressure on their employees to do more in less time. The result is an environment that places workers under a great deal of stress. If you work in this environment, you may be asked to step up your efforts in different ways—do more work, add tasks to your job description, work late nights, keep your cell phone on for work calls on weekends, and so on.

However, there is a boundary—a limit—to what you can do successfully. If you hit that limit and don't overstep it, you may indeed keep your job and earn promotions. If you cross that boundary, your health and the quality of your work can suffer. If you don't work hard enough to approach it, you may lose your job or not advance.

Your challenge is to determine your limit and then monitor yourself to make sure that you work up to potential but don't overdo it. Answer the following questions in the effort to identify the most effective boundary for yourself as an employee:

- Are you willing to take on any job-related task, or do you get upset when people pile work on your desk that is not part of your job description?
- Are you willing to work late to meet a deadline, or do you get upset if you don't leave on time?
- Do you try to do your best work on everything or to get by with doing as little as possible?
- Are you likely to initiate different ideas that will improve your work product and then find ways to make them happen?
- Do you take a leadership position in your work team or try to stay in the background?
- When given a work request, do you tend to say "yes" right away, "no" right away, or take time to think about it thoroughly?
- Do you bring work into your personal life—socialize with coworkers, take work calls on personal time—or do you leave your job behind when you leave the workplace?

Analyze your answers as honestly as possible. Then, answer these questions: How do you think your attitudes will help or hurt you as a team member in your relationships with peers, managers, and others, and how do you think they will affect your career advancement? Check your personal attitude assessment against someone in a field you are interested in to see if you are on target or off base.

If you realize that your attitudes may stand in the way of success in a particular job or career area, consider what specific steps you are willing to take to change them. You might also consider whether you want to rethink your career or company choice to find a position or area that suits you better. Finally, think about how your ability to set effective boundaries may affect your success in school. Working up to your limits, but not too far beyond, will help you become the person you want to be both at school and in the world of work.

SUGGESTED READINGS

Duyff, Roberta Larson. *The American Dietetic Association's Complete Food and Nutrition Guide.* Hoboken, NJ: Wiley, 2003.

Grayson, Paul A., Phil Meilman, and Philip W. Meilman. *Beating the College Blues.* New York: Checkmark Books, 1999.

Kadison, Richard D. and DiGeronimo, Theresa Foy. *College of the Overwhelmed: The Campus Mental Health Crisis and What to Do About It.* San Francisco: Jossey-Bass, 2004.

Kuhn, Cynthia, et al. *Buzzed: The Straight Facts About the Most Used and Abused Drugs from Alcohol to Ecstasy,* 2nd ed. New York: W. W. Norton, 2003.

Mayo Clinic Family Health Book: The Ultimate Home Medical Reference, 3rd ed. New York: HarperResource, 2003.

The Physician's Desk Reference. *The Physician's Desk Reference Family Guide Encyclopedia of Medical Care.* New York: Ballantine Books, 1999.

Schuckit, Marc Alan. *Educating Yourself About Alcohol and Drugs: A People's Primer.* New York: HarperCollins, 1998.

Selkowitz, Ann. *The College Student's Guide to Eating Well on Campus.* Bethesda, MD: Tulip Hill Press, 2000.

Ward, Darrell. *The Amfar AIDS Handbook: The Complete Guide to Understanding HIV and AIDS.* New York: W. W. Norton, 1998.

INTERNET RESOURCES

Prentice Hall Student Success Supersite (fitness and well-being information): www.prenhall.com/success

American Cancer Society (general information, prevention, and early detection tips): www.cancer.org

Columbia University's Health Education Program: www.alice.columbia.edu

Federal Centers for Disease Control and Prevention (disease prevention and health information): www.cdc.gov

It's Your (Sex) Life: www.itsyoursexlife.com/

MayoClinic.com (medical information from this world-renowned medical center): www.mayohealth.org

HIV Prevention: www.thebody.com/safesex.html

ENDNOTES

1. The sources used in this section include Jane E. Brody, "Added Sugars Are Taking a Toll on Health," *New York Times,* September 12, 2000, p. F8; "Diabetes as Looming Epidemic," *New York Times,* January 30, 2001, p. F8; "Extra Soft Drink Is Cited as Major Factor in Obesity," *New York Times,* February 16, 2001, p. A12; Josh Stroud, "No More Fast Forward," *Dallas Business Journal,* January 21, 2000, p. 10C; "U.S. Favors Traditional Weight-Loss Plans," *New York Times,* January 16, 2001, p. F12.

2. Statistics in these bullets taken from K. M. Flegal, M. D. Carroll, C. L. Ogden, and C. L. Johnson,

"Prevalence and Trends in Obesity Among US Adults, 1999–2000," *Journal of the American Medical Association* (2002), 288: 1723–1727.

3. Definitions from "Defining Overweight and Obesity," Centers for Disease Control [on-line]. Available: www.cdc.gov/nccdphp/dnpa/obesity/defining.htm (May 2004).

4. Jennifer Jacobson, "How Much Sports Is Too Much? Athletes Dislike Conferences' Efforts to Give Players More Time to Be Students," *The Chronicle of Higher Education,* December 6, 2002 [on-line]. Available: http://chronicle.com/weekly/v49/i15a03801.htm (March 2004).

5. CBS News, "Help for Sleep-Deprived Students," Durham, NC, April 19, 2004 [on-line]. Available: www.cbsnews.com/stories/2004/04/19/health/main612476.shtml (May 2004).

6. "College Students Sleep Habits Harmful to Health, Study Finds," *The Daily Orange—Feature Issue,* September 25, 2002 [on-line]. Available: www.dailyorange.com/news/2002/09/25/Feature/College.Students.Sleep.Habits.Harmful.To.Health.Study.Finds-280340.shtml (May 2004).

7. Ibid.

8. Herbert Benson, M. D., and Eileen M. Stuart, R.N., C.M.S., et al., *The Wellness Book.* New York: Simon & Schuster, 1992, p. 292; and Gregg Jacobs, Ph.D., "Insomnia Corner," *Talk About Sleep,* 2004 [on-line]. Available: www.talkaboutsleep.com/sleepdisorders/insomnia_corner.htm (May 2004).

9. National Institutes of Health Publication No. 94-3561, National Institutes of Health, 1994.

10. www.save.org/depressed/symptoms.html (SA/VE Web site, accessed 5/9/04).

11. Kim Hubbard, Anne-Marie O'Neill, and Christina Cheakalos, "Out of Control," *People,* April 12, 1999, p. 54.

12. J. McGinnis and W. Foege, "Actual Causes of Death in the United States," *Journal of the American Medical Association (JAMA)* 270.18, American Medical Association, November 10, 1993, p. 2208.

13. National Institute on Alcohol Abuse and Alcoholism, No. 29 PH 357, July 1995.

14. H. Wechsler et al., "Changes in Binge Drinking and Related Problems Among American College Students Between 1993 and 1997," *Journal of American College Health* 47 (September 1998): p. 57.

15. Ibid, pp. 63–64.

16. National Institute on Alcohol Abuse and Alcoholism, No. 29 PH 357, July 1995.

17. Darra Clark, Arizona State Freshman's Comments on EssayEdge.com [on-line]. Available: www.essayedge.com/college/admissions/speakout/arizona.shtml (March 2004).

18. National Institute on Drug Abuse, Capsule Series C-83-08, "Cigarette Smoking," Bethesda, MD: National Institutes of Health, 1994.

19. David Stout, "Direct Link Found Between Smoking and Lung Cancer," *New York Times,* October 18, 1996, pp. A1, A19.

20. *Chicago Tribune,* February 26, 1997, "Secondhand Smoke Blamed in 3,000 Yearly Cancer Deaths" [on-line]. Available: http://archives.chicago.tribune.com (April 1997).

21. National Institutes of Health, Agency for Health Care Policy and Research, "Nicotine: A Powerful Addiction."

22. Anne R. Carey and Bob Laird, "USA Snapshots," "Dollars Up in Smoke," *USA Today,* February 20, 1997, p. D1. Source: Demotech, Inc.

23. National Institute on Drug Abuse, "National Survey Results on Drug Abuse from Monitoring the Future Study," Bethesda, MD: National Institutes of Health, 1994.

24. Drug Enforcement Administration, U.S Department of Justice [on-line]. Available: www.usdoj.gov/dea/concern/mdma/mdmaindex.htm (February 2003).

25. U.S Department of Health and Human Services, "A Condom Could Save Your Life," Publication # 90-4239.

26. Alex P. Kellogg, "'Safe Sex Fatigue' Grows Among Gay Students: Health Officials Change Their HIV-Education Strategies as Condom Use Declines," *The Chronicle of Higher Education,* January 18, 2002 [on-line]. Available: http://chronicle.com/weekly/v38/i19/19a03701.htm (March 2004).

11

Managing Career and Money

REALITY RESOURCES

All of the ways that you grow and learn in college will help you in your future career. Beginning to explore careers now, while you are a student, will help you find a career that suits you, whether it is being a teacher in Minnesota, an attorney in Manhattan, an archaeologist in Egypt, or anything else you dream of.

Money issues are another important concern—now, as you figure out how to finance school costs and manage credit cards, and later, when you are earning money in the working world. This chapter will show you how your successful intelligence can help you explore careers, hunt for jobs effectively, balance work and school, and manage your money so that you can make the most of what you earn.

On the following page, read student Morgan Packard's concerns about how to take a major that interests her and turn it into a career she enjoys.

- How can you prepare for workplace success?
- What does your learning style mean for your career?
- How can you find a career that's right for you?
- What will help you juggle work and school?
- How can you create a budget that works?
- How can you manage your credit cards?

How can I find a career I will enjoy?

I have always had varied interests. Through high school, my extracurricular activities ranged from piano and voice lessons to spending my summers acting in a Renaissance fair and everything in between. I was also continually motivated to keep a high grade point average; though I love my activities, school is my top priority. So, when it came time to choose a college, I looked for one whose reputation in academics, particularly the English department, was balanced by opportunities to participate in the arts.

Now attending college and majoring in English, I am faced with a problem. Since an early age, one of my favorite escapes has been reading. When I chose my major, I did so based on a subject that interested me and that would prepare me to participate in a profession that I would like to turn into my career, editing and publishing. I'm wondering if it is enough to excel in my courses or whether I should try to grow in other ways while at school that will make me a valued employee.

Morgan Packard
Tulane University, New Orleans, Louisiana

Use college to discover what you do well, then . . . find the job you are most suited for.

I think that some of your biggest strengths when you graduate and look for a job will be not only your school affiliation and grades, but those other activities and strengths you acquired along the way. People who strictly adhere to the academic route don't necessarily acquire the skills associated with those activities; they may not have worked in a team environment, which is important in the job market. What is important to businesses today is not your grade point average or your major, but what skills you bring to the table, how flexible you can be to mold and grow into the position for which that company is looking.

I think one of the greatest attributes a person can acquire is to be able to get up in front of a crowd. I've been in the business world long enough to know that you do not have to be brilliant to be a success; however, if you can communicate your ideas, you will be successful.

Life doesn't work within the bounds of a rigid focus. To be successful and happy, you must learn to take life's curve balls. You must assimilate all of those situations that come your way and find the benefit in them. My analytical background and nature have helped me the most in my current career; I have a bachelor's degree in science and a master's in biochemistry and biophysics. I love what I do now, but that doesn't mean that I couldn't do seven other careers and be happy in them too. Use college to discover what you do well; then, when it comes time to leave, you can find the job you are most suited for and be happy in it, staying flexible and always open to the next opportunity that comes your way.

Ramona Z. Locke
Vice President, Senior Financial Consultant,
Merrill Lynch Private Client Group, Dallas, Texas

How can you prepare for *workplace success?*

Whether you have no idea of your career path or have worked for years and are looking for a career change, now is the time to take steps toward a fulfilling career. You are already preparing for career success with your work in this course, because every skill in this book—thinking, teamwork, writing skills, and goal setting, among others—prepares you to thrive in the workplace. Use the following strategies to get more specific in your preparation.

Investigate career paths

The working world changes all the time. You can get an idea of what's out there—and what you think of it all—by exploring potential careers and building knowledge and experience.

Explore potential careers

Career possibilities extend far beyond what you can imagine. Ask instructors, relatives, mentors, and fellow students about careers they are familiar with. Check your library for books on careers or biographies of people who worked in fields that interest you. Explore careers you discover through movies, newspapers, novels, or nonfiction.

Use your analytical thinking skills to broaden your investigation. Look at Key 11.1 for the kinds of questions that will aid your search.

Ask questions like these to analyze how a career area or job may fit you. **key 11.1**

What can I do in this area that I like and do well?	Do I respect the company or the industry? The product or service?
What are the educational requirements (certificates or degrees, courses)?	Does this company or industry accommodate special needs (child care, sick days, flex time)?
What skills are necessary?	Do I need to belong to a union? What does union membership involve?
What wage or salary and benefits can I expect?	Are there opportunities near where I live (or want to live)?
What personality types are best suited to this kind of work?	What other expectations exist (travel, overtime, etc.)?
What are the prospects for moving up to higher-level positions?	Do I prefer the service or production end of this industry?

You may discover that:

A wide array of job possibilities exists for most career fields. For example, the medical world consists of more than doctors and nurses. Administrators run hospitals, researchers test new drugs, pharmacists prepare prescriptions, and so on.

Within each job, there is a variety of tasks and skills. You may know that an instructor teaches, but you may not see that instructors also often write, research, study, design courses, give presentations, and counsel. Take your exploration beyond your first impression of a career.

Common assumptions about salaries don't always hold. Finance, medicine, law, and computer science aren't the only high-paying careers. According to data from the U.S. Labor Department, other careers with high earnings include electricians, public administrators, aircraft mechanics, and more.[1] Remember to place earnings in perspective: Even if you earn a high salary, you may not be happy unless you enjoy your work.

Your school's career center may offer job listings, occupation lists, assessments of skills and personality types, questionnaires to help you pinpoint areas that may suit you, and information about different careers and companies. Visit the center early and work with a counselor to develop a solid career game plan.

Build knowledge and experience

Having knowledge and experience specific to the career you wish to pursue is valuable on the job hunt. Courses, internships, jobs, and volunteering are four great ways to build both.

Courses. When you narrow your career exploration to a couple of areas, try to take a course or two in those areas to determine if you like the material. Find out what courses are required for a major in those areas.

Internships. Companies that offer internships are looking for people who will work hard in exchange for real-world experience they can't get in the classroom. An internship may or may not offer pay. Your career center may be able to help you explore summer or year-round internship opportunities. Focus on areas that interest you, and look for an internship that you can handle while still being able, if needed, to work part-time while at school.

INTERNSHIP

A temporary work program in which a student can gain supervised practical experience in a particular professional field.

Jobs. You may discover career opportunities while earning money during a part-time job. Someone who takes a third-shift legal proofreading job to make extra cash might discover an interest in law. Someone who answers phones for a newspaper company might be drawn into journalism.

Volunteering. Helping others in need can introduce you to careers and increase your experience. Some schools have programs that link you to volunteering opportunities (see Chapter 12). Include volunteer activities on your résumé. Many employers look favorably on volunteering.

Even after you've completed college, the key is to continually build on what you know. With the work world changing so quickly, today's employers value those who are always improving in their skills and knowledge.

Know what employers want

In the jobs you seek after you graduate, employers will look for specific technical skills, work experience, and academic credentials. They will also look for other skills and qualities that indicate that you are a promising candidate.

Important skills

Key 11.2 describes the particular skills and qualities that tell an employer that you are likely to be an efficient and effective employee.

These skills, which you have built throughout this book, are as much a part of your school success as they are of your work success. The more you develop them now, the more employable and promotable you will be.

Employers look for candidates with these important skills.

SKILLS	WHY IS IT USEFUL?
Communication	Good listening, speaking, and writing skills are keys to working with others, as is being able to adjust to different communication styles.
Analytical thinking	An employee who can analyze choices and challenges, as well as assess the value of new ideas, stands out.
Creativity	The ability to come up with new concepts, plans, and products helps companies improve and innovate.
Practical thinking	No job gets done without employees who can think through a plan for achieving a goal, put it into action, and complete it successfully.
Teamwork	All workers interact with others on the job. Working well with others is essential for achieving workplace goals.
Goal setting	Teams fail if goals are unclear or unreasonable. Employees and company benefit from setting realistic, specific goals and achieving them reliably.
Cultural competence	The workplace is increasingly diverse. An employee who can work with, adjust to, and respect people from different backgrounds and cultures is valuable.
Leadership	The ability to influence and motivate others in a positive way earns respect and career advancement.
Positive attitude	Other employees will gladly work with, and often advance, someone who completes tasks with positive, upbeat energy.
Integrity	Acting with integrity at work—communicating promptly, being truthful and honest, following rules, giving proper notice—enhances value.
Flexibility	The most valuable employees understand the constancy of change and have developed the skills to adapt to its challenge.
Continual learning	The most valuable employees take personal responsibility to stay current in their fields.

Emotional intelligence

Another quality employers seek is *emotional intelligence.* In his book *Working with Emotional Intelligence,* psychologist Daniel Goleman states that emotional intelligence can be even more important than IQ and knowledge. He defines emotional intelligence as a combination of these factors:[2]

- *Personal competence* refers to how you manage yourself—your self-awareness, self-regulation, and motivation.
- *Social competence* refers to how you handle relationships with others, including awareness of the needs and feelings of others and ability to encourage others to do things.

Look at Key 11.3 for specific skills that are part of these two factors.

An important part of personal competence is knowledge of your values. Think back to how you explored your values in Chapter 2. These values give you a framework from which to make all kinds of important decisions, including those about your career goals. Because you usually enjoy, excel at, and are most motivated by what is important to you, pursuing a career that incorporates your values increases your chances of fulfillment and success.

The current emphasis on teamwork has made emotional intelligence very important in the workplace. The more adept you are at working comfortably and productively with others (i.e., the more emotionally intelligent you are and the more you use this intelligence), the more likely you are to succeed.

Being emotionally intelligent means developing these key qualities.

key 11.3

PERSONAL COMPETENCE

Self-Awareness

- I know my emotions and how they affect me.
- I understand my strengths and my limits.
- I am confident in my abilities.
- I am open to improvement.

Self-Management

- I can control my emotions and impulses.
- I can delay gratification when there is something more important to be gained.
- I am trustworthy.
- I can adapt to change and new ideas.
- I persist toward my goals despite obstacles.

SOCIAL COMPETENCE

Social Awareness

- I sense the feelings and perspectives of others.
- I help others improve themselves.
- I know how to relate to people from different cultures.
- I can sense how to serve the needs of others.

Social Skills

- I know how to work in a team.
- I can inspire people to act.
- I understand how to lead a group.
- I know how to persuade people.
- I can make positive change happen.

CONNECT VALUES TO CAREER

Use your values as a career exploration guide.

First, look at the following list of "value words." Put a checkmark by those qualities that are most important to you as a working person. Circle your top five.

- Accepting
- Adventurous
- Ambitious
- Calm
- Caring
- Conscientious
- Cooperative
- Creative

- Decisive
- Demonstrating leadership
- Efficient
- Enthusiastic
- Focused on learning
- Honest/fair
- Independent
- Kind

- Loyal
- Organized
- Powerful
- Prompt
- Serious
- Trustworthy
- Wealthy

Keeping your top values in mind, answer the following questions:

The kind of work I enjoy most is

I can't see myself working as a

Self-fulfillment at work consists of

Being in charge of others makes me feel

Being responsible makes me feel

Working independently makes me feel

Working in a team makes me feel

Imagining that I'm being promoted after two years on a job, I think my employer would say it is because of these exemplary characteristics:

Source: Adapted from Gary Izumo et al., *Keys to Career Success*. Upper Saddle River, NJ: Prentice Hall, 2002, pp. 67–69.

Expect change

The working world is always in flux, responding to technological developments, global competition, and other factors. Reading newspapers and magazines, scanning business sites on the Internet, and watching television news all help you keep abreast of what you face as you make career decisions. Think about the following as you prepare to adjust to change.

Growing and declining career areas. Rapid workplace change means that a growth area today may be declining tomorrow—witness the sudden drop in Internet company jobs and fortunes in 2001. The U.S. Bureau of Labor keeps updated statistics on the status of various career areas. For example, for the period 1998–2008, of the 10 fastest growing occupations identified by the Bureau, five are computer-related occupations.

Workplace trends. What's happening now? Companies, to save money, are hiring more temporary employees (temps) and fewer full-time employees. Temporary jobs offer flexibility, few obligations, and often more take-home pay, but have limited benefits. Also, in response to the changing needs of the modern workforce, companies are offering more "quality of life" benefits such as telecommuting, job sharing, and on-site child care.

> Standing still is the fastest way of moving backwards in a rapidly changing world.

LAUREN BACALL

Personal change. Even difficult personal changes can open doors that you never imagined were there. For example, Susan Davenny Wyner, a successful classical singer, was hit by a car while biking. The accident damaged her vocal cords beyond repair. She later discovered that conducting held an opportunity for her to express herself musically in a way she didn't think she could ever do again.[3]

As this story demonstrates, if you think creatively about your marketable skills and job possibilities, you will be able to find new ways to achieve. What you know about your learning style should play an important role in your thinking.

What does your *learning style* mean for your career?

If you don't know what you want to do, you are not alone. Many students who have not been in the workplace—and even some who have—aren't sure what career to pursue. Start with what you know about yourself. Ask yourself questions like the following:

- What do I know best, do best, and enjoy best?
- Out of the jobs I have had, what did I like and not like to do?
- What kinds of careers could make the most of everything I am?

What you know about your learning style from Chapter 3 will give you important clues in the search for the right career. The Multiple Intelligences assessment points to information about your innate learning strengths and challenges, which, in turn, can lead you to careers that involve these strengths. Your Personality Spectrum assessment results are perhaps even more significant to career success, because they provide insight on how you work best with others. Career success depends, in large part, on your ability to function in a team.

Key 11.4 focuses the four dimensions of the Personality Spectrum on career ideas and strategies. Look for your strengths and decide what you may want to keep in mind as you search. Look also at the skills that challenge you because even the most ideal job involves some tasks that may

DIMENSION	STRENGTHS ON THE JOB	CHALLENGES ON THE JOB	LOOK FOR JOBS/CAREERS THAT FEATURE . . .
Thinker	• Problem solving • Development of ideas • Keen analysis of situations • Fairness to others • Efficiency in working through tasks • Innovation of plans and systems • Ability to look strategically at the future	• A need for private time to think and work • A need, at times, to move away from established rules • A dislike of sameness—systems that don't change, repetitive tasks • Not always being open to expressing thoughts and feelings to others	• Some level of solo work/think time • Problem solving • Opportunity for innovation • Freedom to think creatively and to bend the rules • Technical work • Big-picture strategic planning
Organizer	• High level of responsibility • Enthusiastic support of social structures • Order and reliability • Loyalty • Ability to follow through on tasks according to requirements • Detailed planning skills with competent follow-through • Neatness and efficiency	• A need for tasks to be clearly, concretely defined • A need for structure and stability • A preference for less rapid change • A need for frequent feedback • A need for tangible appreciation • Low tolerance for people who don't conform to rules and regulations	• Clear, well-laid-out tasks and plans • Stable environment with consistent, repeated tasks • Organized supervisors • Clear structure of how employees interact and report to one another • Value of, and reward for, loyalty
Giver	• Honesty and integrity • Commitment to putting energy toward close relationships with others • Finding ways to bring out the best in self and others • Peacemaker and mediator • Ability to listen well, respect opinions, and prioritize the needs of coworkers	• Difficulty in handling conflict, either personal or between others in the work environment • Strong need for appreciation and praise • Low tolerance for perceived dishonesty or deception • Avoidance of people perceived as hostile, cold, or indifferent	• Emphasis on teamwork and relationship building • Indications of strong and open lines of communication among workers • Encouragement of personal expression in the workplace (arrangement of personal space, tolerance of personal celebrations, and so on)
Adventurer	• Skillfulness in many different areas • Willingness to try new things • Ability to take action • Hands-on problem-solving skills • Initiative and energy • Ability to negotiate • Spontaneity and creativity	• Intolerance of being kept waiting • Lack of detail focus • Impulsiveness • Dislike of sameness and authority • Need for freedom, constant change, and constant action • Tendency not to consider consequences of actions	• A spontaneous atmosphere • Less structure, more freedom • Adventuresome tasks • Situations involving change • Encouragement of hands-on problem solving • Travel and physical activity • Support of creative ideas and endeavors

not be in your area of comfort. Identifying ways to boost your abilities in those areas will help you succeed.

Keep in mind a few important points as you consider the information in this table:

Use information as a guide, not a label. You may not necessarily have all the strengths and challenges that your dominant areas indicate. Chances are, though, that thinking through them will help you narrow your focus and clarify your abilities and interests.

Avoid thinking that challenges are weaknesses. Work challenges describe qualities that may cause issues in particular work situations. They aren't necessarily weaknesses in and of themselves. For example, not many people would say that a need for structure and stability (a challenge of the Giver) is a weakness. However, it can be a challenge in a workplace that operates in an unstructured manner.

Know that you are capable of change. Use ideas about strengths and challenges as a starting point and make some decisions about how you would like to grow.

Now that you've done your homework, it's time to get to the search. What you know, along with the strategies that follow, will help you along the path to a career that works for you.

NETWORKING

The exchange of information or services among individuals, groups, or institutions.

How can you find a career that's *right for you*?

Maximize your career opportunities by using the resources available to you, making a strategic search plan, and knowing some basics about résumés and interviews.

Use available resources

Use your school's career planning and placement office, your networking skills, classified ads, and on-line services to help you explore possibilities for jobs you need right away and for postgraduation career opportunities.

Your school's career planning and placement office

Generally, the career planning and placement office deals with postgraduation job opportunities, whereas the student employment office, along with the financial aid office, has information about working during school. At either location you might find general workplace information, listings of job opportunities, interview sign-up sheets, and company contact information.

The career office may hold frequent informational sessions on different topics. Your school may also sponsor job or career fairs that give you a chance to explore job opportunities. Start exploring your school's career office early in your college life. The people and resources there can help you at every stage of your career and job exploration process.

If your school has a cooperative education office, it can lead you to job opportunities and can even help you land a job before graduation. Jason Roach, a business computer systems major at New Mexico State University, used the co-op office as a job-referral source. He explains: "The Cooperative Education office works very hard to notify students when companies will be on campus interviewing for jobs. I receive at least ten e-mails a week telling me what company will be on campus and a quick background on the position."[4]

Networking

The most basic type of networking—talking to people about fields and jobs that interest you—is one of the most important job-hunting strategies. Networking contacts can answer questions regarding job hunting, job responsibilities and challenges, and salary expectations. You can network with friends and family members, instructors, administrators, counselors, alumni, employers, coworkers, and others.

You can also network with people you meet through your extracurricular activities. Christine Muñoz, a student at New Mexico State University, chose a campus club that she knew could help her prepare for a business career. "I am currently the president of HBSA—the Hispanic Business Student Association," said Muñoz. "This semester we did several fund-raisers and community service projects. We have bi-weekly meetings, and we also have socials where we all just get together and hang out. Professional speakers from large companies come and speak about résumé building skills and interview skills, something that is beneficial to everyone."[5]

Classified ads

Some of the best job listings are in newspapers. Individual ads describe the position available, including background requirements, and provide contact information. Some ads also include job requirements and salary or wages offered.

On-line services

The Internet has exploded into one of the most fruitful sources of job listings. There are many different ways to hunt for a job on the Web:

- Look up career-focused and job listing Web sites such as CareerBuilder.com, Monster.com, Yahoo Hotjobs, or futurestep.com. In addition to listing and describing different jobs, sites like these offer resources on career areas, résumés, on-line job searching, and more.
- Access job search databases such as the Career Placement Registry and U.S. Employment Opportunities.
- Check the Web pages of individual associations and companies, which may post job listings and descriptions.

If nothing happens right away, keep at it. New job postings appear, new people sign on to look at your

COOPERATIVE EDUCATION

A program, offered by some colleges, that combines credit-earning course work with paid work experience in a field that relates to the course.

CONTACT

A person who serves as a carrier or source of information.

Professors are often valuable resources for information about majors and careers. Don't hesitate to ask questions.

résumé. Plus, sites change all the time. Do a general search using the key-words "hot job sites" or "job search sites" to stay current on what sites are up and running.

Make a strategic job search plan

After gathering information, make a practical plan to achieve your career goals by mapping out your long-term time line and keeping track of specific actions.

Make a big-picture time line

Make a career time line that illustrates the steps toward your goal, as shown in Key 11.5. Write in the steps when you think they should happen. If your plan is five years long, indicate what you plan to do by the fourth, third, and second years, and then the first year, including a six-month goal and a one-month goal for that first year. Your path may change, of course; use your time line as a guide rather than as an inflexible plan.

A career time line helps you plan ahead.

Time	Step
1 month	Enter community college on a part-time schedule
6 months	Meet with advisor to discuss desired major and required courses
1 year	
	Declare major in secondary education
2 years	Switch to full-time class schedule
3 years	Graduate with associate's degree
	Transfer to 4-year college
4 years	Work part-time as a classroom aide
5 years	Student teaching
	Graduate with bachelor's degree and teaching certificate
6 years	Have a job teaching high school

The road to a truly satisfying career can be long. Seek support as you work toward goals. Confide in supportive people, talk positively to yourself, and read books about career planning such as those listed at the end of this chapter.

Keep track of details

After you establish your time frame, make a plan for pursuing the jobs or careers that have piqued your interest. Set goals that establish whom you will talk to, what courses you will take, what skills you will work on, what jobs or internships you will investigate, and any other research you need to do.

Organize your approach according to what you need to do and when you have to do it. Do you plan to make three phone calls per day? Will you fill out one job application each week? Keep a record—on 3 by 5 cards, in a computer file, or in a notebook—of the following:

- people you contact
- companies to which you apply
- jobs you rule out (for example, a job that becomes unavailable)
- responses to your communications (phone calls to you, interviews, written communications), information about the person who contacted you (name, title), and the time and dates of contact

Keeping accurate records enables you to both chart your progress and maintain a clear picture of the process. If you don't get a job now, another one could open up at the same company in a couple of months. In that case, well-kept records enable you to contact key personnel quickly and efficiently. Key 11.6 illustrates a sample file card.

Use a file card like this to keep records of your job search.

key 11.6

Job/company:	Child-care worker at Morningside Day Care
Contact:	Sally Wheeler, Morningside Day Care, 17 Parkside Rd, Silver Spring, MD 20910
Phone/fax/e-mail:	(301) 555-3353 phone, (301) 555-3354 fax, no e-mail
Communication:	Saw ad in paper, sent résumé & cover letter on Oct. 7
Response:	Call from Sally to set up interview —Interview on Oct. 15 at 2 p.m., seemed to get a positive response, said she would contact me again by end of the week
Follow-up:	Sent thank-you note on Oct. 16

Your résumé, cover letter, and interview

Information on résumés, cover letters, and interviews fills entire books. You'll find specific sources listed at the end of the chapter. To get you started, here are a few basic tips on giving yourself the best possible chance at a job.

Résumé and cover letter. Your résumé should always be typed or printed on high-quality paper. Design your résumé neatly, using an acceptable format (books or your career office can show you some standard formats).

Proofread it for errors and have someone else proofread it as well. Type or print it on a heavier bond paper than is used for ordinary copies. Include a cover letter along with your résumé that tells the employer what job you are interested in and why he or she should hire you.

Prospective employers often use a computer to scan résumés. The computer program will select résumés if they contain enough *keywords*—words relating to the job opening or industry. Résumés without enough keywords probably won't even make it to the human resources desk. When you construct your résumé, make sure to include as many keywords as you can. For example, if you are seeking a computer-related job, list computer programs you use and other specific technical proficiencies. To figure out what keywords you need, check out job descriptions, job postings, and other current résumés.[6]

Most schools have a career center where you can research internships, job opportunities, and career areas. These students are taking advantage of what's available at their school's Career Research Library.

Interview. Be clean, neat, and appropriately dressed. Choose a nice pair of shoes—people notice. Bring an extra copy of your résumé and any other materials that you want to show the interviewer, even if you have already

---

MAKE A DREAM RÉSUMÉ

get creative!

Use your imagination to conjure up an ideal work history.

On a separate piece of paper, write your "dream résumé"—the résumé that you would like to have when you graduate college, the résumé that would hit all the high points that you want to achieve and that would open the door at the places where you would most like to work. Use questions like these to brainstorm:

- What would be your academic record?
- What awards and honors would you have?
- What internship or work experience would you have?
- What special skills would you have?

The person who can hand out this résumé is the person you are committed to becoming.

sent a copy ahead of time. Avoid chewing gum or smoking. Offer a confident handshake. Make eye contact. Show your integrity by speaking honestly about yourself. After the interview, no matter what the outcome, follow up right away with a formal but pleasant thank-you note.

Being on time to your interview makes a positive impression—and being late will almost certainly be held against you. If you are from a culture that does not consider being late a sign of disrespect, remember that your interviewer may not agree.

Having a job may not only be a thought for the future; it may be something you are concerned about right now. Many students need to work and take classes at the same time to fund their education. Although you may not necessarily work in an area that interests you, you can hold a job that helps you pay the bills and still make the most of your school time.

What will help you *juggle* work and school?

What you are studying today can prepare you to find a job when you graduate. In the meantime, though, you can make work a part of your student life to make money, explore a career, and increase your future employability through contacts or résumé building.

As the cost of education continues to rise, more and more students are working and taking classes at the same time. Key 11.7 shows statistics related to working for both part-time and full-time college students.

Many people want to work and many need to work to pay for school. Gather information about what you need, analyze the potential positive

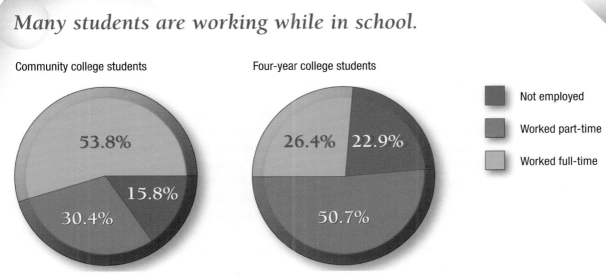

Many students are working while in school.

key 11.7

Community college students

Four-year college students

53.8%
15.8%
30.4%

26.4% 22.9%
50.7%

- Not employed
- Worked part-time
- Worked full-time

Source: U.S. Department of Education, National Center for Educational Statistics. *Profile of Undergraduates in U.S. Postsecondary Education Institutions:* 1999–2000. (NCES 98-084), July 2002, Table 5.1.

and negative effects of working, generate options, and make practical choices that are right for you.

Establish your needs

Think about what you need from a job before you begin your job hunt. Ask questions like these:

- How much money do I need to make—weekly, per semester, for the year?
- What time of day is best for me? Should I consider night or weekend work?
- Can my schedule handle a full-time job or should I look for part-time work?
- Do I want hands-on experience in a particular field? What do I like and dislike doing?
- Does location matter? Where do I want to work and how far am I willing to commute?
- How flexible a job do I need?
- Can I, or should I, find work at my school or as part of a work-study?

Analyze effects of working while in school

Evaluate any job opportunity by looking at these effects. Potential positive effects include:

- money earned.
- general and career-specific experience.
- enhanced school and work performance (working up to 15 hours a week may encourage students to manage time more effectively and build confidence).

  Potential negative effects include:

- demanding time commitment.
- reduced opportunity for social and extracurricular activities.
- having to shift gears mentally from work to classroom.

The right part-time job can help you develop skills that you can use after graduation. For example, "techies" on the University of Denver's Technology Services help-desk learn to solve hardware, software, and Internet problems as they polish their customer-service etiquette. On an average day, each staffer handles nearly 100 calls and visits, many of which involve angry, frustrated people. "We're on the front line, so if something goes wrong, we're the first to know, and we get blamed for everything," said technician Andrew Chan. Because Chan solves problems quickly and efficiently while treating people with respect, he will receive positive recommendations from his supervisors.[7]

No matter where your money comes from—financial aid or one or more jobs—budgeting skills will help you cover your expenses and have some cash left over for savings and fun.

How can you *create a budget* that works?

For the vast majority of college students, money is tight. You may have to rely on loans or money from a job in order to cover tuition, textbooks, and the products and services you need every day. Even if your family pays for your education, you will almost certainly need to monitor your monthly personal expenses. Effective budgeting relieves money-related stress and helps you feel more in control.

Your biggest expense right now is probably the cost of your education, including tuition and room and board. However, that expense may not hit you fully until after you graduate and begin to pay back your student loans. For now, include in your budget only the part of the cost of your education you are paying while you are in school.

Budgeting demands analytical, creative, and practical thinking. You gather information about your resources (money flowing in) and expenditures (money flowing out) and analyze the difference. Next, you come up with ideas about how you can make changes. Finally, you take practical action to adjust spending or earning so that you come out even or ahead. Most people budget on a month-by-month basis.

BUDGETING

Making a plan for the coordination of resources and expenditures; setting goals regarding money.

Figure out what you earn

Add up all of the money you receive during the year—the actual after-tax money you have to pay your bills. Common sources of income include:

- take-home pay from a regular full-time or part-time job during the school year
- take-home pay from summer and holiday employment
- money you earn as part of a work-study program
- money you receive from your parents or other relatives for your college expenses
- scholarships or grants that provide spending money

Money can't buy you happiness. It just helps you look for it in more places.

MILTON BERLE

If you have savings specifically earmarked for your education, decide how much you will withdraw every month for your school-related expenses.

Figure out what you spend

Start by recording every check you write for fixed expenses like rent and telephone. Then, over the next month, record personal expenditures in a small notebook. Indicate any expenditure over five dollars, making sure to count smaller expenditures if they are frequent (for example, a bus pass for a month, soda or newspaper purchases per week).

Some expenses, like automobile and health insurance, may be billed only a few times a year. In these cases, convert the expense to monthly by dividing the yearly cost by 12. Be sure to count only current expenses, not expenses that you will pay after you graduate. Among these are the following:

- rent or mortgage
- tuition that you are paying right now (the portion remaining after all forms of financial aid, including loans, scholarships and grants, are taken into account)
- books, lab fees, and other educational expenses
- regular bills (electric, gas, oil, phone, water)
- food, clothing, toiletries, and household supplies
- child care
- transportation and auto expenses (gas, maintenance)
- credit cards and other payments on credit (car payments)
- insurance (health, auto, homeowner's or renter's, life)
- entertainment and related items (cable TV, movies, eating out, books and magazines)
- computer-related expenses, including the cost of your on-line service
- miscellaneous unplanned expenses

Use the total of all your monthly expenses as a baseline for other months, realizing that your expenditures will vary depending on what is happening in your life.

Evaluate the difference

Focusing again on your current situation, subtract your monthly expenses from your monthly income. Ideally, you have money left over—to save or to spend. However, if you are spending more than you take in, your first job is to analyze the problem by looking carefully at your budget, your spending patterns, and priorities. Use your analytical thinking skills to ask some focused questions.

Question your budget. Did you forget to budget for recurring expenses such as the cost for semiannual dental visits? Or was your budget derailed by an emergency expense that you did not foresee, such as the cost of a new transmission for your car? Is your budget realistic? Is your income sufficient for your needs?

Question your spending patterns and priorities. Did you spend money wisely during the month? Did you go to too many restaurants or movies? Can you afford the luxury of your own car? Are you putting too many purchases on your credit card and being hit by high interest payments? When you are spending more than you are taking in during a "typical month," you may have to adjust your budget over the long term.

Adjust spending or earning

Look carefully at what may cause you to overspend and brainstorm possible solutions that address those causes. Solutions can involve either increasing resources or decreasing spending. To deal with spending, priori-

MULTIPLE INTELLIGENCE STRATEGIES FOR
Budgeting

Looking into the strategies associated with your strongest intelligences helps you identify effective ways to manage your money.

INTELLIGENCE	SUGGESTED STRATEGIES	WHAT WORKS FOR YOU? WRITE NEW IDEAS HERE
Verbal–Linguistic	• Talk over your budget with someone you trust. • Write out a detailed budget outline. If you can, keep it on a computer where you can change and update it regularly.	
Logical–Mathematical	• Focus on the numbers; using a calculator and amounts as exact as possible, determine your income and spending. • Calculate how much money you'll have in 10 years if you start now to put $2,000 in an IRA account each year.	
Bodily–Kinesthetic	• Consider putting money, or a slip with a dollar amount, each month in different envelopes for various budget items—rent, dining out, etc. When the envelope is empty or the number is reduced to zero, your spending stops.	
Visual–Spatial	• Set up a budgeting system that includes color-coded folders and colored charts. • Create color-coded folders for papers related to financial and retirement goals—investments, accounts, etc.	
Interpersonal	• Whenever budgeting problems come up, discuss them right away. • Brainstorm a solid five-year financial plan with one of your friends.	
Intrapersonal	• Schedule quiet time and think about how you want to develop, follow, and update your budget. Consider financial-management software, such as Quicken. • Think through the most balanced allocation of your assets—where you think your money should go.	
Musical	• Include a category of music-related purchases in your budget—going to concerts, buying CDs—but keep an eye on it to make sure you don't go overboard.	
Naturalistic	• Remember to include time and money in your budget to enjoy nature. • Sit in a spot you like. Brainstorm how you will achieve your short- and long-term financial goals.	

tize your expenditures and trim the ones you really don't need to make. Cut out unaffordable extras.

As for resources, investigate ways to take in more money. Start your summer job search early. Taking a part-time job, hunting down scholarships or grants, increasing hours at a current job, or looking for a higher-paying job may also help.

A sample budget

Key 11.8 shows a sample budget of an unmarried student living with two other students in off-campus housing with no meal plan. Included are all regular and out-of-pocket expenses with the exception of tuition expenses, which the student will pay back after graduation in student loan payments. In this case, the student is $164 over budget. How would you make up the shortfall?

Not everyone likes the work involved in keeping a budget. For example, whereas logical–mathematical learners may take to it easily, visual learners may resist the structure and detail of the budgeting process (see Chapter 3). Visual learners may want to create a budget chart such as the

How one student mapped out a monthly budget.

A STUDENT'S SAMPLE MONTHLY BUDGET

- Wages: $10 an hour (after taxes) × 20 hours a week = $200 a week × 4 1/3 weeks (one month) = $866.
- Withdrawals from savings (from summer earnings) = $200
- Total income per month: $1,066

MONTHLY EXPENDITURES

School-related expenses (not covered by student loans, grants, scholarships—including books and supplies)	$ 150
Public transportation	$ 90
Phone	$ 40
Food	$ 450
Credit card payments	$ 100
Rent (including utilities)	$ 200
Entertainment	$ 100
Miscellaneous expenses, including clothes and toiletries	$ 100
Total monthly spending	**$1,230**

$1,066 (income) − $1,230 (spending) = $−164 ($164 over budget) one in the example or use strategies that make budgeting more tangible, such as dumping receipts into a big jar and tallying them at the end of the month. Even if you have to force yourself to use a budget, you will realize that the process can reduce stress and help you take control of your finances and your life.

Make successfully intelligent financial decisions

Every budgetary decision you make has particular effects, often involving a trade-off among options. When you spend $80 for that new pair of sneakers, for example, you may not have enough for movie tickets and dinner with friends that weekend. That is, there is an opportunity cost in addition to money. In this case, the new sneakers deprive you of the chance to attend the movie and go to dinner.

Use decision-making strategies

Being a successfully intelligent money manager means using what you know about decision making (Chapter 4) to think through financial decisions carefully.

1. **Define the decision.** Be honest about what you need and what you just want. Do you really need a new bike? Or can the old one suffice while you pay off some credit card debt?
2. **Generate available options.** Imagine what you can do with your money.
3. **Evaluate options.** Look closely at the positive and negative effects of each option and make a choice.
4. **Take practical action.** Spend it—save it—invest it—whatever you decided to do.
5. **Evaluate the result.** Build knowledge that you can use in the future. What were the positive and negative effects of what you chose? Would you make that choice again?

Balance short-term satisfaction and long-term money growth

Often, making some short-term sacrifices in order to save money can help you tremendously in the long run. However, this doesn't mean you should never spend money on things that bring you immediate satisfaction. The goal is to make choices that provide both short-term satisfaction and long-term money growth. Here are two ways to do just that:

- **Live beneath your means.** Spend less than you make. This helps you create savings. Saved money gives you a buffer that can help with emergencies or bigger expenditures.
- **Pay yourself.** After you pay your monthly bills, put whatever you can save in an account. Paying yourself helps you store money in your savings where it can grow. Make your payment to yourself a high priority so that you honor it as you do your other bills.
- **Use banks to your advantage.** Choose a bank that has reasonable account fees and convenient ATMs—and, if you use it, on-line access for banking and bill payment. Know how much you can maintain in a checking account, and find one that can handle your minimum with the lowest fees.

get practical!

MAP OUT YOUR BUDGET

Arrive at a basic estimate of whether you are operating at a gain or a loss.

Step 1: Estimate your current expenses in dollars per month, using the following table. This may require tracking expenses for a month, if you don't already keep a record of your spending. The grand total is your total monthly expenses.

Expense	Amount Spent
Rent/mortgage or room and board payment	$
Utilities (electric, heat, gas, water)	$
Food (shopping, eating out, meal plan)	$
Telephone (land line and mobile phone)	$
Books, lab fees, other educational expenses	$
Loan payments (educational or bank loans)	$
Car (repairs, insurance, payments, gas)	$
Public transportation	$
Clothing/personal items	$
Entertainment	$
Child care (caregivers, clothing/supplies, etc.)	$
Medical care/insurance	$
Other	$
TOTAL	**$**

Step 2: Calculate your average monthly income. If it's easiest to come up with a yearly figure, divide by 12 to derive the monthly figure. For example, if you have a $6,000 scholarship for the year, your monthly income would be $500 ($6,000 divided by 12).

Income Source	Amount Received
Regular work salary/wages (full-time or part-time)	$
Grants or work-study programs	$
Scholarships	$
Assistance from family members	$
Other	$
TOTAL	**$**

Step 3: Subtract the grand total of your monthly expenses from the grand total of your monthly income:

Income per month	$
Expenses per month	– $
CASH FLOW	$

Step 4: If you have a negative cash flow, you can increase your income, decrease your spending, or both. Think about what's possible for you to accomplish. List here your two most workable ideas about how you can get your cash flow back in the black.

1. _____

2. _____

Use savings strategies

You can save money and still enjoy life. Think carefully about where your money goes and save your splurges for special items or events. Here are some savings suggestions for cutting corners. Small amounts can eventually add up to big savings and may keep you out of debt.

It is thrifty to prepare today for the wants of tomorrow.

AESOP

- Share living space.
- Rent or borrow movies.
- Eat at home more often than at restaurants.
- Use coupons, take advantage of sales, buy store brands, and buy in bulk.
- Find discounted play and concert tickets (students often receive discounts).
- Walk or use public transport.
- Bring your lunch from home.
- Shop in secondhand stores.
- Use e-mail or write letters.
- Ask a relative to help with child care.

How can you manage your *credit cards*?

College students often receive dozens of credit card offers from financial institutions issuing VISA and MasterCard. These offers—and the cards that go along with them—are a double-edged sword: They have the power to help you manage your money, but they also can plunge you into a hole of debt that may take you years to dig out of. Some recent statistics from a Nellie May survey of undergraduates illustrate the challenging situation:[8]

- Average number of credit cards per student—3.2
- Average credit card debt per student—$1,843
- Average available credit card limit—$3,683
- Percentage of students with debt between $3,000 and $7,000— 9 percent
- Percentage of students with more than $7,000 in credit card debt— 5 percent

When used properly, credit cards are a handy alternative to cash. They give you the peace of mind of knowing that you always have money for emergencies and that you have a record of all your purchases. In addition, if you pay your bills on time, you will be building a strong credit history that will affect your ability to take out future loans including auto loans and mortgages.

However, it takes self-control to avoid overspending, especially because it is so easy to hand over your credit card when you see something you like. To avoid excessive debt, ask yourself questions before charging: Would I buy it if I had to pay cash? Can I pay off the balance in full at the end of the first billing cycle? If I buy this, what purchases will I have to forgo? If I buy this, do I have enough to cover emergencies?

How credit cards work

Every time you charge a textbook, a present, or a pair of pants, you are creating a debt that must be repaid. The credit card issuer earns money by charging interest on your unpaid balance. With rates often higher than 20 percent, you may soon find yourself wishing that you had paid cash.

Here's an example of how quickly credit card debt can mount. Say you have a $3,000 unpaid balance on your credit card at an annual interest rate of 18 percent. If you make the $60 minimum monthly payment every month, it will take you 8 long years to pay off your debt, assuming that you make no other purchases. The math—and the effect on your wallet—is staggering:

- Original debt—$3,000
- Cost to repay credit card loan at an annual interest rate of 18 percent for 8 years—$5,760
- Cost of credit—$2,760

By the time you finish, you will repay nearly twice your original debt.

To avoid unmanageable debt that can lead to a personal financial crisis, learn as much as you can about credit cards, starting with the important concepts in Key 11.9. Learn to use credit wisely while you are still in school. The habits you learn today can make a difference to your financial future.

Learn to be a smart credit consumer.

WHAT TO KNOW ABOUT . . .	. . . AND HOW TO USE WHAT YOU KNOW
Account balance—a dollar amount that includes any unpaid balance, new purchases and cash advances, finance charges, and fees. Updated monthly on your card statement.	Charge only what you can afford to pay at the end of the month. Keep track of your balance. Hold on to receipts and call customer service if you have questions about recent purchases.
Annual fee—the yearly cost some companies charge for owning a card.	Look for cards without an annual fee or, if you've paid your bills on time, ask your current company to waive the fee.
Annual percentage rate (APR)—the amount of interest charged on your unpaid balance, meaning the cost of credit if you carry a balance in any given month. The higher the APR, the more you pay in finance charges.	Credit card companies compete by charging different APRs. Shop around, especially on the Web. Two sites with competitive APR information are www.studentcredit.com and www.bankrate.com. Also, watch out for low, but temporary, introductory rates that skyrocket to over 20 percent after a few months. Look for *fixed* rates (guaranteed not to change).
Available credit—the unused portion of your credit line. Determine available credit by deducting your current card balance from your credit limit.	It is important to have credit available for emergencies, so avoid charging to the limit.
Billing cycle—the number of days between the last statement date and the current statement date.	Knowledge of your billing cycle can help you juggle funds. For example, if your cycle ends on the 3rd of the month, holding off on a large purchase until the 4th gives you an extra month to pay without incurring finance charges.
Cash advance—an immediate loan, in the form of cash, from the credit card company. You are charged interest immediately and may also pay a separate transaction fee.	Use a cash advance only in emergencies because the finance charges start as soon as you complete the transaction. It is a very expensive way to borrow money.
Credit limit—the debt ceiling the card company places on your account (e.g., $1,500). The total owed, including purchases, cash advances, finance charges, and fees, cannot exceed this limit.	Credit card companies generally set low credit limits for college students. Many students get around this limit by owning more than one card, which increases the credit available but most likely increases problems as well.
Credit line—a revolving amount of credit that can be used, paid back, then used again for future purchases or cash advances.	Work with the credit line of one card, paying the money you borrow back at the end of each month so you can borrow again.
Delinquent account—an account that is not paid on time or for which the minimum payment has not been met.	Avoid having a delinquent account at all costs. Not only will you be charged substantial late fees, but you also risk losing your good credit rating, affecting your ability to borrow in the future. Delinquent accounts remain part of your credit record for many years.
Due date—the date your payment must be received and after which you will be charged a late fee.	Avoid late fees and finance charges by mailing your payment a week in advance.

WHAT TO KNOW ABOUT . . .	. . . AND HOW TO USE WHAT YOU KNOW
Finance charges—the total cost of credit, including interest and service and transaction fees.	Your goal is to incur no finance charges. The only way to do that is to pay your balance in full by the due date on your monthly statement.
Grace period—the interest-free time period between the date of purchase and the date your payment for that purchase is due once it appears on your statement. For example, a purchase on November 4 may first appear on your November 28 statement with payment due 25 days later.	It is important to know that interest-free grace periods only apply if you have no outstanding balance. If you carry a balance from month to month, all new purchases are immediately subject to interest charges.
Minimum payment—the smallest amount you can pay by the statement due date. The amount is set by the credit card company.	Making only the minimum payment each month can result in disaster if you continue to charge more than you can realistically afford. When you make a purchase, think in terms of total cost, not monthly payments.
Outstanding balance—the total amount you owe on your card.	If you carry a balance over several months, additional purchases are immediately hit with finance charges. Pay cash instead.
Past due—your account is considered "past due" when you fail to pay the minimum required payment on schedule.	Three credit bureaus note past due accounts on your credit history: Experian, Trans Union, and Equifax. You can contact each bureau for a copy of your credit report to make sure there are no errors.

Managing debt

The majority of American citizens have some level of debt, and many people go through periods when they have a hard time paying bills. Falling behind on payments, however, could result in a poor credit rating that makes it difficult for you to make large purchases or take out loans. Particular resources can help you solve credit problems; see Key 11.10 for some ideas.

Avoiding the pitfalls of credit card debt means educating yourself about interest rates, late charges, credit ratings, bankruptcy, and more. Debbie Alford, a student at the University of Central Oklahoma, realized too late how poor financial decisions would affect her future. As a freshman, Debbie charged only "necessities," such as books and tuition, and paid her credit card debt in full when her financial aid check arrived every semester. Her debt began to escalate when she started using her cards to cover expenses, like car repairs, food, and clothes. At age 23, and only a junior in college, Debbie filed for bankruptcy. Looking back, she blames credit card companies for making it so easy to accumulate debt and herself for not understanding the financial hole she was digging until it was too late.[9]

The most basic way to stay in control is to pay bills regularly and on time. On credit card bills, pay at least the minimum amount due. If you get into trouble, deal with it in three steps. First, admit that you made a

National Foundation for Credit Counseling
(tips on credit management)
www.nfcc.org

Springboard Non-profit Consumer
Credit Management
www.ncfe.org

Genus Credit Management
(free debt counseling)
1-888-436-8715

Consumer Credit Counseling Service
(credit counseling)
1-800-338-2227
Spanish 1-800-682-9832

Money Matters for College Students
(free booklet from Citibank)
1-800-833-9666

mistake, even though you may be embarrassed. Then, address the problem immediately to minimize damages. Call the **creditor** and see if you can pay your debt gradually using a payment plan. Finally, examine what got you into trouble and avoid it in the future if you can. Cut up a credit card or two if you have too many. If you clean up your act, your credit history will gradually clean up as well.

CREDITOR

A person or company to whom a debt is owed, usually money.

Sacrifici

In Italy, parents often use the term *sacrifici*, meaning "sacrifices," to refer to tough choices that they make to improve the lives of their children and family members. They may sacrifice a larger home so that they can afford to pay for their children's sports and after-school activities. They may sacrifice a higher-paying job so that they can live close to where they work. They give up something in exchange for something else that is more important to them.

Think of the concept of *sacrifici* as you analyze the sacrifices you can make to get out of debt, reach your savings goals, and prepare for a career that you find satisfying. Many of the short-term sacrifices you are making today will help you do and have what you want in the future.

Developing Successful Intelligence

PUTTING IT ALL TOGETHER

Personal qualities and career success. Much of what brings success in any career area is being able to match who you are to the personal qualities that are valued for a given profession. Use your successful intelligence to investigate where you fit.

Step 1. Think it through: *Analyze who succeeds and why.* Pick one career area to focus on. What are the characteristics of people who are successful in this career? Think about success-promoting qualities that aren't obvious. Investigate, using information from the Internet, conversations with successful working people, and reading.

Career area that interests you:

Qualities and characteristics of people who succeed in this career:

What you have in common with these people:

Do you see yourself and your talents reflected in the people you learned about?

Step 2. Think out of the box: *Generate ideas about what inspires you.* What topics, tasks, and interests make you feel creative, capable, and joyful?

create your future

What motivates you to do more? Brainstorm a few ideas, keeping in mind that career success often comes from pursuing what you love to do.

_____

_____

Step 3. Make it happen: _Look for practical ways to test what you've learned._ From the people you talked to and where they work, make a list of three summer or winter internship possibilities.

_1._ _____

_2._ _____

_3._ _____

On a separate piece of paper, map out a three-month plan for contacting these people, determining the possibility of interning, and applying formally for internships.

Team Building

Building interview skills. Divide into pairs—each student will have a turn interviewing the other about themselves and their career aspirations. Follow these steps.

1. Independently, take three minutes to brainstorm questions you'll ask the other person. Focus on learning style, interests, and initial career ideas. You might ask questions like these:
   - If you could have any job in the world, what would it be?
   - What do you think would be the toughest part of achieving success in that profession?
   - Who are you as a learner and worker—what is your learning style?
   - What sacrifices are you willing to make to realize your dreams?
   - What is your greatest failure, and what have you learned from it?
   - Who is a role model to you in terms of career success?
2. Person A interviews Person B for 5 to 10 minutes and takes notes.
3. Switch roles: Person B interviews Person A and takes notes. Remember that each person uses their own questions that they developed in Step 1.
4. Share with each other what interesting ideas stand out to you from the interviews. If you have any, offer constructive criticism to your interviewee about his or her interview skills.
5. Finally, submit your notes to your instructor for feedback.

   This exercise will build your ability to glean information from others and to answer questions during an interview. You will use this skill throughout your professional life. Probe deeply when interviewing others so that you develop the ability to draw out the best in someone. Be as interested—and interesting—as you can.

Writing

Record your thoughts on a separate piece of paper or in a journal.

Money and you. Describe your relationship with money. What do you buy? How much do you spend? Are you careful? Reckless? Unattentive? Focused on every detail? How much do you use credit cards—and do you pay credit card bills in full each month or run a balance? If you could change how you handle money, what would you do?

Career Portfolio

PLAN FOR SUCCESS

Complete the following in your electronic portfolio or on separate sheets of paper.

Being specific about your job needs. As you consider specific job directions and opportunities, you will have to begin thinking about a variety of job-related factors that different employers offer and that may affect your job experience and personal life. Among these factors are the following:

- Benefits [including health insurance, vacation, 401(k)]
- Integrity of company (What is its reputation?)
- Integrity of organization in its dealings with employees
- Promotion prospects/your chances for advancement
- Job stability
- Training and educational opportunities (Does the company offer in-house training? Will it pay for job-related courses or degrees?)
- Starting salary
- Quality of employees
- Quality of management
- Nature of the work you will be doing (Will you be required to travel extensively? Will you be expected to work long hours? Will you be working in an office or in the field?)
- Your official relationship with the company (Will you be a full-time or part-time employee or an independent contractor?)
- Job title
- Location of your primary workplace
- Company size
- Company's financial performance over time

Think about how important each factor is in your job choice. Then rate each on a scale of 1 to 10, with 1 being the least important and 10 being the most important. As you consider each factor, keep in mind that even if you consider something very important, you may not get it right away if you are just beginning your career.

Finally, consider the results of a recent survey of college students conducted by the National Association of Colleges and Employers. When asked their top two reasons for choosing an employer, students named *integrity of organization in its dealings with employees* as number one and *job stability* as number two. How do these top choices compare to your own?[10]

SUGGESTED READINGS

Adams, Robert Lang, et al. *The Complete Résumé and Job Search Book for College Students.* Holbrook, MA: Adams Publishing, 1999.

Beatty, Richard H. *The Resume Kit,* 5th ed. New York: John Wiley & Sons, 2003.

Boldt, Laurence G. *Zen and the Art of Making a Living: A Practical Guide to Creative Career Design.* New York: Arkana, 1999.

Bolles, Richard Nelson. *What Color Is Your Parachute? 2003: A Practical Manual for Job Hunters and Career Changers.* Berkeley, CA: Ten Speed Press, 2003.

Detweiler, Gerri. *The Ultimate Credit Handbook,* 3rd ed. New York: Plume, 2003.

Goleman, Daniel. *Emotional Intelligence.* New York: Bantam Books, 1997.

Goleman, Daniel. *Working with Emotional Intelligence.* New York: Bantam Books, 2000.

Kennedy, Joyce Lain. *Job Interviews for Dummies.* Foster City, CA: IDG Books Worldwide, 2000.

Tyson, Eric. *Personal Finance for Dummies.* Foster City, CA: IDG Books Worldwide, 2000.

INTERNET RESOURCES

U.S. Bureau of Labor—statistics: www.bls.gov/oco/

Student Advantage—information on discounts: www.studentadvantage.com

Monster.com (on-line job search): www.monster.com

The Motley Fool (money and investment advice): www.fool.com/

1st Steps in the Hunt: Daily News for Online Job Hunters (advice on finding a job via an on-line search): www.interbiznet.com/hunt/

College Grad Job Hunter (advice on résumés, interviews, and a database of entry-level jobs): www.collegegrad.com

Women Working 2000 and Beyond (information for working women): www.womenworking2000.com/

JobWeb (career information site for college students): www.jobweb.com/

Prentice Hall Student Success Supersite—Money Matters: www.prenhall.com/success/MoneyMat/index.html

Career Path: www.prenhall.com/success/CareerPath/index.html

Résumé Edge (résumé advice): www.resumeedge.com

ENDNOTES

1. Peter Passell, "Royal Blue Collars," *New York Times,* March 22, 1998, p. 12.

2. Daniel Goleman, *Working with Emotional Intelligence.* New York: Bantam Books, 1998, pp. 26–27.

3. Women's Review of Books, "Rebuilding a Life: Susan Davenny Wyner Replays Her Transformation from Singer to Conductor," December 2000, reprinted on the Web site for the New England String Ensemble [on-line]. Available: www.newenglandstringensemble.org/ (May 2004).

4. New Mexico State University FAQ, "Does NMSU Do Anything to Help People Get Jobs After They Graduate?" October 2000 [on-line]. Available: www.nmsu.edu/aggieland/students/faq_jobs.html (March 2004).

5. New Mexico State University FAQ, "What Kind of Student Clubs and Organizations Are There?" June 1999 [on-line]. Available: www.nmsu.edu/aggieland/students/faq_orgs.html (March 2004).

6. ResumeEdge.com, "Resume Keyword Search," 2004 [on-line]. Available: www.enetsc.com/ResumeTips23.htm (May 2004).

7. Scott Carlson, "Help-Desk Diary: Tech-Savvy Students Learn People Skills and Patience by Solving Campus Computer Problems," *The Chronicle of Higher Education,* June 20, 2003 [on-line]. Available: http://chronicle.com/weekly/v49/i41a02701.htm (March 2004).

8. Laura A. Bruce, "College Kids' Credit Card Use Can Leave Them Drowning in High-Interest Debt," Bankrate.com, 2001 [on-line]. Available: www.bankrate.com/brm/news/cc/20000815.asp (March 2001).

9. Eric Hoover, "The Lure of Easy Credit Leaves More Students Struggling with Debt: Consumer Advocates Blame Lenders, Congress, and Some Colleges," *The Chronicle of Higher Education,* June 15, 2001 [on-line]. Available: http://chronicle.com/weekly/v47/i40/40a03501.h' (March 2004).

10. Eduardo Porter and Greg Winter, "'04 Grad Learned Lesson in Practicality," *New Yo* May 30, 2004, pp. A1 and A24.

12

IN THIS CHAPTER . . .

You will explore answers to the following questions:

Creating Your Life
BUILDING A SUCCESSFUL FUTURE

As you come to the end of your work in this course, you have built up a wealth of knowledge. You will soon be analyzing how you fared in your first college semester. You are facing important decisions about what direction you want to go in school—and starting to think about where the choices you make now will ultimately lead you.

This chapter will help you connect college to the rest of your life. You will see how the skills and attitudes you acquire in school fuel your future success. You will learn to think of yourself as a member of broader communities and to take on the challenge of being an active participant. You will gather 20 important tools that will help you transfer the power of successful intelligence into your postcollege life. Finally, you will create your personal mission, exploring how to use it to guide your dreams.

On the following page, read how student Rachel Faison is looking for ways in which she can translate her college experience into life success.

- How will what you've learned bring success?
- How can you make a difference in your community?
- How can you continue to activate your succe̅ intelligence?
- How can you create and live your pers̅

What knowledge will help me succeed in a changing world?

At my school, we are required to focus on an area of interest starting in the second semester of sophomore year. At this point I'm planning on studying acting, with an intent to pursue an acting career after I graduate. Since I'm a sophomore now, I will soon have to load my schedule with classes in the theater department. I know that acting is an unreliable profession, but it's what I want to do; plus, these days it seems that you can't find job security anywhere, even in areas that traditionally were pretty solid.

I do want to take time in college to explore other areas of interest. Art history and religion both interest me although I don't know how I would translate those interests into a career. I believe that as long as you have basic areas of knowledge and study a variety of things, you'll have options—you will find something to do and will be able to do it well. I'm just not sure of the specifics of how that works. How will what I'm doing in college serve me, outside of the specific training I'll receive in acting? What will help me keep my footing in a career once I graduate?

Rachel Faison

Bard College, Annandale-on-Hudson, New York

Internship experience and exploring your passions will help you achieve success.

You are absolutely right that if you learn to use your mind to the fullest, you will prepare yourself well for any profession you decide to pursue. The key right now is to develop several skill sets to complement your academic learning so that you will be versatile. Here are some ideas about how to build your general skills and explore your specific passions and interests.

First, work at least two internships before you graduate. You will learn volumes from experiencing the culture and politics in different workplaces and by proving your instincts and skills in the real-world environment. This experience will also help you discover whether you like or dislike the areas in which you intern. Knowing what you don't like can be just as important as knowing what you like. Many students select fields that sound good or pay a lot without discovering what succeeding in that field really entails. Do your homework on what interests you.

Second, look for areas where you can build your leadership skills. What organization can you join? What leadership role can you play? How will that organization be different and better because you have been a part of it? Stretch yourself. Sometimes when we move into areas that scare us, we grow the most. Develop a healthy outlook toward success and failure as you participate and lead within organizations in college.

Finally, think carefully about what you love (and don't love) doing. Ask yourself probing questions regarding your values. Listen to your heart as well as your head. What makes you feel purposeful, creative, joyful, and valued? What makes you want to wake up every morning? You may not come up with answers right away, but committing yourself to the process of asking the questions and "holding" the questions will allow you to dig genuinely and deeply for the way that you can make your mark in the world of work. Good luck and congratulations for being brave enough to ask meaningful questions!

Carol Carter

President and Founder, LifeBound, Denver, Colorado

How will what you've learned *bring success?*

Y ou leave this course with far more than a final grade, a notebook full of work, and a credit hour or three on your transcript. You have gathered important attitudes and skills, developed flexibility, and opened the door to lifelong learning.

New attitudes and skills prepare you to succeed

The attitudes and skills you gained this semester are your keys to success now and in the future (see Key 12.1). As you move through your college years, keep motivation high by reminding yourself that you are creating tools that will benefit you in everything you do.

Flexibility helps you adapt to change

As a citizen of the twenty-first century, you are likely to move in and out of school, jobs, and careers in the years ahead. You are also likely to experience important personal changes. How you react to the changes you experience, especially if they are unexpected and difficult, is almost as important as the changes themselves in determining your future success. The ability to "make lemonade from lemons" is the hallmark of people who always land on their feet.

Successfully intelligent thinking will help you adapt to and benefit from both planned and unexpected changes. Your goal is flexibility as you analyze each change, generate and consider options, make decisions, and take practical actions. With flexibility and resourcefulness, you can adapt to the loss of a job or an exciting job offer, a personal health crisis or a happy change in family status, failing a course or winning an academic scholarship.

Although sudden changes may throw you off balance, the unpredictability of life can open new horizons. Margaret J. Wheatley and Myron Kellner-Rogers, leadership and community experts and founders of the Berkana Institute, explain: People "often look at this unpredictability with resentment, but . . . unpredictability gives us the freedom to experiment. It is this unpredictability that welcomes our creativity."[1] Here are some strategies they recommend for making the most of unpredictable changes:

- **Look for what happens when you meet someone or something new.** Be aware of new feelings or insights that arise. Observe where they lead you.

- **Be willing to be surprised.** Great creative energies can come from the force of a surprise. Instead of turning back to familiar patterns, explore new possibilities.

The word "impossible" is not in my dictionary.

NAPOLEON

- **Use your planning as a guide rather than a rule.** If you allow yourself to follow new paths when changes occur, you are able to grow from what life gives you.

Attitudes and skills acquired in college are tools for lifelong success.

key
12.1

ACQUIRED SKILL	IN COLLEGE, YOU'LL USE IT TO . . .	IN CAREER AND LIFE, YOU'LL USE IT TO . . .
Investigating resources	. . . find who and what can help you have the college experience you want	. . . get acclimated at a new job or in a new town—find the people, resources, and services that can help you succeed
Knowing and using your learning styles	. . . select study strategies that make the most of your learning styles	. . . select jobs, career areas, and other pursuits that suit what you do best
Setting goals and managing stress	. . . complete assignments and achieve educational goals, reduce stress by being in control	. . . accomplish tasks and reach career and personal goals, reduce stress by being in control
Managing time	. . . get to classes on time, juggle school and work, turn in assignments when they are due, plan study time	. . . finish work tasks on or before they are due, balance duties on the job and at home
Analytical, creative, and practical thinking	. . . think through writing assignments, solve math problems, analyze academic readings, brainstorm paper topics, work through academic issues, work effectively on team projects	. . . find ways to improve product design, increase market share, present ideas to customers; analyze life issues, come up with ideas, and take practical action
Reading	. . . read course texts and other materials	. . . read operating manuals, work guidebooks, media materials in your field; read for practical purposes, for learning, and for pleasure at home
Note taking	. . . take notes in class, in study groups, during studying, and during research	. . . take notes in work and community meetings and during important phone calls
Test taking	. . . take quizzes, tests, and final exams	. . . take tests for certification in particular work skills and for continuing education courses
Writing	. . . write essays and reports	. . . write work-related documents, including e-mails, reports, proposals, and speeches; write personal letters and journal entries
Building successful relationships	. . . get along with instructors, students, student groups	. . . get along with supervisors, coworkers, team members, friends, and family members
Staying healthy	. . . stay physically and mentally healthy so that you can make the most of school	. . . stay physically and mentally healthy so that you can be at your best at work and at home
Managing money	. . . stay on top of school costs and make decisions that earn and save you the money you need	. . . budget the money you earn so that you can pay your bills and save for the future
Establishing and maintaining a personal mission	. . . develop a big-picture idea of what you want from your education, and make choices that guide you toward those goals	. . . develop a big-picture idea of what you wish to accomplish in life, and make choices that guide you toward those goals

- **Focus on what is rather than what is supposed to be.** Planning for the future works best as a guide when combined with an awareness of the realities of your situation.

Lifelong learning

As a student, your main focus is on learning—on acquiring knowledge and skills in the courses you take. Though you will graduate knowing much more than you did when you started college, you are not finished learning. On the contrary, with knowledge in many fields doubling every two to three years and with your personal interests and needs changing every day, what you learn in college is just the beginning of lifelong learning. With the *habit* of learning you will be able to achieve your career and personal goals—those that you set out for yourself today and those that you cannot anticipate but that will be part of your future.

You can make learning a habit through asking questions and being open to exploring new ideas and possibilities. Here are some ways to make that happen:

Seeking experiences that broaden your horizons is part of lifelong learning. These students are learning both academic and life lessons during their travel in China.

Investigate new interests. When information and events catch your attention, take your interest one step further and find out more. Instead of dreaming about it, just do it.

Read, read, read. Reading expert Jim Trelease says that people who don't read "base their future decisions on what they used to know. If you don't read much, you really don't know much. You're dangerous."[2] Decrease the danger to yourself and others by opening a world of knowledge and perspectives through reading. Ask friends which books have changed their lives. Keep up with local, national, and world news through newspapers and magazines.

Pursue improvement in your studies and career. After graduation, continue your education both in your field and in the realm of general knowledge. Stay on top of ideas, developments, and new technology in your field by seeking out continuing education courses. Sign up for career-related seminars. Take single courses at a local college or community learning center. Some companies offer additional on-the-job training or pay for their employees to take courses that will improve their knowledge and skills.

CONTINUING EDUCATION
Courses that students can take without having to be part of a degree program.

Spend time with interesting people. When you meet someone new who inspires you and makes you think, keep in touch. Form a study group, a film club, or a walking club. Host a potluck dinner party and invite people from different corners of your life—family, school, work, or neighborhood. Learn something new from everyone you meet.

Talk to people from different generations. Younger people can learn from the experienced, broad perspective of those belonging to older generations;

older people can learn from the fresh and often radical perspective of those younger than themselves. Communication builds mutual respect.

Delve into other cultures. Talk with a friend who has grown up in a culture different from your own. Invite him or her to dinner. Eat food from a country you've never visited. Initiate conversations with people of different races, religions, values, and ethnic backgrounds. Travel internationally and locally. Take a course that deals with some aspect of cultural diversity. Try a semester or year abroad.

Nurture a spiritual life. You don't have to attend a house of worship to be spiritual, although that may be part of your spiritual life. Wherever you find spirituality and soul—in music, organized religion, friendship, nature, cooking, sports, or anything else—they will help you find balance and meaning.

Experience the arts. Art is "an adventure of the mind" (Eugène Ionesco, playwright); "a means of knowing the world" (Angela Carter, author); something that "does not reproduce the visible; rather, it makes visible" (Paul Klee, painter); "a lie that makes us realize truth" (Pablo Picasso, painter); a revealer of "our most secret self" (Jean-Luc Godard, filmmaker). Through art forms you can discover new ideas and shed light on old ones. Seek out whatever moves you—music, visual arts, theater, photography, dance, domestic arts, performance art, film and television, poetry, prose, and more.

Make your own creations. Take a class in drawing, writing, or quilting. Learn to play an instrument. Write poems for your favorite people or

get creative!

THINK 50 POSITIVE THOUGHTS

Appreciate yourself, and plan to expand your horizons.

On a separate piece of paper, list 25 things you like about yourself. You can name anything—things you can do, things you think, things you've accomplished, things you like about your physical self, and so on.

Next, list 25 things you would like to do in your life. These can be anything from trying Vietnamese food to traveling to the Grand Canyon to working for Teach for America. They can be things you'd like to do tomorrow or things that you plan to do in 20 years. At least 5 items on each list should involve your current and future education.

Finally, come up with five things you can plan for the next year that combine what you like about yourself and what you want to do. If you like your strength as a mountain biker and you want to explore a state you've never seen, plan a mountain biking trip. If you like your writing and you want to be a published author, write an essay to submit to a magazine. Be creative. Let everything be possible.

1.
2. _____
3. _____
4. _____
5. _____

stories to read to your children. Concoct a new recipe. Design and build a set of shelves for your home. Create a memoir of your life. Express yourself, and learn more about yourself, through art.

Lifelong learning is the master key that unlocks every door you encounter on your journey. If you keep it firmly in your hand, you will discover worlds of knowledge—and a place for yourself within them.

You are part of a world community of people who depend on one another. Giving what you can of your time, energy, and resources to those who need help makes you a valued community member.

How can you *make a difference* in your community?

Everyday life is demanding. You can become so caught up in your own issues that you neglect to pay attention to anything else. However, you can make a difference in your community—by helping others; being an active, involved citizen; and doing your share for the environment.

COMMUNITY
(1) A group of people living in the same locality.
(2) A group of people having common interests.
(3) A group of people forming a distinct segment of society.

You can help others

What you do for others has enormous impact. Giving others hope, comfort, or help can improve their ability to cope. Reaching out to others can also enhance your career. Being involved in causes and the community shows caring and community spirit, qualities companies look for in people they hire.

You can help others by volunteering, participating in service learning, and setting an example in how you live your life.

Volunteering

Look for a volunteering activity that you can fit into your schedule. Key 12.2 lists organizations that provide volunteer opportunities; you might also look into more local efforts or private clearinghouses that set up smaller projects.

Never doubt that a small group of committed citizens can change the world; indeed, it's the only thing that ever has.

MARGARET MEAD

Many schools, realizing the importance of community involvement, sponsor volunteer groups or have committees that organize volunteering opportunities. For example, the University of Virginia has a student volunteer center called Madison House, which connects UVa students to the surrounding community through projects such as youth mentoring, housing improvement, and a crisis hotline.

- AIDS-related organizations
- American Red Cross
- Amnesty International
- Audubon Society
- Battered women shelters
- Big Brothers and Big Sisters
- Churches, synagogues, temples, mosques, and affiliated organizations such as the YM/WCA or YM/WHA
- Educational support organizations

- Environmental awareness/support organizations such as Greenpeace and Sierra Club
- Health-focused organizations such as the Avon Foundation for Breast Cancer or the Childhood Leukemia Foundation
- Hospitals
- Hotlines
- Kiwanis/Knights of Columbus/Lions Club/Rotary

- Libraries
- Meals on Wheels
- Nursing homes
- Planned Parenthood
- School districts
- Scouting organizations
- Share Our Strength/other food donation organizations
- Shelters and organizations supporting the homeless
- World Wildlife Fund

Volunteerism is also getting attention on the national level. Ameri-Corps, a federal volunteer clearinghouse, offers financial awards for education in return for community service. If you work for AmeriCorps and you are enrolled in the National Service Trust, you will receive an award that you can use to pay current tuition expenses or repay student loans. You may work either before, during, or after your college education.

Service learning

In the past few years, looking for a way to help students become involved citizens as well as successful learners, many colleges have instituted *service learning* programs. The basic concept of service learning is to provide the community with service and the students with knowledge, creating positive change for both and including specific opportunities for students to reflect on and analyze their experiences.[3]

In service learning, schools set up a system whereby students provide services in the context of a course for which they receive credit. The service and related assignments are required. The National Service Learning Clearinghouse presents this example of the difference between volunteering and service learning:

> If school students collect trash out of an urban streambed, they are providing a service to the community as volunteers; a service that is highly valued and important. When school students collect trash from an urban streambed, then analyze what they found and possible sources so they can share the results with residents of the neighborhood along with suggestions for reducing pollution, they are engaging in service-learning. In the service-learning example, the students are providing an important service to the community AND, at the same time, learning about water quality and laboratory analysis, developing an understanding of pollution issues, learning to interpret science issues to the public, and practicing communications skills by speaking to residents.[4]

Service learning builds a sense of civic responsibility, helps students learn useful skills through doing, and promotes values exploration and personal change. If you are interested in seeing these benefits firsthand, talk to your advisor about whether your school offers service learning programs. Service learning is a "win-win" situation—everyone has something to gain.

Setting an example

The most basic—and perhaps the most important—way you can make a difference is to live your life in a way that sets an example for others. If you make life choices that show a value of learning and hard work, perseverance, commitment, responsibility, and love, you will inspire others to strive for their own personal best.

When you reach for the heights, you also leave an inspiring legacy to any children you have now or may one day have. A 31-year-old returning student and mother of four at Palo Alto College in San Antonio, Texas, is keenly aware of the relationship between what she is doing in school and her children's future. She explains:

> Having waited so long [to go to college] after high school and having a family has put a new perspective and priority on seeking a degree and my goals I want to accomplish in life. Throughout my high school years and even into my twenties, I didn't have any desire to pursue a degree or have any higher ambitions about work. I decided to go back to college after I realized that I could not get a job that paid more than minimum wage.
>
> Hopefully, I am setting a great example for my children. I want them to be confident in their talents and discover their skills. I know that I live in a very stressful environment and everything doesn't go the way I plan for it to go. That is why I try to stay open and flexible to the changes that occur. There is still a lot of spontaneity and it mostly feels like chaos around this house, but it is more of a controlled chaos. And there is always tomorrow.[5]

You can get involved locally and nationally

Being an active citizen is another form of involvement. On a local level, you might take part in your community's debate over saving open space from developers. On a state level, you might contact legislators about building sound barriers along an interstate highway that runs through your town. On a national level, you might write letters to your congressional representative to urge support of an environmental, energy, or patients' rights bill. Work for political candidates who adopt the views you support, and consider running for office yourself—in your district, city, or state, or nationally.

Most important, vote in every election. Your votes and your actions can make a difference—and getting involved will bring you the power and satisfaction of being a responsible citizen. Having the right to vote places you in a privileged minority among people around the world who have no voice in how they live. In the booklet

College is a great time to discover more about how to be an active citizen. This student group is involved in a voter registration campaign.

get analytical! EVALUATE YOUR INVOLVEMENT IN COMMUNITIES[6]

Look closely at your ties to communities important to you.

Thinking about the definition of "community" that you read in the margin on page 000, come up with a list of communities to which you belong—professional, family, spiritual, academic, athletic, political, and so on. Write them here.

_____

_____

_____

Choose two of these communities that are especially important to you. On a separate sheet of paper, answer the following questions for each community. These questions will help you analyze your involvement and how you and your communities benefit.

- How do I help others in this community?
- How do others in this community help me?
- Do I get more than I give, or give more than I get, from this community?
- What about this community concerns me?
- What have I done, or can I do, to address my concerns?
- What is the extent of my commitment to this community and to its success?

"Everything You Wanted to Know About Registering to Vote and Voting in the United States," Caty Borum writes:

> For some young people, a feeling of being disconnected from government, or that "politicians don't listen to me" is the reason they say they don't vote. But elected officials must be responsive to their constituents, so your vote is actually your way of telling leaders what you care about. There may be many reasons people give for not taking advantage of the right to vote, but it's never too late to actually jump into the game, rather than sitting it out on the sidelines. There are too many issues that affect young people—such as education, jobs, health care, crime and violence—to sit it out on Election Day.
>
> *Here's the bottom line: If you don't vote, someone else is deciding your future for you.* It's that simple. If you have an opinion about the cost of college tuition, jobs, the economy, or tons of other laws and issues that affect you, then you're already involved. Now take advantage of your right to determine your future. What are you waiting for?[7]

You can help to preserve your environment

Your environment is your home. When you help to maintain a clean, safe, and healthy place to live, your actions have an impact not only on your immediate surroundings but also on others around you and on the future of the planet. Every environmentally aware person, saved bottle, and reused bag is a step in the right direction. Take responsibility for what you can control—your own habits—and develop sound practices that contribute to the health of the environment.

Recycle anything that you can. Many communities have some kind of recycling program. If you live on campus, your college may have its own recycling program set up. What you can recycle—plastics, aluminum, glass, newspapers, magazines, other scrap paper—depends on how extensive the program is. Products that use recycled materials are often more expensive, but if they are within your price range, try to reward the company's dedication by purchasing them.

Respect the outdoors. Use products that reduce chemical waste. Pick up after yourself. Through volunteering, voicing your opinion, or making monetary donations, support the maintenance of parks and the preservation of natural, undeveloped land. Be creative: One young woman planned a cleanup of a local lakeside area as the main group activity for the guests at her birthday party (she joined them, of course). Everyone benefits when each person takes responsibility for maintaining the fragile earth.

Remember that valuing yourself is the base for valuing all other things. Improving the earth is possible when you value yourself and think you deserve the best living environment possible. Part of valuing yourself is doing whatever you can to create the life you want to live. Activating your successful intelligence and developing your personal mission are two ways to guide yourself to that life.

How can you continue to activate your *successful intelligence?*

Throughout this text you have connected analytical, creative, and practical thinking to academic and life skills. You have put them together in order to solve problems and make decisions. You have seen how these skills, used consistently and balanced, can help you succeed.

As you complete your work in the course, know that you are only just beginning your career as a successfully intelligent learner. You will continue to discover the best ways to use your analytical, creative, and practical thinking skills to achieve goals that are meaningful to you.

Robert Sternberg has found that successfully intelligent people, despite differences in thinking and in personal goals, have several particular characteristics in common. He calls them "self-activators"—things that get you moving and keep you going. According to Sternberg, successfully intelligent people:[8]

1. **Motivate themselves.** They make things happen, spurred on by a desire to succeed and a love of what they are doing.

2. **Learn to control their impulses.** Instead of going with their first quick response, they sit with a question or problem. They allow time for thinking and let ideas surface before making a decision.

3. **Know when to persevere.** When it makes sense, they push past frustration and stay on course, confident that success is in their sights. They also are able to see when they've hit a dead end—and, in those cases, to stop pushing.

4. **Know how to make the most of their abilities.** They understand what they do well and capitalize on it in school and in work.

5. **Translate thought into action.** Not only do they have good ideas; they are able to turn those ideas into practical actions that bring ideas to fruition.

6. **Have a product orientation.** They want results; they focus on what they are aiming for rather than on how they are getting there.

7. **Complete tasks and follow through.** With determination, they finish what they start. They also follow through to make sure all the loose ends are tied and the goal has been achieved.

8. **Are initiators.** They commit to people, projects, and ideas. They make things happen rather than sitting back and waiting for things to happen to them.

9. **Are not afraid to risk failure.** Because they take risks and sometimes fail, they often enjoy greater success and build their intellectual capacity. Like everyone, they make mistakes—but tend not to make the same mistake twice.

10. **Don't procrastinate.** They are aware of the negative effects of putting things off, and they avoid them. They create schedules that allow them to accomplish what's important on time.

11. **Accept fair blame.** They strike a balance between never accepting blame and taking the blame for everything. If something is their fault, they accept the responsibility and don't make excuses.

12. **Reject self-pity.** When something goes wrong, they find a way to solve the problem. They don't get caught in the energy drain of feeling sorry for themselves.

13. **Are independent.** They can work on their own and think for themselves. They take responsibility for their own schedule and tasks.

14. **Seek to surmount personal difficulties.** They keep things in perspective, looking for ways to remedy personal problems and separate them from their professional lives.

15. **Focus and concentrate to achieve their goals.** They create an environment in which they can best avoid distraction and they focus steadily on their work.

16. **Spread themselves neither too thin nor too thick.** They strike a balance between doing too many things, which results in little progress on any of them, and too few things, which can reduce the level of accomplishment.

17. **Have the ability to delay gratification.** While they enjoy the smaller rewards that require less energy, they focus the bulk of their work on the goals that take more time but promise the most gratification.

18. **Have the ability to see the forest and the trees.** They are able to see the big picture and to avoid getting bogged down in tiny details.

19. **Have a reasonable level of self-confidence and a belief in their ability to accomplish their goals.** They believe in themselves enough to get

through the tough times, while avoiding the kind of overconfidence that stalls learning and growth.

20. **Balance analytical, creative, and practical thinking.** They sense what to use and when to use it. When problems arise, they combine all three skills to arrive at solutions.

Make these characteristics your personal motivational tools. Return to them when you need reactivation. Use them to make sure that you move ahead toward the goals that mean most to you.

How can you *create and live* your personal mission?

If the trees are your goals, the forest is the big picture of what you are aiming for in life—your personal mission. To define your mission, craft a *personal mission statement*.

Dr. Stephen Covey, author of *The Seven Habits of Highly Effective People*, defines a mission statement as a philosophy outlining what you want to be (character), what you want to do (contributions and achievements), and the principles by which you live (your values). He describes

EXPLORE YOUR PERSONAL MISSION

get practical!

Work toward a concrete description of your most important life goals.

As a way of exploring what you most want out of life, consider one or more of the following questions, which ask you to look back at the life you imagine you will have. Freewrite some answers on a separate piece of paper.

1. You are at your retirement dinner. You have had an esteemed career in whatever you ended up doing in your life. Your best friend stands up and talks about the five aspects of your character that have taken you to the top. What do you think they are?

2. You are preparing for a late-in-life job change. Updating your résumé, you need to list your contributions and achievements. What would you like them to be?

3. You have been told that you have one year to live. Talking with your family, you reminisce about the values that have been central to you in your life. Based on that discussion, how do you decide you want to spend your time in this last year? How will your choices reflect what is most important to you?

Thinking about your answers, draft a personal mission statement here, up to a few sentences long, that reflects what you want to achieve in life. Focus on the practical—on what you want to do and the effects you want to have on the world.

_____

_____

_____

_____

_____

the statement as "a personal constitution, the basis for making major, life-directing decisions."[9]

Here is a mission statement written by Carol Carter, one of the authors of *Keys to Success*.

> My mission is to use my talents and abilities to help people of all ages, stages, backgrounds, and economic levels achieve their human potential through fully developing their minds and their talents. I aim to create opportunities for others through work, service, and family. I also aim to balance work with people in my life, understanding that my family and friends are a priority above all else.

How can you start formulating a mission statement? Try using Covey's three aspects of personal mission as a guide. Think through the following:

- **Character.** What aspects of character do you think are most valuable? When you consider the people you admire most, which of their qualities stand out?

- **Contributions and achievements.** What do you want to accomplish in your life? Where do you want to make a difference?

- **Values.** How do the values you established in your work in Chapter 2 inform your life goals? What in your mission could help you live according to what you value most highly? For example, if you value community involvement, your mission may reflect a life goal of holding elected office, which may translate into an interim goal of running for class office at college.

Because what you want out of life changes as you move from one phase to the next—from single person to spouse, from student to working citizen—your personal mission should remain flexible and open to revision. If you frame your mission statement carefully so that it truly reflects your goals, it can be your guide in everything you do, helping you to live with integrity and to work to achieve your personal best.

Live with integrity

ETHICS
A system of moral values; a sense of what is right to do.

Having integrity puts your ethics into day-to-day action. When you act with integrity, you earn trust and respect from others. If people can trust you to be honest, to be sincere in what you say and do, and to consider the needs of others, they will be more likely to encourage you, support your goals, and reward your work.

Living with integrity helps you believe in yourself and in your ability to make good choices. A person of integrity isn't a perfect person, but is one who makes the effort to live according to values and principles, continually striving to learn from mistakes and to improve. Take responsibility for making the right moves, and you will follow your mission with strength and conviction.

JOE A. MARTIN JR. Professor of Communications, University of West Florida, Tallahassee

Growing up around people who've been hampered by difficulties can inspire a person to make different choices. Joe Martin made the effort to achieve as a student—but that wasn't enough for him. His main focus now is his life mission to use his abilities to help and inspire others. Read the account, then use a separate piece of paper to answer the questions on page 369.

I grew up in the housing projects of Miami, Florida. My mother didn't finish high school, and no one in my family even considered going to college, including me. My low GPA and SAT scores seemed to indicate I wasn't "college material."

While I was in high school, six of my friends died as a result of crime, drugs, or murder. At least 12 people I knew were in prison, five from my own family. I made a vow that if I survived the projects, I would do something constructive with my life and give something back to the community. I initially wanted to join the military, but after the recruiter told me I wasn't smart enough to go to college, I decided to prove him wrong.

I enrolled in college and, given my academic background, was shocked by my success. I ended up graduating at the top of my class, with a bachelor's degree in public relations, and was voted "Student of the Year" among 10,000 students. Competing against more than 400 other candidates, I landed a job right out of college working for the federal government. Within a year, I was able to move my mother out of the projects and afford almost anything I wanted. Life was great, but I didn't like my job and the person I was becoming.

Around that time, I heard a motivational speaker talk about the need for young professionals to give back to the community. I suddenly realized that I hadn't kept my vow. I was indulging myself, but I didn't have any passion or purpose for what I was doing with my life.

After his presentation, I asked the speaker for advice. I jotted down his suggestions on a napkin and began to implement his ideas. I discovered that I could make money doing what I do best—talking. I became a motivational speaker for students and found that my true passion was teaching. Through teaching, whether on stage or in the classroom, I discovered that I could make a difference in the lives of students who were growing up in poverty as I had.

I've given over 300 presentations and spoken to more than a quarter of a million people about student success. I've written books, recorded audio- and videotapes of my programs, and have my own television show. However, my biggest accomplishment so far has been the creation of a Web site called "Real World University." With the Web site, I'm now able to reach more than 100,000 students a month in 26 different countries.

I believe the reason many students fail is because they have no clue about their gifts and talents or about how they can use those gifts and talents to serve others. Many people are on what I call the "Treadmill Trench" of life—motivated to stay busy, but too scared to live their dreams.

My main question to students is: "If you knew you couldn't fail, what would you attempt to do professionally?" The answer to this question can help anyone find their purpose and passion in life. I also stress to students the importance of meeting a model of success—not someone you'll probably never meet, like Michael Jordan, but someone who is doing what you love to do. Then spend time with that person to find out how they did it. Once students have a clear vision of what they want to become, they're destined to succeed.

Aim for your personal best

Your personal best is simply the best that you can do, in any situation. It may not be the best you have ever done. It may include mistakes, for nothing significant is ever accomplished without making mistakes and taking risks. It may shift from situation to situation. As long as you aim to do your best, though, you are inviting growth and success.

And life is what we make it, always has been, always will be.

GRANDMA MOSES

Aim for your personal best in everything you do. As a lifelong learner, you will always have a new direction in which to grow and a new challenge to face. Seek constant improvement in your personal, educational, and professional life. Dream big, knowing that incredible things are possible for you if you think positively and act with successful intelligence. Enjoy the richness of life by living each day to the fullest, developing your talents and potential into the achievement of your most valued goals.

Kaizen is the Japanese word for "continual improvement." Striving for excellence, finding ways to improve on what already exists, and believing that you can effect change are at the heart of the industrious Japanese spirit. The drive to improve who you are and what do you provides the foundation of a successful future.

Think of this concept as you reflect on yourself, your goals, your lifelong education, your career, and your personal pursuits. Create excellence and quality by continually asking yourself, "How can I improve?" Living by *kaizen* helps you to be a respected friend and family member, a productive and valued employee, and a truly contributing member of society. You can change the world.

BUILDING SKILLS

FOR COLLEGE, CAREER, AND LIFE SUCCESS

Developing Successful Intelligence

PUTTING IT ALL TOGETHER

Learn from the experiences of others. Look back to Joe Martin's Personal Triumph on page 367. After you've read his story, relate his experience to your own life by completing the following:

Step 1. Think it through: *Analyze your experience and compare it to Joe's.* What was a "missing piece" in Joe's life and how did he fill it? What do you consider a missing piece in your life, and how do you think you could fill the gap?

Step 2. Think out of the box: *Imagine ways to contribute.* Think about the ways in which you could serve. How might your talents and skills give something to others? Brainstorm ideas about how you could use what you do well to help others in your community.

Step 3. Make it happen: *Make a practical plan to get involved.* Decide on a specific way to help others, then form a plan to pursue this goal. As you think about your decision, consider your "missing piece": Is there a way to contribute that also somehow fills that missing piece? Write down what you intend to do and the specific steps you will take to do it.

create your future

Team Building

COLLABORATIVE SOLUTIONS

Giving back. In your group, research volunteering opportunities in your community. Each group member should choose one possibility to research. Answer questions such as the following: What is the situation or organization? What are its needs? Do any volunteer positions require an application, letters of reference, or background checks? What is the time commitment? Is any special training involved? Are there any problematic or difficult elements to this experience?

When you have the information, meet together so that each group member can describe each volunteering opportunity to the other members. Choose one that you feel you will have the time and ability to try next semester. Name your choice and tell why you selected it.

Writing

DISCOVERY THROUGH JOURNALING

Record your thoughts on a separate piece of paper or in a journal.

Your learning for life. Review the strategies for lifelong learning on pages 357 to 359. Which three do you feel you already do well? Which three do you think you need to develop further? For the three you want to develop, brainstorm ideas for how you will grow in those areas. Include your prediction for how this effort will benefit you.

Career Portfolio

PLAN FOR SUCCESS

Complete the following in your electronic portfolio or on separate sheets of paper. When you have finished, read through your entire career portfolio. You have gathered information to turn to again and again on your path to a fulfilling, successful career.

A Wheel for Life. In Key 12.3 you see a blank Wheel of Life. Without looking at the first wheel from the beginning of the semester, evaluate yourself as you are right now, after completing this course: Where would you rank yourself in the eight categories? After you have finished, compare this wheel with your previous wheel. Look at the changes: Where have you grown? How has your self-perception changed? Let what you learn from this new wheel inform you about what you have accomplished and what you plan for the future.

Continue to update your Wheel of Life so that it reflects your growth and development, helping to guide you through the changes that await you in the future. Add or change the categories as your college, career, and life priorities evolve.

Use this new wheel to evaluate your progress.

Rate yourself in each area of the wheel on a scale of 1 to 10, 1 being least developed (near the center of the wheel) and 10 being most developed (the outer edge of the wheel). In each area, at the level of the number you choose, draw a curved line and fill in the wedge below that line. Be honest—this is for your benefit only. Finally, look at what your wheel says about the balance in your life. If this were a real wheel, how well would it roll?

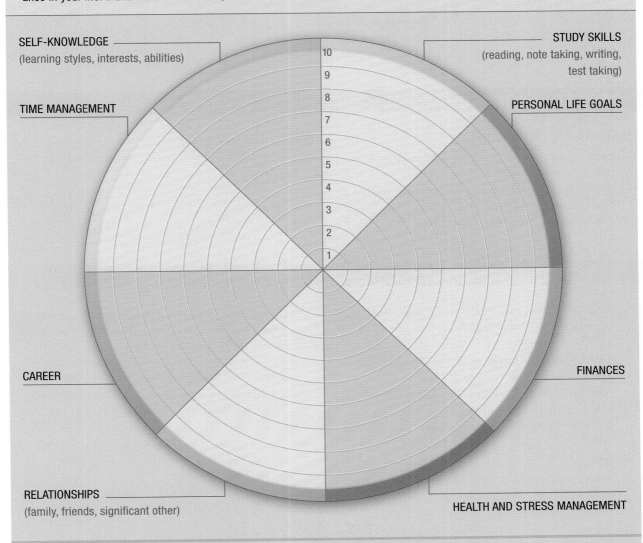

SELF-KNOWLEDGE
(learning styles, interests, abilities)

TIME MANAGEMENT

CAREER

RELATIONSHIPS
(family, friends, significant other)

STUDY SKILLS
(reading, note taking, writing, test taking)

PERSONAL LIFE GOALS

FINANCES

HEALTH AND STRESS MANAGEMENT

Source: Based on "The Wheel of Life" model developed by the Coaches Training Institute, © Co-Active Space 2000.

SUGGESTED READINGS

Blaustein, Arthur I. *Make a Difference: America's Guide to Volunteering and Community Service.* San Francisco: Jossey-Bass, 2003.

Delany; Sarah and Elizabeth Delany with Amy Hill Hearth. *Book of Everyday Wisdom.* New York: Kodansha America, 1996.

Jones, Laurie Beth. *The Path: Creating Your Mission Statement for Work and for Life.* New York: Hyperion, 1998.

Moore, Thomas. *Care of the Soul: How to Add Depth and Meaning to Your Everyday Life.* New York: HarperCollins, 1998.

Wheatley, Margaret J. and Myron Kellner-Rogers. *A Simpler Way.* San Francisco: Berrett-Koehler Publishers, 1998.

INTERNET RESOURCES

(AmeriCorps): www.americorps.org

Campus Compact (site for citizenship and community service): www.compact.org

Hearts and Minds (clearinghouse for volunteer opportunities and civic involvement): www.heartsandminds.org/ index.htm

Queendom.com Soul Search (self-tests, personal exploration, and growth): www.queendom.com/

ENDNOTES

1. Margaret J. Wheatley and Myron Kellner-Rogers, "A Simpler Way," *Weight Watchers Magazine* 30.3 (1997), pp. 42–44.

2. Linton Weeks, "The No-Book Report: Skim It and Weep," *Washington Post*, May 14, 2001 p. C8.

3. National Service Learning Clearinghouse, "Service Learning Is . . . ," 2004 [on-line]. Available: www.servicelearning.org/article/archive/35/ (May 2004).

4. Ibid.

5. Student essay submitted by the First Year Experience students of Patty Parma, Palo Alto College, San Antonio, Texas, January 2004.

6. Adapted from Katherine Woodward Thomas, *Calling In the One.* New York: Three Rivers Press, 2004, pp. 298–299.

7. Caty Borum, "Everything You Wanted to Know About Registering to Vote and Voting in the United States," 2004, Declare Yourself website [on-line]. Available: www.declareyourself.com/press/voter_guides/voter_guide_download.pdf (November 2004).

8. List and descriptions based on Robert J. Sternberg, *Successful Intelligence.* New York: Plume, 1997, pp. 251–269.

9. Stephen Covey, *The Seven Habits of Highly Effective People.* New York: Simon & Schuster, 1989, pp. 70–144, 309–318.

**Demonstrate
What You Know
in an Oral Exam**

In an oral exam, your instructor asks you to verbally present your responses to exam questions or to discuss a pre-assigned topic. Exam questions may be similar to essay questions on written exams. They may be broad and general, or they may focus on a narrow topic that you are expected to explore in depth.

The material in this Study Break is designed to help you master the skills you need to perform well during an oral exam. These skills have lifelong benefits. The more comfortable you are speaking in front of instructors, the more prepared you will be for any kind of public speaking situation—in school, in the community, and at work.

Keep in mind that if you have a documented learning disability that limits your ability to express yourself effectively in writing, you may need to take all your exams orally. Speak with your advisor and instructors to set up an oral exam schedule.

Preparation strategies

Because oral exams require that you speak logically and to the point, your instructors will often give you the exam topic in advance and may even allow you to bring your notes to the exam room. Other instructors ask you to study a specified topic and they then ask questions about the topic during the exam.

Speaking in front of others—even an audience of one, your instructor—involves developing a presentation strategy before you enter the exam room:

Learn your topic.   Study for the exam until you have mastered the material. Nothing can replace subject mastery as a confidence booster.

Plan your presentation.   Dive into the details. Brainstorm your topic if it is pre-assigned, narrow it with the prewriting strategies you learned in Chapter 8, determine your central idea or argument, and write an outline that will be the basis of your talk. If the exam uses a question-and-answer format, make a list of the most likely questions, and formulate the key points of your response.

Do, or do not. There is no "try."

YODA (THE EMPIRE STRIKES BACK)

Use clear thinking.   Make sure your logic is solid and that your evidence supports your thesis. Work on an effective beginning and ending that focus on the exam topic.

Draft your thoughts. To get your thoughts organized for the exam, make a draft, using "trigger" words or phrases that will remind you of what you want to say.

Practice your presentation

The element of performance distinguishes speaking from writing. As in any performance, practice is essential. Use the following strategies to guide your efforts:

Know the parameters. How long do you have to present your topic? Where will you be speaking? Will you have access to a podium, table, chair, or white board?

Use index cards or notes. If your instructor doesn't object, bring note cards to the presentation. Keep them out of your face, however; it's tempting to hide behind them.

Pay attention to the physical. Your body positioning, voice, eye contact, and what you wear contribute to the impression you make; therefore, try to look good and sound good.

Time your practice sessions to determine whether you should add or cut material. If you are given your topic in advance, make sure you can state your points in the allotted time. During the exam, make sure you don't speak too quickly.

Try to be natural. Use words you are comfortable with to express concepts you know. Be yourself as you show your knowledge and enthusiasm for the topic.

Be prepared for questions

After your formal presentation, your instructor may ask you topic-related questions. Your responses and the way you handle the questions will affect your grade. Here are some strategies for answering questions effectively:

Take the questions seriously. The exam is not over until the question-and-answer period ends.

Jot down keywords from the questions. This is especially important if the question has several parts, and you intend to address one part at a time.

Ask for clarification. Ask the instructor to rephrase a question you don't understand.

Think before you speak. Take a moment to organize your thoughts and to write down keywords for the points you want to cover.

Answer only part of a question if that's all you can do. Emphasize what you know best and impress the instructor with your depth of knowledge. If you draw a blank, simply tell the instructor that you don't know the answer.

Handling your nerves during an exam

If you are nervous, there are things you can do to help yourself:

Keep your mind on your presentation, not yourself. Focus on what you want to say and how you want to say it.

Take deep breaths right before you begin, and carry a bottle of water. Deep breathing will calm you, and the water will ease a dry mouth.

Visualize your own success. Create a powerful mental picture of yourself acing the exam. Then visualize yourself speaking with knowledge, confidence, and poise.

Establish eye contact with your instructor and realize that he or she wants you to succeed. You'll relax when you feel that your instructor is on your side.

Decide how well these techniques work for you

Practice makes perfect, especially when it comes to public speaking. Gauge your ability to speak effectively during an oral exam with the following team exercise:

- Team up with another student to prepare for a written essay, then quiz each other as if you were taking an actual oral exam. How did your partner evaluate your presentation? What were your strengths? Your weaknesses?

  _____

  _____

- Do you think that your answers demonstrated all you know about the subject or that you could have done better in writing? If the latter, what obstacles prevented you from doing your best in your oral presentation?

  _____

  _____

- Describe three actions you will take to improve your next presentation.

1. _____

2. _____

3. _____

Index